W9-BZK-587

WESTMAR
COLLEGE
LIBRARY
LE MARS
IOWA
Gift of
Dr. Kalas

John Knox's History of the Reformation in Scotland

Volume Two

John Knox's
History of the Reformation in Scotland

Edited by

William Croft Dickinson D.Lit.

Volume Two

PHILOSOPHICAL LIBRARY
NEW YORK

Published 1950 by the Philosophical Library Inc.
15 East 40th Street, New York, N.Y.

Printed in Great Britain by
Thomas Nelson and Sons Ltd, Edinburgh and London

CONTENTS

VOLUME II

THE FOURTH BOOK
OF THE PROGRESS AND CONTINUANCE OF TRUE RELIGION WITHIN SCOTLAND

PREFATIO

In the former Books, gentle reader, thou may clearly see how potently God hath performed in these our last and wicked days, as well as in the ages that have passed before us, the promises that are made to the servants of God, by the prophet Isaiah, in these words: "They that wait upon the Lord shall renew their strength; they shall lift up the wings as the eagles; they shall run, and not be weary; they shall walk, and not faint." This promise, we say, such as Sathan hath not utterly blinded may see performed in us, the professors of Christ Jesus within this realm of Scotland, with no less evidence than it was in any age that ever hath passed before us. For what was our force? What was our number? Yea, what wisdom or worldly policy was into us, to have brought to a good end so great an enterprise? Our very enemies can bear witness. And yet in how great purity God did establish amongst us his true religion, as well in doctrine as in ceremonies! To what confusion and fear were idolaters, adulterers, and all public transgressors of God's commandments within short time brought? The public order of the Church, yet by the mercy of God preserved, and the punishments executed against malefactors, can testify unto the world. For, as touching the doctrine taught by our ministers, and as touching the administration of Sacraments used in our Churches, we are bold to affirm that there is no realm this day upon the face of the earth, that hath them in greater purity; yea (we must speak the truth whomsoever we offend), there is none (no realm, we mean) that hath them in the like purity. For all others (how sincere that ever the doctrine be, that by some is taught), retain in their Churches, and the ministers thereof, some footsteps of Antichrist, and some dregs of papistry; but we (all praise to God alone) have nothing within our Churches that ever flowed from that Man of Sin.[1] And this we acknowledge to be the strength given unto us by God, because we esteemed not ourselves wise in our own eyes, but understanding our whole wisdom to be but mere foolishness before our God, laid it aside, and followed only that which we found approved by himself.

In this point could never our enemies cause us to faint, for our first petition was, "That the reverent face of the primitive and

[1] *Cf. infra*, 266–267, in The Confession of Faith, c. xviii.

The first Petition of the Protestants of Scotland

apostolic Church should be reduced [1] again to the eyes and knowledge of men." [2] And in that point, we say, our God hath strengthened us till that the work was finished, as the world may see. And as concerning the suppressing of vice, yea, and of the abolishing of all such things as might nourish impiety within the realm, the acts and statutes of the principal towns reformed will yet testify. For what adulterer, what fornicator, what known mass-monger, or pestilent Papist, durst have been seen in public, within any reformed town within this realm, before that the Queen arrived? And this victory to his word, and terror to all filthy livers, did our God work by such as yet live and remain witnesses (whether they will or not) of the foresaid works of our God. We say, our God suffered none of those, whom he first called to the battle, to perish or to fall till that he made them victors of their enemies. For even as God suffered none of those whom he called from Egypt to perish in the Red Sea, how fearful that ever the danger appeared, so suffered he none of us to be oppressed, nor yet to be taken from this life, till that more Pharaohs than one were drowned, and we set at freedom without [3] all danger of our enemies: to let both us and our posterity understand that such as follow the conducting of God cannot perish, albeit that they walked in the very shadow of death.

But from whence (alas) cometh this miserable dispersion of God's people within this realm, this day, anno 1566, in May? [4] And what is the cause that now the just are compelled to keep silence; good men are banished; murderers, and such as are known unworthy of the common society (if just laws were put in due execution) bear the whole regiment and swing [5] within this realm? We answer, Because that suddenly the most part of us declined from the purity of God's word, and began to follow the world; and so again to shake hands with the Devil, and with idolatry, as in this Fourth Book we will hear.

The cause of the troubles of the Kirk within Scotland flowed from the courtiers that seemed to profess the Evangel

For while that Papists were so confounded that none within the

[1] *brought back* [2] *Cf. supra*, i, 151–152

[3] *outside*, that is, "beyond all danger from. . ."

[4] That is, when, following the murder of Riccio (9 March 1566) and Mary's escape with Darnley to Dunbar, Mary had summoned her forces in arms, the murderers had been denounced as rebels, many of "the godly" had fled from Edinburgh, and Knox himself had taken refuge in Kyle. According to the *Diurnal of Occurrents* (94) the Lords "with dolorous hearts" left Edinburgh on 17 March at seven in the morning, and Knox left the same day at two in the afternoon "with a great mourning of the godly of religion." This date, coming in the body of the text, and in the text hand (folio 301 *verso*) shows that at least the Preface to Book IV was written during Knox's retirement in the south-west. [5] *sway*

realm durst more avow the hearing or saying of Mass than the thieves of Liddesdale durst avow their stowth[1] in presence of an upright judge, there were Protestants found that ashamed not at tables, and other open places, to ask, "Why may not the Queen have her own Mass, and the form of her religion? What can that hurt us or our religion?" And from these two, "Why" and "What," at length sprang out this affirmative, "The Queen's Mass and her priests will we maintain: this hand and this rapier shall fight in their defence, etc."

The inconvenients were shown, both by tongue and pen; but the advertisers were judged to be men of unquiet spirits. Their credit was defaced at the hands of such as before were not ashamed to have used their counsel in matters of greater importance than to have resisted the Mass. But then, my Lord, my Master, may not be thus used: he has that honour to be the Queen's brother; and therefore we will that all men shall understand that he must tender her as his sister; and whosoever will counsel him to displease her, or the least that appertains unto her, shall not find him their friend; yea, they are worthy to be hanged that would so counsel him, etc.[2]

The corruption that entered in the Queen's court. The theology of the court, and their reasons

These and the like reasons took such deep root in flesh and blood that the truth of God was almost foryett[3]; and from this fountain (to wit, that flesh and blood was, and yet, alas, is preferred to God, and to his messengers rebuking vice and vanity) hath all our misery proceeded. For as before, so even yet, although the ministers be set to beg, the guard and the men-of-war must be served.[4] Though the blood of the ministers be spilled, it is the Queen's servant that did it. Although Masses be multiplied in all quarters of the realm, who can stop the Queen's subjects to live of the Queen's religion? Although innocent men be imprisoned, it is the Queen's pleasure: she is offended at such men. Although under pretence of justice innocents be cruelly murdered; the lords shall weep, but the Queen's mind must be satisfied. Nobles of the realm, barons and councillors are banished, their escheats disponed, and their lives most unjustly pursued; the Queen has lost her trusty servant Davy[5]; he was dear unto her; and therefore, for her honour's sake, she

[1] *theft*

[2] The chief "advertiser" and "unquiet spirit" was, of course, Knox. "My Lord, my Master" was the Lord James Stewart, Mary's half-brother. Knox had openly broken with him at the end of May, 1563 (*infra*, 78), and in June 1564 they were still so estranged that "neither by word nor write was there any communication betwix them." (*Infra*, 134)

[3] *forgot* [4] See the note *infra*, 103, *note* 6 [5] David Riccio

must show rigour to revenge his death. And yet further, albeit that some know that she has plainly purposed to wreck the religion within this realm; that to that Roman Antichrist she hath made her promise; and that from him she hath taken money to uphold his pomp within this realm; yet will they let the people understand that the Queen will establish religion, and provide all things orderly, if she were once delivered.

This was written when the second rank of the Lords was banished[1]

If such dealings, which are common amongst our Protestants, be not to prefer flesh and blood to God, to his truth, to justice, to religion, and unto the liberty of this oppressed realm, let the world judge. The plagues have been, and in some part are present, that were before threatened; the rest approach. And yet who from the heart cries, "I have offended; the Lord knows. In Thee only is the trust of the oppressed; for vain is the help of man." But now return we to our HISTORY.

[1] See *supra*, 4, *note* 4

THE nineteenth day of August, the year of God 1561, betwix seven and eight hours before noon, arrived MARIE QUEEN OF SCOTLAND, then widow, with two galleys forth of France. In her company (besides her gentlewomen called the Maries [1]), were her three uncles, the Duke d'Aumale,[2] the Grand Prior,[3] and the Marquis d'Elbœuf.[4] There accompanied her also, Damville,[5] son to the Constable of France, with other gentlemen of inferior condition,[6] besides servants and officers. The very face of heaven, the time of her arrival, did manifestly speak what comfort was brought unto this country with her, to wit, sorrow, dolour, darkness, and all impiety. For, in the memory of man, that day of the year was never seen a more dolorous face of the heaven than was at her arrival, which two days after did so continue; for besides the surface wet, and corruption of the air, the mist was so thick and so dark that scarce might any man espy another the length of two pair of boots. The sun was not seen to shine two days before, nor two days after. That fore-warning gave God unto us; but alas, the most part were blind.

The Queen's last arrival in Scotland

At the sound of the cannons which the galleys shot, the multitude being advertised, happy was he and she that first might have the presence of the Queen. The Protestants were not the slowest, and thereinto they were not to be blamed. Because the Palace of Holyroodhouse was not thoroughly put in order (for her coming was more sudden than many looked for [7]), she remained in Leith till towards

[1] That is, Mary Fleming, Mary Seton, Mary Beaton, and Mary Livingstone. (See "The Queen's Maries" in *Scot. Hist. Review,* ii, 363–371) See also Lesley, *Historie of Scotland* (Bannatyne Club), 209.

[2] Claude of Lorraine (1526–73), Marquis de Mayenne, Duc d'Aumale.

[3] Francis of Lorraine (1534–63), Duc de Guise (1550–63), Grand Prior of the Order of the Knights of St. John of Jerusalem (at Malta).

[4] René of Lorraine (1536–66), Marquis d'Elbœuf.

[5] Henry de Montmorency, Count of Damville, son of Anne de Montmorency, Marshal and Constable of France.

[6] The "others" included Pierre de Bourdeille, better known as the Sieur de Brantôme.

[7] Mary's arrival had not been expected until the end of the month (*Calendar of Scottish Papers,* i, No. 1001; Hay Fleming, *Mary Queen of Scots,* 253, *note* 4). In July, 1561, Elizabeth was of opinion that Mary's return would "alter many things for the worse," and the English Queen kept in touch with the Hamiltons (*Calendar of Scottish Papers,* i, No. 992). Her refusal to grant a safe-conduct to Mary, and her patrolling fleet, may have been intended to drive Mary to take the western route to Dumbarton, that is, into Hamilton country. Knowledge of this might account for Mary's earlier return; certainly it was to her interest to return to Scotland as soon as possible and, once there, to rely on her half-brother, the Lord James Stewart.

The Queen's first grace in despite of religion

the evening, and then repaired thither.[1] In the way betwixt Leith and the Abbey, met her the rebels of the crafts (of whom we spake before [2]), to wit, those that had violated the authority of the magistrates, and had besieged the Provost. But because she was sufficiently instructed that all they did was done in despite of the religion, they were easily pardoned. Fires of joy were set forth all night, and a company of the most honest, with instruments of music and with musicians, gave their salutations at her chamber window. The melody (as she alleged) liked her well; and she willed the same to be continued some nights after.

With great diligence the lords repaired unto her from all quarters. And so was nothing understood but mirth and quietness till the next Sunday, which was the xxiv of August, when preparation began to be made for that idol the Mass to be said in the Chapel; which pierced the hearts of all. The godly began to bolden; and men began openly to speak, "Shall that idol be suffered again to take place within this realm? It shall not." The Lord Lindsay (then but Master [3]), with the gentlemen of Fife, and others, plainly cried in the close, "The idolater priest should die the death," according to God's law. One that carried in the candle was evil effrayed; but then began flesh and blood to show itself. There durst no Papist neither yet any that came out of France whisper. But the Lord James [4] (the man whom all the godly did most reverence) took upon him to keep the Chapel door. His best excuse was, that he would stop all Scottish men to enter in to the Mass. But it was, and is, sufficiently known that the door was kept that none should have entry to trouble the priest, who, after the Mass, was committed to the protection of Lord John of Coldingham [5] and Lord Robert of Holyroodhouse,[6] who then were both Protestants, and had communicated at the Table of the Lord. Betwix them two was the priest convoyed to his chamber.[7]

The Queen's first Mass

Lord James's fact

Convoyers of the Priest

And so the godly departed with great grief of heart, and at afternoon repaired to the Abbey in great companies, and gave plain signification that they could not abide that the land which God by his power had purged from idolatry should in their eyes be

[1] Hay Fleming, *op. cit.*, 253, *note* 2 [2] *Supra*, i, 355–359

[3] Patrick, eldest son of John, fifth Lord Lindsay of the Byres, became Patrick, sixth Lord Lindsay, after the death of his father in December 1563.

[4] The Lord James Stewart, later Earl of Moray.

[5] The Lord John Stewart, a natural son of James V, and Commendator of Coldingham.

[6] The Lord Robert Stewart, a natural son of James V, and Commendator of Holyrood.

[7] See Hay Fleming, *Mary Queen of Scots*, 46–47, 257, *notes* 14 and 15

polluted again. Which understood, there began complaint upon complaint. The old dountybours,[1] and others that long had served in the Court and have no remission of sins but by virtue of the Mass, cried, "They would to France without delay: they could not live without the Mass." The same affirmed the Queen's uncles. And would to God that that menzie,[2] together with the Mass, had taken good-night at this realm for ever; for so had Scotland been rid of an unprofitable burden of devouring strangers, and of the malediction of God that has stricken and yet will strike for idolatry.

The end is not yet seen

The Council assembled, disputation was had of the next remedy. Politic heads were sent unto the gentlemen with these and the like persuasions, "Why, alas, will ye chase our Sovereign from us? She will incontinent return to her galleys; and what then shall all realms say of us? May we not suffer her a little while? We doubt not but she shall leave it. If we were not assured that she might be won, we should be as great enemies to her Mass as ye should be. Her uncles will depart, and then shall we rule all at our pleasure. Would not we be as sorry to hurt the Religion as any of you would be?"

The persuasion of the courtiers

With these and the like persuasions (we say) was the fervency of the Brethren quenched; and an Act[3] was framed, the tenor whereof followeth:

APUD EDINBURGH, XXV^to AUGUSTI ANNO &C. LXI°

Forsamekle as the Queen's Majesty has understood the great inconvenients that may come through the division presently standing in this Realm for the difference in matters of religion, that her Majesty is most desirous to see [it] pacified by a good order, to the honour of God, and tranquillity of her Realm, and means to take the same by advice of her Estates so soon as conveniently may be; and that her Majesty's godly resolution therein may be greatly hindered, in case any tumult or sedition be raised amongst the lieges if any sudden alteration or novation be pressed [at] or attempted before that the order may be established: Therefore, for eschewing of the

[1] Later (*infra*, 87) the word seems to be used in the sense of *courtesans*. A possible derivation would be from *donte* (the rounded *belly* of a musical instrument) and *bourrés* (stuffed or filled). [2] *company*

[3] Laing thought that this Act had not survived in the extant Register of the Privy Council (Laing's *Knox*, ii, 272, *note*); but the Act *is* contained in the Register, though not in its proper place. (See *Reg. Privy Council of Scotland*, i, 266–67; and the important editorial comment, *ibid.*, Intro., xxxvi–xl)

said inconvenients, her Majesty ordains letters to be directed [1] to charge all and sundry her lieges, by open proclamation at the Market Cross of Edinburgh, and other places needful, that they and every one of them, contain themselves in quietness, [and] keep peace and civil society amongst themselves : And in the meantime, while [2] the Estates of this Realm may be assembled, and that her Majesty have taken a final order by their advice and public consent, which her Majesty hopes shall be to the contentment of the whole, that none of them take upon hand, privately or openly, to make alteration or innovation of the state of religion, or attempt anything against the form which her Majesty found publicly and universally standing at her Majesty's arrival in this her Realm, under the pain of death : With certification, that if any subject of the Realm shall come in the contrary hereof, he shall be esteemed and held a seditious person and raiser of tumult, and the said pain shall be executed upon him with all rigour, to the example of others. Attour, [3] her Majesty by the advice of the Lords of her Secret Council, commands and charges all her lieges that none of them take upon hand to molest or trouble any of her domestical servants, or persons whatsomever, come forth of France in her Grace's company at this time, in word, deed, or countenance, for any cause whatsomever, either within her palace or without, or make any derision or invasion upon any of them, under whatsomever colour or pretence, under the said pain of death : Albeit her Majesty be sufficiently persuaded that her good and loving subjects would do the same, for the reverence they bear to her person and authority, notwithstanding that no such commandment were published.

This Act and Proclamation, penned and put in form by such as before professed Christ Jesus (for in the Council then had Papists neither power nor vote), it was publicly proclaimed at the Market Cross of Edinburgh, upon Monday foresaid. No man reclaimed, nor made repugnance to it, except the Earl of Arran only who, in open audience of the Heralds and people protested, " That he dissented that any protection or defence should be made to the Queen's domestics, or to any that came from France, to offend God's Majesty, and to violate the laws of the Realm, more than to any other subject. For God's law had pronounced death against the idolater, and the laws of the Realm had appointed punishment for sayers and hearers of Mass ; which (said he), I here protest, be universally observed,

[1] For the issue of the Letters, see *Accounts Lord High Treasurer*, xi, 63, 64.

[2] *until* [3] *moreover*

and that none be exempted, unto such time as a law, as publicly made, and as consonant to the law of God, have disannulled the former." And thereupon he took documents, as the tenor of this his Protestation doth witness:

In so far as by this Proclamation it is understood to the Kirk of God, and members thereof, that the Queen's Grace is minded that the true religion and worshipping, else [1] established, proceed forward, that it may daily increase, unto the Parliament, that order then may be taken for extirpation of all idolatry within this Realm: We render most heartly thanks to the Lord our God for her Grace's good mind, earnestly praying that it may be increased in her Highness to the honour and glory of his name, and weal of his Kirk within this Realm. And as touching the molestation of her Highness's servants, we suppose that none dare be so bold as once to move their finger at them, in doing of their lawful business; and as for us, we have learned at our master Christ's school, "to keep peace with all men"; and therefore, for our part, we will promise that obedience unto her Majesty (as is our duty), that none of her servants shall be molested, troubled, or once touched by the Kirk, or any member thereof, in doing their lawful affairs. But, since that God has said, "The idolater shall die the death," we Protest solemnly, in presence of God, and in the ears of the whole people that hear this Proclamation, and specially in presence of you, Lyon Herald, and of the rest of your colleagues, &c., makers of this Proclamation, that if any of her servants shall commit idolatry, specially say Mass, participate therewith, or take the defence thereof, (which we were loth should be in her Grace's company), in that case, that this Proclamation be not extended to them in that behalf, nor be not a safeguard or gyrth [2] to them in that behalf, no more nor if they commit slaughter or murder, seeing the one is mekle more abominable and odious in the sight of God than is the other: But that it may be lawful to inflict upon them the pains contained in God's word against idolaters, wherever they may be apprehended, but [3] favour. And this our Protestation we desire you to notify unto her, and give her the copy hereof, lest her Highness should suspect an uproar, if we should all come and present the same. At Edinburgh, the day and year foresaid.

This boldness did somewhat exasperate the Queen, and such as favoured her in that point. As the Lords, called of the Congregation,

[1] *already* [2] *sanctuary* [3] *without*

repaired unto the town, at the first coming they showed themselves wondrously offended that the Mass was permitted; so that every man as he came accused them that were before him: but after that they had remained a certain space, they were as quiet as were the former. Which thing perceived, a zealous and godly man, Robert Campbell of Kinzeancleuch, said unto the Lord Ochiltree, "My Lord, now ye are come, and almost the last of all the rest; and I perceive, by your anger, that the fire-edge is not off you yet; but I fear, that after that the holy water of the Court be sprinkled upon you, that ye shall become as temperate as the rest. For I have been here now five days, and at the first I heard every man say, 'Let us hang the priest'; but after that they had been twice or thrice in the Abbey, all that fervency was past. I think there be some enchantment whereby men are bewitched." And in very deed so it came to pass. For the Queen's flattering words, upon the one part, ever still crying, "Conscience, conscience: it is a sore thing to constrain the conscience"; and the subtle persuasions of her supposts [1] (we mean even of such as sometimes were judged most fervent with us [2]) upon the other part, blinded all men, and put them in this opinion: she will be content to hear the preaching, and so no doubt but she may be won. And thus of all it was concluded to suffer her for a time.

Robert Campbell to the Lord Ochiltree

The Queen's practices at the first

The judgment of John Knox upon the suffering of the Queen's Mass

The next Sunday,[3] John Knox, inveighing against idolatry, showed what terrible plagues God had taken upon realms and nations for the same; and added, "That one Mass (there was no more suffered at the first) was more fearful to him than if ten thousand armed enemies were landed in any part of the realm, of purpose to suppress the whole religion. For (said he) in our God there is strength to resist and confound multitudes if we unfeignedly depend upon him; whereof heretofore we have had experience; but when we join hands with idolatry, it is no doubt but that both God's amicable presence and comfortable defence leaveth us, and what shall then become of us? Alas, I fear that experience shall teach us, to the grief of many." At these words, the guiders of the Court mocked, and plainly spake, "That such fear was no point of their faith: it was beside his text, and was a very untimely admonition." But we heard this same John Knox,[4] in the audience of the same

The courtiers

[1] *supporters*

[2] A reference to the Lord James and Maitland of Lethington, in particular.

[3] That is, Sunday 31 August 1561; though Knox had already "thundered" from the pulpit on Sunday 24 August (*Calendar of Scottish Papers*, i, No. 1010).

[4] An attempt at impersonal narration.

men, recite the same words again in the midst of troubles; and, in the audience of many, ask [of] God mercy that he was not more vehement and upright in the suppressing of that idol in the beginning.[1] "For (said he), albeit that I spake that which offended some (which this day they see and feel to be true), yet did I not [that] which I might have done; for God had not only given unto me knowledge and tongue to make the impiety of that idol known unto this realm, but he had given unto me credit with many, who would have put in execution God's judgments, if I would only have consented thereto. But so careful was I of that common tranquillity, and so loth was I to have offended those of whom I had conceived a good opinion, that in secret conference with earnest and zealous men, I travailed rather to mitigate, yea, to slaken, that fervency that God had kindled in others, than to animate or encourage them to put their hands to the Lord's work. Whereintill I unfeignedly acknowledge myself to have done most wickedly; and from the bottom of my heart, ask of my God grace and pardon, for that I did not what in me lay to have suppressed that idol in the beginning." These and other words did many hear him speak in public place, in the month of December, the year of God 1565, when such as at the Queen's arrival only maintained the Mass, were exiled the realm, summoned upon treason, and decreet of forfeiture intended against them.[2] But to return from whence we have digressed.

John Knox's confession

Whether it was by counsel of others, or of the Queen's own desire, we know not; but the Queen spake with John Knox, and had long reasoning with him, none being present except the Lord James[3] (two gentlewomen stood in the other end of the house[4]). The sum of their reasoning was this. The Queen accused him that he had raised a part of her subjects against her mother, and against herself: That he had written a book against her just authority (she meant the treatise against the Regiment of Women), which she had, and should cause the most learned in Europe to write against it:

The first reasoning betwix the Queen and John Knox

[1] Writing to Cecil on 7 October 1561, Knox laments that he "did not more zealously gainstand that idol at the first erecting," though "men delighting to swim betwix two waters have often complained upon my severity." (Laing's *Knox*, vi, 131)

[2] That is, when, following the Roundabout or Chase-about Raid, Châtelherault, Moray, Glencairn, Rothes, Boyd, Ochiltree and others were summoned to compear before the next Parliament on a charge of treason. (Hay Fleming, *Mary Queen of Scots*, 113ff; *Reg. Privy Council of Scotland*, i, 355ff, 409; *Diurnal of Occurrents*, 80ff, 85-86; *infra*, 161ff)

[3] This "first reasoning betwix the Queen and John Knox" apparently took place on Thursday, 4 September 1561. (*Calendar of Scottish Papers*, i, No. 1017)

[4] *chamber*

That he was the cause of great sedition and great slaughter in England: and That it was said to her that all which he did was by necromancy, &c.

To the which the said John answered, " Madam, it may please your Majesty patiently to hear my simple answers. And first (said he) if to teach the truth of God in sincerity, if to rebuke idolatry, and to will a people to worship God according to his word, be to raise subjects against their princes, then cannot I be excused; for it has pleased God of his mercy to make me one (amongst many) to disclose unto this realm the vanity of the Papistical religion, and the deceit, pride and tyranny of that Roman Antichrist. But, Madam, if the true knowledge of God, and his right worshipping be the chief causes that must move men from their heart to obey their just princes (as it is most certain that they are) wherein can I be reprehended? I think, and am surely persuaded, that your Grace has had, and presently has, a sunfeigned obedience of such as profess Jesus Christ within this realm as ever your father or other progenitors had of those that were called bishops. And touching that book which seemeth so highly to offend your Majesty, it is most certain that I wrote it, and am content that all the learned of the world judge of it. I hear that an Englishman hath written against it,[1] but I have not read him. If he have sufficiently improved my reasons, and established his contrary proposition, with as evident testimonies as I have done mine, I shall not be obstinate, but shall confess my error and ignorance. But to this hour I have thought, and yet thinks, myself alone to be more able to sustain the things affirmed in that my work than any ten in Europe shall be able to confute it."

" Ye think then (quod she), that I have no just authority? "

" Please your Majesty (said he) that learned men in all ages have had their judgments free, and most commonly disagreeing from the common judgment of the world; such also have they published, both with pen and tongue, and yet notwithstanding they themselves have lived in the common society with others, and have borne patiently with the errors and imperfections which they could not amend. Plato, the philosopher, wrote his Books of the Commonwealth, in the which he damneth many things that then were maintained in the world, and required many things to have been reformed; and yet, notwithstanding, he lived even under such policies as then were universally received without further troubling of any estate. Even so, Madam, am I content to do, in uprightness

[1] That is, John Aylmer. (See *supra*, i, 290, *note* 3; and Laing's *Knox*, iv, 354-355)

of heart, and with a testimony of a good conscience. I have communicated my judgment to the world. If the realm finds no inconvenience from the regiment of a woman, that which they approve shall I not further disallow than within my own breast, but shall be as well content to live under your Grace as Paul was to live under Nero; and my hope is, that so long as that ye defile not your hands with the blood of the saints of God, that neither I nor that book shall either hurt you or your authority: for in very deed, Madam, that book was written most especially against that wicked Jezebel of England." [1]

"But (said she), ye speak of women in general."

"Most true it is, Madam (said the other), and yet it appeareth to me that wisdom should persuade your Grace never to raise trouble for that which to this day hath not troubled your Majesty, neither in person nor yet in authority. For of late years many things which before were held stable have been called in doubt; yea they have been plainly impugned. But yet, Madam (said he), I am assured that neither Protestant nor Papist shall be able to prove that any such question was at any time moved in public or in secret. Now, Madam (said he), if I had intended to have troubled your estate, because ye are a woman, I might have chosen a time more convenient for that purpose than I can do now, when your own presence is within the realm.

"But now, Madam, shortly to answer to the other two accusations. I heartly praise my God, through Jesus Christ, that Sathan, the enemy of mankind, and the wicked of the world, hath no other crimes to lay to my charge than such as the very world itself knoweth to be most false and vain. For in England I was resident only the space of five years. The places were Berwick, where I abode two years; so long in the New Castle; and a year in London.[2] Now, Madam, if in any of these places, during the time that I was there, any man shall be able to prove that there was either battle, sedition or mutiny I shall confess that I myself was the malefactor and the shedder of the blood. I ashame not, Madam, further to affirm that God so blessed my weak labours that in Berwick (where commonly before there used to be slaughter by reason of quarrels that used to arise amongst soldiers) there was as great quietness all the time that I remained there as there is this day in Edinburgh. And where they slander me of magic, necromancy, or of any other art forbidden of God, I have witnesses (besides my own conscience) all [the] congrega-

[1] That is, Mary Tudor, Queen of England

[2] See *supra*, i, 110

tions that ever heard me, what I spake both against such arts, and against those that use such impiety. But, seeing the wicked of the world said, That my Master, the Lord Jesus, was possessed with Beelzebub, I must patiently bear, albeit that I, wretched sinner, be unjustly accused of those that never delighted in the verity."

The Queen's second objection

"But yet (said she), ye have taught the people to receive another religion than their princes can allow. And how can that doctrine be of God, seeing that God commands subjects to obey their princes?"

[*Answer*]

"Madam (said he), as right religion took neither original strength nor authority from worldly princes but from the Eternal God alone, so are not subjects bound to frame their religion according to the appetites of their princes. For oft it is that princes are the most ignorant of all others in God's true religion, as we may read in the histories as well before the death of Christ Jesus, as after. If all the seed of Abraham should have been of the religion of Pharaoh, whom to they were long subjects, I pray you, Madam, what religion should there have been in the world? Or, if all men in the days of the Apostles should have been of the religion of the Roman Emperors, what religion should there have been upon the face of the earth? Daniel and his fellows were subjects to Nebuchadnezzar, and unto Darius, and yet, Madam, they would not be of their religion, neither of the one or of the other. For the three children said, 'We make it known unto thee, O King, that we will not worship thy gods'; and Daniel did pray publicly unto his God against the expressed commandment of the King. And so, Madam, ye may perceive that subjects are not bound to the religion of their princes, albeit they are commanded to give them obedience."

The third objection

"Yea (quod she), but none of those men raised the sword against their princes."

[*Answer*]

"Yet Madam (quod he), ye cannot deny but that they resisted: for those that obey not the commandments that are given, in some sort resist."

Question

"But yet (said she), they resisted not by the sword?"

[*Answer*]

"God (said he), Madam, had not given unto them the power and the means."

"Think ye (quod she), that subjects having power may resist their princes?"

"If their princes exceed their bounds (quod he), Madam, and do against that wherefore they should be obeyed, it is no doubt but they may be resisted, even by power. For there is neither greater honour nor greater obedience to be given to kings or princes, than God has commanded to be given unto father and mother. But so it is, Madam, that the father may be stricken with a frenzy, in the which he would slay his own children. Now, Madam, if the children arise, join themselves together, apprehend the father, take the sword or other weapons from him, and finally bind his hands, and keep him in prison till that his frenzy be overpast; think ye, Madam, that the children do any wrong? Or, think ye, Madam, that God will be offended with them that have stayed their father to commit wickedness? It is even so (said he), Madam, with princes that would murder the children of God that are subject unto them. Their blind zeal is nothing but a very mad frenzy; and therefore, to take the sword from them, to bind their hands, and to cast themselves in prison till that they be brought to a more sober mind, is no disobedience against princes, but just obedience, because that it agreeth with the will of God."

Question to answer the former

Blind zeal what

When this was written there was no appearance of Marie's imprisonment[1]

At these words, the Queen stood as it were amazed, more than the quarter of an hour. Her countenance altered, so that Lord James began to entreat her, and to demand, "What has offended you, Madam?"

At length, she said, "Well, then, I perceive that my subjects shall obey you,[2] and not me; and shall do what they list, and not what I command: and so must I be subject to them, and not they to me."

The Queen's conclusion

"God forbid (answered he), that ever I take upon me to command any to obey me, or yet to set subjects at liberty to do what pleaseth them. But my travail is that both princes and subjects obey God. And think not (said he), Madam, that wrong is done unto you when ye are willed to be subject unto God: for it is He that subjects people under princes, and causes obedience to be given unto them; yea, God craves of kings That they be as it were foster-fathers to his Church, and commands queens to be nurses unto his people. And this subjection, Madam, unto God, and unto his troubled Church, is the greatest dignity that flesh can get upon the face of the earth, for it shall carry them to everlasting glory."

"Yea (quod she), but ye are not the Kirk that I will nourish. I will defend the Kirk of Rome for I think it is the true Kirk of God."

The Queen's Kirk

"Your will (quod he), Madam, is no reason; neither doth your thought make that Roman harlot to be the true and immaculate

[1] In the manuscript (folio 307 *recto*), this marginal note is in the same hand as that of the text. The reference is evidently to the imprisonment of Queen Mary in Lochleven Castle, June 1567, and thus this part of the *History* must have been transcribed between 16 June 1567 and 2 May 1568 (see *supra*, i, ciii).

[2] Namely, John Knox

spouse of Jesus Christ. And wonder not, Madam, that I call Rome a harlot; for that Church is altogether polluted with all kind of spiritual fornication, as well in doctrine as in manners. Yea, Madam, I offer myself further to prove that the Church of the Jews that crucified Christ Jesus was not so far degenerated from the ordinances and statutes which God gave by Moses and Aaron unto his people when that they manifestly denied the Son of God, as that the Church of Rome is declined, and more than five hundred years hath declined, from the purity of that religion which the Apostles taught and planted."

"My conscience (said she), is not so."

"Conscience, Madam (said he), requires knowledge; and I fear that right knowlege ye have none."

"But (said she), I have both heard and read."

"So (said he), Madam, did the Jews that crucified Christ Jesus read both the Law and the Prophets, and heard the same interpreted after their manner. Have ye heard (said he), any teach but such as the Pope and his Cardinals have allowed? And ye may be assured that such will speak nothing to offend their own estate."

Question

"Ye interpret the Scriptures (said she), in one manner, and they interpret in another. Whom shall I believe? And who shall be judge?"

Answer

"Ye shall believe (said he), God that plainly speaketh in his word: and further than the word teaches you, ye neither shall believe the one or the other. The word of God is plain in the self; and if there appear any obscurity in one place, the Holy Ghost, which is never contrarious to himself, explains the same more clearly in other places: so that there can remain no doubt but unto such as obstinately remain ignorant.[1] And now (said he), Madam, to take one of the chief points which this day is in controversy betwix the Papists and us: for example, the Papists allege, and boldly have affirmed, That the Mass is the ordinance of God, and the institution of Jesus Christ, and a sacrifice for the sins of the quick and the dead. We deny both the one and the other, and affirm that the Mass as it is now used is nothing but the invention of man; and, therefore, is an abomination before God, and no sacrifice that ever God commanded. Now, Madam, who shall judge betwix us two thus contending? It is no reason that either of the parties be further believed than they are able to prove by unsuspect witnessing. Let them lay down the book of God, and by the plain words thereof prove their affirmatives, and

Mass

[1] Compare the *Confession of Faith*, c. xviii (*infra*, 267).

we shall give unto them the plea granted. But so long as they are bold to affirm, and yet do prove nothing, we must say that, albeit all the world believed them, yet believe they not God, but receive the lies of men for the truth of God. What our Master Jesus Christ did, we know by his Evangelists: what the priest doth at his Mass, the world seeth. Now, doth not the Word of God plainly assure us that Christ Jesus neither said, nor yet commanded Mass to be said at his Last Supper, seeing that no such thing as their Mass is made mention of within the whole Scriptures?"

"Ye are oure sair [1] for me (said the Queen), but and if they were here that I have heard, they would answer you." [2]

"Madam (quod the other), would to God that the learnedest Papist in Europe, and he that ye would best believe, were present with your Grace to sustain the argument; and that ye would patiently abide to hear the matter reasoned to the end. For then I doubt not, Madam, but that ye should hear the vanity of the Papistical religion and how small ground it hath within the word of God."

"Well (said she), ye may perchance get that sooner than ye believe."

"Assuredly (said the other), if ever I get that in my life, I get it sooner than I believe. For the ignorant Papists cannot patiently reason, and the learned and crafty Papist will never come in your audience, Madam, to have the ground of their religion searched out; for they know that they are never able to sustain an argument, except fire and sword and their own laws be judges."

"So say ye," (quod the Queen).

"But I can believe that it has been so to this day, (quod he). For how oft have the Papists in this and other realms been required to come to conference, and yet could it never be obtained, unless that themselves were admitted for judges. And therefore, Madam, I must yet say again that they dare never dispute but where themselves are both judge and party. And whensoever that ye shall let me see the contrary, I shall grant myself to have been deceived in that point."

And with this the Queen was called upon to dinner, for it was after noon. [3] At departing, John Knox said unto her, "I pray God,

[1] *too hard*

[2] It is to be noted, however, that Mary's library included many books relating to the religious revolution of her time. (See *Inventaires de la Royne Descosse*, Bannatyne Club, Preface, cxi–cxiii)

[3] The Queen apparently dined at noon (*cf. Diurnal of Occurrents*, 67).

Madam, that ye may be as blessed within the Commonwealth of Scotland, if it be the pleasure of God, as ever Deborah was in the Commonwealth of Israel."

Of this long Conference, whereof we only touch a part, were divers opinions. The Papists grudged, and feared that which they needed not. The godly, thinking at least that she would have heard the preaching, rejoiced ; but they were allutterly [1] deceived, for she continued in her Massing ; and despised and quietly mocked all exhortations.

John Knox's judgment of the Queen at the first, and ever since

John Knox's own judgment being by some of his familiars demanded, What he thought of the Queen ? " If there be not in her (said he), a proud mind, a crafty wit, and an indurate heart against God and his truth, my judgment faileth me." [2]

When the whole Nobility were convened, the Lords of Privy Council were chosen : who were appointed, the Duke's Grace,[3] the Earls of Huntly,[4] Argyll,[5] Atholl,[6] Morton,[7] Glencairn,[8] Marischal,[9] Bothwell[10] ; Lords Erskine,[11] &c., Lord James,[12] &c.[13] Of these were a certain [number] appointed to wait upon [the] Court by course [14] ; but that order continued not long.

[The] Duke d'Aumale [15] returned with the galleys to France. The Queen entered in her progresses,[16] and in the month of September travelled from Edinburgh to Linlithgow, Stirling, Saint Johnston, Dundee, [and] Saint Andrews ; which all parts she polluted with her idolatry. Fire followed her very commonly in that journey.[17] The towns propined [18] her liberally, and thereof were the French enriched.

[1] *utterly*

[2] Writing to Cecil on 7 October 1561, Knox says " In communication with her, I espied such craft as I have not found in such age." (Laing's *Knox*, vi, 132)

[3] James, second Earl of Arran, Duke of Châtelherault

[4] George, fourth Earl of Huntly

[5] Archibald, fifth Earl of Argyll

[6] John Stewart, fourth Earl of Atholl

[7] James Douglas, fourth Earl of Morton

[8] Alexander, fourth Earl of Glencairn

[9] William, fourth Earl Marischal

[10] James Hepburn, fourth Earl of Bothwell

[11] John, sixth Lord Erskine, later Earl of Mar

[12] Lord James Stewart, later Earl of Moray

[13] The sederunt and choice of the Privy Council was at Holyrood, 6 September 1561. (*Reg. Privy Council of Scotland*, i, 157–158)

[14] *in turn*

[15] See *supra*, 7, *note* 2. According to the *Diurnal of Occurrents* (67), he left on 1 September 1561 with the two galleys which had brought the Queen home.

[16] See Hay Fleming, *Mary Queen of Scots*, 51–52 ; *Diurnal of Occurrents*, 69

[17] But apparently only at Stirling, where a candle set the curtains and tester of her bed on fire while she was asleep. (Randolph to Cecil, 24 September 1561, in *Calendar of Scottish Papers*, i, No. 1023)

[18] *made presents to*

In the beginning of October,[1] she returned to Edinburgh, and at the day appointed she was received in the Castle. Great preparations were made for her entry in the town. In farces, in masking, and in other prodigalities, fain would fools have counterfeited France.[2] Whatsoever might set forth her glory, that she heard, and gladly beheld. The keys were delivered unto her by a pretty boy, descending as it were from a cloud. The verses of her own praise she heard, and smiled. But when the Bible was presented,[3] and the praise thereof declared, she began to frown : for shame she could not refuse it. But she did no better, for immediately she gave it to the most pestilent Papist within the realm, to wit, to Arthur Erskine.[4] Edinburgh since that day has reaped as they sowed. They gave her some taste of their prodigality ; and because the liquor was sweet, she has licked of that buist [5] ofter than twice since. All men know what we mean : the Queen can not lack, and the subjects have.

Balfour's doctrine [6]

In Edinburgh it hath been an ancient and laudable custom that the Provost, Bailies, and Council after their election, which useth to be at Michaelmas, caused publicly proclaim the Statutes and Ordinances of the town.[7] And therefore Archibald Douglas, Provost, Edward Hope, Adam Fullarton [John Preston and David Somer],[8] Bailies, caused proclaim, according to the former Statutes of the town, that no adulterer [no fornicator], no noted drunkard, no mass-

[1] Knox has here confused the date and the order of events. Mary had returned to Edinburgh from her " progresses " by the end of September, but the " entry " and reception Knox now describes took place on Tuesday, 2 September. (See the detailed account in *Diurnal of Occurrents*, 67–69, and Robertson's note in *Inventaires de la Royne Descosse*, Preface, lxxiv, *note* 1)

[2] But in July 1572 Knox himself attended a mask or " play " at the marriage of Mr. John Davidson, one of the Regents at the University of St. Andrews, wherein " the Castle of Edinburgh was besieged, taken, and the Captain, with one or two with him, hanged in effigy." (*Autobiography and Diary of Mr. James Melvill*, Wodrow Society, 27)

[3] A Bible and a Psalm Book were presented to her. " If, as Lord Herries alleges [*Historical Memoirs*, 56], the Psalm Book was in ' Scots vers,' it may have been Wedderburn's version ; but his statement that the Bible was in the ' Scots languadge ' is altogether incredible." (Hay Fleming, *Mary Queen of Scots*, 255, *note* 10)

[4] Arthur Erskine of Blackgrange, son of John, fifth Lord Erskine. He is said to have been Mary's favourite equerry and on his horse she is said to have escaped from Holyrood after the murder of Riccio. But see Pollen, *Papal Negotiations with Mary Queen of Scots*, 271, *note* 4.

[5] *chest* or *coffer* ; here used in the sense of a container for food or drink

[6] That is, Sir James Balfour

[7] This was the usual practice in the Scottish burghs.

[8] In the manuscript (folio 308 *verso*), a blank space is left for these names. They have been supplied from the list given in *Edinburgh Burgh Records*, iii, 301. But these men were the officers for the year 1559–60, and the officers who were discharged by order of the Queen were Archibald Douglas, provost, and David Forster, Robert Ker, Alexander Home, and Allan Dickson, bailies. (*Ibid.*, iii, 126)

monger, no obstinate Papists that corrupted the people, such as priests, friars, and others of that sort, should be found within the town within forty-eight hours thereafter, under the pains contained in the statutes.[1] Which blown in the Queen's ears, there began pride and maliciousness to show the self; for without further cognition of the cause, were the Provost and Bailies charged to ward in the Castle; and immediately was commandment given, that other Provost and Bailies should be elected.[2]

The Queen's first pride after her arrival

Some gainstood for a while the new election,[3] alleging, that the Provost and Bailies whom they had chosen, and to whom they had given their oath, had committed no offence wherefore that justly they ought to be deprived. But while charge was doubled upon charge, and no man was found to oppose themselves to iniquity, Jezebel's letter and wicked will is obeyed as a law. And so was Mr. Thomas McCalzean chosen for the other.[4] The man, no doubt, was both discreet and sufficient for that charge; but the deposition of the other was against all law. God be merciful to some of our own; for they were not all blameless that her wicked will was so far obeyed.[5]

The Queen's true lieges, who?

A contrary proclamation was publicly made that the town should be patent unto all the Queen's lieges; and so murderers, adulterers, thieves, whores, drunkards, idolaters, and all malefactors got protection under the Queen's wings, under that colour, because they were

[1] The proclamation was made on 2 October 1561 and was against "monks, friars, priests, nuns, adulterers, fornicators, and all such filthy persons" (*Edinburgh Burgh Records*, iii, 125). On 20 September 1560 the Council had proclaimed the Act of Parliament against hearing or saying Mass (*ibid.*, iii, 82), and on 24 March 1561 a proclamation had been made against priests, monks, friars, canons, nuns, and others of the ungodly sects and opinions, and against sayers and maintainers of the Mass, whoremongers, adulterers and fornicators (*ibid.*, iii, 101–102). The October 1561 proclamation, with its reference to the Roman Catholic priesthood as "filthy persons" was naturally resented by the Queen.

[2] There is no reference in the Burgh Records that the provost and bailies were charged to enter themselves in ward in the Castle. In a letter to Cecil of 7 October 1561 Knox writes: "At this very instant are the Provost of Edinburgh and Baillies thereof, commanded to ward in their Tolbooth, by reason of their proclamation against Papists and whoremongers. The whole blame lieth upon the necks of the two forenamed," viz. Lord James Stewart and Lethington. (Laing's *Knox*, vi, 132) The Queen's letters charging the burgh to deprive the provost and bailies of their offices, and to choose others, were read in presence of the bailies and council on 5 October. (*Edinburgh Burgh Records*, iii, 125)

[3] A protestation appears in the records on behalf of the Council and community. (*Ibid.*, iii, 126)

[4] On 8 October effect was given to the Queen's letters; Mr Thomas McCalzean was elected provost, and James Thomson, John Adamson, Mr John Marjoriebanks, and Alexander Acheson, bailies. (*Ibid.*, iii, 126)

[5] A reference to Lord James Stewart and Maitland of Lethington. (See *note* 2 above)

of her religion.[1] And so got the Devil freedom again, where that before he durst not have been seen in the daylight upon the common streets. "Lord deliver us from that bondage."

The Devil getting entry with his finger, will shoot forth his whole arm

The Devil finding his reins loose, ran forwards in his course; and the Queen took upon her greater boldness than she and Baal's bleating priests durst have attempted before. For upon All Hallows Day[2] they blended up their Mass with all mischievous solemnity. The ministers thereat offended, in plain and public place declared the inconvenients that thereupon should ensue. The nobility were sufficiently admonished of their duties. But affection caused men to call that in doubt wherein shortly before they seemed to be most resolute, to wit, "Whether that subjects might put to their hand to suppress the idolatry of their Prince?" And upon this question convened in the house of Mr. James M'Gill,[3] the Lord James, the Earl of Morton, the Earl Marischal, Secretary Lethington, the Justice-Clerk,[4] and Clerk of Register[5]; who all reasoned for the part of the Queen, affirming, "That the subjects might not lawfully take her Mass from her." In the contrary judgment were the principal ministers, Mr. John Row, Master George Hay, Master Robert Hamilton, and John Knox. The reasons of both parties we will omit because they will be explained after, where the same question, and others concerning the obedience due unto Princes, were long reasoned in open assembly. The conclusion of that first reasoning was, "That the question should be formed, and letters directed to Geneva for the resolution of that Church," wherein John Knox offered his labours.[6] But Secretary Lethington (alleging that there stood mekle in the

[1] Here Knox is guilty of exaggeration, though possibly he would have argued that "murderers" and "thieves" were but synonyms for Papists. The Queen's contrary proclamation is not inserted in the MS. Burgh Records, but, writing to Cecil on 7 October, Knox says that Mary "set forth proclamations contrary." (Laing's *Knox*, vi, 131)

[2] All Hallows, or All Saints' Day, 1 November

[3] Sir James M'Gill of Nether Rankeillor, the Clerk Register

[4] Sir John Bellenden of Auchnoull

[5] Sir James M'Gill of Nether Rankeillor

[6] This meeting was apparently held after All Hallows (1 November), and if that is so, Knox deliberately conceals the fact that *he had already written.* His letter to Calvin, dated 24 October 1561, is printed with a facsimile and a translation in Laing's *Knox*, vi, 133–135, and with a facsimile in Teulet, *Papiers d'État*, ii, 12–14. Laing later noticed this point (Laing's *Knox*, vi, 687–688) and observes that Knox had nothing to gain by his concealment of what he may have considered to be a *private letter* as opposed to a formal letter to be sent in the name of those present at the meeting. But, three years later, when the question again arose, Knox does not openly admit his letter to Calvin but, refusing to write, contents himself with saying that he has already had letters of many on this same question, and has heard the opinions of the most godly and learned in Europe. (*Infra*, 134)

information [1]), said that he should write. But that was only to drive time, as the truth declared its self. The Queen's party urged, " That the Queen should have her religion free in her own chapel, to do, she and her household, what they list." The ministers both affirmed and voted the contrary, adding, " That her liberty should be their thraldom ere it was long." But neither could reason nor threatening move the affections of such as were creeping in credit. And so did the votes of the lords prevail against the ministers.

For the punishment of theft and of reif, which had increased upon the Borders and in the South, from the Queen's arrival, was the Lord James made Lieutenant.[2] Some suspected that such honour and charge proceeded from the same heart and counsel that Saul made David captain against the Philistines. But God assisted him, and bowed the hearts of men both to fear and obey him. Yea, the Lord Bothwell himself [3] at that time assisted him (but he had remission for Liddesdale). Sharp execution was made in Jedburgh, for twenty-eight of one clan and others were hanged at that Justice Court.[4] Bribes, budds,[5] nor solicitation saved not the guilty, if he might be apprehended ; and therefore God prospered him in that his integrity.

That same time the said Lord James spake the Lord Grey of England [6] at Kelso, for good rule to be kept upon both the Borders, and agreed in all things.

The Queen's first fray [7] in Holyroodhouse

Before his returning, the Queen upon a night took a fray [7] in her bed, as if horsemen had been in the close and the Palace had been enclosed about. Whether it proceeded of her own womanly fantasy, or if men put her in fear for displeasure of the Earl of Arran, and for other purposes, as for the erecting of the guard, we know not. But the fear was so great that the town was called to the watch. Lords Robert of Holyroodhouse, and John of Coldingham [8] kept the watch by course.[9] Scouts were sent forth, and sentinels were commanded under the pain of death to keep their stations. And yet

[1] This might mean either that the question was of great importance, or, and more significantly, that much depended upon the way the question was put. (See *infra*, 133)

[2] The arrangements for this Justice Court and the instructions given to the Lord James are printed in *Reg. Privy Council of Scotland*, i, 163–64, 184–87.

[3] James Hepburn, fourth Earl of Bothwell

[4] Randolph, writing to Cecil, 7 December 1561, says the Lord James burned many houses, hanged twenty-two or twenty-three [men], and " brought in " forty or fifty. (*Calendar of Scottish Papers*, i, No. 1049)

[5] *gifts* intended as bribes

[6] William, Lord Grey de Wilton, then Warden of the East Marches of England.

[7] *fright*

[8] The Lords Robert Stewart and John Stewart, natural brothers of the Queen.

[9] *in turn*

they feared where there was no fear: neither yet could ever any appearance or suspicion of such things be tried.[1]

Short after the returning of the Lord James, there came from the Queen of England, Sir Peter Mewtas,[2] with commission to require the ratification of the Peace made at Leith. His answer was even such as we have heard before: that she behoved to advise, and then she should send answer.[3]

In presence of her Council she kept herself [very] grave, (for under the dule weed,[4] she could play the hypocrite in full perfection); but how soon that ever her French fillocks,[5] fiddlers, and others of that band got the house alone there might be seen skipping not very comely for honest women.[6] Her common talk was, in secret, she saw nothing in Scotland but gravity, which repugned altogether to her nature, for she was brought up in joyousity[7]; so termed she her dancing and other things thereto belonging.

Division betwix the Lords and the Ministers

The General Assembly of the Church approached, held in December after the Queen's arrival; in the which began the rulers of the Court to draw themselves apart from the society of their brethren, and began to stir and grudge that anything should be consulted upon without their advice. Master John Wood, who before had shown himself very fervent in the cause of God, and forward in giving of his counsel in all doubtful matters, plainly refused ever to assist the Assembly again, whereof many did wonder. The courtiers drew unto them some of the lords, who would not convene with their brethren, as before they were accustomed, but kept them in the Abbey. The principal commissioners of the churches, the superintendents, and some ministers passed unto

[1] Buchanan says that the whole affair was arranged by the Queen herself in order to secure a bodyguard without arousing the suspicions of the people (Aikman's *Buchanan*, ii, 450–51). Randolph says the "hurly-burly" took place about 9 p.m. on Sunday, 16 November, and gives a full account of it, indicating that the Queen seized the opportunity to put Arran in disgrace (*Calendar of Scottish Papers*, i, No. 1049). Later, he inclines to the opinion that there were grounds for the "trouble," and that "unadvised" words had passed Arran (*ibid.*, i, No. 1058). Certainly the affair led to the establishment of a small bodyguard for the Queen of which James Stewart [of Cardonald] was captain (*ibid.*, i, No. 1058). See also Hay Fleming, *Mary Queen of Scots*, 271, *note* 66, and Pollen, *Papal Negotiations with Mary Queen of Scots*, 271, *note* 4.

[2] The commission to Sir Peter Mewtas is dated 17 September 1561. (*Foreign Calendar, Elizabeth*, iv, No. 506)

[3] Mary apparently answered that as there were divers matters in the Treaty which touched her late husband, it would be better to have a new meeting for such matters as touched her only. Therein she was almost certainly thinking of her succession to the English throne. (See *Foreign Calendar, Elizabeth*, iv, No. 648)

[4] *mourning* [5] *fillies; wanton young women* [6] See *infra*, 68

[7] See *infra*, 36

them, where they were convened in the Abbot's lodging within Holyroodhouse. Both the parties began to open their grief. The lords complained that the ministers drew the gentlemen into secret, and held councils without their knowledge. The ministers denied that they had done anything in secret, or otherwise than the common order commanded them ; and accused the lords (the flatterers of the Queen we mean) that they kept not the Convention with their brethren, considering that they knew the order, and that the same was appointed by their own advice, as the Book of Discipline, subscribed with the most part of their own hands, would witness. Some began to deny that ever they knew such a thing as the Book of Discipline ; and called also in doubt, whether it was expedient that such conventions should be or not ; for gladly would the Queen and her Secret Council have had all assemblies of the godly discharged.

The reasoning was sharp and quick on either part. The Queen's faction alleged that it was suspicious to princes that subjects should assemble themselves and keep conventions without their knowledge. It was answered, That without knowledge of the Prince, the Church did nothing. For the Prince perfectly understood that within this realm there was a Reformed Church, and that they had their orders and appointed times of convention ; and so without knowledge of the Prince they did nothing. "Yea," said Lethington, "the Queen knew and knowest it well enough ; but the question is, Whether that the Queen allows such conventions ?" It was answered, "If the liberty of the Church should stand upon the Queen's allowance or disallowance, we are assured not only to lack assemblies, but also to lack the public preaching of the Evangel." That affirmative was mocked, and the contrary affirmed. "Well (said the other),[1] time will try the truth ; but to my former words this will I add, take from us the freedom of Assemblies, and take from us the Evangel [2] ; for without Assemblies, how shall good order and unity in doctrine be kept? It is not to be supposed that all ministers shall be so perfect but that they shall need admonition, as well concerning manners as doctrine, as it may be that some be so stiff-necked that they will not admit the admonition of the simple ; as also it may be that fault may be found with ministers without just offence committed : and yet if order be not taken both with the complainer and the persons com-

[1] Certainly Knox

[2] Or, in the ultimate resort, the lieges must be able to convocate to protect the religion they have secured.

plained upon, it cannot be avoided but that many grievous offences shall arise. For remedy whereof, of necessity it is that General Assemblies must be, in the which the judgment and the gravity of many may concur to correct or to repress the follies or errors of a few." Hereunto consented the most part, as well of the nobility as of the barons, and willed the reasoners for the part of the Queen to will her Grace, if that she stood in any suspicion of anything that was to be entreated in their Assemblies, that it would please her Grace to send such as she would appoint to hear whatsoever was proponed or reasoned.

Lethington opposed him to the Book of Discipline[2]

Hereafter was the Book of Discipline proponed, and desired to have been ratified by the Queen's Majesty. That was scripped at,[1] and the question was demanded, "How many of those that had subscribed that Book would be subject unto it?" It was answered, "All the godly." "Will the Duke?"[3] said Lethington. "If he will not," answered the Lord Ochiltree,[4] "I would that he were scraped out, not only of that book, but also out of our number and company. For to what purpose shall labours be taken to put the Kirk in order, and to what end shall men subscribe, and then never mean to keep word of that which they promise?" Lethington answered, "Many subscribed there *in fide parentum*, as the bairns are baptized." One, to wit John Knox,[5] answered, "Albeit ye think that scoff proper, yet as it is most untrue so is it most improper. That Book was read in public audience, and by the space of divers days the heads thereof were reasoned, as all that here sit know well enough, and ye yourself cannot deny; so that no man was required to subscribe that which he understood not." "Stand content (said one), that Book will not be obtained." "Let God (said the other), require the lack which this poor commonwealth shall have of the things therein contained, from the hands of such as stop the same."

The barons perceiving that the Book of Discipline was refused, presented unto the Council certain articles requiring idolatry to be suppressed, their churches to be planted with true ministers, and some certain provision to be made for them, according to equity and conscience; for unto that time the most part of the ministers had

[1] *mocked*

[2] In the manuscript (folio 312 *recto*) this marginal note is not in the text hand.

[3] Châtelherault

[4] Andrew Stewart, second Lord Ochiltree

[5] In the manuscript (folio 312 *recto*) after "One" there is a caret and the words "to wit Jone Knox" are added above the line; there is a second caret after "ansuered" and the words "to wit Jo^{n} Knox" are added in the margin, in Knox's own hand. A facsimile of this page is given in *National Manuscripts of Scotland*, iii, No. 60.

lived upon the benevolence of men. For many held into their own hands the fruits that the Bishops and others of that sect had before abused; and so some part was bestowed upon the ministers. But then the Bishops began to grip again to that which most unjustly they called their own; for the Earl of Arran was discharged of Saint Andrews and Dunfermline, wherewith before, by virtue of a factory, he had intromitted [1]: and so were many others. And therefore the barons required that order might be taken for their ministers, or else they would no more obey the Bishops, neither yet suffer any thing to be lifted up to their use after the Queen's arrival, than that they did before; for they verily supposed that the Queen's Majesty would keep promise made unto them, which was, not to alter their religion, which could not remain without ministers, and ministers could not live without provision: and therefore they heartly desired the Council to provide some convenient order in that head.

That somewhat moved the Queen's flatterers; for the rod of impiety was not then strengthened in her and their hands. And so began they to practise how they should please the Queen and yet seem somewhat to satisfy the faithful; and so devised they that the church men [2] should have intromission with the two parts of their benefices, and that the third part should be lifted up by such men as thereto should be appointed, for such uses, as in the Acts [of Secret Council] is more fully expressed.[3]

. . . .

The names of the Nobility and Lords that were present at the making of the foresaid Acts [4] hereafter follow:

James, Duke of Châtelherault
George, Earl Huntly
Archibald, Earl Argyll
William, Earl Marischal
John, Earl Atholl
James, Commendator of Saint Andrews and Pittenweem
John, Lord Erskine
John Bellenden of Auchnoull, knight, Justice Clerk

[1] With which he had *intermeddled* by virtue of letters under authority of the Privy Council authorizing the appointment of a *factor* or chamberlain to ingather the revenues (*infra*, 330).

[2] That is, the old hierarchy of the Roman Catholic Church.

[3] In the manuscript, "as in these subsequent Acts are more fully expressed"; and Knox then inserts the relevant Acts of the Privy Council, under which the old church was to be allowed to retain two-thirds of the rents of all benefices, and the remaining one-third of the rents was to be ingathered, by Collectors appointed by the Queen, to meet "the charges to be borne for the common weal of the realm," and also "the sustentation of the Preachers" of the Reformed Kirk. These are printed *infra*, Appendix IX

[4] See *infra*, Appendix IX

William, Earl Montrose	The Treasurer
James, Earl Morton	The Clerk of Register, and
Alex^r^., Earl of Glencairn	The Secretary [1]

After the first Act, the Earl of Huntly said, jestingly, "Good day, my Lords of the Two part."

The whole Rentals being gathered, the sum of the Third, according to their own calculation, was found to extend to. . . .[2]

The Ministers, even in the beginning, in public sermons opposed themselves to such corruption, for they foresaw the purpose of the Devil, and clearly understood the butt whereat the Queen and her flatterers shot; and so in the stool of Edinburgh, John Knox said: "Well, if the end of this order, pretended to be taken for sustentation of the ministers, be happy, my judgment faileth me; for I am assured that the Spirit of God is not the author of it; for, first, I see two parts freely given to the Devil, and the third must be divided betwix God and the Devil. Well, bear witness to me that this day I say it, ere it be long the Devil shall have three parts of the Third; and judge you then what God's portion shall be." [3] This

John Knox's judgment of the Thirds

[1] These names are those of the *sederunt* of the Privy Council at its meeting on 22 December 1561 (*infra*, 326); the *sederunt* differed at each of the subsequent meetings of the Council when the arrangement was under consideration. In the manuscript this *sederunt* is repeated on the immediately following page (folio 317 *verso*) with the addition of the Comptroller who, however, does not appear in the *sederunt* in the Register of the Privy Council. The officials whose names are not given were: Mr. Robert Richardson, *Treasurer*; Mr. James McGill of Nether Rankeillor, *Clerk of Register*; William Maitland of Lethington, *Secretary*; and Sir John Wishart of Pittarrow, *Comptroller*.

[2] In the manuscript (folio 317 *verso*), a space of two lines has been left blank for the sum to be inserted. The Accounts of the Collectors of the Thirds of the Benefices are now being edited by Dr. Gordon Donaldson, for the Scottish History Society, from the records still extant in the General Register House, and I have had the advantage of reading the draft of Dr. Donaldson's introduction to the forthcoming volume. Exact figures are impossible, because of exceptions, deductions, remissions, and variations from year to year; but it would appear that the amount of the "Thirds" in 1562 was well over £76,000, of which about £72,500 came in and of which £26,000 went in stipends to the ministers. But in succeeding years, as the *History* shows, there were more and more remissions, the difficulties of collection increased, and more and more the ministers were "frustrated of their stipends." A number of the records were earlier examined by Bishop Keith in the first half of the eighteenth century, and his extracts and calculations will be found in *History of the Affairs of Church and State in Scotland* (Spottiswoode Society), iii, 370–387. According to Keith, the total sum of the "Thirds" came to £72,491, of which the Reformed Kirk received £24,231.

[3] In a supplication to the Queen, of July 1562, the ministers state that they are all "so cruelly entreated by this last pretended Order taken for sustentation of ministers, that their latter misery far surmounteth the former. For now the poor labourers of the ground are so oppressed by the cruelty of those that pay their Third, [in] that they for the most part advance upon the poor whatsoever they pay to the Queen, or to any other." (*Infra*, 49; *Booke of the Universall Kirk*, i, 22)

was an unsavoury saying in the ears of many. Some ashamed not to affirm, "The ministers being sustained, the Queen will not get at the year's end to buy her a pair of new shoes." And this was Secretary Lethington.

There were appointed to modify [1] the ministers' stipends, the Earls Argyll, Moray, and Morton, Lethington, the Justice Clerk, and Clerk of Register. The Laird of Pittarrow was appointed to pay the ministers' stipends according to their modification.[2] Who would have thought that when Joseph ruled Egypt that his brethren should have travelled for victuals, and have returned with empty sacks unto their families? Men would rather have thought that Pharaoh's pose,[3] treasure, and garnalls [4] should have been diminished, ere that the household of Jacob should stand in danger to starve for hunger.

Let this be noted

But so busy and circumspect were the Modificators (because it was a new office, the term must also be new), that the ministers should not be over wanton,[5] that a hundred marks [6] was sufficient to a single man, being a common minister. Three hundred marks was the highest that was appointed to any, except unto the Superintendents, and unto a few others. Shortly, whether it was the niggardness of their own hearts, or the care that they had to enrich the Queen, we know not, but the poor Ministers, Readers, and Exhorters cried out to the heaven (as their complaints in all Assemblies do witness) that neither were they able to live upon the stipends appointed, neither could they get payment of that small thing that was appointed. So fain would the Comptroller [7] have played the good valet, and have satisfied the Queen, or else his own profit in every point, that he got this dicton [8] and proverb, "The good Laird of Pittarrow was an earnest professor of Christ; but the mekle Devil receive the Comptroller, for he and his Collectors are become greedy factors." [9]

A proverb

[1] *assess*, or determine the amount of

[2] Sir John Wishart of Pittarrow, who had been appointed as Comptroller on 16 February 1562, was appointed as Collector General of the "Thirds" on 1 March 1562. (MS. Register of the Privy Seal, xxxi, 3, 5)

[3] *hoard* [4] *granaries* [5] *extravagant*

[6] The mark was not a coin; it was a reckoning of two-thirds of a pound, that is, thirteen shillings and fourpence. One hundred marks was thus £66, 13s. 4d. It should be noted that these amounts were not greatly different from those recommended in the *Book of Discipline* (*infra*, 289); and it is therefore difficult to understand Knox's petulance

[7] Sir John Wishart of Pittarrow

[8] *saying*. (More usually *ditton*; but from French *dicton*)

[9] But when Wishart relinquished office he was about £5,000 out of pocket.

To put an end to this unpleasing matter: when the Brethren complained of their poverty, it was disdainfully answered of some, "There are many Lords have not so much to spend." When men did reason that the vocation of Ministers craved of them books, quietness, study, and travel, to edify the Kirk of Jesus Christ, when that many Lairds were waiting upon their worldly business, and therefore, that the stipends of ministers, who had none other industry, but to live upon that which was appointed, ought not to be modified according to the livings of common men, who might, and did daily augment their rents by some other industry; when such reasons were laid before them, they got none other answer, but "The Queen can spare no greater sums." Oft was it cried into their ears, "O happy servants of the Devil, and miserable servants of Jesus Christ, if that after this life there were not hell and heaven." For to the servants of the devil, to your dumb dogs and horned bishops, to one of those idle bellies (I say) ten thousand was not enough; but to the servants of Christ that painfully preach his evangel, a thousand pounds; how can that be sustained?

One day, in reasoning of this matter, the Secretary burst out in a piece of his choler, and said, "The ministers have this much paid unto them by year, and who yet ever bade the Queen 'grand-mercies' for it? Was there ever a minister that gave thanks to God for her Majesty's liberality towards them?" One [1] smiled and answered, "Assuredly, I think, that such as receive anything gratis of the Queen, are unthankful if they acknowledge it not, both in heart and mouth. But whether that the ministers be of that rank or not, I greatly doubt. Gratis, I am assured, they receive nothing; and whether they receive anything at all from the Queen, wise men may reason.[2] I am assured that neither third nor two part ever appertained to any of her predecessors within this realm these thousand years bypast, neither yet has the Queen better title to that which she usurps, by giving it to others, or in taking [it] to herself, than such as crucified Christ Jesus had to divide his garments amongst them. And if the truth may be spoken, she has not so good title as they had; for such spoil used to be the reward of such men. And in that point those soldiers were more gentle than the Queen and her flatterers, for they parted not the garments of our Master till that he himself was hung upon the cross; but she and her flatterers do part the spoil while as [3] poor Christ is yet preaching

[1] Undoubtedly Knox [2] *question*

[3] In the manuscript (folio 319 *recto*) "till that" has been corrected to "while as."

amongst you. But the wisdom of our God takes trial of us by these means, knowing well enough what she and her faction have purposed to do. Let the Papists, who have the two parts, some that have their thirds free,[1] and some that have got Abbacies and feu lands thank the Queen, and sing, *Placebo Dominæ.* The poor preachers will not yet flatter for feeding of their bellies." These words were judged proud and intolerable, and engendered no small displeasure to the speaker.

This we put in memory, that the posterities to come may know that God once made his truth to triumph ; but because that some of ourselves delighted more in darkness than in light, God hath restrained our freedom, and put the whole body in bondage. Yea, the greatest flatterers have not escaped so free as they supposed ; yea, the latter plagues appear yet to be worse than the first. " Be merciful to us, O Lord, and entreat us not according to our deservings ; but look thou to the equity of the cause which thou hast put into our hands, and suffer not iniquity to oppress thy truth, for thy own name's sake, O Lord."

Marriage of the Earl of Mar

In this meantime, to wit in February, the year of God 1561,[2] was the Lord James first made Earl of Mar,[3] and then married upon Agnes Keith, daughter to the Earl Marischal. The marriage was public in the church of Edinburgh.[4] In the marriage they both got an admonition to behave themselves moderately in all things : " For, (said the preacher [5] to him), unto this day the Kirk of God hath received comfort by you, and by your labours ; in the which, if hereafter ye shall be found fainter than that ye were before, it will be said that your wife hath changed your nature." The greatness of the banquet, and the vanity used thereat, offended many godly. There began the masking which from year to year hath continued

[1] That is, those to whom remissions had been granted

[2] That is, February 1562

[3] The Lord James Stewart was created Earl of Mar on 7 February 1562 (*Antiquities of Aberdeen and Banff*, Spalding Club, iv, 743) ; he resigned the earldom a few months later (*Scots Peerage*, vi, 314), and by February 1563 he had assumed the title of Earl of Moray, that earldom having been granted to him by charter as early as January 1562.

[4] According to the *Diurnal of Occurrents* (70), the marriage of the Lord James Stewart with Agnes Keith, eldest daughter of William, fourth Earl Marischal, was celebrated on 8 February 1562, " with sik solemnitie as the lyk hes not bene sein befoir ; the haill nobilitie of this realme being thair present, and convoyit thame doun to the Abbay of Halyrudhous, quhair the banket wes maid, and the Quenis Grace thairat." Randolph, however, dates the banquet as 10 February (*infra*, 33, *note* 2). 8 February was a Sunday.

[5] The preacher was John Knox.

since.[1] Master Randolph, agent for the Queen of England, was then, and sometime after, in no small conceit with our Queen ; for his Mistress's sake, she drank to him [in] a cup of gold, which he possessed with greater joy, for the favour of the giver, than of the gift and value thereof ; and yet it was honourable.[2]

The things that then were in handling betwix the two Queens, whereof Lethington, Secretary Cecil, and Master Randolph were ministers, were of great weight, as we will after hear.

This winter, the Earl Bothwell, the Marquis d'Elbœuf, and Lord John of Coldingham, played the riot in Edinburgh, misordered the whole town, broke Cuthbert Ramsay's yetts[3] and doors, [and] sought his house for his good-daughter [4] Alison Craik. And this was done in despite of the Earl of Arran, whose whore the said Alison was suspected to have been.[5] The horror of this fact, and the rarity of it, highly commoved all godly hearts. The Assembly, and also the nobility, for the most part were in the town ; and so they concluded to crave justice, as that they did, as by this subsequent Supplication doth appear :

TO THE QUEEN'S MAJESTY AND HER SECRET AND GREAT COUNCIL, HER GRACE'S FAITHFUL AND OBEDIENT SUBJECTS, THE PROFESSORS OF CHRIST JESUS HIS HOLY EVANGEL, WISH THE SPIRIT OF RIGHTEOUS JUDGMENT.[6]

The fear of God conceived of his holy word, the natural and unfeigned love we bear unto your Grace, the duty which we owe to the quietness of our country, and the terrible threatenings which our God pronounces against every realm and city in the which horrible crimes are openly committed, and then by the committers obstinately defended, compel us, a great part of your subjects, humbly

[1] Knox is here unjust to the Lord James Stewart with whom he had recently differed with regard to the Queen's Mass (*supra*, 5, 8). Masking did not begin with this marriage ; there had been masking at Holyrood as early as October 1561. (Robertson, *Inventaires de la Royne Descosse*, Preface, lxxv)

[2] This is reported by Randolph in a letter of 12 February to Cecil, where he says that Mary drank to Elizabeth and then sent him the cup of gold which weighed eighteen or twenty ounces. Randolph speaks of the banquet being held on " Shrove Tuesday at night," that is, on 10 February. (*Calendar of Scottish Papers*, i, No. 1077)

[3] *gates* [4] *daughter-in-law*, but in the modern sense of *step-daughter*

[5] According to Randolph, writing to Cecil on 27 December 1561, Arran was " known to have had company of a good handsome wench, a merchant's daughter." (See his account of the " disorder " in *Calendar of Scottish Papers*, i, No. 1056)

[6] *Booke of the Universall Kirk*, i, 11–12. The Supplication is prefaced with a particular recitation of the " horrible fact and impiety committed . . . under silence of night by the Marquis d'Elbœuf and his colleagues in breaking up of Cuthbert Ramsay's yets and doors, and searching and seeking his daughter-in-law to oppress her."

to crave of your Grace upright and true judgment against such persons as have done what in them lies to kindle God's wrath against this whole realm. The impiety by them committed is so heinous and so horrible, that as it is a fact most vile and rare to be heard of within this realm, and principally within the bowels of this city, so should we think ourselves guilty in the same, if negligently, or yet for worldly fear we pass it over with silence. And therefore your Grace may not think that we require anything (while that we crave open malefactors condignly to be punished) but that which God has commanded us to crave, and has also commanded your Grace to give to every one of your subjects ; for by this link has God knit together the prince and the people, that as he commands honour, fear, and obedience to be given to the powers established by him, so does he in expressed words command and declare what the prince oweth unto the subjects, to wit, that as he is the Minister of God, bearing his sword for vengeance to be taken on evil doers, and for the defence of peaceable and quiet men, so ought he to draw the same without all partiality so oft as in God's name he is required thereto. Seeing so it is (Madam), that this crime so recently committed, and that in the eyes of your whole realm now presently assembled, is so heinous, for who heretofore have heard within the bowels of Edinburgh, yetts and doors under silence of night burst up, houses ryped [1] (and that with hostility), seeking a woman as [it] appeared to oppress her ; seeing, we say, that this crime is so heinous, that all godly men fear not only God's sore displeasure to fall upon you and your whole realm, but also that such liberty breed contempt, and in the end sedition, if remedy in time be not provided, which in our judgment is impossible, if severe punishment be not executed for the crime committed ; Therefore, we most humbly beseech your Grace, that all affection set aside, ye declare yourself so upright in this case that ye may give evident demonstration to all your subjects that the fear of God, joined with the love of the common tranquillity, have principal seat and dominion in your Grace's heart. This further, Madam, of conscience we speak, that as your Grace in God's name does crave of us obedience (which to render in all things lawful we are most willing) so in the same name do we, the whole Professors of Christ's Evangel within this your Grace's Realm, crave of you and of your Council sharp punishment of this crime ; and for performance thereof, that without all delay the principal actors of this most heinous crime, and the pursuers of this pretended [2] villainy, may be called

[1] *searched* [2] *attempted*

before the Chief Justice of this Realm, to suffer an assize, and to be punished according to the laws of the same : And your Grace's answer most humbly we beseech.

This Supplication was presented by divers gentlemen. The flatterers of the Court at the first stormed, and asked, " Who durst avow it ? " To whom the Master, now Lord Lindsay [1] answered, " A thousand gentlemen within Edinburgh." Others were ashamed to oppose themselves thereto in public ; but they suborned the Queen to give a gentle answer unto such time as the Convention was dissolved. And so she did ; for she lacks no craft, both to cloak and to maintain impiety (and whoredom in especial). She alleged, " That her Uncle [2] was a stranger, and he had a young company ; but she should put such order unto him, and unto all others, that hereafter they should have no occasion to complain." And so deluded she the just petition of her subjects ; and no wonder, for how shall she punish in others that vice which in France is free without punishment, and which Kings and Cardinals use most commonly, as the mask and dancing of Orleans can witness, wherein virgins and men's wives were made as common to King Harry [3] and Charles, the Cardinal,[4] [and] unto their Court and pages, as common harlots of the bordel [5] are unto their companions. The manner was thus :

The mask of Orleans

At the entry of King Harry of France in the town of Orleans, the matrons, virgins, and men's wives, were commanded to present themselves in the King's palace at night, to dance : and they obeyed ; for commonly the French nation is not hard to be entreated to vanity. After fiddling and flinging, and when the Cardinal of Lorraine had espied his prey, he said to the King, " *Sire, la primiere est vostre, et faut que je suis le second.*" That is to say, " Sire, the first choice is yours, and I must be the second." And so the King got the pre-eminence, that he had his first election. But because Cardinals are companions to Kings, the Cardinal of Lorraine had the next : And thereafter the torches were put out, and every man commanded to provide for himself the best he might. What cry was there of husbands for their wives ; of wives, for their husbands ; of ancient matrons for their daughters ; and of virgins for their friends, or for some honest man to defend their pudicity, Orleans will remember more king's days than one.

This horrible villainy, a fruit of the Cardinal of Lorraine's religion,

[1] Patrick, later sixth Lord Lindsay of the Byres
[2] That is, René, Marquis d'Elbœuf [3] Henry II, King of France
[4] Charles, Cardinal of Lorraine, another of Mary's uncles [5] *brothel*

we shortly touch to let all the world understand what subjects may look of such magistrates ; for such pastime to them is but joyousity, wherein our Queen was brought up.[1] We call her not a whore (albeit her dame heard more than we will write), but she was brought up in the company of the wildest whoremongers (yea, of such as no more regarded incest than honest men regard the company of their lawful wives) ; in the company of such men (we say), was our Queen brought up. What she was, and is, herself best knows, and God (we doubt not), will further declare.

Our Queen's education

[G]od has now [d]one it, 1567 [2]

But punishment of that enormity and fearful attemptat [3] we could get none : but more and more they presumed to do violence, and frequented nightly masking. Some, as Robin Craig's house, because his daughter was fair, delighted therein : others lamented, and began to bear the matter very heavily. At length the Lord Duke's friends assembled upon a night upon the calsey.[4] The Abbot of Kilwinning [5] (who then was joined to the Church, and so, as we understand, yet abideth) was the principal man at the beginning. To him repaired many faithful ; and amongst others came Andrew Stewart, Lord Ochiltree, a man rather born to make peace than to brag upon the calsey, and demanded the quarrel ; and being informed of the former enormity said, " Nay, such impiety shall not be suffered so long as God shall assist us. The victory that God in his mercy hath given us, we will by his grace maintain." And so he commanded his son, Andrew Stewart, then Master,[6] and his servants to put themselves in order, and to bring forth their spears and long weapons ; and so did others. The word came to the Earl Bothwell and his, that the Hamiltons were upon the gait.[7] Vows were made, " That the Hamiltons should be doung,[8] not only out of the town, but also out of the country." Lord John of Coldingham had married the said Earl Bothwell's sister (a sufficient woman for such a man [9])—allia [10] drew the Lord Robert [11] ; and so they joined

The Hamiltons against Bothwell and the Marquis

[1] *Cf. supra*, i, 103 ; ii, 25

[2] This marginal note must have been added subsequently. It is not in the hand of the text (Hand A), and may be compared with the marginal note, *supra*, i, 103.

[3] *unlawful enterprise*

[4] A brief account of this further " incident " is given in *Diurnal of Occurrents* (70) under the date 19 December 1561.

[5] Gavin Hamilton, Commendator of Kilwinning

[6] Andrew Stewart, eldest son of Andrew Stewart, second Lord Ochiltree, predeceased his father.

[7] That is, were waiting to attack them in the street.

[8] *driven*

[9] The Lord John Stewart, Commendator of Coldingham, a natural son of James V, married Jean Hepburn, daughter of Patrick, third Earl of Bothwell, in January 1562.

[10] *alliance*

[11] Lord Robert Stewart, Commendator of Holyrood, also a natural son of James V.

both with the said Earl Bothwell. But the stoutness of the Marquis Le Bœuf (d'Elbœuf they call him) is most to be commended; for in his chamber, within the Abbey, he started to a halberd, and ten men were scarce able to hold him; but as hap was [1] the inner yett of the Abbey kept him that night; and the danger was betwix the Cross and the Salt Trone [2]; and so he was a large quarter of [a] mile from the shot and sklenting [3] of bolts. The Master of Maxwell [4] gave declaration to the Earl Bothwell, "That if he stirred forth of his lodging, he, and all that would assist him, should resist him in the face"; whose words did somewhat beat down that blast. The Earls of Huntly and Moray, being in the Abbey where the Marquis was, came with their companies, sent from the Queen to stay that tumult, as that they did; for Bothwell and his were commanded, under pain of treason, to keep their lodgings. [5]

It was whispered of many that the Earl of Moray's displeasure was as much sought as any haitterent that the Hamiltons bare against the Earl Bothwell, or yet he against them. And in very deed, either had the Duke very false servants, or else by Huntly and the Hamiltons the Earl of Moray's death was ofter conspired than once: the suspicion whereof burst forth so far that, upon a day, the said Earl, being upon horse to have come to the sermon, was charged by one of the Duke's own servants to return and abide with the Queen. The bruit thereof spread over all. What ground it had we cannot say; but short thereafter the Duke and some of the Lords convened at Glasgow; their conclusion was not known. The Earl of Arran came to Edinburgh, where the Earl Bothwell lay. The Queen and the Court were departed to Fife, and remained sometimes in Saint Andrews and sometimes in Falkland. [6]

The Earl Bothwell, by the means of James Barron, burgess, and then merchant of Edinburgh, desired to speak with John Knox secretly; which the said John gladly granted, and spake him upon a night, first in the said James's lodging, and thereafter in his own study. The sum of all their communication and conference was:

[1] *as it happened*

[2] That would be in the present High Street, between the Market Cross and the Tron Church. [3] the *crossfire*

[4] John, second son of Robert, fifth Lord Maxwell; later Lord Herries.

[5] Randolph, writing to Cecil on 27 December 1561, says that to avoid trouble Bothwell was to leave the town until 8 January (*Calendar of Scottish Papers*, i, No. 1056); the *Diurnal of Occurrents* (70) says that Bothwell "departed with his friends furth of Edinburgh at the Queen's command" on 21 December.

[6] Apparently from early in March until early in May, 1562. (See the Itinerary in Hay Fleming, *Mary Queen of Scots*, 518)

The Earl Bothwell. His communing with John Knox

The said Earl lamented his former inordinate life, and especially that he was provoked by the enticements of the Queen Regent to do that which he sore repented, as well against the Laird of Ormiston,[1] whose blood was spilt, albeit not in his default. But his chief dolour was that he had misbehaved himself against the Earl of Arran,[2] whose favours he was most willing to redeem, if possible it were that so he might; and desired the said John to give him his best counsel, "For (said he), if I might have my Lord of Arran's favours, I would await upon the Court with a page and few servants, to spare my expenses, where now I am compelled to keep, for my own saftey, a number of wicked and unprofitable men, to the utter destruction of my living that is left."

To the which the said John answered, "My Lord, would to God that in me were counsel or judgment that might comfort and relieve you. For albeit that to this hour it hath not chanced me to speak with your Lordship face to face, yet have I borne a good mind to your house; and have been sorry at my heart of the troubles that I have heard you to be involved in. For, my Lord, my grandfather, goodsire, and father,[3] have served your Lordship's predecessors, and some of them have died under their standards[4]; and this is a part of the obligation of our Scottish kindness[5]: but this is not the chief. But as God has made me his public messenger of glad tidings, so is my will earnest that all men may embrace it, which perfectly they cannot, so long as that there remaineth in them rancour, malice, or envy. I am very sorry that ye have given occasion unto men to be offended with you; but I am more sorry that ye have offended the Majesty of God, who by such means oft punishes the other sins of man. And therefore my counsel is, that ye begin at God, with whom if ye will enter in perfect reconciliation, I doubt not but he shall bow the hearts of men to forget all offences. And as for me, if ye will continue in godliness, your Lordship shall command me as boldly as any that serves your Lordship."

[1] See *supra*, i, 258–259. But as recently as March 1562, Bothwell and eight companions had "lain again in wait for the Laird of Ormiston." (*Calendar of Scottish Papers*, i, No. 1089) [2] See *Calendar of Scottish Papers*, i, No. 1089; Laing's *Knox*, vi, 140

[3] That is, Knox's great-grandfather, his grandfather, and his father. This terminology is even used in the Glasgow MS. (See Laing's *Knox*, vi, 688)

[4] This statement is interesting and important. It is our only reliable information with regard to Knox's family.

[5] *Kindness* is here used in the sense of *kinship*. Earlier Knox has referred to Hailes as being "the principal place that then [1546] the Earl Bothwell had in Lothian" (*supra*, i, 71). Hailes is in the parish of Prestonkirk, East Lothian. Did the Knox family hold lands in that neighbourhood?

The said Lord desired him that he would tempt [1] the Earl of Arran's mind, if he would be content to accept him in his favours, which he promised to do ; and so earnestly travailed in that matter, that it was once [2] brought to such an end as all the faithful praised God for that agreement. The greatest stay [3] stood upon the satisfaction of the Laird of Ormiston, who, beside his former hurt, as is before declared,[4] was even in that same time of the communing, pursued by the said Lord Bothwell, his son Master Alexander Cockburn taken by him, and carried with him to Borthwick ; but gently enough sent back again.[5]

That new trouble so greatly displeased John Knox that he almost gave over further travailing for amity. But yet, upon the excuse of the said Earl, and upon the declaration of his mind, he re-entered in labours, and so brought it to pass that the Laird of Ormiston referred his satisfaction in all things to the judgment of the Earls of Arran and Moray, whom to the said Earl Bothwell submitted himself in that head, and thereupon delivered his hand write. And so was convoyed by certain of his friends to the lodging of the Kirk-of-Field, where the Earl of Arran was with his friends, and the said John Knox with him, to bear witness and testification of the end of the agreement.[6] As the said Earl Bothwell entered at the chamber door, and would have done those honours that friends had appointed (Master Gavin Hamilton and the Laird of Riccarton,[7] were the chief friends that communed), the said Earl of Arran gently passed unto him, embraced him, and said, "If the hearts be upright, few ceremonies may serve and content me."

Reconciliation betwix the Earl of Arran and Earl Bothwell, etc.

The said John Knox, in audience of them both, and of their friends, said, "Now, my Lords, God hath brought you together by the labours of simple men, in respect of such as would have travailed therein. I know my labours are already taken in an evil part ; but because I have the testimony of a good conscience before my God, that whatsoever I have done, I have done it in his fear, for the profit of you both, for the hurt of none and for the tranquillity of this Realm ; seeing (I say), that my conscience beareth witness to me what I have sought and continually seek, I the more patiently bear the misreports and wrangous judgments of men. And now I leave

[1] *test* [2] *at one time* [3] *obstacle* [4] *Supra*, i, 258–259

[5] See the account of this incident in Randolph's letter to Cecil of 31 March 1562. There Randolph says the son was "led away till near Crichton, where the neighbours of the country (the Laird's friends) rescued him, driving Bothwell into his own house." (*Calendar of Scottish Papers*, i, No. 1089) [6] That is, the *reaching* of the agreement

[7] Alexander Hepburn of Whitsome and Riccarton

you in peace, and desire you that are the friends to study that amity may increase, all former offences being forgot." The friends on either party embraced other, and the two Earls departed to a window, and talked by themselves familiarly a reasonable space. And thereafter the Earl Bothwell departed for that night; and upon the next day in the morning returned, with some of his honest friends, and came to the sermon with the Earl foresaid; whereat many rejoiced. But God had another work to work than the eyes of men could espy.

The Thursday next [1] they dined together; and thereafter the said Earl Bothwell and Master Gavin Hamilton rode to my Lord Duke's Grace, who then was in Kinneil.[2] What communication was betwix them it is not certainly known, but by the report which the said Earl of Arran made to the Queen's Grace, and unto the Earl of Moray, by his writings.[3] For upon Friday,[4] the fourth day after their reconciliation, the sermon being ended, the said Earl of Arran came to the house of the said John Knox, and brought with him Master Richard Strang and Alexander Guthrie, to whom he opened the grief of his mind before that John Knox was called; for he was occupied (as commonly he used to be after his sermons) in directing of writings. Which ended, the said Earl called the three together, and said, "I am treasonably betrayed"; and with these words began to weep. John Knox demanded, "My Lord, who has betrayed you?" "A Judas, or other (said he); but I know it is but my life that is sought: I regard it not." The other said, "My Lord, I understand not such dark manner of speaking: if I shall give you any answer, ye must speak more plain." "Well (said he), I take you three to witness that I open this unto you, and I will write it unto the Queen. An act of treason is laid to my charge; the Earl Bothwell has shown to me in council, that he shall take the Queen, and put her in my hands in the Castle of Dumbarton; and that he shall slay the Earl of Moray, Lethington, and others that now misguide her: and so shall I and he rule all. But I know that this is devised to accuse me of treason; for I know that he will inform the Queen of it: But I take you to witness, that I open it here unto you; and I will pass incontinent and write to the Queen's Majesty, and unto my brother the Earl of Moray."

John Knox demanded, "Did ye consent, my Lord, to any part

[1] 26 March 1562 [2] Kinneil House, West Lothian

[3] For further accounts of the subsequent strange story see Randolph's letters (*Calendar of Scottish Papers*, i, Nos. 1089, 1090, 1091, 1095) and *Diurnal of Occurrents*, 71.

[4] Good Friday, 27 March 1562

of that treason ?" He answered, "Nay." "Then (said he), in my judgment, his words, albeit they were spoken, can never be treason unto you ; for the performance of the fact depends upon your will, whereto ye say ye have dissented ; and so shall that purpose evanish and die by the self, unless that ye waken it ; for it is not to be supposed that he will accuse you of that which he himself [has] devised, and whereto ye would not consent." "O (said he), ye understand not what craft is used against me : It is treason to conceal treason." "My Lord (said he), Treason must import consent and determination, which I hear upon neither of your parts. And therefore, my Lord, in my judgment it shall be more sure and more honourable to you to depend upon your [own] innocence, and to abide the unjust accusation of another (if any follow thereof, as I think there shall not), than ye to accuse (especially after so late reconciliation) and have none other witnesses but your own affirmation." "I know (said he) that he will offer the combat unto me ; but that would not be suffered in France ; but I will do that which I have purposed." And so he departed, and took with him to his lodging the said Alexander Guthrie and Mr. Richard Strang ; from whence was dited and written a letter to the Queen's Majesty, according to the former purpose, which letter was directed with all diligence to the Queen's Majesty, who then was in Falkland.

The Earl himself rode after to Kinneil, to his father, the Duke's Grace. How he was entreated, we have but the common bruit ; but from thence he wrote another letter with his own hand, in cipher, to the Earl of Moray, complaining upon his rigorous handling and entreatment by his own father, and by his friends ; and affirmed further, that he feared his life, in case that he got not sudden rescue. But thereupon he remained not, but broke the chamber wherein he was put, and with great pain passed to Stirling, and from thence he was convoyed to the Hallyards,[1] where he was kept till that the Earl of Moray came unto him, and convoyed him to the Queen, then being in Falkland, who then was sufficiently instructed of the whole matter ; and upon suspicion conceived, had caused apprehend Master Gavin Hamilton and the Earl Bothwell foresaid ; who knowing nothing of the former advertisements, came to Falkland, which augmented the former suspicion.

But yet the letters of John Knox made all things to be used more circumspectly ; for he did plainly forewarn the Earl of Moray that he espied the Earl of Arran to be stricken with frenzy, and therefore

[1] Hallyards, Auchtertool, Fife. At that time a seat of Kirkcaldy of Grange.

willed not over great credit to be given unto his words and inventions. And as he advertised, so it came to pass; for within few days his sickness increased; he devised of wondrous signs that he saw in the heavens; he alleged that he was bewitched; he would have been in the Queen's bed, and affirmed that he was her husband; and finally, he behaved himself in all things so foolishly, that his frenzy could not be hid. And yet were the said Earl Bothwell and Abbot of Kilwinning[1] kept in the Castle of Saint Andrews, and convened before the Council, with the said Earl of Arran, who ever stood firm that the Earl Bothwell proponed to him such things as he advertised the Queen's Grace of; but stiffly denied that his father, the said Abbot, or friends, knew anything thereof, either yet that they intended any violence against him; but alleged that he was enchanted[2] so to think and write. Whereat the Queen, highly offended, committed him to prison, with the other two, first in the Castle of Saint Andrews, and thereafter caused them to be convoyed to the Castle of Edinburgh.[3] James Stewart of Cardonald, called Captain James,[4] was evil bruited [of] for the rigorous entreatment that he showed to the said Earl in his sickness, being appointed keeper unto him.

To consult upon these accusations, the whole Council was assembled at Saint Andrews, the 18 day of April,[5] in the year of God 1562; in which it was concluded that, in consideration of the former suspicion, the Duke's Grace should render to the Queen the Castle of Dumbarton, the custody whereof was granted unto him by appointment, till that lawful succession should be seen of the Queen's body. But will prevailed against reason and promises, and so was the said Castle delivered to Captain Anstruther, as having power from the Queen and Council to receive it.[6]

Things ordered in Fife, the Queen returned to Edinburgh, and then began dancing to grow hot; for her friends began to triumph

[1] Gavin Hamilton [2] *bewitched*

[3] On 4 May 1562, according to the *Diurnal of Occurrents* (72). According to the Collector's Accounts of the Thirds of the Benefices (from which the Earl of Arran was allowed £2 a day for his upkeep in the castle of Edinburgh), Arran's second year of confinement began on 3 May 1563. He was released 1 May 1566.

[4] He was Captain of the Queen's bodyguard. (See *supra*, 25, *note* 1)

[5] On Monday 20 April 1562, according to Randolph. (*Calendar of Scottish Papers*, i, No. 1095)

[6] Apparently Captain Robert Anstruther, and in April 1562. (*Accounts Lord High Treasurer*, xi, 161, 162, 198) See also *Diurnal of Occurrents*, 72. It should be noted that Buchanan gives a different version of this strange story. According to Buchanan Bothwell first endeavoured to embroil the Earl of Moray against the Hamiltons and, that failing, then endeavoured to embroil the Hamiltons in a plot to murder Moray. (See Aikman's *Buchanan*, ii, 453–456; Calderwood's *History of the Kirk of Scotland*, ii, 177–179)

in France.[1] The certainty hereof came to the ears of John Knox, for there were some that showed to him, from time to time, the estate of things [2]; and, amongst others, he was assured that the Queen had danced excessively [3] till after midnight, because that she had received letters that persecution was begun again in France, and that her uncles were beginning to stir their tails,[4] and to trouble the whole Realm of France. Upon occasion of this text, "And now understand, O ye Kings, and be learned, ye that judge the earth," he began to tax the ignorance, the vanity, and the despite of Princes against all virtue, and against all those in whom haitterent of vice and love of virtue appeared.

Psal. 2

The report hereof made unto the Queen, the said John Knox was sent for.[5] Mr. Alexander Cockburn, who before had been his scholar,[6] and then was very familiar with him, was the messenger, who gave him some knowledge both of the report and of the reporters. The Queen was in her bedchamber, and with her, besides the ladies and the common servants, were the Lord James, the Earl of Morton, Secretary Lethington, and some of the guard that had made the report. He was called and accused, as one that had irreverently spoken of the Queen, and that travailed to bring her in haitterent and contempt of the people, and that he had exceeded the bounds of his text: And upon these three heads, made the Queen herself a long harangue or orison [7]; whereto the said John answered as follows:

The second communing of John Knox with the Queen

"Madam, this is oftentimes the just recompense which God giveth to the stubborn of the world, that because they will not hear God speaking to the comfort of the penitent, and for amendment of the wicked, they are oft compelled to hear the false report of others to their greater displeasure. I doubt not but that it came to the ears

[1] Queen Mary had returned to Edinburgh before 12 May 1562 (Hay Fleming, *Mary Queen of Scots*, 518); but the "massacre at Vassy" had already taken place on 1 March 1562, there had been a "massacre" at Sens, and Orleans had been seized by the Huguenots. Certainly war between the Huguenots and the Catholics had become inevitable, but there was as yet no "triumph" for Mary's "friends." According to Randolph, writing to Cecil on 29 May 1562, Mary regretted the "unadvised enterprise" of the Guises and feared their overthrow. (*Calendar of Scottish Papers*, i, No. 1107)

[2] *Cf. supra*, i, 351

[3] According to Sir James Melville, Mary did not dance "so high and disposedly" as Elizabeth. (*Memoirs*, Bannatyne Club, 125)

[4] *bestir themselves*

[5] Knox has here confused the order of events. Mary was back in Edinburgh before 12 May 1562, but Knox delivered his sermon in which "he inveighed sore against the Queen's dancing" on Sunday 13 December 1562, and the interview with Mary took place on Tuesday 15 December 1562—that is, after the Queen's "progress" in the North in the autumn of 1562, and not after her stay in Fife in the spring. (See Randolph's letter to Cecil of 16 December 1562, in Laing's *Knox*, vi, 147 and *Calendar of Scottish Papers*, i, No. 1155)

[6] *Supra*, i, 82

[7] *oration*

of proud Herod, that our Master Christ Jesus called him a fox; but they told him not how odious a thing it was before God to murder an innocent, as he had lately done before, causing to behead John the Baptist, to reward the dancing of a harlot's daughter. Madam, if the reporters of my words had been honest men, they would have reported my words, and the circumstances of the same. But because they would have credit in Court, and lacking virtue worthy thereof, they must have somewhat to please your Majesty, if it were but flattery and lies. But such pleasure (if any your Grace take in such persons) will turn to your everlasting displeasure. For, Madam, if your own ears had heard the whole matter that I entreated; if there be into you any sparkle of the Spirit of God, yea, of honesty or wisdom, ye could not justly have been offended with anything that I spake. And because that ye have heard their report, please your Grace to hear myself rehearse the same, so near as memory will serve." (It was even upon the next day after that the sermon was made).[1] "My text (said he), Madam, was this, 'And now, O Kings, understand; be learned, ye judges of the earth.' After, Madam (said he), that I had declared the dignity of kings and rulers, the honour whereinto God has placed them, the obedience that is due unto them, being God's lieutenants, I demanded this question,—But, O alas! what compte [2] shall the most part of princes make before that Supreme Judge, whose throne and authority so manifestly and shamefully they abuse? That the complaint of Solomon is this day most true, to wit, 'That violence and oppression do occupy the throne of God here in this earth': for while that murderers, bloodthirsty men, oppressors, and malefactors dare be bold to present themselves before kings and princes, and the poor saints of God are banished and exiled, what shall we say but that the devil hath taken possession in the throne of God, which ought to be fearful to all wicked doers, and a refuge to the innocent oppressed. And how can it otherwise be? For princes will not understand; they will not be learned as God commands them. But God's law they despise; his statutes and holy ordinances they will not understand; for in fiddling and flinging they are more exercised than in reading or hearing of God's most blessed word; and fiddlers and flatterers (which commonly corrupt the youth) are more precious in their eyes than men of wisdom and gravity, who by wholesome admonition might beat down into them some part of that vanity and pride whereinto all are born, but in

[1] According to Randolph the interview was on the Tuesday following the sermon on the Sunday. (*Supra* 43, *note* 5) [2] *account*

princes take deep root and strength by wicked education. And of dancing, Madam, I said, that albeit in Scriptures I found no praise of it, and in profane writers that it is termed the gesture rather of those that are mad and in frenzy than of sober men ; yet do I not utterly damn it, providing that two vices be avoided : the former, That the principal vocation of those that use that exercise be not neglected for the pleasure of dancing ; Secondly, That they dance not, as the Philistines their fathers, for the pleasure that they take in the displeasure of God's people. For if any of both they do, so they shall receive the reward of dancers, and that will be drink in hell,[1] unless they speedily repent, so shall God turn their mirth in sudden sorrow : for God will not always afflict his people, neither yet will he always wink at the tyranny of tyrants. If any man, Madam (said he), will say that I spake more, let him presently [2] accuse me ; for I think I have not only touched the sum, but the very words as I spake them." Many that stood by bare witness with him, that he had recited the very words that publicly he spake.

The Queen looked about to some of the reporters, and said, "Your words are sharp enough as ye have spoken them ; but yet they were told to me in another manner. I know (said she) that my uncles and ye are not of one religion, and therefore I cannot blame you albeit you have no good opinion of them. But if ye hear any thing of myself that mislikes you, come to myself and tell me, and I shall hear you."

"Madam," quod he, "I am assured that your uncles are enemies to God, and unto his Son Jesus Christ ; and that for maintenance of their own pomp and worldly glory that they spare not to spill the blood of many innocents ; and therefore I am assured that their enterprises shall have no better success than others have had that before them have done that [which] they do now. But as to your own personage, Madam, I would be glad to do all that I could to your Grace's contentment, provided that I exceed not the bounds of my vocation. I am called, Madam, to a public function within the Kirk of God, and am appointed by God to rebuke the sins and vices of all. I am not appointed to come to every man in particular to show him his offence ; for that labour were infinite.[3]

[1] The meaning is obvious ; but there may also be reference to the custom of drinking at dances, referred to in an old musical MS. : 'The tune is to be played even through once over every time : so the first couple has time to take their drink.' (Dauney's *Ancient Scottish Melodies*, Bannatyne Club, 260, cited Hay Fleming, *Mary Queen of Scots*, 275)

[2] *now*, at this present time

[3] It should be noted, however, that private admonition, in certain cases, had been prescribed by the *Book of Discipline*. (*Infra*, 306)

If your Grace please to frequent the public sermons, then doubt I not but that ye shall fully understand both what I like and mislike, as well in your Majesty as in all others. Or if your Grace will assign unto me a certain day and hour when it will please you to hear the form and substance of doctrine which is proponed in public to the churches of this Realm, I will most gladly await upon your Grace's pleasure, time and place. But to wait upon your chamber-door, or elsewhere, and then to have no further liberty but to whisper my mind in your Grace's ear, or to tell to you what others think and speak of you, neither will my conscience nor the vocation whereto God hath called me suffer it. For albeit at your Grace's commandment I am here now, yet cannot I tell what other men shall judge of me, that at this time of day am absent from my book and waiting upon the Court."

"You will not always," said she, "be at your book," and so turned her back. And the said John Knox departed with a reasonable merry countenance; whereat some Papists, offended, said, "He is not afraid." Which, heard of him, he answered, "Why should the pleasing face of a gentlewoman effray me? I have looked in the faces of many angry men, and yet have not been afraid above measure." And so left he the Queen and the Court for that time.

In this meantime, the negotiation and credit was great betwix the Queen of England and our Sovereign: letters, couriers, and posts ran very frequent. Great bruit there was of the interview and meeting of the two Queens at York, and some preparation was made therefor in both the Realms. But that failed upon the part of England, and that by occasion of the troubles moved in France (as was alleged), which caused the Queen and her Council attend upon the south parts of England, for avoiding of inconvenients.[1]

That summer, there came an Ambassador from the King of Sweden, requiring marriage of our Sovereign to his Master the King.[2] His entertainment was honourable; but his petition liked our Queen nothing; for such a man was too base for her estate; for had not she been great Queen of France? Fye of Sweden! What

[1] For these negotiations and the proposed "interview and meeting of the two Queens" see Hay Fleming, *Mary Queen of Scots*, 70–73 and supporting notes.

[2] According to the *Diurnal of Occurrents* (72, 73) the Swedish ambassador "Here Petir Groif" arrived on 24 April 1562 and departed with his [negative] answer on 1 June 1562. Randolph speaks of the news of his arrival on 25 April, says he is called the Earl of Wismar, and reports his departure early in the morning of Tuesday 2 June, after leaving a picture of his king to be presented to the Queen. (*Calendar of Scottish Papers*, i, Nos. 1095, 1097, 1111) Erik XIV of Sweden married Catharine Jagello in the following October.

is it? But happy was the man that of such a one was forsaken. And yet she refused not one far inferior to a virtuous King.

The Earl of Lennox and his wife were committed to the Tower of London for trafficking with Papists.[1] The young Laird of Barr[2] was a travailer in that business, and was apprehended with some letters, which were the cause of his and their trouble.

Hawick raid

The Earl of Moray made a privy raid to Hawick upon the fair-day thereof, and apprehended fifty thieves; of which number were seventeen drowned; others were executed in Jedburgh. The principals were brought to Edinburgh and there suffered, according to their merits upon the Burgh Muir.[3] The Queen was nothing content of the prosperity and good success that God gave to the Earl of Moray in all his enterprises, for she hated his upright dealing, and the image of God which evidently did appear into him; but at that time she could not well have been served without him.

Sharp left preaching and took him to the law

The Assembly of the Kirk at Midsummer, the [29][4] of June, anno 1562, approached, in the which were many notable heads entreated concerning good order to be kept in the Church; for the Papists and the idolatry of the Queen began to trouble the former good order. Some ministers, such as Master John Sharp, had left their charges, and entered into other vocations more profitable for the belly; against whom were acts made, although to this day they have not been put in execution.

Anno 1566 in May[5]

The tenor of the Supplication read in open audience, and approved by the whole Assembly to be presented to the Queen's Majesty, was this:

TO THE QUEEN'S MAJESTY, AND HER MOST HONOURABLE PRIVY COUNCIL, THE SUPERINTENDENTS AND MINISTERS OF THE EVANGEL OF JESUS CHRIST WITHIN THIS REALM, TOGETHER WITH THE COMMISSIONERS OF THE WHOLE CHURCHES, DESIRE GRACE AND PEACE FROM GOD THE FATHER OF OUR LORD JESUS CHRIST, WITH THE SPIRIT OF RIGHTEOUS JUDGMENT.[6]

[1] Matthew, fourth Earl of Lennox, and his wife, Lady Margaret Douglas, daughter of Archibald, sixth Earl of Angus. Their son was Henry Lord Darnley, who later married Mary Queen of Scots. Randolph, writing to Cecil on 31 March 1562, reports that "it is not lamented here [in Scotland] that Lennox is in the Tower." (*Calendar of Scottish Papers*, i, No. 1089)

[2] John Lockhart, younger, of Barr

[3] An account of this "raid" on the thieves of Teviotdale and Liddesdale is given by Randolph in a letter to Cecil of 8 July 1562. (*Calendar of Scottish Papers*, i, No. 1123)

[4] In the manuscript (folio 329 *recto*) the date is given, erroneously, as "the 24 of June"; but see *Booke of the Universall Kirk* (Bannatyne Club) i, 13–24.

[5] This marginal note (folio 329 *recto*) is in the text hand.

[6] *Booke of the Universall Kirk*, i, 20–24

Having in mind that fearful sentence pronounced by the Eternal God against the watchmen that see the sword of God's punishment approach, and do not in plain words forewarn the people, yea, the princes and rulers, that they may repent, we cannot but signify unto your Highness, and unto your Council, that the estate of this Realm is such for this present, that unless redress and remedy be shortly provided, that God's hand can not long spare in his anger, to strike the head and the tail, the inobedient Prince and sinful people : For as God is unchangeable and true, so must he punish in these our days, the grievous sins that before we read he has punished in all ages, after that he has long called for repentance, and none is shown.

And that your Grace and Council may understand what be the things we desire to be reformed, we will begin at that which we assuredly know to be the fountain and spring of all other evils that now abound in this Realm, to wit, that idol and bastard service of God, the Mass ; the fountain, we call it, of all impiety, not only because that many take boldness to sin by reason of the opinion which they have conceived of that idol, to wit, that by the virtue of it, they get remission of their sins ; but also because that under the colour of the Mass, are whores, adulterers, drunkards, blasphemers of God, of his holy Word and Sacraments, and such other manifest malefactors, maintained and defended : for let any Mass-sayer, or earnest maintainer thereof be deprehended [1] in any of the fore-named crimes, no execution can be had, for all is done in haiterent of his religion ; and so are wicked men permitted to live wickedly, cloaked and defended by that odious idol. But supposing that the Mass were occasion of no such evils, yet in the self it is so odious in God's presence, that we cannot cease with all instance to desire the removing of the same, as well from yourself as from all others within this Realm, taking heaven and earth, yea, and your own conscience to record, that the obstinate maintenance of that idol shall in the end be to you destruction of soul and body.

This causes the Queen's religion to have many favourers

If your Majesty demand, why that now we are more earnest than we have been heretofore ; we answer (our former silence nowise excused), because we find us frustrate of our hope and expectation ; which was, that in process of time, your Grace's heart should have been mollified, so far as that ye would have heard the public doctrine taught within this Realm ; by the which, our further hope was, that God's Holy Spirit should so have moved your heart, that ye should

[1] *apprehended*

have suffered your religion (which before God is nothing but abomination and vanity) to have been tried by the true touchstone, the written word of God[1]; and that your Grace finding it to have no ground nor foundation in the same, should have given that glory unto God, that ye would have preferred his truth unto your own preconceived vain opinion, of what antiquity that ever it has been. Whereof we in a part now discouraged can no longer keep silence, unless we would make ourselves criminal before God of your blood, perishing in your own iniquity; for we plainly admonish you of the dangers to come.

The second that we require, is punishment of horrible vices, such as are adultery, fornication, open whoredom, blasphemy, contempt of God, of his Word and Sacraments; which in this Realm, for lack of punishment, do even now so abound that sin is reputed to be no sin. And therefore, as that we see the present signs of God's wrath now manifestly appear, so do we forewarn that he will strike, ere it be long, if his law without punishment be permitted thus manifestly to be contemned. If any object that punishments cannot be commanded to be executed without a Parliament, we answer that the eternal God in his Parliament has pronounced death to be the punishment for adultery and for blasphemy; whose acts if ye put not to execution (seeing that kings are but his lieutenants, having no power to give life, where he commands death), as that he will repute you, and all others that foster vice, patrons of impiety, so will he not fail to punish you for neglecting of his judgments.

Our third request concerneth the poor, who be of three sorts: the poor labourers of the ground; the poor desolate beggars, orphans, widows, and strangers; and the poor ministers of Christ Jesus his holy evangel, which are all so cruelly entreated by this last pretended Order taken for sustentation of Ministers, that their latter misery far surmounteth the former. For now the poor labourers of the ground are so oppressed by the cruelty of those that pay their Third, [in] that they for the most part advance upon the poor whatsoever they pay to the Queen, or to any other.[2] As for the very indigent and poor, to whom God commands a sustentation to be provided of the Teinds, they are so despised that it is a wonder that the sun giveth heat and light to the earth where God's name is so frequently called upon and no mercy (according to his commandment) shown to his creatures. And also for the Ministers, their livings are so appointed that the most part shall live but a beggar's life. And all

Grudging of the nobility one against the other

[1] See *supra*, 12 [2] See also the *Book of Discipline*, *infra*, 303

cometh of that impiety, that the idle bellies of Christ's enemies must be fed in their former delicacy.

We dare not conceal from your Grace and Honours our conscience, which is this, that neither by the law of God, neither yet by any just law of man, is anything due unto them who now most cruelly do exact of the poor and rich the Two parts of their Benefices, as they call them: and therefore we most humbly require, that some other Order may be taken with them, nor that they be set up again to empire above the people of God, either yet above any subject within this Realm. For we fear that such usurpation to their former estate be neither in the end pleasing to themselves, nor profitable to them that would place them in that tyranny. If any think that a competent living is to be assigned to them, we repugn not, provided that the labourers of the ground be not oppressed, the poor be not utterly neglected, and the Ministers of the word so sharply entreated as now they are. And, finally, that those idle bellies, who by law can crave nothing, shall confess that they receive their sustentation, not of debt, but as of benevolence. Our humble request is, therefore, that some sudden order may be taken, that the poor labourers may find some relief, and that in every parish some portion of the Teinds may be assigned to the sustentation of the poor within the same; and likewise that some public relief may be provided for the poor within burghs; that collectors may be appointed to gather, and that sharp compts [1] may be taken, as well of their receipt as of their deliverance. The further consideration to be had to our Ministers, we in some part remit to your Wisdoms, and unto their particular complaints.

Our fourth petition is for the manses, yards, and glebes, justly appertaining to the Ministers, without the which it is impossible unto them quietly to serve their charges; and therefore we desire order to be taken thereinto without delay.

Our fifth concerneth the inobedience of certain wicked persons, who not only trouble, and have troubled Ministers in their function, but also disobey the Superintendents in their visitation; whereof we humbly crave remedy; which we do not so much for any fear that we and our Ministers have of the Papists, but for the love that we bear to the common tranquillity. For this we cannot hide from your Majesty and Council, that if the Papists think to triumph where they may, and to do what they list, where there is not a party able to resist them, that some will think that the godly must begin where

[1] *accounts*

they left, who heretofore have borne all things patiently, in hope that laws should have bridled the wicked ; whereof if they be frustrate (albeit that nothing be more odious to them than tumults and domestical discord), yet will men attempt the uttermost, before that in their own eyes they behold that House of God demolished, which with travail and danger God hath within this Realm erected by them.

Last, we desire that such as have received remission of their Thirds be compelled to sustain the Ministry within their bounds,[1] or else we forewarn your Grace and Council that we fear that the people shall retain the whole in their hands unto such time as their ministry be sufficiently provided. We further desire the kirks to be repaired according to an Act set forth by the Lords of Secret Council, before your Majesty's arrival in this country ; That Judges be appointed to hear the causes of divorcement, for the Kirk can no longer sustain that burden, especially because there is no punishment for the offenders ; That sayers and hearers of Mass, profaners of the Sacraments, such as have entered in[to] benefices by the Pope's Bulls, and such other transgressors of the law made at your Grace's arrival within this Realm, may be severely punished ; for else men will think that there is no truth meant in making of such laws.

Further, We most humbly desire of your Grace and Honourable Council, a resolute answer to every one of the heads forewritten that, the same being known, we may somewhat satisfy such as be grievously offended at manifest iniquity now maintained, at oppression under pretext of law done against the poor, and at the rebellious disobedience of many wicked persons against God's word and holy ordinance.

God the Father of our Lord Jesus Christ so rule your hearts and direct your Grace and Council's judgments by the ditement and illumination of his Holy Spirit that ye may answer so as that your consciences may be absolved in the presence of that righteous Judge, the Lord Jesus ; and then we doubt not but ye yourselves shall find felicity, and this poor Realm, that long has been oppressed by wicked men, shall enjoy tranquillity and rest, with the true knowledge of God.

These things read in public Assembly,[2] as said is, were approved of all (and some wished that more sharpness had been used, because

[1] That is, within their ecclesiastical boundaries. An account of the many remissions of " Thirds " is given by Dr. G. Donaldson in his work on the Collectors' Accounts.

[2] On 4 July 1562, at the sixth session. (*Booke of Universall Kirk*, i, 18–19)

that the time so craved), but the monzeors [1] of the Court, and Secretary Lethington above others, could not abide such hard speaking: " For whoever saw it written (said he) to a Prince, that God would strike the head and the tail: that if Papists did what they list, men would begin where they left." But above all others, that was most offensive that the Queen was accused, as that she would raise up Papists and Papistry again. To put that in the people's head was no less than treason; for oaths durst be made that she never meant such thing. To whom it was answered,[2] " That the Prophet Isaiah used such manner of speaking; and it was no doubt but he was well acquainted in the Court, for it was supposed he was of the King's stock. But howsoever it was, his words make manifest that he spake to the Court and Courtiers, to Judges, Ladies, Princes, and Priests: And yet (says he), 'The Lord shall cut away the head and the tail,' &c." " And so," said the first writer, " I find that such [a] phrase was once used before us. And if this offend you, that we say, 'Men must begin where they left,' in case that Papists do as they do, we would desire you to teach us, not so much how we shall speak, but rather what we shall do, when our Ministers are stricken, our Superintendents disobeyed, and a plain rebellion decreed against all good order." " Complain," said Lethington. " Whom to?" said the other. " To the Queen's Majesty," said he. " How long shall we do so?" quod the whole. " Till that ye get remedy," said the Justice Clerk [3]: " give me their names, and I shall give you letters." [4] " If the sheep," said one, " shall complain to the wolf that the wolves and whelps have devoured their lambs, the complainer may stand in danger; but the offender, we fear, shall have liberty to hunt after his prey." " Such comparisons," said Lethington, " are very unsavoury; for I am assured that the Queen will neither erect nor yet maintain Papistry." " Let your assurance," said another, " serve yourself but it cannot assure us, for her manifest proceedings speak the contrary."

Isaiah

Answer to Lethington

After such taunting reasoning of both the sides, the multitude concluded that the Supplication, as it was conceived, should be presented, unless that the Secretary would form one more agreeable to the present necessity. He promised to keep the substance of ours, but he would use other terms, and ask things in a more gentle manner. The first writer answered, " That he served the Kirk at their com-

[1] Possibly a derisive form of *monsieurs*, *mounseers*; or possibly intended for *monzeons*, that is, *minions*. [2] Undoubtedly by Knox

[3] Sir John Bellenden of Auchnoull [4] That is, letters of summonds

mandment, and was content that in his ditement should men use the liberty that best pleased them, provided that he was not compelled to subscribe to the flattery of such as more regarded the persons of men and women, than the simple truth of God." And so was this former Supplication given to be reformed as Lethington's wisdom thought best. And in very deed he framed it so, that when it was delivered by the Superintendents of Lothian and Fife, and when that she had read somewhat of it, she said, " Here are many fair words : I cannot tell what the hearts are." And so for our painted oratory we were termed the next name to flatterers and dissemblers. But for that Session the Kirk received none other answer.

John Gordon and Ogilvy

Short after [1] the convention of the Kirk chanced that unhappy pursuit which John Gordon, Laird of Findlater,[2] made upon the Lord Ogilvy,[3] who was evil hurt and almost yet abides mutilated. The occasion was for certain lands and rights which old Findlater had resigned to the said Lord, which he was pursuing, and was in appearance to obtain his purpose. Whereat the said John and his servants were offended, and therefore made the said pursuit upon a Saturday, at night, betwix nine and ten. The friends of the said Lord were either not with him, or else not well willing to fight that night ; for they took strokes, but gave few that left marks. The said John was taken, and put in the Tolbooth, where he remained certain days, and then broke his ward, some judged, at his father's commandment ; for he was making preparation for the Queen's coming to the North, as we will after hear.

The interview and meeting of the two Queens delayed till the next year, our Sovereign took purpose to visit the North, and departed from Stirling in the month of August. Whether there was

[1] As already noted (*supra*, 47, *note* 4) Knox gave the 24 June as the date of the meeting of the General Assembly instead of the 29 June. Thus for " short after " we should here read " short before." The conflict between Sir John Gordon and James, fifth Lord Ogilvy of Airlie, in which the latter was hurt in " the three principal members " of his right arm so seriously " that if he bleeds again the same will be his death," took place in Edinburgh on Saturday night, 27 June. (See *Edinburgh Burgh Records*, Burgh Record Society, iii, 138–139)

[2] Sir John Gordon was the third son of George, fourth Earl of Huntly. Alexander Ogilvy of Deskford and Findlater had disinherited his son, James Ogilvy of Cardell, in 1545, and had settled his lands and baronies in Aberdeen and Banff, and the name and arms of Ogilvy on John Gordon, whom failing, on his brothers William, James, and Adam Gordon, in succession. (*Registrum Magni Sigilli*, iii, No. 3157) Randolph, reporting this fight in Edinburgh, speaks of John Gordon as " named the Laird of Findlater." (*Calendar of Scottish Papers*, i, No. 1121) The endeavour of the Ogilvies to regain these lands, and the unwillingness of the Gordons to relinquish them, lie in the background of Corrichie and the forfeiture of Huntly. (See *Scots Peerage*, iv, 21–25)

[3] James, fifth Lord Ogilvy of Airlie

any secret paction and confederacy betwix the Papists in the South, and the Earl of Huntly and his Papists in the North; or, to speak more plainly, betwix the Queen herself and Huntly, we cannot certainly say. But the suspicions were wondrous vehement that there was no good will borne to the Earl of Moray, nor yet to such as depended upon him at that time. The history we shall faithfully declare, and so leave the judgment free to the readers.

That John Gordon broke his ward, we have already heard, who immediately thereafter repaired to his father George, then Earl of Huntly [1]; and understanding the Queen's coming, made great provision in Strathbogie, and in other parts, as it were to receive the Queen. At Aberdeen the Queen and Court remained certain days to deliberate upon the affairs of the country; where some began to smell that the Earl of Huntly was under gathering, as hereafter shall be declared.

Bothwell broke ward

While things were so working in the North, the Earl Bothwell broke his ward, and came forth of the Castle of Edinburgh,[2] the 28th of August. Some say that he broke the stancheour [3] of the window; others whispered that he got easy passage by the yetts. One thing is certain, to wit, the Queen was little offended at his escaping. There passed with him a servant of the Captain's, named James Porterfield. The said Earl showed himself not very afraid, for his common residence was in Lothian. The Bishop of Saint Andrews [4] and Abbot of Crossraguel [5] kept secret convention that same time in Paisley, to whom resorted divers Papists; yea, the said Bishop spake the Duke,[6] unto whom also came the Lord Gordon [7] from the Earl of Huntly, requiring him "to put to his hands in the South, as he should do in the North; and so it should not be Knox's crying nor preaching that should stay that purpose." The Bishop, be he never so close, could not altogether hide his mind, but at his own table said, "The Queen is gone into the North, belike to seek disobedience: she may perchance find the thing that she seeks." It was constantly affirmed that the Earl Bothwell and the said Lord Gordon spake together, but of their purpose we heard no mention.[8]

The false bishop and his traffic

[1] George, fourth Earl of Huntly [2] See *supra*, 42
[3] *stanchion* [4] John Hamilton [5] Quintin Kennedy
[6] The Duke of Châtelherault
[7] George, Lord Gordon, second son of George, fourth Earl of Huntly; later George, fifth Earl of Huntly.
[8] Their "purpose" is revealed in the reduction of the sentence of forfeiture passed against George, Lord Gordon. (*Acts Parl. Scot.*, ii, 577*a*) Briefly, it was that Bothwell should raise men to serve Huntly.

That same year, and at that instant time, were appointed Commissioners by the General Assembly to Carrick and Cunningham Master George Hay who, the space of a month, preached with great fruit in all the churches of Carrick; to Kyle, and to the parts of Galloway, was appointed John Knox who, beside the doctrine of the Evangel shown unto the common people, forewarned some of the Nobility and Barons of the dangers that he feared, and that were appearing shortly to follow, and exhorted them to put themselves in such order as that they might be able to serve the authority, and yet not to suffer the enemies of God's truth to have the upper hand. Whereupon a great part of the Barons and Gentlemen of Kyle and Cunningham and Carrick, professing the true doctrine of the Evangel, assembled at Ayr, and, after exhortations made and conference had, subscribed this Band, the tenor whereof follows:

Commissioners

We, whose names are underwritten, do promise, in the presence of God, and in the presence of his Son our Lord Jesus Christ, that we, and everyone of us, shall and will maintain and assist the preaching of his holy Evangel, now of his mere mercy offered unto this Realm; and also will maintain the ministers of the same against all persons, power, and authority, that will oppose themselves to the doctrine proponed, and by us received. And further, with the same solemnity, we protest and promise, that every one of us shall assist others; yea, and the whole body of the Protestants within this Realm, in all lawful and just actions, against all persons; so that whosoever shall hurt, molest, or trouble any of our body, shall be reputed enemy to the whole, except that the offender will be content to submit himself to the judgment of the Kirk now established amongst us. And this we do, as we desire to be accepted and favoured of the Lord Jesus, and reaccompted [1] worthy of credit and honesty in the presence of the godly. At the Burgh of Ayr, the fourth day of September, the year of God 1562.

Subscribed by all these with their hands, as follows:

Mr. Michael Wallace, Provost of Ayr	Glencairn [3]
	Ro. Boyd [4]
James Lockhart [2]	R. Failford [5]

[1] *accounted* [2] Probably Sir James Lockhart of Lee

[3] Alexander, fourth Earl of Glencairn [4] Robert, fifth Lord Boyd

[5] Robert Cunningham, a younger son of William, third Earl of Glencairn. He was "minister" of Fail, or Failford, and Provincial of the Order of the Holy Trinity (Trinitarians) in Scotland. The head of a Trinitarian House was called the "minister"; and we find the designation "minister of Fail" as early as 1413. (*Laing Charters*, No. 93)

William Montgomery
John Crawford of Walston
John Mure in Wole
Hew Wallace of Cairnhill
James Chalmers of Gadgirth
Hew Montgomery of Hesilhead
John Fullarton of Dreghorn
I, William Cunningham, with my hand
Skeldon [1]
Fergushill [2]
Mr. of Boyd [3]
John Lockhart of Barr
William Cunningham of Caprington younger
Robert Ker of Kersland
Robert Crawford
David Crawford
William Cunningham
Charles Campbell, Burgess of Ayr
James Dalrymple of Stair
Mungo Mure
James Reid
James Kennedy, Burgess of Ayr
George Lockhart, Burgess there
Robert Shaw, Burgess there
John Dunbar of Blantyre
Robert Chalmers of Martnaham
Robert Hunter of Hunterston
Robert Rankin
Archibald Boyle
Alexander Nisbet
James Lockhart
William Stewart of Halrig
Hector Dunbar of Clugstone
James Campbell of Lochlee
Adam Cathcart of Bardarroch
George Reid of Chapelhouse
Matthew Campbell of Loudoun, Knight [4]
Alan Lord Cathcart [5]
John Cunningham of Caprington
Cunninghamhead [6]
Ochiltree [7]
George Crawford of Leiffnoris
John Mure of Rowallan
Hew Cunningham of Waterstoun
Robert Cunningham [of] Auchenharvie
Middleton [8]
John Wallace of Craigie
John Boyd of Naristoun
Robert Campbell of Kinzeancleuch
Gilbert Eccles
Thomas Cathcart, with my hand
Alan Cathcart of Clavannis
Adam Reid of Barskimming
John Cathcart of Gibsyard
John Reid, with my hand
John . . . [9]
Robert Boyd of Piedmont
William Campbell of Horsecleuch
William Cathcart, brother to the Lord Cathcart [10]
John Macquhidaill
George Corry of Kelwood
William Kennedy of Ternganoch
John Kennedy of Kirkmichael
Thomas MacAlexander of Crosslays
Hew Wallace of the Meinford
Robert Campbell of Craigdow
Andrew Niven of Monkredding
William Cathcart
David Crawford of the Kerse
John Kennedy of Ternganoch
Patrick Kennedy of Daljarrock
Alan Cathcart of Carleton

[1] William Campbell of Skeldon
[2] John Fergushill of that Ilk
[3] Thomas, Master of Boyd, son of Robert, fifth Lord Boyd
[4] Sir Matthew Campbell of Loudoun, had succeeded his father Sir Hugh Campbell of Loudoun in February 1561. In the manuscript (folio 335 *recto*), "Crawfurd of" has been deleted and "Mathew Campbell of" added above the line.
[5] Alan, fourth Lord Cathcart
[6] William Cunningham of Cunninghamhead
[7] Andrew Stewart, second Lord Ochiltree
[8] The Laird of Middleton (unidentified)
[9] Blank in manuscript
[10] Presumably a natural son of Alan, third Lord Cathcart. If so, he has escaped the peerage writers.

These things done at Ayr, the said John passed to Nithsdale and Galloway where, in conference with the Master of Maxwell,[1] a man of great judgment and experience, he communicated with him such things as he feared; who, by his motion, wrote to the Earl Bothwell to behave himself as it became a faithful subject, and to keep good quietness in the parts committed to his charge, and so would his crime of the breaking of the ward be the more easily pardoned. John Knox wrote unto the Duke's Grace, and earnestly exhorted him neither to give ear to the Bishop his bastard brother,[2] nor yet to the persuasions of the Earl of Huntly; for if he did, he assured him that he and his House should come to a sudden ruin.

By such means were the South parts kept in reasonable quietness during the time that the troubles were in brewing in the North. And yet the Bishop and the Abbot of Crossraguel,[3] did what in them lay to have raised some trouble; for besides the fearful bruits that they sparsed [4] abroad (sometimes that the Queen was taken; sometimes that the Earl of Moray and all his band were slain; and sometimes that the Queen had given herself unto the Earl of Huntly —besides such bruits) the Bishop, to break the country of Kyle, where quietness was greatest, raised the Crawfords against the Reids for the payment of the Bishop's Pasche fines [5]; but that was stayed by the labours of indifferent men [6] who favoured peace.

Disputation

The Abbot of Crossraguel required disputation of John Knox for maintenance of the Mass, which was granted unto him, and which [was] held in Maybole three days. The Abbot had the advantage that he required, to wit, he took upon him to prove that Melchisedek offered bread and wine unto God, which was the ground that the Mass was built upon to be a Sacrifice, &c. But in the travail of three days there could no proof be produced for Melchisedek's oblation, as in the same disputation (which is to be had in print [7]) clearly may appear. The Papists constantly looked for a wolter,[8] and therefore they would make some brag of reasoning. The Abbot further presented himself to the pulpit, but the voice of Master George Hay so effrayed him that after once he wearied of that exercise.[9]

Crossraguel offered him once to preach

[1] Sir John Maxwell, second son of Robert, fifth Lord Maxwell; later fourth Lord Herries [2] That is, John Hamilton, Archbishop of St. Andrews

[3] Quintin Kennedy, fourth son of Gilbert, second Earl of Cassillis

[4] *spread* [5] Easter offerings [6] *neutral men*

[7] Printed by Robert Lekprevik, Edinburgh, 1563; reprinted in Laing's *Knox*, vi, 169–220 [8] Literally an *overturning*, that is, a counter-revolution

[9] Mr. George Hay's controversy with Quintin Kennedy was also published by Robert Lekprevik under the title *The Confutation of the Abbote of Crosraguells Masse* (Edinburgh, 1563).

After [1] that the Queen was somewhat satisfied of hunting and other pastime, she came to Aberdeen, where the Earl of Huntly met her, and his Lady, with no small train, [and] remained in Court. [He] was supposed to have the greatest credit, departed with the Queen to Buchan, [and] met her again at Rothiemay, looking that she should have passed with him to Strathbogie. But in the journey certain word came to her that John Gordon had broken promise in not re-entering in ward; for his father the Earl had promised that he should enter again within the Castle of Stirling, and there abide the Queen's pleasure. But whether with his father's knowledge and consent, or without the same we know not, but he refused to enter; which so offended the Queen that she would not go to Strathbogie, but passed through Strathisla to Inverness, where the Castle thereof was denied unto her. The Captain was commanded to keep it, and looked for relief, for so had John of Gordon promised; but being thereof frustrated, the Castle was rendered, and the Captain named Gordon was executed; the rest were damned,[2] and the hands of some bound, but [they] escaped.

This was the beginning of further trouble; for the Earl of Huntly, thereat offended, began to assemble his folks, and spared not to speak that he would be revenged. But always his wife bore fair countenance to the Queen; and it is verily supposed that no other harm than the Queen herself could easily have stood content with was meant unto her own person. But the whole malice lay upon the Earl of Moray, Secretary Lethington, and upon the Laird of Pittarrow. Yet the Queen began to be afraid, and by proclamation caused warn Stirling, Fife, Angus, Mearns and Strathearn charge all substantial men to be in Aberdeen the fifth day of October, there to remain the space of twenty days. In her returning from Inverness, she required the Castle of Findlater, which was likewise denied, and so was Auchindoune, which more inflamed [3] the Queen. The Earl of Huntly was charged to cause deliver the said houses, under pain of treason. To show some obedience, he caused the keys of both to be presented by his servant, Mr. Thomas Keir. But before had the Queen sent young Captain Stewart,[4] (son to Captain James who,

[1] For further details of Mary's northern progress, the Battle of Corrichie, and Huntly's overthrow, see Hay Fleming, *Mary Queen of Scots*, chapter vii and supporting notes.

[2] *condemned*

[3] In the manuscript (folio 337 *recto*) the scribe had written "in," and Knox has completed the word by crowding "flammed" into the space left before the word "the".

[4] Apparently Captain Alexander Stewart, son of Captain James Stewart of Cardonald. (See *supra*, 25, *note* 1)

to this day, has neither been stout, happy, nor true), with six score of soldiers, to lie about the said place of Findlater. They lodged in Cullen, not far distant from the said place. Upon a night, John Gordon came with a company of horsemen, took the Captain, slew certain of the soldiers, and disarmed the rest. This fact, done (as the Queen alleged) under trust, so inflamed her, that all hope of reconciliation was past ; and so the said Earl of Huntly was charged, under pain of putting of him to the horn,[1] to present himself and the said John before the Queen and Council within six days : which charge he disobeyed, and so was denounced rebel. Whether it was law or not, we dispute little therein ; but it was a preparative to others that after were served with that same measure. He was sought at his place of Strathbogie, but escaped.

So was the Duke, the Earls Argyll, Moray, and Glencairn, with all their companies after served[2]

The evil increased, for the Earl assembled his folk out of all parts of the North. He marched forward towards Aberdeen, and upon the twenty-two day of October, the year of God 1562, came to the Loch of Skene. His army was judged to seven or eight hundred men. The Queen's army, both in number and manhood, far surmounted his, and yet he took no fear ; for he was assured of the most part of them that were with the Queen, as the issue did witness. Within the town they stood in great fear ; and therefore it was concluded that they would assail the uttermost upon the fields.[3] The Forbeses, Hays, and Leslies took the vanguard, and promised to fight the said Earl without any other help. They passed forth of the town before ten hours. They put themselves in array, but they approached not to the enemy till that the Earl of Moray and his company were come to the fields ; and that was after two at afternoon ; for he was appointed with his company only to have beholden the battle. But all things turned otherwise than the most part of men supposed.

The Earl of Huntly was the night before determined to have retired himself and his company ; but that morning he could not be wakened before it was ten hours, and when he was up on foot his spirits failed him (by reason of his corpulency), so that rightly a long time he could do nothing. Some of his friends, fearing the danger, left him. When that he looked upon both the companies, he said, " This great company that approacheth nighest to us will do us no harm, they are our friends. I only fear yonder small com-

[1] To be " put to the horn " was to be proclaimed an outlaw or rebel. The proclamation was accompanied by *three blasts upon a horn*, which gave rise to the term.

[2] That is, they were denounced rebels and " at the horn " in August and September 1565, after Mary's marriage with Darnley and preceding the " Chase-about Raid."

[3] That is, put up the strongest defence outside the town.

pany that stand upon the hill-side, yon are our enemies. But we are enough for them, if God be with us." And when he had thus spoken, he fell upon his knees, and made his prayer in this form: "O Lord, I have been a bloodthirsty man, and by my means has mekle innocent blood been spilt; but wilt thou give me victory this day, and I shall serve thee all the days of my life."—Note and observe, good reader, he confessed that he had been a bloodthirsty man, and that he had been the cause of the shedding of much innocent blood: but yet would he have had victory; and what was that else, but to have had power to have shed more, and then would he have satisfied God for all together. Wherein is expressed the nature of hypocrites, which neither further feareth nor loveth God than present danger or profit suadeth. But to our History.

The Earl of Huntly's prayer

The Leslies, Hays, and Forbeses, espying the Earl of Moray and his to be lighted upon their foot, made forward against the Earl of Huntly and his, who stood in Corrichie Burn (some call it Fare Bank) [1]; but ere they approached, nigh by the space of the shot of an arrow, they cast from them their spears and long weapons, and fled directly in the face of the Earl of Moray and his company. The danger espied, the Laird of Pittarrow, a man both stout and of a ready wit,[2] with the Master, now Lord Lindsay,[3] and [the] Tutor of Pitcur,[4] said, "Let us cast down spears [5] to the foremost, and let them not come amongst us, for there is no doubt but that this flying is by treason." And so they did: so that they that fled kept themselves apart from the few number that were marching upon foot in order. The Earl of Huntly, seeing the vanguard flee, said unto his company, "Our friends are honest men, they have kept promise: let us now rencounter [6] the rest." And so he and his, as sure of victory, marched forward.

Corrichie Burn, or Fare Bank

The treasonable fact of the North

The Secretary, in few words, made a vehement orison,[7] and willed every man to call upon his God, to remember his duty, and not to fear the multitude; and, in the end, concluded thus: "O Lord, thou that rules the heaven and the earth, look upon us thy servants, whose blood this day is most unjustly sought, and to man's judgment is sold and betrayed: Our refuge is now unto thee and our hope

Secretary Lethington. His orison at Corrichie

[1] Corrichie is a marshy hollow almost surrounded by the heights of the Hill of Fare in Banchory-Ternan parish, on the border of Kincardineshire and Aberdeenshire. The battle of Corrichie was fought on 28 October 1562.

[2] Sir John Wishart of Pittarrow

[3] Patrick, eldest son of John, fifth Lord Lindsay of the Byres; became sixth Lord Lindsay following the death of his father in December 1563.

[4] James Haliburton, Tutor of Pitcur, and Provost of Dundee

[5] That is, *level our spears* [6] *meet* [7] *oration*

is in thee. Judge thou, O Lord, this day, betwix us and the Earl of Huntly, and the rest of our enemies. If ever we have unjustly sought his or their destruction and blood, let us fall in the edge of the sword. And, O Lord, if thou knowest our innocence, maintain thou and preserve us for thy great mercy's sake."

Short after the speaking of these and the like words, the former ranks joined, for Huntly's company made great haste. They were repulsed by the Master of Lindsay and the companies of Fife and Angus. Some of them that fled returned, and followed the Earl of Moray, but gave no strokes till that Huntly's company gave back. In the front there were slain about eighteen or twenty-four men, and in the fleeing there fell nigh a hundred. There was taken a hundred, and the rest were spared. The Earl himself was taken alive; his two sons, John foresaid, and Adam Gordon, were taken with him. The Earl, immediately after his taking, departed this life without any wound, or yet appearance of any stroke whereof death might have ensued [1]; and so, because it was late, he was casten over-thorte [2] a pair of creels, and so was carried to Aberdeen, and was laid in the Tolbooth thereof, that the response which his wife's witches had given might be fulfilled, who all affirmed (as the most part say) that that same night should he be in the Tolbooth of Aberdeen without any wound upon his body. When his Lady got knowledge thereof, she blamed her principal witch, called Janet; but she stoutly defended herself (as the devil can ever do), and affirmed that she gave a true answer, albeit she spake not all the truth; for she knew that he should be there dead: but that could not profit my Lady.[3] She was angry and sorry for a season, but the Devil, the Mass, and witches have as great credit of her this day as they had seven years ago.

The response of the Earl of Huntly's witches

12 *June* 1566 [4]

The Earl of Moray sent message unto the Queen of the marvellous victory, and humbly prayed her to show that obedience to God as

[1] Randolph, writing to Cecil from Aberdeen at 11 p.m. on the night of the battle, says that Huntly, after he was taken "without either blow or stroke, being set upon horseback before him that was his taker, suddenly falleth from his horse stark dead." (*Calendar of Scottish Papers*, i, No. 1148) The accounts in the *Diurnal of Occurrents* (74) and in Herries's *Historical Memoirs* (Abbotsford Club edition, 66) say that Huntly's "taker" was one Andrew Ridpath, one of the Queen's guard. Probably Huntly died of an apoplectic stroke (see *Records of Aboyne*, New Spalding Club, 467). For the numbers engaged in the battle, see Hay Fleming, *Mary Queen of Scots*, 305, *note* 28.

[2] *athwart*

[3] Elizabeth Keith, sister of William, fourth Earl Marischal, and daughter of Robert, eldest son of William, third Earl Marischal.

[4] This marginal note is in the hand of the text; a later caret has been added after the word "day" (folio 339 *recto*).

publicly to convene with them to give thanks unto God for his notable deliverance. She glowmed both at the messenger and at the request, and scarcely would give a good word or blithe countenance to any that she knew earnest favourers of the Earl of Moray, whose prosperity was, and yet is, a very venom to her boldened heart against him for his godliness and upright plainness.[1] Of many days she bare no better countenance; whereby it might have been evidently espied that she rejoiced not greatly of the success of that matter; and albeit she caused execute John Gordon and divers others, yet it was the destruction of others that she sought.

The Lady Forbes. Her words

Upon the morrow after the discomfiture, the Lady Forbes,[2] a woman both wise and fearing God, came amongst many others to visit the corpse of the said Earl; and seeing him lie upon the cold stones, having only upon him a doublet of cammoise,[3] a pair of Scottish gray hose, and covered with an arras-work, she said, "What stability shall we judge to be into this world? There lieth he that yesterday in the morning was holden the wisest, the richest, and a man of greatest power that was within Scotland." And in very deed she lied not; for, in man's opinion, under a prince, there was not such a one these three hundred years in this realm produced. But felicity and worldly wisdom so blinded him that in the end he perished in them, as shall all those that despise God and trust in themselves.

John Gordon, at his death, confessed many horrible things, devised by his father, by his brother, and by himself.[4] There were letters found in the Earl's pocket, that disclosed the treason of the Earl of Sutherland,[5] and of divers others. Mr. Thomas Keir,[6] who before was the whole counsellor to the Earl foresaid, disclosed whatsoever he understood might hurt the Gordons and their friends:

[1] Buchanan simply says that "the Queen betrayed no symptom of joy, either in her countenance or speech" (Aikman's *Buchanan*, ii, 464), without directing Mary's hatred solely against Moray and his supporters.

[2] Elizabeth Keith, daughter of Sir William Keith of Inverugie, and wife of William, seventh Lord Forbes. It should be noted, in view of the context, that at this time no love was lost between the Gordons and the Forbeses.

[3] Usually a fine silken cloth (*cammes*), though Knox may have intended to convey the sense of a coarse cloth of rough weave (*cammas*).

[4] For John Gordon's confessions, see *Calendar of Scottish Papers*, i, Nos. 1149, 1152.

[5] John, tenth Earl of Sutherland. He was later accused of treason and condemned and forfeited by Parliament in May 1563, but the forfeiture was reduced in 1567 (*Acts Parl. Scot.*, ii, 579, c. 25). See also Fraser's *Sutherland Book*, i, 123–125; iii, 135–139, where it appears that he was rehabilitated in December 1565 and received a new charter of his Earldom in March 1566.

[6] In the manuscript (folio 339, *verso*) "keyth" has been scored through and "keir" added in the margin—possibly in Knox's own hand.

and so the treason [was] plainly disclosed, which was, that the Earl of Moray with certain others should have been murdered in Strathbogie; the Queen should have been taken, and kept at the devotion of the said Earl of Huntly.

These things (we say) revealed, the Queen left the North, and came to Dundee, Saint Johnston, Stirling, and then to Edinburgh. The Earl of Huntly's body was carried about in a boat, and laid without burial in the Abbey of Holyroodhouse,[1] till the day of his forfaltour,[2] as after shall be declared.[3] The Duke apprehended the Lord Gordon, his son-in-law,[4] because that the Queen had straitly commanded him so to do, if he repaired within his bounds. Before he delivered him, the Earl of Moray laboured at the Queen's hand for the safety of his life, which hardly was granted[5]; and so was he delivered within the Castle of Edinburgh, the twenty-eighth day of November, where he remained till the eighth of February, when he was put to an assize, accused, and convicted of treason; but was restored again, first to the Castle foresaid, and thereafter was transported to Dunbar, where he remained prisoner till the month of August, the year of God 1565, as we will after hear.[6]

1562

In this meantime the troubles were hot in France; and the intelligence and outward familiarity betwix the two Queens[7] was great. Lethington was directed with large commission both to the Queen of England and unto the Guisians. The marriage of our Queen was in all men's mouths. Some would have Spain; some the Emperor's brother; some Lord Robert Dudley; some Duke de Nemours; and some unhappily guessed at the Lord Darnley.[8]

Men's judgments of the Queen's marriage

[1] The Treasurer's Accounts give details of the expenses of bringing Huntly's body to Edinburgh and of the expenses of its rough embalment in order that it might be laid before parliament and arraigned for treason. (*Accounts Lord High Treasurer*, xi, 205, 226) See also Hay Fleming, *Mary Queen of Scots*, 80 and supporting notes; *Inventaires de la Royne Descosse*, Preface, xxii and notes.

[2] *forfeiture* [3] *Infra*, 77

[4] George, Lord Gordon (later fifth Earl of Huntly) had married Anne, youngest daughter of the Duke of Châtelherault.

[5] According to Keith (*History*, ii, 180–181) Châtelherault had already interceded in vain. In contradistinction to Knox's statement, Moray is said to have surreptitiously obtained Mary's signature to a letter ordering Gordon's execution, but the story needs to be better authenticated (see Hay Fleming, *Mary Queen of Scots*, 306, *note* 32).

[6] But only from Knox's continuator (*infra*, 157)

[7] That is, between Mary and Elizabeth

[8] These "dukes, brethren to Emperors, and Kings," who were spoken of for Mary's hand were Don Carlos, son of Philip II of Spain; the Archduke Charles of Austria, a younger son of the Emperor Ferdinand I, and brother of Maximilian II; Robert, Lord Dudley, later Earl of Leicester; James, Duc de Nemours; and Henry, Lord Darnley, whom Mary eventually married in 1565. See also *infra*, 81.

What Lethington's credit was, we know not [1]; but short after there began much to be talked of the Earl of Lennox, and of his son, the Lord Darnley. It was said that Lethington spake the Lady Margaret Douglas,[2] and that Robert Melville [3] received a horse to the Secretary's use, from the Earl of Lennox, or from his wife. Howsoever it was, Master Fowler, servant to the said Earl, came with letters to the Queen's Grace, by the which licence was permitted to the Earl of Lennox to come to Scotland, to travail in his lawful business.[4] That same day that the licence was granted, the said Secretary said, "This day have I taken the deadly haiterent of all the Hamiltons within Scotland, and have done unto them no less displeasure than that I had cut their throats."

The Earl Bothwell who before had broken ward, fearing apprehension, prepared to pass to France; but by storm of weather was driven into England, where he was stayed, and was offered to have been rendered by the Queen of England. But our Queen's answer was that he was no rebel, and therefore she requested that he should have liberty to pass where it pleaseth him. And thereto Lethington helped not a little; for he travailed to have friends in every faction of the Court. And so obtained the said Earl licence to pass to France.

The preachers railed upon of [5] the courtiers

The preachers' admonition after the death of the Earl Huntly

The winter after the death of the Earl of Huntly, the Court remained for the most part in Edinburgh. The Preachers were wondrous vehement in reprehension of all manner of vice, which then began to abound; and especially avarice, oppression of the poor, excess, riotous cheer, banqueting, immoderate dancing, and whoredom, that thereof ensues. Whereat the Courtiers began to storm, and began to pick quarrels against the Preachers, alleging that all their preaching was turned to railing. Whereunto one of them [6] gave answer as followeth: "It comes to our ears that we are called railers, whereof albeit we wonder, yet we are not ashamed, seeing that the most worthy servants of God that before us have travailed in this vocation, have so been styled. But unto you do I say, that that same God, who from the beginning has punished the contempt of his word, and has poured forth his vengeance upon such

[1] Likewise the *Diurnal of Occurrents* (75) reports that on 13 February 1563 Lethington went on embassy to France, "to what effect non knowis." The instructions given to Lethington for his English embassy are printed in Keith, *History*, ii, 188–192.

[2] Wife of Matthew, fourth Earl of Lennox, and mother of Darnley.

[3] Sir Robert Melville of Murdocairnie, later Lord Melville of Monimail.

[4] But Lennox did not return to Scotland until the early autumn of 1564 (*Calendar of Scottish Papers*, ii, No. 97).

[5] *by*

[6] Undoubtedly Knox

proud mockers, shall not spare you ; yea, he shall not spare you before the eyes of this same wicked generation, for the pleasure whereof ye despise all wholesome admonitions. Have ye not seen one greater than any of you sitting where presently ye sit, pick his nails, and pull down his bonnet over his eyes, when idolatry, witchcraft, murder, oppression, and such vices were rebuked? Was not his common talk, When those knaves have railed their fill, then will they hold their peace? Have ye not heard it affirmed to his own face, that God should revenge that his blasphemy, even in the eyes of such as were witnesses to his iniquity? Then was the Earl Huntly accused by you, as the maintainer of idolatry, and only hinderer of all good order. Him has God punished, even according to the threatenings that his and your ears heard ; and by your hands hath God executed his judgments. But what amendment in any case can be espied in you? Idolatry was never in greater rest : virtue and virtuous men were never in more contempt : vice was never more bold, nor less feared punishment. And yet who guides the Queen and Court? Who but the Protestants? O horrible slanderers of God, and of his holy Evangel. Better it were unto you plainly to renounce Christ Jesus, than thus to expose his blessed Evangel to mockage. If God punish not you, that this same age shall see and behold your punishment, the Spirit of righteous judgment guides me not."

Huntly

Let the world judge now, 1571, for Lethington then was the father of all mischief[1]

This vehemence provoked the hatterent,[2] not only of the Courtiers, but also of divers others against the speaker ; for such as be in credit never lack flatterers. "Their brethren of the Court were irreverently handled. What was that, but to raise the hearts of the people against them? They did what they might ; such speaking would cause them do less." And this was the fruit the Preachers gathered of their just reprehensions.

The defence of the courtiers

The General Assembly of the Church, held the twenty-fifth of December, the year of God 1562, approached, in the which,[3] great complaints were made, that churches lacked Ministers ; that Ministers lacked their stipends ; that wicked men were permitted to be Schoolmasters, and so to infect the youth ; amongst whom

[1] This marginal note (folio 341 *recto*) is not in the hand of the text and not in Knox's hand. The hand is that of a later commentator who also added the note on the preceding page "The preachers railed upon of the courtiers." The words "then was" refer, of course, to the period 1562–63. The comment "Let the world judge now, 1571" refers to Lethington's adherence to the cause of the Queen and to his arrival in Edinburgh Castle in April of that year to join Kirkcaldy of Grange, who was then holding the Castle for Mary. [2] *hatred* [3] See *Booke of the Universall Kirk*, i, 25–30

one, Master Robert Cumin, schoolmaster in Aberbrothok,[1] was complained upon by the Laird of Dun,[2] and sentence was pronounced against him. It was further complained, that idolatry was erected in divers parts of the Realm; for redress whereof, some thought best that new supplication should be presented to the Queen's Grace. Others demanded, what answer was received of the former? The Superintendent of Lothian [3] confessed the deliverance of it, "But," said he, "I received no answer." It was answered for the part of the Queen (for her supposts [4] were ever there), "That it was well known to the whole Realm what troubles had occurred since the last Assembly; and therefore that they should not wonder albeit that the Queen had not answered: but betwix that and the Parliament which was appointed in May, they doubted not but that such order should be taken as all men should have occasion to stand content." This satisfied, for that time, the whole assembly: And this was the practice of the Queen and of her Council, with fair words to drive time, as before we have said.

The Queen's practice

The Assembly, notwithstanding, proceeded forward in establishing of such orders, as whereby vice might be punished, and virtue might be maintained. And because that there was a great slander risen upon Paul Methven, of whom mention is made in the Second Book of this History,[5] commission and charge was given unto John Knox, minister of Edinburgh, and unto certain of the elders of the Kirk of Edinburgh, to pass to the town of Jedburgh, where the said slander was raised, and to be found there the third of January next, for the trial to be taken in the slander raised, and to hear the articles and complaint of the said Paul; and after the trial to report the truth to the Session of the Church of Edinburgh; to whom, with the assistance of the Superintendent of Lothian, commission was given to decern therein. The trial and examination of that crime was difficult. The slander was universal in that town and country. The servant woman of the said Paul had betwix terms left his house; she had borne a child; no father to it could she find; but alleged herself to have been oppressed late in one evening. The said Paul constantly affirmed himself innocent, and would have given his public purgation; but because that his accusators had taken upon them to prove their accusation, that was denied. Many witnesses were produced, of whom some deponed so clearly that the Commissioners suspected

[1] Arbroath
[2] John Erskine of Dun, Superintendent of Angus and Mearns
[3] John Spottiswoode [4] *supporters* [5] *Supra*, i, 148

that they had been suborned, and therefore they required to have inspection of the places, where some said they saw, and some said they heard them in the very act of iniquity. The sight and consideration of the places augmented greatly the suspicion. But one thing was most suspicious of all others; for the wife of the said Paul, an ancient matron, was absent from him the space of eight or nine weeks in Dundee; which time (or at least a great part thereof) they suspected, and he lay nightly in a house, without other company than a child of seven or eight years of age.

The Judges, notwithstanding these suspicions, having a good opinion of the honesty and godliness of the man, travailed what they could (conscience not hurt) to purge him of the slander. But God, who would not that such villainy should be cloaked and concealed within his Church, otherwise had decreed; for he brought the brother of the guilty woman to the town, having no mind of such matters, who, being produced by the accusators as one that was privy of the fact, and knew the verity with all circumstances: This witness (we say), which could not be suspected, being produced, made the matter so plain and clear that all suspicion was removed; for he it was that convoyed the woman away; he it was that caused the child to be baptised, alleging it to be his own: he it was that carried frequent message betwix them, and from Paul carried money and clothes divers times. How soon that ever the said Paul saw that man produced as witness, he withdrew himself, and left the town, by that means plainly taking upon him the crime; and so the Commissioners with full information returned to Edinburgh, and notified the fact unto the Church, who caused publicly summon the said Paul to hear the sentence pronounced; who not compearing, in the end, for his odious crime and contumacy, was publicly excommunicated, and deprived of all function within the Churches of Scotland[1]: and so left he the Realm.

Here the iniquity of Paul Methven was clearly proven

For two causes we insert this horrible fact, and the order kept in punishment of the same. Former, to forewarn such as travail in that vocation that, according to the admonition of the Apostle, "Such as stand, take heed lest they fall." No man in the beginning of the Evangel was judged more fervent and more upright, and yet we have heard how far Sathan has prevailed against him. God grant that we may hear of his repentance.[2] Neither yet ought his fall anything to prejudge the authority of the doctrine which he

[1] *Booke of the Universall Kirk*, i, 31

[2] See *ibid.*, 55–56, 79–81; and also Knox's continuator, *infra*, 187–188

taught; for the doctrine of God has authority of no creature, but has the assurance of God himself, how weak or imperfect that ever the instruments be by whom it pleases God to publish the same.[1] The treason of Judas, the adultery of David, and the abnegation of Peter, did derogate nothing to the glory of Christ's evangel, nor yet to the doctrine which before they had taught; but declared the one to be a reprobate, and the other to be instruments in whom mercy must needs surmount judgment. The other cause is, That the world may see what difference there is betwix light and darkness, betwix the uprightness of the Church of God, and the corruption that ringes[2] in the synagogue of Sathan, the Papistical rabble; for how many of that sort hath been, and still remain openly known whoremongers, adulterers, violaters of virgins, yea, and committers of such abominations as we will not name; and yet are they called and permitted to be Bishops, Archbishops, Cardinals, and Popes themselves. For what sins can unable[3] the sworn servants of simony, and of his father the devil? For brag what they list of Christ, of Peter, and of Paul, their lives and conversations bear witness whom to they belong. But we return to our History of things done in Court.

Amongst the monzeons[4] of the Court, there was one named Monsieur Chattelett,[5] a Frenchman, that at that time passed all others in credit with the Queen. In dancing of the Purpose (so term they that dance, in the which man and woman talk secretly—wise men would judge such fashions more like to the bordell[6] than to the comeliness of honest women),[7] in this dance the Queen chose Chattelett, and Chattelett took the Queen. Chattelett had the best dress. All this winter Chattelett was so familiar in the Queen's cabinet, ayre[8] and late that scarcely could any of the Nobility have access unto her. The Queen would lie upon Chattelett's shoulder, and sometimes privily she would steal a kiss of his neck. And all this was honest enough; for it was the gentle entreatment of a stranger. But the familiarity was so great that, upon a night, he privily did convoy himself under the Queen's bed; but, being espied, he was commanded away. But the bruit arising, the Queen called the Earl of Moray, and bursting forth in a womanly affection, charged him,

Chattelett and the Queen

[1] Though this is a different attitude from that taken against the Roman clergy in Books I, II, and III. [2] *reigns* [3] *disqualify* [4] *minions*

[5] For a detailed analysis of the Châtelard incident see Hay Fleming, *Mary Queen of Scots*, 312, *note* 5. See also *Inventaires de la Royne Descosse*, Preface, lxxv, *note*.

[6] *brothel* [7] *Cf. supra*, 25, 44–45 [8] *early*

"That as he loved her, he should slay Chattelett, and let him never speak word." The other, at the first, made promise so to do; but after calling to mind the judgments of God pronounced against the shedders of innocent blood, and also that none should die, without the testimony of two or three witnesses, returned and fell upon his knees before the Queen, and said, "Madam, I beseech your Grace, cause not me take the blood of this man upon me. Your Grace has entreated him so familiarly before that ye have offended all your Nobility; and now if he shall be secretly slain at your own commandment, what shall the world judge of it? I shall bring him to the presence of Justice, and let him suffer by law according to his deserving." "Oh," said the Queen, "ye will never let him speak?" "I shall do," said he, "Madam, what in me lieth to save your honour." [1]

The Queen's desire concerning Chattelett's death

Poor Chattelett was brought back from Kinghorn to Saint Andrews, examined, put to an assize, and so beheaded, the twenty-two day of February, the year of God 1562.[2] He begged licence to write to France the cause of his death, which, said he, in his tongue, was, "Pour estre trouvé en lieu trop suspect"; that is, "Because I was found in a place too much suspect." At the place of execution, when he saw that there was no remedy but death, he made a godly confession, and granted, that his declining from the truth of God, and following of vanity and impiety, was justly recompensed upon him. But in the end he concluded, looking unto the heavens, with these words, "O cruel Dame," that is, "Cruel Mistress".[3] What that complaint imported, lovers may divine. And so received Chattelett the reward of his dancing; for he lacked his head, that his tongue should not utter the secrets of our Queen. "Deliver us, O Lord, from the rage of such inordinate rulers."

The year of God a thousand five hundred threescore three years, there was a universal dearth in Scotland. But in the northland,

[1] The latter part of this conversation between Mary and the Earl of Moray, and particularly Mary's insistence that Châtelard should not be allowed to speak, is probably apocryphal. Randolph, writing to Cecil on 15 February 1563, says that Moray was sent for, and Mary "incontinent commanded" him "to put his dagger" in Châtelard; which had been done "if God had not put into his mind" to reserve him to be justified according to law. So this day [15 February] the Lord Chancellor, the Justice-Clerk, and other Councillors are sent for over the water to meet the Queen at St. Andrews. (*Calendar of Scottish Papers*, i, No. 1170)

[2] That is, 22 February 1563

[3] Despite the following sentence, Knox can here be using "mistress" only in the sense of a woman who is loved and courted by a man. According to Brantôme, the words spoken by Chastelard were "Adieu, the most beautiful and the most cruel Princess of the world." (Laing's *Knox*, ii, 369, *note*)

The punishment of God for maintaining and erecting of the Mass

Dearth and famine in the north

where the harvest before the Queen had travelled, there was an extreme famine, in the which many died in that country. The dearth was great over all, but the famine was principally there. The boll [1] of wheat gave six pounds; the boll of bear,[2] six marks [3] and a half; the boll of meal, four marks; the boll of oats, fifty shillings; an ox to draw in the pleuch,[4] xx marks; a wether thirty shillings. And so all things appertaining to the sustentation of man, in triple and more exceeded their accustomed prices.[5] And so did God, according to the threatening of his law, punish the idolatry of our wicked Queen, and our ingratitude that suffered her to defile the land with that abomination again, that God so potently had purged by the power of his word. For the riotous feasting and excessive banqueting, used in Court and country, wheresoever that wicked woman repaired, provoked God to strike the staff of bread and to give his malediction upon the fruits of the earth. But, O alas, who looked, or yet looks to the very cause of all our calamities.

Pasche or Easter

Lethington was absent, as before we have heard,[6] in the Queen's affairs. The Papists, at that Pasche, anno 1563,[7] in divers parts of the Realm, had erected up that idol, the Mass; amongst whom the Bishop of Saint Andrews,[8] the Prior of Whithorn,[9] with divers others of their faction, would avow it. Besides the first proclamation, there had letters passed in the contrary, with certification of death to the contravener.

The stoutness of the Protestants in the West

The brethren universally offended, and espying that the Queen, by her proclamations, did but mock them, determined to put to their own hands, and to punish for example of others. And so some Priests in the westland were apprehended,[10] intimation made unto others (as unto the Abbot of Crossraguel,[11] the Parson of Sanquhar,[12] and such), that they [13] should neither complain to Queen nor Council, but should execute the punishment that God has appointed to

[1] A measure for grain which, despite the Acts of 1426 (*Acts Parl. Scot.*, ii, 12*a*) varied in different parts of the country. [2] *barley* (of an inferior quality)

[3] A *mark* was not a coin; it was the amount of thirteen shillings and fourpence (two-thirds of a pound). [4] *plough*

[5] An Act of the Privy Council of 11 February 1563 refers to "the tempestuous storms of the winters past" whereby the animals were lost, suffocated, or died, so that the price of meat had risen "to such extreme dearth that the like has not been seen within this realm." (*Register Privy Council of Scotland*, i, 235) [6] *Supra*, 63–64

[7] Easter Sunday, 11 April [8] John Hamilton

[9] Malcolm Fleming, second son of John, second Lord Fleming

[10] Randolph, writing to Cecil on 1 May 1563, says that at Easter five or six priests were apprehended in the West country for saying Mass and ministering to the people. (*Calendar of Scottish Papers*, ii, No. 6) [11] Quintin Kennedy

[12] Mr. Robert Crichton [13] That is, "the brethren"

idolaters in his law, by such means as they might, wherever they should be apprehended.

The Queen stormed at such freedom of speaking, but she could not amend it; for the Spirit of God, of boldness and of wisdom had not then left the most part of such as God had used instruments in the beginning. They were of one mind to maintain the truth of God, and to suppress idolatry. Particularities had not divided them; and therefore could not the devil, working in the Queen and Papists, do then what they would; and, therefore, she began to invent a new craft. She sent for John Knox to come unto her, where she lay at Lochleven.[1] She travailed with him earnestly two hours before her supper, that he would be the instrument to persuade the people, and principally the gentlemen of the West, not to put hands to punish any man for the using of themselves in their religion as pleased them. The other, perceiving her craft, willed her Grace to punish malefactors according to the laws, and he durst promise quietness upon the part of all them that professed the Lord Jesus within Scotland. But if her Majesty thought to delude the laws, he said, he feared that some would let the Papists understand that, without punishment, they should not be suffered so manifestly to offend God's Majesty.

John Knox sent for by the Queen

"Will ye," quod she, "allow that they shall take my sword in their hand?"

Reasoning betwix the Queen and John Knox

"The Sword of Justice," quod he, "Madam, is God's, and is given to princes and rulers for one end, which, if they transgress, sparing the wicked, and oppressing innocents, they that in the fear of God execute judgment where God has commanded, offend not God, although kings do it not; neither yet sin they that bridle kings to strike innocent men in their rage. The examples are evident; for Samuel feared not to slay Agag, the fat and delicate king of Amalek, whom king Saul had saved. Neither spared Elijah Jezebel's false prophets, and Baal's priests, albeit that king Ahab was present. Phinehas was no magistrate, and yet feared he not to strike Cozbi and Zimri in the very act of filthy fornication. And so, Madam, your Grace may see that others than chief magistrates may lawfully punish, and have punished, the vice and crimes that God commands to be punished. And in this case I would earnestly pray your Majesty to take good advisement, and that your Grace should let the Papists understand that their attemptates will not be suffered un-

[1] This interview probably took place in April 1563 (see Hay Fleming, *Mary Queen of Scots*, 523). According to Laing, Mary left Lochleven for Perth on 15 April. (Laing's *Knox*, ii, 371)

punished. For power, by Act of Parliament, is given to all judges within their own bounds, to search [for] massmongers, or the hearers of the same, and to punish them according to the law. And therefore it shall be profitable to your Majesty to consider what is the thing your Grace's subjects look to receive of your Majesty, and what it is that ye ought to do unto them by mutual contract. They are bound to obey you, and that not but in God. Ye are bound to keep laws unto them. Ye crave of them service: they crave of you protection and defence against wicked doers. Now, Madam, if ye shall deny your duty unto them (which especially craves that ye punish malefactors) think ye to receive full obedience of them? I fear, Madam, ye shall not."

Herewith she, being somewhat offended, passed to her supper. The said John Knox left her, informed the Earl of Moray of the whole reasoning, and so departed of final purpose to have returned to Edinburgh, without any further communication with the Queen. But before the sun, upon the morn, were two directed (Watt Melville [1] was the one) to him, commanding him not to depart while that he spake the Queen's Majesty; which he did, and met her at the hawking be-west Kinross. Whether it was the night's sleep, or a deep dissimulation locked in her breast, that made her to forget her former anger, wise men may doubt; but thereof she never moved word, but began divers other purposes: such as the offering of a ring to her by the Lord Ruthven,[2] "Whom," said she, "I cannot love (for I know him to use enchantment), and yet is he made one of my Privy Council."

"Who blames your Grace," said the other, "thereof?"

"Lethington," said she, "was the whole cause."

"That man is absent," said he, "for this present, Madam; and therefore I will speak nothing in that behalf."

"I understand," said the Queen, "that ye are appointed to go to Dumfries, for the election of a Superintendent to be established in those countries."

"Yes," said he, "those quarters have great need, and some of the gentlemen so require."

"But I hear," said she, "that the Bishop of Athens [3] would be Superintendent."

[1] Walter Melville, a younger son of Sir John Melville of Raith and brother of Sir James Melville of Hallhill. (*Scots Peerage*, vi, 93)

[2] Patrick, third Lord Ruthven. For the giving of the ring to Mary—a little ring with a pointed diamond in it, which had a "virtue" to keep the Queen from poisoning—see Keith, *History of the Affairs of Church and State in Scotland*, Spottiswoode Soc., iii, 271.

[3] Alexander Gordon, titular Archbishop of Athens, Bishop of Galloway

"He is one," said the other, "Madam, that is put in election." [1]

"If ye knew him," said she, "as well as I do, ye would never promote him to that office, nor yet to any other within your Kirk." [2]

"What he has been," said he, "Madam, I neither know nor yet will I enquire; for, in time of darkness, what could we do but grope and go wrong even as darkness carried us? But if he fear not God now, he deceives many more than me. And yet (said he), Madam, I am assured God will not suffer his Church to be so far deceived as that an unworthy man shall be elected, where free election is, and the Spirit of God is earnestly called upon to decide betwix the two."

"Well," says she, "do as ye will, but that man is a dangerous man."

The Queen's judgment of the Bishop of Athens

And therein was not the Queen deceived; for he had corrupted most part of the gentlemen, not only to nominate him, but also to elect him; which perceived by the said John [Knox], Commissioner, [he] delayed the election and left [it] with the Master of Maxwell [and] Mr. Robert Pont (who was put in election with the foresaid Bishop), to the end that his doctrine and conversation might be the better tried of those that had not known him before. And so was the Bishop frustrated of his purpose for that present. And yet was he, at that time, the man that was most familiar with the said John, in his house, and at table. But now to the former conference.

When the Queen had long talked with John Knox, and he being oft willing to take his leave, she said, "I have one of the greatest matters that have touched me since I came in this Realm to open unto you, and I must have your help into it." And she began to make a long discourse of her sister, the Lady Argyll,[3] how that she was not so circumspect in all things as that she wished her to be. "And yet," said she, "my Lord, her husband, whom I love, entreats her not in many things so honestly and so godly as I think ye yourself would require."

"Madam," said he, "I have been troubled with that matter before, and once I put such an end to it (and that was before your

[1] See *Booke of the Universall Kirk*, i, 28 (29 December 1562)

[2] He was the son of a natural daughter of James IV, and was thus cousin to the Queen.

[3] Lady Jane Stewart, a natural daughter of James V, who had married Archibald, fifth Earl of Argyll—"a wayward and unloving wife who had forsaken her husband's home for the court of Holyrood" (Robertson, *Inventaires de la Royne Descosse*, Preface, xxxviii and *notes*). For the history of her subsequent divorce from the Earl, see Riddell, *Inquiry into the Law and Practice in Scottish Peerages*, i, 547–552.

Grace's arrival), that both she and her friends seemed fully to stand content. And she herself promised before her friends, that she should never complain to creature, till that I should first understand the controversy by her own mouth, or else [by an] assured messenger. I now have heard nothing of her part; and therefore I think there is nothing but concord."

"Well," said the Queen, "it is war [1] than ye believe. But do this mekle [2] for my sake, as once again to put them at unity; and if she behave not herself so as she ought to do, she shall find no favours of me. But, in anywise (said she) let not my Lord know that I have requested you in this matter, for I would be very sorry to offend him in that or any other thing. And now (said she), as touching our reasoning yesternight, I promise to do as ye required; I shall cause summon all offenders, and ye shall know that I shall minister justice."

"I am assured then," said he, "that ye shall please God, and enjoy rest and tranquillity within your Realm; which to your Majesty is more profitable than all the Pope's power can be." And thus they departed.

This conference we have inserted to let the world see how deeply Mary, Queen of Scotland, can dissemble; and how that she could cause men to think that she bore no indignation for any controversy in religion, while that yet in her heart was nothing but venom and destruction, as short after did appear.

John Knox departed, and prepared himself for his journey appointed to Dumfries [3]; and from Glasgow, according to the Queen's commandment, he wrote this Letter to the Earl of Argyll, the tenor whereof follows:

"*The Lord cometh and shall not tarry, &c.*

"After commendation of my service unto your Lordship, if I had known of your Lordship's sudden departing, the last time it chanced me to see and speak you, I had opened unto you somewhat of my grief. But supposing that your Lordship should have remained still with the Queen's Grace, I delayed at that time to utter any part of that which now my conscience compelleth me to do. Your behaviour toward your wife is very offensive unto many godly. Her

[1] *worse* [2] *much*

[3] As one of the commissioners for the election of the Superintendent of Galloway. (*Booke of the Universall Kirk*, i, 28)

complaint is grievous, that ye altogether withdraw the use of your body from her. If so be, ye have great need to look well to your own estate, for albeit that ye, within yourself, felt no more repugnance than any flesh this day on earth, yet by promise made before God are ye debtor unto her, as reasonably ye shall be required of her. But if that ye burne [1] on the one side (albeit ye do no worse), and she in your default upon the other, ye are not only mensworn before God, but also doeth what in you lieth to kindle against yourself his wrath and heavy displeasure. These words are sharp, and God is witness that in dolour of heart I write them ; but because they are true, and pronounced by God himself, I dare not but admonish you, perceiving you, as it were, sleeping in sin. The proud stubbornness, whereof your Lordship hath oft complained, will not excuse you before God ; for if ye be not able to convict her of one crime, ye ought to bear with other imperfections, and that ye would that she should bear with you, in the like. In the bowels of Christ Jesus, I exhort you, my Lord, to have respect to your own salvation, and not to abuse the lenity and long suffering of God : for that is a fearful treasure [2] that ye heap upon your own head, while that He calleth you to repentance, and you obstinately continue in your own impiety ; for impiety it is, that ye abstract your comfort and company from your lawful wife. I write nothing in defence of her misbehaviour towards your Lordship in any sort ; but I say, if ye be not able to convict her of adultery committed since your last reconciliation, which was in my presence, that ye can never be excused before God of this freammed [3] and strange intreatment of your wife. And if by you such impiety be committed as is bruited, then, before God, and unto your own conscience I say, that every moment of that filthy pleasure shall turn to you in a year's displeasure; yea, it shall be the occasion and cause of everlasting damnation, unless speedily ye repent : and repent ye cannot, except that ye desist from that impiety. Call to mind, my Lord, ' That the servant knowing the will of his Lord, and doing the contrary, shall be plagued with many plagues.' Sin, my Lord, is sweet in drinking, but in digesting more bitter than the gall. The Eternal move your heart earnestly to consider how fearful a thing it is ever to have God to be [an] enemy.

" In the end, I most heartily pray your Lordship not to be absent from Edinburgh the nineteen of this instant for such causes as I will

[1] *deceive ;* or *play false* [2] So in the manuscript. ? *lege* " measure "
[3] *distant, foreign*

not write.[1] This much only I forewarn your Lordship, that it will not be profitable for the common quietness of this Realm that the Papists brag and that justice be mocked that day. And thus I cease further to trouble your Lordship, whom God assist. In haste from Glasgow, the 7 of May 1563. Your Lordship's to command in godliness.

(*Sic subscribitur*)
"JOHN KNOX."

This bill was not well accepted of the said Earl; and yet did he utter no part of his displeasure in public, but contrarily showed himself most familiar with the said John. He kept the diet, and sat in judgment himself, where the Bishop and the rest of the Papists were accused, as after follows.

The summonds were directed against the mass-mongers with expedition, and in the straitest form. The day was appointed the xix of May, a day only before the Parliament.[2] Of the Pope's knights compeared [3] the Bishop of Saint Andrews,[4] the Prior of Whithorn,[5] the Parson of Sanquhar,[6] William Hamilton of Cambuskeith, John Gordon of Barskeoch, with others divers. The Protestants convened whole to crave for justice. The Queen asked counsel of the Bishop of Ross [7] and of the old Laird of Lethington [8] (for the younger was absent, and so the Protestants had the fewer unfriends) who affirmed, "That she must see her laws kept, or else she would get no obedience." And so was preparation made for their accusations. The Bishop, and his band of the exempted sort, made it nice [9] to enter before the Earl of Argyll who sat in judgment [10]; but at last he was compelled to enter within the bar. A merry man (who now sleeps in the Lord), Robert Norwell, instead of the Bishop's cross, bore before him a steel hammer; whereat the Bishop and his band were not a little offended, because the Bishop's privileges were not then current in Scotland (which day God grant our posterity may see of longer continuance than we possessed it.) The Bishop and his fellows, after much ado and long drift of time, came in the Queen's will, and were committed to ward, some to one place, some

Robert Norwell's fact [11]

[1] For the trial of the Papists, as in the immediately following paragraphs.
[2] A parliament had been summoned for 20 May 1563, but it did not meet until 26 May. (*Diurnal of Occurrents*, 75, 76; *Calendar of Scottish Papers*, ii, No. 9)
[3] To *compear* is to appear before a court in response to a summons.
[4] John Hamilton [5] Malcolm Fleming [6] Mr. Robert Crichton
[7] Henry Sinclair, Bishop of Ross, and President of the Court of Session
[8] Sir Richard Maitland of Lethington [9] *made some scruple*
[10] As hereditary Justice-General [11] *deed*

to another.[1] The Lady Erskine [2] (a sweet morsel for the Devil's mouth) got the Bishops for her part.[3] All this was done of a most deep craft, to abuse the simplicity of the Protestants, that they should not press the Queen with any other thing concerning matters of religion at that Parliament, which began within two days thereafter.[4] She obtained of the Protestants whatsoever she desired; for this was the reason of many, "We see what the Queen has done; the like of this was never heard of within the Realm: we will bear with the Queen; we doubt not but all shall be well." Others were of a contrary judgment, and forespake things, as after they came to pass, to wit, that nothing was meant but deceit; and that the Queen, how soon that ever Parliament was past, should set the Papists at freedom [5]: and therefore willed the nobility not [to] be abused. But because many had their private commodity to be handled at that Parliament, the common cause was the less regarded.

The judgment of some

The Earl of Huntly, whose corpse had lain unburied till that time, was brought to the Tolbooth: he was accused; his arms rent off him; the Earl of Sutherland,[6] and eleven Barons and Lairds, bearing Gordon to surname, were that day forfalted.[7] The Lady Huntly craftily protested, and asked the support of a man of law. In that Parliament were restored the Laird of Grange in Fife, Master Henry Balnaves, John Leslie, and Alexander Whitelaw.[8]

Huntly forfalted

Such stinking pride of women as was seen at that Parliament, was never seen before in Scotland. Three sundry days the Queen rode to the Tolbooth. The first day she made a painted orison [9];

The pride of women at that Parliament

[1] For details of the trial and of the subsequent wardings, see Pitcairn, *Criminal Trials*, i, *427–*430. For the general background, see Herkless and Hannay, *Archbishops of St. Andrews*, v, 152–57.

[2] Annabella Murray, daughter of Sir William Murray of Tullibardine, and wife of John, sixth Lord Erskine, later (1565) Earl of Mar and (1571) Regent of Scotland. Knox has already called her a "very Jezebel" (*supra*, i, 344 and *note*).

[3] The Archbishop of St. Andrews was committed to ward in the Castle of Edinburgh, of which Lord Erskine was then keeper.

[4] But see *supra*, 76, *note* 2

[5] See *infra*, 84

[6] John, tenth Earl of Sutherland

[7] *forfeited*. For fuller details, see *Diurnal of Occurrents*, 76; *Records of Aboyne*, New Spalding Club, 467–468. Mary herself was present at the grim ceremony (*Calendar of Scottish Papers*, ii, No. 9).

[8] No record of the reduction of the forfeitures of Sir William Kirkcaldy of Grange, Henry Balnaves of Halhill, John Leslie of Parkhill (younger son of William, third Earl of Rothes), and Alexander Whitelaw has been preserved in the official register.

[9] *Lege* "oration." In his Preface to the *Registrum Honoris de Morton* (Bannatyne Club, i, xxvi–xxvii), Cosmo Innes printed what appear to be the "heads" of Morton's reply to the Queen's speech. The "three sundry days" and the "stinking pride of women" of Knox's account are borne out by Randolph (see Hay Fleming, *Mary Queen of Scots*, 490; *Calendar of Scottish Papers*, ii, No. 9). *Painted* is used for *artificial*, that is *insincere*.

and there might have been heard among her flatterers, "*Vox Dianæ!* The voice of a goddess (for it could not be *Dei*), and not of a woman! God save that sweet face! Was there ever orator spake so properly and so sweetly!"

Flatterers enough

All things misliking the Preachers, they spake boldly against the tarejatting of their taillies,[1] and against the rest of their vanity, which they affirmed should provoke God's vengeance, not only against those foolish women, but against the whole Realm; and especially against those that maintained them in that odious abusing of things that might have been better bestowed. Articles were presented for order to be taken for apparel, and for reformation of other enormities; but all was scripped at.[2] The Earldom of Moray needed confirmation, and many things were to be ratified that concerned the help of friends and servants; and therefore they might not urge the Queen, for if they so did, she would hold no Parliament; and what then should become of them that had melled [3] with the slaughter of the Earl of Huntly? Let that Parliament pass over, and when the Queen asked anything of the nobility, as she must do before her marriage, then should the Religion be the first thing that should be established.[4] It was answered, that the poets and painters erred not altogether, that feigned and painted Occasion with a bald hind-head: for the first, when it is offered, being lost, is hard to be recovered again. The matter fell so hot betwix the Earl of Moray and some others of the Court, and John Knox, that familiarly after that time they spake not together more than a year and half [5]; for the said John, by his letter, gave a discharge to the said Earl of all further intromission or care with his affairs. He made unto him a discourse of their first acquaintance; in what estate he was when that first they spake together in London [6]; how God had promoted him, and that above man's judgment; and in the end made this conclusion, "But seeing that I perceive myself frustrate of my expectation, which was, that ye should ever have

Why religion and the commonwealth were both neglected

Variance betwix the Earl of Moray and John Knox

[1] Decorating the *ends* of their dresses with *tassels* [2] *mocked*

[3] *meddled*

[4] Although Knox here seems anxious that the reformed religion should be "established," almost immediately afterwards (*infra*, 81) he argues that it *had been* established. The root of the matter was that Mary consistently refused to ratify the Acts of the Reformation Parliament of 1560.

[5] Knox's *History*, closing in June 1564, ends with a note that he was still at variance with the Earl of Moray (*infra*, 134 and *notes* 3 and 4).

[6] It is difficult to say when this meeting took place. Possibly it was in July 1552, when the Lord James Stewart was on his way to France, or in December 1552 on his return. (But see M'Crie's *Knox*, 5th edition, ii, 85, *note*)

preferred God to your own affection, and the advancement of his truth to your singular commodity, I commit you to your own wit, and to the conducting of those who better can please you. I praise my God, I this day leave you victor of your enemies, promoted to great honours, and in credit and authority with your Sovereign. If so ye long continue, none within the Realm shall be more glad than I shall be: but if that after this ye shall decay (as I fear that ye shall), then call to mind by what means God exalted you; which was neither by bearing with impiety, neither yet by maintaining of pestilent Papists."

John Knox's discharge to the Earl of Moray

This bill and discharge was so pleasing to the flatterers of the said Earl, that they triumphed of it, and were glad to have got their occasion; for some envied that so great familiarity was betwix the said Earl and John Knox. And therefore from the time that they got once that occasion to separate them, they ceased not to cast oil in the burning flame, which ceased not to burn, till that God by water of affliction, began to slaken it, as we shall after hear. But lest that they [1] should altogether have been seen to have forsaken God (as in very deed both God and his Word was far from the hearts of the most part of the courtiers in that age, a few excepted [2]), they began a new shift, to wit, to speak [3] of the punishment of adultery, of witchcraft, and to seek the restitution of the glebes and manses [4] to the Ministers of the Kirk, and of the reparation of churches: and thereby they thought to have pleased the godly that were highly offended at their slackness.

The Act of Oblivion passed, because some of the Lords had interest [5]; but the acts against adultery, and for the manses and glebes, were so modified that no law and such law might stand *in eodem predicamento*: to speak plain, no law and such Acts were both

[1] In the manuscript (folio 349 *verso*) there is a caret after "they" and the words "Lethingtoun and his companyons" have been added in the margin by a different hand and then scored through.

[2] In the manuscript (folio 349 *verso*) the words "of the courteouris in that aige a fewe excepted" have been added in the margin.

[3] In the manuscript (folio 349 *verso*) the words "to speak" have been scored through, and the words "a newe schift, to wit, to speak" have been added in the margin.

[4] In the manuscript (folio 349 *verso*) the words "of gleibis and manssis" have been scored through, and the words "and to seik the restitution of the gleibes and manses to the ministeris of the Kirk" have been added in the margin.

[5] In accordance with the concessions of 1560 (*supra*, i, 327). For the Act of Oblivion see *Acts Parl. Scot.*, ii, 535–537. For the Acts against adultery and witchcraft see *ibid.*, ii, 539. For Keith's and Spottiswoode's observations on the passing of the Act of Oblivion see Keith's *History*, ii, 200–201.

alike.[1] The Acts are in print [2]: let wise men read, and then accuse us if without cause we complain.

John Knox's sermon

In the progress of this corruption, and before the Parliament dissolved,[3] John Knox, in his sermon before the most part of the Nobility began to enter in a deep discourse of God's mercies which that Realm had felt, and of that ingratitude which he espied almost in the whole multitude, which God had marvellously delivered from the bondage and tyranny both of body and soul. "And now, my Lords," said he, "I praise my God, through Jesus Christ, that in your own presence I may pour forth the sorrows of my heart; yea, yourselves shall be witness, if that I shall make any lie in things that are bypast. From the beginning of God's mighty working within this Realm, I have been with you in your most desperate tentations.[4] Ask your own consciences, and let them answer you before God, if that I (not I, but God's Spirit by me), in your greatest extremity willed you not ever to depend upon your God, and in his name promised unto you victory and preservation from your enemies, so that [5] ye would only depend upon his protection, and prefer his glory to your own lives and worldly commodity. In your most extreme dangers I have been with you: Saint Johnston, Cupar Muir, and the Craigs of Edinburgh are yet recent in my heart; yea, that dark and dolorous night wherein all ye, my Lords, with shame and fear left this town, is yet in my mind [6]; and God forbid that ever I forget it. What was (I say) my exhortation unto you, and what is fallen in vain of all that ever God promised unto you by my mouth, ye yourselves yet live to testify. There is not one of you against whom was death and destruction threatened, perished in that danger. And how many of your enemies has God plagued before your eyes! Shall this be the thankfulness that ye shall render unto your God, to betray his cause, when ye have it in your own hands to establish it as ye please? The Queen, say ye, will not agree with us. Ask ye of her that which by God's word ye may justly require, and if she will not agree with you in God, ye are not bound to agree with her in the Devil. Let her plainly understand so far of your minds; and steal not from your former stoutness in God, and he shall prosper you in

[1] But the Act against adultery (*Acts Parl. Scot.*, ii, 539, c. 10) seems severe enough, and Randolph seems to have thought it severe enough to be "notable." (*Calendar of Scottish Papers*, ii, No. 13)

[2] The Acts of this Parliament were printed by Robert Lekprevik, Edinburgh, 1565; and later, in the "Black Acts" of 1566.

[3] Parliament opened on 26 May and closed on 6 June. (*Calendar of Scottish Papers*, ii, Nos. 9, 13)

[4] *trials*

[5] *provided that*

[6] *Supra*, i, 264–265

your enterprises. But I can see nothing but such a recoiling from Christ Jesus, as the man that first and most speedily flyeth from Christ's enseignzie,[1] holdeth himself most happy. Yea, I hear that some say that we have nothing of our Religion established, neither by Law or Parliament. Albeit that the malicious words of such can neither hurt the truth of God, nor yet us that thereupon depend, yet the speaker for his treason against God committed, and against this poor Commonwealth, deserves the gallows. For our Religion being commanded, and so established by God, is accepted within this Realm in public Parliament[3]; and if they will say that was no Parliament, we must and will say, and also prove, that that Parliament was as lawful as ever any that passed before it within this Realm. Yea, if the King then living[4] was King, and the Queen now in this Realm be lawful Queen, that Parliament cannot be denied.

The speaker was the Dean of Restalrig[2]

"And now, my Lords, to put end to all, I hear of the Queen's marriage: Dukes, brethren to Emperors, and Kings, strive all for the best game.[5] But this, my Lords, will I say, (note the day, and bear witness after), whensoever the Nobility of Scotland professing the Lord Jesus,[6] consents that an infidel (and all Papists are infidels) shall be head to your Sovereign, ye do so far as in ye lieth to banish Christ Jesus from this Realm; ye bring God's vengeance upon the country, a plague upon yourself, and perchance ye shall do small comfort to your Sovereign."

John Knox's affirmation

These words, and this manner of speaking were judged intolerable. Papists and Protestants were both offended; yea, his most familiars disdained him for that speaking. Placeboes[7] and flatterers posted to the Court to give advertisement that Knox had spoken against the Queen's marriage. The Provost of Lincluden,[8] Douglas of Drumlanrig,[9] by surname, was the man that gave the charge that the said John should present himself before the Queen: which he did soon

[1] *ensign*

[2] Mr. John Sinclair, Dean of Restalrig, later (1565) Bishop of Brechin and President of the Court of Session.

[3] But see *supra*, 78 and *note* 4

[4] Francis II, Mary's first husband. He died 5 December 1560.

[5] See *supra*, 63, *note* 8, and *infra*, 98

[6] In the manuscript (folio 351 *recto*) the words "professing the Lord Jesus" are added in the margin in the hand of the text.

[7] "*Yes-men*"

[8] In the manuscript (folio 351 *recto*) the words "persone" and "dundrannan" have been scored through, and the words "proveist" and "glyncluden" added in the margin.

[9] Robert Douglas, Provost of the Collegiate Church of Lincluden, was a natural son of Sir James Douglas of Drumlanrig.

after dinner.[1] The Lord Ochiltree and divers of the faithful bore him company to the Abbey; but none passed into the Queen with him in the cabinet but John Erskine of Dun, then Superintendent of Angus and Mearns.

The Queen's fume against John Knox

The Queen, in a vehement fume, began to cry out that never Prince was handled as she was. "I have," said she, "borne with you in all your rigorous manner of speaking, both against myself and against my uncles; yea, I have sought your favours by all possible means. I offered unto you presence and audience whensoever it pleased you to admonish me; and yet I cannot be quit of you. I avow to God, I shall be once revenged." And with these words, scarcely could Marnock, her secret chamber-boy,[2] get napkins to hold her eyes dry for the tears; and the howling, besides womanly weeping,[3] stayed her speech.

Answer

The said John did patiently abide all the first fume, and at opportunity answered, "True it is, Madam, your Grace and I have been at divers controversies, into the which I never perceived your Grace to be offended at me. But when it shall please God to deliver you from that bondage of darkness and error in the which ye have been nourished, for the lack of true doctrine, your Majesty will find the liberty of my tongue nothing offensive. Without the preaching place, Madam, I think few have occasion to be offended at me; and there, Madam, I am not master of myself, but must obey Him who commands me to speak plain, and to flatter no flesh upon the face of the earth."[4]

"But what have ye to do," said she, "with my marriage?"

"If it please your Majesty," said he, "patiently to hear me, I shall show the truth in plain words. I grant your Grace offered unto me more than ever I required; but my answer was then, as it is now, that God hath not sent me to await upon the courts of Princesses, nor upon the chambers of Ladies; but I am sent to preach the Evangel of Jesus Christ to such as please to hear it; and it hath two parts, Repentance and Faith. And now, Madam, in preaching repentance, of necessity it is that the sins of men be so noted that

[1] Since Knox's sermon was preached "before the Parliament dissolved," this interview with Mary apparently took place between 26 May and 6 June 1563. (See *supra*, 80, *note* 3)

[2] Apparently the same as Merna, Mernan, Marnac who, in the *Inventaires de la Royne Descosse* (11, 82) receives gifts of pearls. [3] See *infra*, 94, 98

[4] In 1565 Knox wrote, "For in the publike place I consulte not with flesh and bloud what I shall propone to the people, but as the Spirit of my God who hath sent me, and unto whome I must answere, moveth me, so I speake." (Laing's *Knox*, vi, 230)

they may know wherein they offend ; but so it is that the most part of your Nobility are so addicted to your affections, that neither God's word, nor yet their Commonwealth, are rightly regarded. And therefore it becomes me so to speak, that they may know their duty."

"What have ye to do," said she, "with my marriage? Or what are ye within this Commonwealth?"

"A subject born within the same," said he, "Madam. And albeit I neither be Earl, Lord, nor Baron within it, yet has God made me (how abject that ever I be in your eyes), a profitable member within the same [1]: Yea, Madam, to me it appertains no less to forewarn of such things as may hurt it, if I foresee them, than it does to any of the Nobility ; for both my vocation and conscience crave plainness of me. And therefore, Madam, to yourself I say that which I speak in public place : Whensoever that the Nobility of this Realm shall consent that ye be subject to an unfaithful husband,[2] they do as much as in them lieth to renounce Christ, to banish his truth from them, to betray the freedom of this Realm, and perchance shall in the end do small comfort to yourself."

Let Papists judge this day. 1567 [3]

At these words, howling was heard, and tears might have been seen in greater abundance than the matter required. John Erskine of Dun, a man of meek and gentle spirit, stood beside and entreated what he could to mitigate her anger, and gave unto her many pleasing words of her beauty, of her excellence, and how that all the Princes of Europe would be glad to seek her favours.[4] But all that was to cast oil in the flaming fire. The said John stood still, without any alteration of countenance for a long season, while that the Queen gave place to her inordinate passion ; and in the end he said, "Madam, in God's presence I speak : I never delighted in the weeping of any of God's creatures ; yea, I can scarcely well abide the tears of my own boys whom my own hand corrects,[5] much less can I rejoice in your Majesty's weeping. But seeing that I have offered unto you no just occasion to be offended, but have spoken

[1] "Modern democracy was born in that answer." (*Glasgow Quatercentenary Studies of George Buchanan*, 29) [2] That is, a husband not of the reformed faith

[3] This marginal note (folio 352 *recto*) is in the hand of the text.

[4] See *infra*, 98

[5] One of the rare references by Knox, in all his works, to his own household. Nathaniel, Knox's elder son, was born at Geneva in May 1557, and Eleazer, the second son, was born at Geneva in (probably November) 1558. Both were children by his first wife, Marjory Bowes. Both were educated at the University of Cambridge. Nathaniel died young in 1580; Eleazer, who was collated to the Vicarage of Clacton Magna, in the Archdeaconry of Colchester, in 1587, died in 1591. (See Laing's *Knox*, vi, lxiii–lxv)

the truth, as my vocation craves of me, I must sustain (albeit unwillingly) your Majesty's tears rather than I dare hurt my conscience, or betray my Commonwealth through my silence."

Herewith was the Queen more offended, and commanded the said John to pass forth of the cabinet, and to abide further of her pleasure in the chamber. The Laird of Dun tarried, and Lord John of Coldingham came into the cabinet, and so they both remained with her near the space of an hour. The said John stood in the chamber, as one whom men had never seen (so were all afraid), except that the Lord Ochiltree bore him company : and therefore began he to forge talking of the ladies who were there sitting in all their gorgeous apparel ; which espied, he merrily said, "O fair Ladies, how pleasing were this life of yours if it should ever abide, and then in the end that we might pass to heaven with all this gay gear. But fie upon that knave Death, that will come whether we will or not ! And when he has laid on his arrest, the foul worms will be busy with this flesh, be it never so fair and so tender ; and the silly [1] soul, I fear, shall be so feeble, that it can neither carry with it gold, garnishing, targetting, [2] pearl, nor precious stones." And by such means procured he the company of women ; and so passed the time till that the Laird of Dun willed him to depart to his house while new advertisement.[3] The Queen would have had the censement [4] of the Lords of [the] Articles, if that such manner of speaking deserved not punishment ; but she was counselled to desist : and so that storm quieted in appearance, but never in the heart.

John Knox's talk amongst the Queen's ladies

Short after the Parliament, Lethington returned from his negotiation in England and France.[5] God, in the February before, had stricken that bloody tyrant the Duke of Guise,[6] which somewhat broke the fard [7] of our Queen for a season. But short after the returning of Lethington pride and malice began to show themselves again. She set at liberty the Bishop of Saint Andrews, and the rest of the Papists that before were put in prison for violating of the laws.[8] Lethington, at his returning, showed himself not a little offended that any bruit should have risen of the Queen's marriage with the King of Spain ; for he took upon him that such thing never entered in her heart : but how true that was we shall after hear. The end of all his acquittance and complaint was to discredit John Knox,

The Bishop of St. Andrews set at liberty

[1] *weak* [2] *tasselling* [3] *until new notification* was made to him

[4] *judgment*

[5] Lethington reached Edinburgh on 24 June 1563. (*Calendar of Scottish Papers*, ii, No. 17)

[6] Francis, second Duke of Guise, was shot by Jean Poltrot de Méré on 18 February 1563. [7] *ardour* ; *violence* [8] *Supra*, 76–77

who had affirmed that such a marriage was both proposed and, upon the part of our Queen, by the Cardinal[1] accepted.[2] Lethington in his absence, had run into a very evil bruit among the nobility for too much serving the Queen's affections against the Commonwealth; and therefore had he, as one that lacketh no worldly wisdom, made provision both in England and in Scotland. For in England he travailed for the freedom of the Earl Bothwell, and by that means obtained promise of his favour. He had there also taken order for the home-coming of the Earl of Lennox, as we shall after hear. In Scotland he joined with the Earl of Atholl[3]: him he promoted, and set forward in Court; and so began the Earl of Moray to be defaced.[4] And yet to the said Earl, Lethington at all times showed a fair countenance.

Lethington's practices

The rest of that summer the Queen spent in her progress through the West country, where in all towns and gentlemen's places she had her Mass. Which, coming to the ears of John Knox, he began that form of prayer which ordinarily he sayeth after thanksgiving at his table: "1. Deliver us, O Lord, from the bondage of idolatry. 2. Preserve and keep us from the tyranny of strangers. 3. Continue us in quietness and concord amongst ourselves, if thy good pleasure be, O Lord, for a season," &c. While that divers of the familiars of the said John asked of him why he prayed for quietness to continue for a season, and not rather absolutely that we should continue in quietness, his answer was, "That he durst not pray but in faith; and faith in God's word assured him that constant quietness could not continue in that Realm where idolatry had been suppressed and then was permitted to be erected again."[5]

John Knox's answer towards his prayer

From the West country, the Queen passed in Argyll to the hunting,[6] and after returned to Stirling. The Earl of Moray, the Lord Robert of Holyroodhouse, and Lord John of Coldingham passed to the Northland. Justice Courts were held; thieves and murderers were punished; two witches were burned: the eldest was so blinded

[1] Charles de Guise, Cardinal of Lorraine

[2] See Hay Fleming, *Mary Queen of Scots*, 84–92 and supporting notes.

[3] John, fourth Earl of Atholl

[4] *defamed*; literally, *to lose face*

[5] In a letter to Cecil, of 6 October 1563, Knox laments that "the conveying of the Mass through those quarters which longest have been best reformed hath so dejected the hearts of many that men appear not to have that courage they had before." (Laing's *Knox*, vi, 528–529; *Calendar of Scottish Papers*, ii, No. 34)

[6] Randolph, writing to Cecil on 13 June 1563, refers to the "Hyeland apparell" prepared for the visit to Argyll, and his own attempt to be "in outer shape" as "like unto the rest." (*Calendar of Scottish Papers*, ii, No. 13) For Mary's hunting, see Robertson's *Inventaires de la Royne Descosse*, Preface, lxx, *note*.

with the Devil that she affirmed, "That no Judge had power over her."

That same time Lord John of Coldingham departed this life in Inverness.[1] It was affirmed that he commanded such as were beside him to say unto the Queen, "That unless she left her idolatry that God would not fail to plague her. He asked God mercy that he had so far borne with her in her impiety, and had maintained her in the same [3]: And that no one thing did him more regret than that he had flattered, fostered, and maintained her in her wickedness against God and his servants." And in very deed great cause had he to have lamented his wickedness; for, besides all his other infirmities, in the end, he, for the Queen's pleasure, became enemy to virtue and all virtuous men, and a patron to impiety to the uttermost of his power: yea, his venom was so kindled against God and his word, that in his rage he bursted forth these words: "Or [4] I see the Queen's Majesty so troubled with the railing of these knaves, I shall have the best of them sticked in the pulpit." What further villainy came forth of both their stinking throats and mouths,[5] modesty will not suffer us to write; whereof, if he had grace to unfeignedly repent, it is no small document to God's mercies. But howsoever God wrought with him, the Queen regarded his words as wind or else thought them to have been forged by others, and not to have proceeded from himself; and affirmed plainly that they were devised by the Laird of Pittarrow and Mr. John Wood, whom she both hated, because they flattered her not in her dancing and other doings. One thing in plain words she spake "That God took always from her those persons in whom she had greatest pleasure," and that she repented; but of further wickedness no mention.

The last commendation of Lord John to the Queen [2]

[1] The exact date of his death is unknown; it occurred probably in October or November 1563.

[2] In the manuscript (folio 353 *verso*) the words "quhairof more is spoken after" follow here and have been scored through.

[3] In the manuscript (folio 355 *recto*) the following words "When suche thingis war schauin unto the quene, Thei war but mocked at sche affirmyng that thei war devisit by maister Johne Wode and by the Lard of pettarrow, as we sall after more planelie heare" are scored through, and a marginal direction, in Knox's own hand, runs "tak in this that Is sewed in this place quhar it is scraped out," with the catchwords, "And that no one thing, etc." There is attached a separate slip of paper (folio 354), which contains, again in Knox's hand, the rest of this paragraph running from "And that no one thing" down to "Whill the Quene lay at Streveling with hir Idolatrie in hir chapell"—these last words forming catchwords for the beginning of the paragraph of the main text (folio 355 *recto*). See *supra*, i, civ.

[4] *ere*

[5] The "both" seems to refer to the Queen and to her half-brother, the dead Lord John Stewart of Coldingham.

While the Queen lay at Stirling, with her idolatry in her chapel, in the Palace of Holyroodhouse were left certain dontybours,[1] and others of the French menzie,[2] who raised up their Mass more publicly than they had done at any time before. For upon those same Sundays that the Church of Edinburgh had the ministration of the Lord's Table, the Papists in great number resorted to the Abbey, to their abomination. Which understood, divers of the brethren, being sore offended, consulted how to redress that enormity ; and so were appointed certain of the most zealous and most upright in the religion to await upon the Abbey, that they might note such persons as resorted to the Mass. And perceiving a great number to enter into the chapel, some of the brethren burst also in ; whereat the Priest and the French dames being afraid, made the shout to be sent to the town ; and Madame Raylie,[3] mistress to the Queen's dontibours [4] (for maids that Court could not then bear), posted on with all diligence to the Comptroller, the Laird of Pittarrow,[5] who then was in Saint Giles Kirk at the sermon, and cried for his assistance to save her life, and to save the Queen's Palace. Who, with greater haste than need required, obeyed her desire, and took with him the Provost, the Bailies, and a great part of the faithful. But when they came where the fear was bruited to have been, they found all things quiet, except the tumult they brought with themselves, and peaceable men looking to the Papists and forbidding them to transgress the laws. True it is, a zealous brother, named Patrick Cranstoun, passed into the chapel, and finding the altar covered, and the Priest ready to go to that abomination, said, " The Queen's Majesty is not here : how dare thou then be so malapert, as openly to do against the law ? " No further was done nor said, and yet the bruit hereof was posted to the Queen, with such information as the Papists could give : which found such credit as their hearts could have wished for. It was so heinous a crime in her eyes, that satisfaction for that sin was there none without blood. And therefore, without delay were summoned Andrew Armstrong and Patrick Cranstoun, to find surety to underlie the law, for forethought felony, hamesucken, violent invasion of the Queen's Palace, and for spoliation of the same.[6]

These letters divulged, and the extremity feared, [the] Brethren

[1] See the note *supra*, 9, *note* 1 [2] *retinue* or *following*

[3] The wife of Monsieur Raulet, or Roulet, Mary's private secretary. (See *Calendar of Scottish Papers*, ii, Index, *s.v. Raulet*)

[4] Here the word seems to be used in the sense of *courtesans*.

[5] Sir John Wishart of Pittarrow

[6] See Pitcairn's *Criminal Trials*, i, *434–*435. *Hamesucken* is *forcible entry and assault*. (See Skene's *De Verborum Significatione*, *s.v. Haimsuken*)

(the few that were within the town) consulted upon the next remedy; and in the end concluded that John Knox (to whom the charge was given to make advertisements whensoever danger should appear) [1] should write to the Brethren in all quarters, giving information as the matter stood, and requiring their assistance: which he did in tenor [2] as here follows:

The Superscription

The superscription

"*Wheresoever two or three are gathered together in my name, there am I in the midst of them*

"It is not unknown unto you, dear Brethren, what comfort and tranquillity God gave unto us, in times most dangerous, by our Christian assemblies and godly conferences, as oft as any danger appeared to any member or members of our body; and how that since we have neglected, or at the least not frequented, our conventions and assemblies, the adversaries of Christ Jesus his holy Evangel have enterprised, and boldened themselves publicly and secretly, to do many things odious in God's presence, and most hurtful to the liberty of true religion, now of God's great favour granted unto us. The holy Sacraments are abused by profane Papists. Masses have been (and yet are) openly said and maintained. The blood of some of our dearest ministers has been shed, without fear of punishment or correction craved by us. And now last, are two of our dear brethren, Patrick Cranstoun and Andrew Armstrong, summoned to underlie the law, in the town of Edinburgh, the 24th of this instant October, 'For forethought felony, pretended murder, and for invading the Queen's Majesty's Palace of Holyroodhouse, with unlawful convocation, &c.' This terrible summons is directed against our Brethren because that they, with two or three more, passed to the Abbey upon Sunday, the 15th of August, to behold and note what persons repaired to the Mass; and that because that the Sunday before (the Queen's Grace being absent), there resorted to that idol a rascal multitude, having openly the least [5] devilish ceremony (yea even the conjuring of their accursed water) that ever

Mr. Robert Pont stricken in the head with a whinger [3] by Captain Lauder [4]

[1] For this charge to Knox see *Booke of the Universall Kirk*, i, 38–39, and *infra*, 101.

[2] In the manuscript (folio 356 *recto*) this phrase originally ran "in tennour as after we shall heare," and thereafter, for thirteen further lines, the scribe continues, "The brethren advertissed etc," as *infra*, 90. The whole of these thirteen lines have been scored through; the words "after we shall heare" have been scored through; the words "heir followes" have been added in the text hand; and Knox's letter begins on folio 356 *verso.*

[3] *knife* or *a short sword*; really a *hanger*

[4] In July 1565 Randolph refers to him as "Robert Lauder, of the Guard, that struck the minister." (*Calendar of Scottish Papers*, ii, No. 214)

[5] ? *lege* "most"

they had in the time of greatest blindness. Because (I say), our said Brethren passed, and that in most quiet manner, to note such abusers, these fearful summons are directed against them, to make (no doubt) preparation upon a few, that a door may be opened to execute cruelty upon a greater multitude. And if so it come to pass, God, no doubt, has justly recompensed our former negligence and ingratitude towards him and his benefits received in our own bosoms. God gave to us a most notable victory of his and our enemies: he broke their strength, confounded their counsels: he set us at freedom, and purged this Realm (for the most part) of open idolatry; to the end that we, ever mindful of so wondrous a deliverance, should have kept this Realm clean from such vile filthiness and damnable idolatry. But we, alas! preferring the pleasure of flesh to the pleasure and commandment of our God, have suffered that idol, the Mass, to be erected again, and therefore justly suffers he us now to fall in that danger that to look to an idolator, going to his idolatry, shall be reputed a crime little inferior to treason. God grant that we fall not further. And now I, whom God has of his mercy made one amongst many to travail in setting forward of his true religion within this Realm, seeing the same in danger of ruin, cannot but of conscience crave of you, my Brethren, of all estates, that have professed the truth, your presence, comfort, and assistance, at the said day, in the Town of Edinburgh, even as that ye tender the advancement of God's glory, the safety of your brethren, and your own assurance, together with the preservation of the Kirk in these appearing dangers. It may be, perchance, that persuasions be made in the contrary, and that ye may be informed that either your assembly is not necessary, or else that it will offend the upper powers. But my good hope is that neither flattery nor fear shall make you so far to decline from Christ Jesus as that, against your public promise and solemn band, ye will leave your brethren in so just a cause. And albeit there were no great danger, yet cannot our assembly be unprofitable; for many things require consultation, which cannot be had unless the wisest and godliest convene. And thus, doubting nothing of the assistance of our God, if that we uniformly [1] seek his glory, I cease further to trouble you, committing you heartly to the protection of the Eternal.

"JOHN KNOX.

"From Edinburgh, the 8th [2] of October 1563."

[1] In the manuscript (folio 358 *recto*) *unfaynedlie* scored through and *uniformlie* added in the margin in the hand of the text.

[2] The copy endorsed by Randolph is dated 9 October 1563. (*Foreign Calendar*, *Elizabeth*, vi, No. 1279)

The Brethren, advertised[1] by this bill, prepared themselves, so many as were thought expedient for every town and province, to keep the day appointed. But by the means of false brethren, the letter came to the hands of the Queen, and the manner was this: It was read in the town of Ayr, where was present Robert Cunningham, minister of Failford,[2] who then was held an earnest professor of the Evangel; who (by what means we know not) got the said letter, and sent it with his token to Master Henry Sinclair, then President of the Seat and College of Justice, and styled Bishop of Ross, a perfect hypocrite, and a conjured enemy to Christ Jesus, whom God after struck according to his deservings.[3] The said Mr. Henry being enemy to all that unfeignedly professed the Lord Jesus, but chiefly to John Knox, for the liberty of his tongue—for he had affirmed, as ever still he doth affirm, that a Bishop that receives profit, and feeds not the flock, even by his own labours, is both a thief and a murderer—the said Mr. Henry, we say, thinking himself happy that had found so good occasion to trouble him, whose life he hated, posted the said letter with his counsel to the Queen, who then lay in Stirling.

The minister of Fail, and Bishop of Ross

The letter being read, it was concluded by the Council of the Cabinet, that is, by the most Secret Council, that it imported treason: whereof the Queen was not a little rejoiced, for she thought once to be revenged of that her great enemy. It was concluded that the Nobility should be written for, that the condemnation should have the greater authority. The day was appointed about the midst of December; which was kept of the whole Council, and of divers others, such as the Master of Maxwell,[4] the old Laird of Lethington,[5] and the said President.[6]

In the meantime the Earl of Moray returned from the North, to whom the Secretary Lethington opened the matter as best pleased him. The Master of Maxwell gave unto the said John, as it had been, a discharge of the familiarity which before was great betwix them, unless that he would satisfy the Queen at her own sight.

The master of Maxwell's discharge to John Knox

[1] In the manuscript (folio 358 *recto*) *admonished* scored through and *advertissed* written immediately following.

[2] Failford, or Fail, was a House of the Trinitarians, or Red Friars, and the head of the House was styled *Minister* (see *supra*, 55, *note* 5). Robert Cunningham, Minister of Failford, was a younger son of William, third Earl of Glencairn.

[3] He died in Paris, after an operation for stone, in January 1565. (*Diurnal of Occurrents*, 77, 79)

[4] John, second son of Robert, fifth Lord Maxwell; later, John, Lord Herries.

[5] Sir Richard Maitland of Lethington, father of William Maitland of Lethington, the Secretary.

[6] Henry Sinclair

Reasoning betwix the Master of Maxwell and John Knox

[1] The answer [of John Knox] was, " He knew no offence done by him to the Queen's Majesty, and therefore he wist not what satisfaction to make."

" No offence ! " said the other. " Have ye not written letters desiring the Brethren from all parts to convene to Andrew Armstrong and Patrick Cranstoun's day ? "

" That I grant," said the other ; " but therein I acknowledge no offence done by me."

" No offence," said he, " to convocate the Queen's lieges ? "

" Not for so just a cause," said the other ; " for greater things were reputed no offence within these two years."

" The time," said he, " is now other ; for then our Sovereign was absent, and now she is present."

" It is neither the absence nor the presence of the Queen," said he, " that rules my conscience, but God speaking plainly in his word ; what was lawful to me last year, is yet lawful, because my God is unchangeable."

" Well," said the Master, " I have given you my counsel, do as ye list ; but I think ye shall repent it, if ye bow not unto the Queen."

" I understand not," said he, " Master, what ye mean. I never made myself an adversary party unto the Queen's Majesty, except in to the head of religion, and therein I think ye will not desire me to bow."

" Well," said he, " ye are wise enough ; but ye will find that men will not bear with you in times to come, as they have done in times bypast."

" If God stand my friend," said the other, " as I am assured he of his mercy will, so long as I depend upon his promise, and prefer his glory to my life and worldly profit, I little regard how men behave themselves towards me ; neither yet know I wherein any man has borne with me in times past, unless it be that of my mouth they have heard the word of God, which in times to come, if they refuse, my heart will be pierced, and for a season will lament ; but the incommodity will be their own."

[1] That part of the manuscript which, from internal evidence, appears to have been transcribed in 1566, terminates at the beginning of this paragraph (folio 359 *recto*). The remainder of the manuscript, extending to twenty-nine folios, cannot have been transcribed earlier than December 1571 (though still in Knox's lifetime). This concluding portion is " hastily written, more like a scroll copy from dictation, than an accurate transcript." (See Laing's *Knox*, ii, 399, *note* 2). Many of the words are omitted or inaccurately written, and various minute corrections have been adopted from Laing's collation with the manuscript in the University Library, Glasgow. See the Bibliographical Note, *supra*, i, cv–cvi, cix.

And after these words, whereinto the Laird of Lochinvar [1] was witness, they departed. But unto this day, the 17 of December 1571,[2] they met not in such familiarity as they had before.

The bruit of the accusation of John Knox being divulged, Mr. John Spens of Condie, Advocate,[3] a man of gentle nature and one that professed the doctrine of the Evangel, came, as it were in secret, to John Knox, to inquire the cause of that great bruit. To whom the said John was plain in all things, and showed unto him the double of the letter. Which heard and considered, he said, "I thank my God. I came to you with a fearful and sorrowful heart, fearing that ye had done such a crime as laws might have punished, which would have been no small trouble to the hearts of all such as have received the word of life which ye have preached; but I depart greatly rejoiced, as well because I perceive your own comfort, even in the midst of your troubles, as that I clearly understand that ye have committed no such crime as ye are burdened with: Ye will be accused (said he), but God will assist you." And so he departed.

Before they disdained not to come to his own house

The Earl of Moray and the Secretary sent for the said John to the Clerk of Register's house, and began to lament that he had so highly offended the Queen's Majesty, the which they feared should come to a great inconvenience to himself, if he were not wisely foreseen. They showed what pains and travail they had taken to mitigate her anger, but they could find nothing but extremity, unless he himself would confess his offence, and put him in her Grace's will. To which heads the said John answered as follows:

The Secretary's counsel to John Knox

John Knox's answer

"I praise my God, through Jesus Christ, I have learned not to cry conjuration and treason at every thing that the godless multitude does condemn, neither yet to fear the things that they fear. I have the testimony of a good conscience that I have given no occasion to the Queen's Majesty to be offended with me; for I have done nothing but my duty, and so, whatsoever shall thereof ensue, my good hope is that my God will give me patience to bear it. But to confess an offence where my conscience witnesseth there is none, far be it from me."

"How can it be defended?" said Lethington: "Have ye not made convocation of the Queen's lieges?"

"If I have not," said he, "a just defence for my fault, let me smart for it."

[1] Sir John Gordon of Lochinvar

[2] This date, which forms part of the text, proves that this concluding part of the *History* must have been written at that time.

[3] Mr. John Spens of Condie was Queen's Advocate.

"Let us hear," said they, "your defences; for we would be glad that ye might be found innocent."

"Nay," said the other, "for I am informed, and that by divers, and even by you, my Lord Secretary, that I am already condemned, and my cause prejudged: Therefore I might be reputed a fool, if I would make you privy to my defences."

This was the first time that the Earl of Moray spake to the said John after the Parliament [1]

At those words they seemed both offended; and so the Secretary departed. But the said Earl remained still, and would have entered in further discourse of the estate of the Court with the said John, who answered, "My Lord, I understand more than I would of the affairs of the Court; and therefore it is not needful that your Lordship trouble you with the recounting thereof. If ye stand in good case, I am content; and if ye do not, as I fear you do not already, or else ye shall not do ere it be long, blame not me. Ye have the Councillors whom ye have chosen; my weak judgment both ye and they despised: I can do nothing but behold the end, which, I pray God, be other than my troubled heart feareth."

John Knox called before the Queen and Council in anno 1563

Within four days, the said John was called before the Queen and Council betwix six and seven hours at night [2]: the season of the year was the midst of December. The bruit rising in the town, that John Knox was sent for by the Queen, the brethren of the Kirk followed in such number that the inner close was full, and all the stairs, even to the chamber door where the Queen and Council sat; who had been reasoning amongst themselves before, but had not fully satisfied the Secretary's mind. And so was the Queen retired to her cabinet, and the Lords were talking each one with other, as occasion served. But upon the entry of John Knox, they were commanded to take their places, and so they did, sitting as Councillors one against another.

The Duke,[3] according to his dignity, began the one side. Upon the other side sat the Earl of Argyll, and consequently followed the Earl of Moray, the Earl of Glencairn, the Earl Marischal, the Lord Ruthven, the common officers, Pittarrow then Comptroller, the Justice-Clerk, Mr. John Spens of Condie, Advocate; and divers

[1] See *supra*, 78–79

[2] Randolph, in a letter to Cecil of 21 December 1563, states that the Lords had assembled for three causes of which the last was "that the Quene fyndethe her greeved with a letter that Mr. Knox wrote unto hys brethrene the prechers, to assyst two honest men of the congregation, whome the Quene wolde have had punished, for troblinge a prest that, her Grace beinge in Argile, saide masse unto the reste of her howseholde remayninge in the Abbaye of Hollie-roode howse." (Laing's *Knox*, vi, 527; *Calendar of Scottish Papers*, ii, No. 42) There is no record in the Register of the Privy Council of Scotland.

[3] Châtelherault

others stood by. Removed from the table sat old Lethington, father to the Secretary, Mr. Henry Sinclair, then Bishop of Ross, and Mr. James M'Gill, Clerk Register.

Things thus put in order, the Queen came forth, and with no little worldly pomp was placed in the chair, having two faithful supports, the Master of Maxwell upon the one tor,[1] and Secretary Lethington on the other tor of the chair; whereupon they waited diligently all [the] time of that accusation, sometimes the one occupying her ear, sometimes the other. Her pomp lacked one principal point, to wit, womanly gravity. For when she saw John Knox standing at the other end of the table bare-headed, she first smiled, and after gave a gawf [of] laughter,[2] whereat when her place-boes [3] gave their *plaudite*, affirming with like countenance, "This is a good beginning," she said, "But wat ye [4] whereat I laugh? Yon man gart me [5] greit,[6] and grat never tear himself: I will see if I can gar him greit." At that word the Secretary whispered her in the ear, and she him again, and with that gave him a letter. After the inspection thereof, he directed his visage and speech to John Knox in this manner:

"The Queen's Majesty is informed that ye have travailed to raise a tumult of her subjects against her, and for certification thereof, there is presented to her your own letter subscribed in your name.[7] Yet because her Grace will do nothing without a good advisement, she has convened you before this part of the Nobility, that they may witness betwix you and her."

"Let him acknowledge," said she, "his own handwrite, and then shall we judge of the contents of the letter."

And so was the letter presented from hand to hand to John Knox who, taking inspection of it, said, "I gladly acknowledge this to be my handwrite: and also I remember, I dited a letter in the month of October, giving signification to the brethren in sundry quarters, of such things as displeased me. And that good opinion have I of the fidelity of the scribes that willingly they would not adulterate my original, albeit I left divers blanks subscribed with them; and so I acknowledge both the handwrite and the ditement."

"Ye have done more," said Lethington, "than I would have done."

"Charity," said the other, "is not suspicious."

"Well, well," said the Queen, "read your own letter, and then answer to such things as shall be demanded of you."

[1] *arm* [2] *guffaw* [3] "*yes-men*" [4] *know ye* [5] *made me*
[6] *weep* [7] That is, the letter of 8 October 1563 (*supra*, 88–89)

" I shall do the best I can," said the other ; and so with loud voice he began to read as before expressed.

After that the letter was read to the end, it was presented again to Mr. John Spens ; for the Queen commanded him to accuse, as he after did, but very gently. After, we say, that the letter was read, the Queen, beholding the whole table, said, " Heard ye ever, my Lords, a more despiteful and treasonable letter ? "

While that no man gave answer, Lethington addressed him to John Knox, and said, " Master Knox, are ye not sorry from your heart, and do ye not repent that such a letter has passed your pen, and from you is come to the knowledge of others."

John Knox answered, " My Lord Secretary, before I repent I must be taught of my offence."

" Offence," said Lethington, " if there were no more but the convocation of the Queen's lieges, the offence cannot be denied."

" Remember yourself, my Lord," said the other, " there is a difference betwix a lawful convocation, and an unlawful. If I have been guilty in this, I have oft offended sen [1] I came [last] in Scotland : for what convocation of the brethren has ever been to this day into which my pen served not ? Before this no man led it to my charge as a crime."

" Then was then," said Lethington, " and now is now : We have no need of such convocations as sometimes we have had."

John Knox answered, " The time that has been is even now before my eyes ; for I see the poor flock in no less danger nor it has been at any time before, except that the Devil has got a vissorne [2] upon his face. Before, he came in with his own face discovered [3] by open tyranny, seeking the destruction of all that has refused idolatry ; and then I think ye will confess the brethren lawfully assembled themselves for defence of their lives. And now the Devil comes under the cloak of Justice, to do that which God would not suffer him to do by strength."

" What is this ? " said the Queen. " Methink ye trifle with him. Who gave him authority to make convocation of my lieges ? Is not that treason ? "

" No, Madam," said the Lord Ruthven, " for he makes convocation of the people to hear prayer and sermon almost daily, and whatever your Grace or others will think thereof, we think it no treason."

[1] *since* [2] a *vizor*, that is, a *mask* [3] *exposed*

"Hold your peace," said the Queen, "and let him make answer for himself."

"I began [Madam]" said John Knox, "to reason with the Secretary, whom I take to be a far better dialectician than your Grace is, that all convocations are not unlawful; and now my Lord Ruthven has given the instance, which if your Grace will deny, I shall address me for the proof."

"I will say nothing," said the Queen, "against your religion, nor against your convening to your sermons: But what authority have ye to convocate my subjects when ye will, without my commandment?"

"I have no pleasure," said John Knox, "to decline from the former purpose. And yet, Madam, to satisfy your Grace's two questions, I answer, that at my will I never convened four persons in Scotland; but at the order that the brethren has appointed, I have given divers advertisements, and great multitudes have assembled thereupon. And if your Grace complain that this was done without your Grace's commandment, I answer, so has all that God has blessed within this Realm from the beginning of this action. And therefore, Madam, I must be convicted by a just law, that I have done against the duty of God's messenger in writing of this letter, before that either I be sorry, or yet repent for the doing of it, as my Lord Secretary would persuade me. For what I have done, I have done [at] the commandment of the general Kirk of this Realm; and therefore, I think, I have done no wrong."

"Ye shall not escape so," said the Queen. "Is it not treason, my Lords, to accuse a Prince of cruelty? I think there be Acts of Parliament against such whisperers." That was granted of many.

"But wherein," said John Knox, "can I be accused?"

"Read this part of your own bill," said the Queen, which began, "These fearful summons are directed against them (to wit, the brethren foresaid), to make, no doubt, preparation upon a few, that a door may be opened to execute cruelty upon a greater multitude."[1] "Lo," said the Queen, "what say ye to that?"

While many doubted what the said John should answer, he said unto the Queen, "Is it lawful for me, Madam, to answer for myself? Or shall I be damned before I be heard?"

"Say what ye can," said she; "for I think ye have enough ado."

"I will first [then] desire this of your Grace, Madam, and of this

[1] *Supra*, 89

most honourable audience, whether if your Grace knows not, that the obstinate Papists are deadly enemies to all such as profess the Evangel of Jesus Christ, and that they most earnestly desire the extermination of them, and of the true doctrine that is taught within this Realm ? "

The Queen held her peace : but all the Lords, with common voice said, " God forbid that either the lives of the faithful, or yet the staying of the doctrine, stood in the power of the Papists : for just experience has told us what cruelty lies in their hearts."

" I must proceed then," said John Knox, " seeing that I perceive that all will grant that it were a barbarous cruelty to destroy such a multitude as profess the Evangel of Jesus Christ within this Realm, which ofter than once or twice they have attempted to do by force, as things done of late days do testify, whereof they, by God and his providence, being disappointed, have invented more crafty and dangerous practices, to wit, to make the Prince party under colour of law : and so what they could not do [by] open force, they shall perform by crafty deceit. For who thinks, my Lords, that the insatiable cruelty of the Papists, within this Realm, I mean, shall end in the murdering of these two brethren now unjustly summoned, and more unjustly to be accused. I think no man of judgment can so esteem, but rather the direct contrary, that is, that by this few number they intend to prepare a way to their bloody enterprises against the whole. And therefore, Madam, cast up when ye list the Acts of your Parliament. I have offended nothing against them ; I accuse not in my letter your Grace, nor yet your nature of cruelty. But I affirm yet again, that the pestilent Papists, who have inflamed your Grace without cause against those poor men at this present, are the sons of the devil ; and therefore must obey the desires of their father, who has been a liar and a murderer from the beginning."

" Ye forget yourself," said one ; " ye are not now in the pulpit."

" I am in the place," said the other, " where I am demanded of conscience to speak the truth ; and therefore I speak. The truth I speak, impugn it whoso list. And hereunto [I add], Madam, that honest, gentle, and meek natures by appearance, by wicked and corrupt councillors may be converted and alter to the direct contrary. Example we have of Nero who, in the beginning of his empire, we find having some natural shame ; but after that his flatterers had encouraged him in all impiety, alleging that nothing was either unhonest nor yet unlawful for his personage, who was Emperor above others : when he had drunk of this cup, I say, to what enormities

Let the world judge what after shortly ensued

he fell, the histories bear witness. And now, Madam, to speak plainly, Papists and conjured enemies to Jesus Christ have your Grace's ear patent at all times. I assure your Grace they are dangerous councillors, and that your mother found."

As this was said, Lethington smiled, and spake secretly to the Queen in her ear. What it was, the table heard not, but immediately she addressed her visage, and spake to John Knox, and said, " Well, ye speak fair enough here before my Lords ; but the last time I spake with you secretly, ye caused me weep many salt tears, and said to me stubbornly, ' Ye set not by my greiting.' "[1]

" Madam," said the other, " because now the second time your Grace has burdened me with that crime,[2] I must answer, lest for my silence I be held guilty. [If your Grace] be ripely remembered, the Laird of Dun, yet living to testify the truth, was present at that time whereof your Grace complains. Your Grace accused me that I had irreverently handled you in the pulpit ; that I denied. Ye said, What ado had I to speak of your marriage? What was I, that I should mell[3] with such matters ? I answered, As touching nature, I was a worm of this earth, and yet a subject of this Commonwealth ; but as touching the office wherein it has pleased God to place me, I was a watchman, both over the Realm, and over the Kirk of God gathered within the same ; by reason whereof I was bound in conscience to blow the trumpet publicly, so oft as ever I saw any upfall,[4] any appearing danger, either of the one or of the other. But so it was, that a certain bruit affirmed that traffick of marriage was betwix your Grace and the Spanish allya[5]; whereinto I said, that if your Nobility and Estates did agree, unless that both ye and your husband should be so straitly bound that neither of you might hurt this Commonwealth, nor yet the poor Kirk of God within the same, that in that case I would pronounce that the consenters were troublers of this Commonwealth, and enemies to God, and to his promise planted within the same. At these words, I grant, your Grace stormed and burst forth into an unreasonable weeping. What mitigation the Laird of Dun would have made, I suppose your Grace has not forgot.[6] But while that nothing was able to stay your weeping, I was compelled to say, I take God to record, that I never took pleasure to see any creature weep, [yea, not my children when my own hands had beaten them], meikle less can I rejoice to see your Grace make such regret. But seeing I have offered your Grace no

[1] That is, ' Ye set naught by my weeping.' See *supra*, 83-84. [2] *Supra*, 94
[3] *meddle* [4] *relapse* [5] *alliance* [6] *Supra*, 83

such occasion, I must rather suffer your Grace to take your own pleasure, ere that I dare conceal the truth, and so betray both the Kirk of God and my Commonwealth. These were the most extreme words that I spake that day."

After that the Secretary had conferred with the Queen, he said, "Mr. Knox, ye may return to your house for this night."

"I thank God and the Queen's Majesty," said the other. "And, Madam, I pray God to purge your heart from Papistry, and to preserve you from the counsel of flatterers; for how pleasing that they appear to your ear and corrupt affection for the time, experience has told us in what perplexity they have brought famous princes."

Lethington and the Master of Maxwell [were] that night the two stoups [1] of her chair.

John Knox being departed, the Table of the Lords and others that were present were demanded, every man by his vote, if John Knox had not offended the Queen's Majesty. The Lords voted uniformly they could find no offence. The Queen was passed to her cabinet. The flatterers of the Court, and Lethington principally, raged. The Queen was brought again, and placed in her chair, and they commanded to vote over again: which thing highly offended the whole Nobility, who began to speak in open audience, "What! shall the Laird of Lethington have power to control us: or shall the presence of a woman cause us to offend God, and to damn an innocent against our conscience for pleasure of any creature?" And so the whole Nobility absolved John Knox again, and praised God for his modesty, and for his plain and sensible answers. Yet before the end, one thing is to be noted, to wit, that amongst so many placeboes, we mean the flatterers of Court, there was not one that plainly durst condemn the poor man that was accused, this same God ruling their tongue that sometimes ruled the tongue of Balaam, when gladly he would have cursed God's people.

The taunt of the Queen to Mr. Henry Sinclair

This perceived, the Queen began to upbraid Mr. Henry Sinclair, then Bishop of Ross, and said, hearing his vote to agree with the rest, "Trouble not the bairn: I pray you trouble him not; for he is newly wakened out of his sleep. Why should not the old fool follow the footsteps of them that have passed before him." The Bishop answered coldly, "Your Grace may consider, that it is neither affection to the man, nor yet love to his profession that moved me to absolve him; but the simple truth, which plainly appears in his defence, draws me after it, albeit that others would have condemned

[1] *props*

him." And this being said, the Lords and whole assisters arose and departed. That night was neither dancing nor fiddling in the Court; for Madam was disappointed of her purpose, which was to have had John Knox in her will by vote of her Nobility.

The craft of the Court

John Knox, absolved by the votes of the greatest part of the Nobility from the crime intended against him, even in the presence of the Queen, she raged, and the placeboes of the Court stormed. And so began new assaults to be made at the hands of the said John, to confess an offence, and to put him in the Queen's will, and they should promise that his greatest punishment should be to go within the Castle of Edinburgh, and immediately to return to his own house. He answered, "God forbid that my confession should damn[1] those noble men that of their conscience, and with displeasure of the Queen, have absolved me. And further, I am assured, ye will not in earnest desire me to confess an offence, unless that therewith ye would desire me to cease from preaching: for how can I exhort others to peace and Christian quietness, if I confess myself an author and mover of sedition?"

Which began the 25 of December.

The Court refused the Ministers

The General Assembly of the Kirk approached. But the just petitions of the Ministers and Commissioners of Kirks were despised at the first, and that with these words, "As Ministers will not follow our counsels, so will we suffer Ministers to labour for themselves, and see what speed they come." And when the whole Assembly said, "If the Queen will not [provide for our Ministers] we must; [for] both Third and Two parts are rigorously taken from us, and from our tenants." "If others," said one, "will follow my counsel, the guard and the Papists shall complain as long as our Ministers have done." At these words the former sharpness was coloured, and the speaker alleged that he meant not of all Ministers, but of some to whom the Queen was no debtor; for what Third received she of Burghs? Cristopher Goodman answered, "My Lord Secretary, if ye can show me what [just] title either the Queen has to the Third or the Papists to the Two parts, then I think I should solve whether she were debtor to Ministers within Burghs or not." But thereto he received this check for answer, "*Ne sit peregrinus curiosus in aliena republica*"; that is, "Let not a stranger be curious in a strange commonwealth."[2] The man of God answered, "Albeit I be a stranger in your policy, yet so am I not in the Kirk of God; and

[1] *condemn*

[2] Christopher Goodman was an Englishman. A short account of him is given in M'Crie's *John Knox*, 5th edn., ii, 331–334.

therefore the care thereof does no less appertain to me in Scotland than if I were in the midst of England."

Many wondered at the silence of John Knox; for in all those quick reasonings he opened not his mouth. The cause thereof he himself expressed in these words: "I have travailed, right honourable and beloved Brethren, sen my last arrival within this Realm in an upright conscience before my God, seeking nothing more, as he is [my] witness, than the advancement of his glory, and the stability of his Kirk within this Realm; and yet of late days I have been accused as a seditious man, and as one that usurps unto myself power that becomes me not. True it is, I have given advertisements into the brethren in divers quarters, of the extremity intended against certain faithful for looking to a priest going to Mass, and for observing of those that transgressed just laws; but [that] therein I have usurped further power than is given unto me, till that by you I be damned,[1] I utterly deny; for I say that by you, that is by the charge of the General Assembly, I have as just power to advertise the brethren from time to time of dangers appearing, as that I have to preach the word of God in the pulpit of Edinburgh; for by you I was appointed to the one and to the other; and therefore, in the name of God, I crave your judgments. The danger that appeared to me in my accusation was not so fearful as the words that came to my ears were dolorous to my heart; for these words were plainly spoken, and that by some Protestants, 'What can the Pope do more than send forth his Letters, and require them to be obeyed?' Let me have your judgments thereof, whether that I have usurped any power to myself, or if I have but obeyed your commandment."

Knox falsely reported of

The flatterers of the Court, amongst whom Sir John Ballantyne, Justice-Clerk, was then not the least, began to storm, and said, "Shall we be compelled to justify the rash doings of men?" "My Lord," said John Knox, "ye shall speak your pleasure for the present: of you I crave nothing; but if the Kirk that is here present do not either absolve me, or else condemn me, never shall I in public or in private as a public minister, open my mouth in doctrine or in reasoning."

After long contention, the said John being removed, the whole Kirk found that a charge was given unto him to advertise the Brethren in all quarters as oft as ever danger appeared; and therefore avowed that fact not to be his only, but to be the fact of all.[2]

[1] *condemned*

[2] *Booke of the Universall Kirk*, i, 38–39; *supra*, 88

Thereat were the Queen's claw-backs [1] more enraged than ever they were, for some of them had promised to the Queen to get the said John convicted, both by the Council and by the Kirk; and being frustrated of both, she and they thought themselves not [a little] disappointed.

1563

In the very time of the General Assembly, there comes to public knowledge a heinous murder committed in the Court, yea, not far from the Queen's own lap; for a French woman, that served in the Queen's chamber had played the whore with the Queen's own apothecary. The woman conceived and bore a child, whom with common consent the father and the mother murdered. Yet were the cries of a new born bairn heard; search was made, the child and mother were both deprehended [2]; and so were both the man and the woman damned [3] to be hanged upon the public street of Edinburgh. The punishment was notable, because the crime was heinous.[4] But yet was not the Court purged of whores and whoredom, which was the fountain of such enormities; for it was well known that shame hastened marriage betwix John Sempill, called the Dancer, and Marie Livingstone, surnamed the Lusty.[5] What bruit the Maries and the rest of the dancers of the Court had, the ballads of that age did witness, which we for modesty's sake omit.[6] But this was the common complaint of all godly and wise men, that if they thought that such a Court should long continue, and if they looked for no other life to come, they would have wished their sons and daughters rather to have been brought up with fiddlers and dancers, and to have been exercised in flinging upon a floor, and in the rest that thereof follows, than to have been nourished in the company of the godly, and exercised in virtue, which in that Court was hated, and filthiness not only maintained, but also rewarded. Witness the Lordship of Abercorn, the barony of Auchtermuchty, and divers others pertaining to the patrimony of the Crown, given in heritage to scoupars,[7] dancers, and dalliers with dames.[8] This was the

Whoredom and murder in the court

Sempill and Livingstone

Marie's regiment

[1] *back-scratchers,* that is, *flatterers* [2] *apprehended* [3] *condemned*

[4] See Randolph's letters to Cecil in *Calendar of Scottish Papers*, ii, Nos. 42, 45.

[5] John Sempill was a natural son of Robert, third Lord Sempill. He married Marie, daughter of Alexander, fifth Lord Livingstone, and one of Queen Mary's "Maries." But, as Robertson has shown (*Inventaires de la Royne Descosse*, Preface, xlvii, *note*), Knox's statement that "shame hastened marriage" is a libel. See also, *Calendar of Scottish Papers*, ii, Nos. 132, 147.

[6] No copy of these ballads is known to be extant. [7] *skippers*

[8] Sir James Melville says that on his return to Scotland in May 1564 the Queen would have given him in heritage the lands of Auchtermuchty, beside Falkland, which he refused, for it was "the nerest part of hir propertie"; but, he adds, "another, hearen that sche was sa weill harted, socht it and gat it." (*Memoirs*, Bannatyne Club, 111)

beginning of the regiment of Mary Queen of Scots, and they were the fruits that she brought forth of France.[1] "Lord, look upon our miseries, and deliver us from the tyranny of that whore, for thy own mere mercy's sake."

Prayed and written when she was in greatest authority[2]

God from heaven, and upon the face of the earth, gave declaration that he was offended at the iniquity that was committed even within this Realm; for upon the 20th day of January there fell wet in great abundance, which in the falling freezed so vehemently that the earth was but a sheet of ice. The fowls both great and small freezed, and might not fly: many died, and some were taken and laid beside the fire, that their feathers might resolve. And in that same month the sea stood still, as was clearly observed, and neither ebbed nor flowed the space of 24 hours. In the month of February, the 15th and 18th day thereof, was seen in the firmament battles arrayed, spears, and other weapons, and as it had been the joining of two armies.[3] These things were not only observed, but also spoken and constantly affirmed by men of judgment and credit. But the Queen and our Court made merry. There was banqueting upon banqueting. The Queen would banquet all the Lords; and that was done upon policy, to remove the suspicioun of her displeasure against them, because they would not at her devotion damn[4] John Knox. To remove, we say, that jealousy, she made the banquet to the whole Lords, whereat she would have the Duke amongst the rest. It behoved them to banquet her again; and so did banqueting continue till Fastron's-eve[5] and after. But the poor Ministers were mocked, and reputed as monsters; the guard, and the affairs of the kitchen were so gripping, that the Ministers' stipends could not be payed[6]; and yet at the Assembly preceding,[7] solemnly promise was made in the Queen's name, by the mouth of Secretary

Great wet and frost in January 1563

Wonders seen in February

Banqueting in the court, but contempt of the ministers

[1] See *supra*, i, 103

[2] Probably in the autumn of 1565 or the early months of 1566. (But see *supra*, i, cix)

[3] Presumably the Northern Lights. Randolph, writing to Cecil on 5 February 1565, reports a foolish story then current that "these three nights past there have been about midnight many armed men walking about the streets, fighting one with the other. The strokes they say are heard, the clamours of men great, no bloodshed." (*Calendar of Scottish Papers*, ii, No. 143) Knox may be mistaking the year, for his chronology is here somewhat confused; the marginal dates would, of course, be 1564 according to the modern calendar.

[4] *condemn*

[5] The eve of Lent, or Shrove Tuesday (14 February 1564)

[6] In his work on the Collectors' Accounts Dr. Donaldson has analysed the amounts paid from the "Thirds" to the Queen's Household and to the "Guard"; and his analysis shows how both these "needs" of the Crown increased.

[7] If Knox is referring to Lent 1564, then he should have written "the Assembly *following*" (*infra*, 104, *note* 2).

The Queen's promise

Lethington, in the audience of many of the Nobility and of the whole Assembly, who affirmed, that he had commandment of her Highness to promise unto them full contentation [1] to all the Ministers within the Realm of things bygone; and of such order to be kept in all times to come, that the whole body of the Protestants should have occasion to stand content. The Earl of Moray affirmed the same, with many other fair promises given by writ by Lethington himself; as in the register of the Acts done in the General Assembly may be seen.[2] But how that, or yet any other thing promised by her, or in her name, unto the Kirk of God, was observed, the world can witness.

The Ministers perceiving all things tend to ruin, discharged their conscience in public and in private; but they received for their labours hatred and indignation; and amongst others, that worthy servant of God, Mr. John Craig, speaking against the manifest corruption that then without shame or fear declared itself, said, "Sometimes were hypocrites known by their disguised habits, and we had men to be monks, and women to be nuns; but now all things are so changed, that we cannot discern the Earl from the Abbot, nor the nun from such as would be held the noble women; so that we have got a new order of monks and nuns. But (said he), seeing that ye ashame not of that unjust profit, would God that therewith ye had the cowl of the nun, the veil, yea, and the tail joined with all, that so ye might appear in your own colours."

Lethington twice defied the servants of God

This liberty did so provoke the choler of Lethington, that in open audience he gave him unto the Devil, if that ever after that day he should regard what became of Ministers, [and] that he should do what he could that his companions should have a skair [3] with him; "And let them bark and blow," said he, "as loud as they list." And so that was the second time that he had given [his] defiance to the servants of God. And hereupon rose whispering and complaints, all by the flatterers of the Court, complaining that men were not charitably handled: "Might not sins be reproved in general, albeit that men were not so specially taxed that all the world might know of whom the preacher spake?" Whereunto was the answer made, "Let men ashame publicly to offend, and the Ministers shall abstain from specialities; but so long as Protestants are not ashamed manifestly to do against the evangel of Jesus Christ, so long cannot the Ministers of God cease to cry that God will be revenged upon such abusers of his holy word."

[1] *satisfaction* [2] *Booke of the Universall Kirk*, i, 47–48 (28 June 1564) [3] *part*

And thus had the servants of God a double battle, fighting upon the one side against the idolatry and the rest of the abominations maintained by the Queen ; and upon the other part, against the unthankfulness of such as sometime would have been esteemed the chief pillars of the Kirk within the Realm.

The threatenings of the preachers were fearful ; but the Court thought itself in [such] security that it could not miscarry. The Queen, after the banqueting, kept a diet [by direction of] Monsieur Lusury,[1] Frenchman, who had been acquainted with her malady before, being her physician. And thereafter she, for the second time, made her progresses in the North,[2] and commanded to ward in the Castle of Edinburgh the Earl of Caithness,[3] for a murder committed by his servants upon the Earl of Marischal's [4] men. He obeyed, but he was suddenly relieved ; for such bloodthirsty men and Papists, such as he is, are best subjects to the Queen. "Thy kingdom come, O Lord ; for in this Realm is nothing (amongst such as should punish vice and maintain virtue) but abominations abounding without bridle."

1564

The flatterers of the Court did daily enrage against the poor Preachers : happiest was he that could invent the most bitter taunts and disdainful mockings of the Ministers. And at length they began to jest at the term of Idolatry, affirming, "That men wist not what they spake, when they called the Mass Idolatry." Yea, some proceeded further, and feared not at open tables to affirm, "That they would sustain the argument that the Mass was no Idolatry." These things coming to the ears of the preachers, were proclaimed in public pulpit of Edinburgh, with this complaint directed by the speaker [5] to his God. "O Lord, how long shall the wicked prevail against the just ? How long shalt thou suffer thyself and thy blessed Evangel to be despised of men ? Of men, we say, that make themselves defenders of the truth ! For of thy manifest and known enemies we complain not, but of such as unto whom thou hast revealed thy light : for now it comes into our ears, that men, not Papists, we say, but chief

[1] Jacques Lusgerie, who had been Mary's physician in France. Again the chronology is somewhat confused. After the autumn of 1563 it was noticed that Mary was occasionally greatly depressed and wept without apparent cause ; in December she took to her bed and complained of a pain in her right side. But Lusgerie does not seem to have left Paris until the end of April 1564, remaining in Scotland until March 1565. (Hay Fleming, *Mary Queen of Scots*, 93, 94, 321, *note* 40)

[2] Mary left Edinburgh for her second northern progress on 22 July 1564, and was back in Edinburgh on 15 September. (Hay Fleming, *op. cit.*, 96, 529)

[3] George, fourth Earl of Caithness

[4] William, fourth Earl Marischal

[5] John Knox

Protestants, will defend the Mass to be no Idolatry. If so were, O Lord, miserably have I been deceived, and miserably, alas, O Lord, have I deceived thy people; which thou knowest, O Lord, I have ever more abhorred than a thousand deaths. But," said he, turning his face towards the rowme [1] where such men as so had affirmed, sat, "If I be not able to prove the Mass to be the most abominable Idolatry that ever was used since the beginning of the World, I offer myself to suffer the punishment appointed by God to a false teacher; and it appears unto me," said the preacher, "that the affirmers should be subject to the same law: for it is the truth of God that ye persecute and blaspheme; and it is the invention of the Devil, that obstinately against his Word, ye maintain. Whereat, albeit ye now flirt [2] and ye flyre,[3] as [though] that all [that] were spoken were but wind, yet am I [as] assured, as I am assured that my God liveth, that some that hear this your defection and railing against the truth and servants of God, shall see a part of God's judgments poured forth upon this Realm (and principally upon you that fastest cleaves to the favour of the Court), for the abominations that are by you maintained." Albeit that such vehemency provoked tears of some, yet those men that knew themselves guilty, in a mocking manner said, "We must recant, and burn our bill; for the Preachers are angry."

Lethington's countenance at the threatenings of the preachers

Let the world judge whether this has come to pass or not, and what has fallen out since that time

The General Assembly, held in June 1564, approached, unto the which [a] great part of the Nobility, of those that are called Protestants, convened; some for assistance of the ministers, and some to accuse them, as we will after hear.

A little before the troubles which Sathan raised in the body of the Kirk, began Davie [4] to grow great in Court.[5] The Queen used him for Secretary in things that appertained to her secret affairs, in France [6] or elsewhere. Great men made court unto him, and their suits were the better heard. But of the beginning and progress, we delay now further to speak, because his end will require the description of the whole.

This was never done by this author [7]

[1] *place* [2] *scoff* [3] *ridicule* [4] David Riccio

[5] *Cf.* Aikman's *Buchanan*, ii, 476. See also *infra*, 141 (marginal note). A year later, Randolph, writing to Leicester on 3 June 1565, says that David "now works all; chief secretary to the Queen, and only governor to her good man . . . his pride is intolerable, his words not to be borne" (*Calendar of Scottish Papers*, ii, No. 191). See also Laing's *Knox*, ii, 595–598; and Hay Fleming, *Mary Queen of Scots*, 120–129 and supporting notes.

[6] Randolph, writing to Cecil early in March 1565, reports that Riccio has become Mary's Secretary for French affairs, having displaced Raulet (*Calendar of Scottish Papers*, ii, No. 153. See also *ibid.*, No. 124).

[7] This note is in the hand of the text. In later manuscripts there is the further note, "And refers it unto such as God shall raise up to do the same".

The first day of the General Assembly, the Courtiers nor the Lords that depended upon the Court presented not themselves in the session with their Brethren. Whereat many wondering, an ancient and honorable man, the Laird of Lundie,[1] said, "Nay, I wonder not of their present absence ; but I wonder that at our last Assembly they drew themselves apart, and joined not with us, but drew from us some of our ministers, and willed them to conclude such things as were never proponed in the public Assembly [which appears to me to be a thing], very prejudicial to the liberty of the Kirk. And, therefore, my judgment is, that they shall be informed of this offence, which the whole Brethren have conceived of their former fault ; humbly requiring them, that if they be Brethren, they will assist their Brethren with their presence and counsel, for we had never greater need. And if they be minded to fall back from us, it were better we knew it now than afterwards." Thereto agreed the whole Assembly, and gave commission to certain Brethren to signify the minds of the Assembly to the Lords ; which was done that same day after noon.[2]

The Courtiers at first seemed not a little offended that they should be as it were suspected of defection : yet, nevertheless, upon the morrow, they joined with the Assembly, and came into it. But they drew themselves, like as they did before, apart, and entered the Inner Council-house. There was the Duke's Grace, the Earls Argyll, Moray, Morton, Glencairn, Marischal, Rothes ; the Master of Maxwell, Secretary Lethington, the Justice-Clerk, the Clerk of Register, and the Comptroller, the Laird of Pittarrow.

After a little consultation they directed a messenger, Mr. George Hay, then called the Minister of the Court,[3] requiring the Superintendents, and some of the learned ministers, to confer with them. The Assembly answered, "That they convened to deliberate upon the common affairs of the Kirk ; and, therefore, that they could not lack their Superintendents and chief ministers, whose judgments were so necessary that without them the rest should sit as it were idle ; and therefore willing them (as of before) that if they acknow-

[1] Walter Lundie of that Ilk. Randolph also speaks of him as "a grave, ancient man, white head and white beard." (*Calendar of Scottish Papers*, ii, No. 159)

[2] According to Calderwood, "The Laird of Lundie and the Superintendent of Lothian were appointed to request the Lords of Secret Council to assist the Assembly with their presence and counsel" on 26 June 1564. (*Booke of the Universall Kirk*, i, 46)

[3] He was minister of Eddleston ; Commissioner of the Diocese of Aberdeen and Banff ; minister of Ruthven. In Calderwood's account of the proceedings of the General Assembly, 30 December 1563, he is called "minister to the privie counsell." (*Booke of the Universall Kirk*, i, 42)

ledge themselves members of the Kirk, that they would join with the Brethren, and propone in public such things as they pleased ; and so they should have the assistance of the whole in all things that might stand to God's commandment. But to send from themselves a portion of their company, they understood that thereof hurt and slander might arise, rather than any profit or comfort to the Kirk : for they feared that all men should not stand content with the conclusion, where the conference and reasons were heard but of a few."

This answer was not given without cause ; for no small travail was made to have drawn some ministers to the faction of the Courtiers, and to have sustained their arguments and opinions. But when it was perceived by the most politic amongst them, that they could not prevail by that means, they proponed the matter in other terms, purging themselves, first, that they never meant to divide themselves from the society of their brethren ; but, because they had certain heads to confer with certain ministers, therefore, for avoiding of confusion, they thought it more expedient to have the conference before a few, rather than in the public audience. But the Assembly did still reply, "That secret conference would they not admit in those heads that should be concluded by general vote." The Lords promised, "That no conclusion should be taken, neither yet vote required, till that both the propositions and the reasons should be heard and considered of the whole body." And upon that condition were directed unto them, with expressed charge to conclude nothing without the knowledge and advice of the Assembly, the Laird of Dun, Superintendent of Angus,[1] the Superintendents of Lothian[2] and Fife,[3] Mr. John Row, Mr. John Craig, William Christison, Mr. David Lindsay, ministers, with the Rector of Saint Andrews,[4] and Mr. George Hay ; the Superintendent of Glasgow, Mr. John Willock, was Moderator, and John Knox waited upon the Scribe. And so they were appointed to sit with the Brethren. And that because the principal complaint touched John Knox, he was also called for.

Lethington's harangue at the Assembly in June 1564

Secretary Lethington began the harangue, which contained these heads : First, How much we were addebted unto God, by whose providence we had liberty of religion under the Queen's Majesty, albeit that she was not persuaded in the same : Secondly, How necessary a thing it was that the Queen's Majesty, by all good offices (so spake he), of the Kirk, and of the ministers principally, should be retained in that constant opinion, that they unfeignedly favoured her

[1] John Erskine of Dun [2] John Spottiswoode [3] John Winram
[4] John Douglas, Rector of the University of St. Andrews

advancement, and procured her subjects to have a good opinion of her: And, last, How dangerous a thing it was, that ministers should be noted one to disagree from another, in form of prayer for her Majesty, or in doctrine concerning obedience to her Majesty's authority: "And in these two last heads (said he), we desire you all to be circumspect; but especially we must crave of you our brother, John Knox, to moderate yourself, as well in form of praying for the Queen's Majesty, as in doctrine that ye propone touching her estate and obedience. Neither shall ye take this (said he), as spoken to your reproach, *quia mens interdum in corpore pulchro*, but because that others, by your example, may imitate the like liberty, albeit not with the same modesty and foresight; and what opinion may ingather in the people's heads, wise men do foresee."

The said John prepared him for answer, as follows: "If such as fear God have occasion to praise him, that because that idolatry is maintained, the servants of God despised, wicked men placed again in honour and authority (Mr. Henry Sinclair was of short time before made President, who before durst not have sat in judgment [1]); and, finally (said he), if we ought to praise God because that vice and impiety overfloweth this whole Realm without punishment, then have we occasion to rejoice and to praise God: But if those and the like used to provoke God's vengeance against realms and nations, then, in my judgment, the godly within Scotland ought to lament and mourn, and so to prevent [2] God's judgments, lest that He, finding all in a like security, strike in his hot indignation, beginning [perchance] at such as think they offend not."

"That is one head," said Lethington, "whereinto ye and I never agreed; for how are ye able to prove that ever God stroke or plagued a nation or people for the iniquity of their Prince, if that [they] themselves lived godly?"

"I looked," said he, "my Lord, to have audience, till that I had absolved the other two parts; but seeing it pleases your Lordship to cut me off before the midst, I will answer to your question. The Scripture of God teaches me that Jerusalem and Judah were punished for the sin of Manasseh; and if ye will allege that they were punished because that they were wicked, and offended with their King, and not because their King was wicked, I answer, that albeit the Spirit of God makes for me, saying in expressed words,

[1] Henry Sinclair, Bishop of Ross, succeeded Robert Reid, Bishop of Orkney, as President of the Court of Session. The exact date of his appointment cannot be traced, but it was probably early in 1559. No love was lost between the President and John Knox. (*Cf. supra*, 90) [2] *act in anticipation of*

'For the sin of Manasseh,' yet will I not be so obstinate as to lay the whole sin, and plagues that thereof followed, upon the King, and utterly absolve the people ; but I will grant with you, that the whole people offended with the King : but how, and in what fashion, I fear that ye and I shall not agree. I doubt not but the great multitude accompanied him in all abominations which he did ; for idolatry and a false religion hath ever been, is, and will be pleasing to the most part of men. But to affirm that all Judah committed really the acts of his impiety, is but to affirm that which neither has certainty, nor yet appearance of a truth : for who can think it to be possible that all those of Jerusalem should so shortly turn to external idolatry, considering the notable reformation lately before had in the days of Hezekiah ? But yet, says the text, 'Manasseh made Judah and the inhabitants of Jerusalem to err.' True it is ; for the one part, as I have said, willingly followed him in his idolatry, and the other, by reason of his authority, suffered him to defile Jerusalem, and the temple of God, with all abominations, and so were they all criminal for his sin ; the one by act and deed, the other by suffering and permission : even as all Scotland is guilty this day of the Queen's idolatry, and ye, my Lords, especially above all others."

"Well," said Lethington, "that is the chief head wherein we never agreed ; but of that we shall speak hereafter. What will ye say as touching the moving of the people to have a good opinion of the Queen's Majesty, and as concerning obedience to be given to her authority, as also of the form of the prayer which commonly ye use, "&c.

"My Lord," said he, "more earnestly to move the people, or yet otherwise to pray than heretofore I have done, a good conscience will not suffer me ; for He who knows the secret of hearts, knows that privily and publicly I have called to God for her conversion, and have willed the people to do the same, showing them the dangerous estate wherein not only she herself stands, but also the whole Realm, by the reason of her indurate blindness," &c.

"That is it," said Lethington, "wherein we find greatest fault. Your extremity against her Mass, in particular, passes measure. Ye call her a slave to Sathan ; ye affirm that God's vengeance hangs over the Realm, by reason of her impiety ; and what is this else but to rouse up the hearts of the people against her Majesty, and against them that serve her."

There was heard an exclamation of the rest of the flatterers, that such extremity could not profit. The Master of Maxwell said in plain words, " If I were in the Queen's Majesty's place, I would not suffer such things as I hear."

The Master of Maxwell's words in the Assembly

" If the words of preachers," said John Knox, " shall always be reft to the worst part,[1] then will it be hard to speak anything so circumspectly, provided that the truth be spoken, which shall not escape the censure of the calumniator. The most vehement and, as ye speak, excessive manner of prayer that I use in public is this, ' O Lord, if thy pleasure be, purge the heart of the Queen's Majesty from the venom of idolatry, and deliver her from the bondage and thraldom of Sathan, in the which she has been brought up, and yet remains, for the lack of true doctrine ; and let her see, by the illumination of thy Holy Spirit, that there is no means to please Thee but by Jesus Christ thy only Son, and that Jesus Christ cannot be found but in thy holy word, nor yet received but as it prescribes ; which is, to renounce our own wits and preconceived opinion, and worship Thee as Thou commands ; that in so doing she may avoid that eternal damnation which abides all [them that are] obstinate and impenitent unto the end ; and that this poor Realm may also escape that plague and vengeance which inevitably follows idolatry, maintained against thy manifest word and the open light thereof.' This (said he), is the form of my common prayer,[2] as yourselves can witness. Now, what is worthy [of] reprehension in it I would hear ? "

John Knox's prayer for the Queen

" There are three things," said Lethington, " that never liked unto me. And the first is, Ye pray for the Queen's Majesty with a condition saying, ' Illuminate her heart, if thy good pleasure be ' ; whereby it may appear that ye doubt of her conversion. Where have ye the example of such prayer ? "

" Wheresoever the examples are," said the other, " I am assured of the rule, which is this, ' If we shall ask anything according to his will, he shall hear us '; and our Master, Christ Jesus, commanded us to pray unto our Father, ' Thy will be done.' "

" But," said Lethington, " where ever find ye any of the Prophets so to have prayed ? "

" It sufficeth me," said the other, " my Lord, that the Master and teacher of both Prophets and Apostles has taught me so to pray."

[1] That is, twisted to the worst interpretation

[2] As early as 24 October 1561, Randolph, writing to Cecil, had reported Knox's *daily* prayer for the Queen " that God will turn her obstinate heart against God and his truth, or if his holy will be otherwise, to strengthen the heart and hand of his chosen and elect, stoutly to withstand the rage of all tyrants, etc., in words terrible enough." (*Calendar of Scottish Papers*, i, No. 1035)

" But in so doing," said he, " ye put a doubt in the people's head of her conversion."

" Not I, my Lord," said the other, " but her own obstinate rebellion causes more than me to doubt of her conversion."

" Whereinto," said he, " rebels she against God ? "

" In all the actions of her life," said he, " but in these two heads especially ; former, That she will not hear the preaching of the blessed evangel of Jesus Christ ; and secondly, That she maintains that idol, the Mass."

" She thinks not that rebellion," said Lethington, " but good religion."

" So thought they," said the other, " that sometimes offered their children unto Moloch, and yet the Spirit of God affirms that they offered them unto devils, and not unto God. And this day the Turks think to have a better religion than the Papists have ; and yet, I think, ye will excuse neither of them both from committing rebellion against God : neither yet justly can ye do the Queen, unless that ye will make God to be partial."

" But yet," said Lethington, " why pray ye not for her without moving any doubt ? "

" Because," said the other, " I have learned to pray in faith. Now faith, ye know, depends upon the words of God, and so it is that the word teaches me that prayers profit the sons and daughters of God's election, of which number, whether she be one or not, I have just cause to doubt ; and, therefore, I pray God ' illuminate her heart, if his good pleasure be.' "

" But yet," said Lethington, " ye can produce the example of none that so has prayed before you."

" Thereto I have already answered," said John Knox ; " but yet for further declaration, I will demand a question, which is this, Whether if ye think that the Apostles prayed themselves as they commanded others to pray."

" Who doubts of that ? " said the whole company that were present.

" Well then," said John Knox, " I am assured that Peter said these words to Simon Magus, ' Repent therefore of this thy wickedness, and pray to God, that if it be possible the thought of your heart may be forgiven thee.' Here we may clearly see that Peter joins a condition with his commandment, That Simon should repent and pray, to wit, if it were possible that his sin might be forgiven ; for he was not ignorant that some sins were unto the death, and so without all hope of repentance or remission. And think ye not, my Lord Secretary (said he), but the same doubt may touch my heart, as touching the Queen's conversion, that then touched the heart of the Apostle ?"

"I would never," said Lethington, "hear you or any other call that in doubt."

"But your will," said the other, "is no assurance to my conscience : And to speak freely, my Lord, I wonder if ye yourself doubt not of the Queen's conversion ; for more evident signs of induration have appeared, and still do appear in her, than Peter outwardly could have espied in Simon Magus. For albeit sometimes he was a sorcerer, yet joined he with the Apostles, believed, and was baptised ; and albeit that the venom of avarice remained in his heart, and that he would have bought the Holy Ghost, yet when he heard the fearful threatenings of God pronounced against him, he trembled, desired the assistance of the prayers of the Apostles, and so humbled himself, so far as the judgment of man could perceive, like a true penitent, and yet we see that Peter doubts of his conversion. Why then may not all the godly justly doubt of the conversion of the Queen, who has used idolatry which is no less odious in the sight of God than is the other, and still continues in the same, yea, that despises all threatenings, and refuses all godly admonitions ?"

"Why say ye that she refuses admonition ?" said Lethington. "She will gladly hear any man."

"But what obedience," said the other, "to God or to his word, ensues of all that is spoken unto her ? Or when shall she be seen to give her presence to the public preaching ?"

"I think never," said Lethington, "so long as she is thus entreated."

"And so long," said the other, "ye and all others must be content that I pray so as I may be assured to be heard of my God, that his good will may be done, either in making her comfortable to his Kirk, or if that he has appointed her to be a scourge to the same, that we may have patience, and she may be bridled."

"Well," said Lethington, "let us come to the Second Head. Where find ye that the Scripture calls any the bound slaves to Sathan, or that the Prophets of God speak so irreverently of kings and princes ?"

"The Scripture," said John Knox, "says, that 'by nature we are all the sons of wrath.' Our Master, Christ Jesus, affirms, 'that such as do sin are servants to sin,' and that it is the only Son of God that sets men at freedom. Now what difference there is betwix the sons of wrath and the servants of sin, and the slaves to the devil, I understand not, except I be taught; and if the sharpness of the term offended you, I have not invented that phrase of speech, but have learned it out of God's Scripture, for those words I find spoken unto Paul, 'Behold, I send thee to the Gentiles, to open their eyes, that they may turn from darkness to light, and from the power of Sathan unto God.' Mark these words, my Lord, and sture not at [1] the speaking of the Holy Ghost. And the same Apostle writing to his scholar Timothy, says, 'Instruct with meekness those that are contrary minded, if that God at any time will give them repentance, that they may know the truth, and that they may come to amendment, out of the snare of the Devil, which are taken of him at his will.' If your Lordship rightly consider these sentences, ye shall not only find my words to be the words of the Holy Ghost, but also the conditions which I [am in] use to add, to have the assurance of God's Scriptures."

Acts 26

2 Tim 2

"But they spake nothing against kings in special," said Lethington, "and yet your continual crying is, 'The Queen's idolatry, the Queen's Mass, will provoke God's vengeance.'"

"In the former sentences," said the other, "I hear not kings and queens excepted, but all unfaithful are pronounced to stand in one rank, and to be in bondage to one tyrant, the Devil. But belike, my Lord, ye little regard the estate wherein they stand, when ye would have them so flattered, that the danger therefor should neither be known, neither yet declared to the poor people."

"Where will ye find," said Lethington, "that any of the Prophets did so entreat kings and queens, rulers or magistrates?"

"In more places than one," said the other. "Ahab was a King, and Jezebel was a Queen, and yet what the Prophet Elijah said to the one and to the other, I suppose ye be not ignorant?"

"That was not cried out before the people," said Lethington, "to make them odious unto their subjects."

"That Elijah said, 'Dogs shall lick the blood of Ahab,'" said John Knox, "'and eat the flesh of Jezebel,' the Scriptures assure me; but that it was whispered in their own ear, or in a corner, I read not. But the plain contrary appears to me, which is, that both the people and the Court understood well enough what the Prophet had promised; for so witnesseth Jehu, after that God's vengeance had stricken Jezebel."

[1] *be not discontented with*

"They were singular motions of the Spirit of God," said Lethington, "and appertain nothing to this our age."

"Then has the Scripture far deceived me," said the other; "for Saint Paul teaches me, that 'Whatsoever is written within the Holy Scriptures, the same is written for our instruction.' And my Master said, that 'Every learned and wise scribe brings forth his treasure, both things old and things new.' And the Prophet Jeremiah affirms, that 'Every realm and every city that likewise offends as then did Jerusalem, should likewise be punished.' Why then the facts of the ancient Prophets, and the fearful judgments of God executed before us upon the disobedient, appertain not unto this our age, I neither see nor yet can understand. But now, to put end to this head, my Lord (said he), the Prophets of God have not spared to rebuke wicked kings, as well in their face as before the people and subjects. Elisha feared not to say to King Jehoram, 'What have I to do with thee? Get thee to the Prophets of thy father, and to the Prophets of thy mother; for as the Lord of Hosts lives, in whose sight I stand, if it were not that I regard the presence of Jehosaphat, the King of Judah, I would not have looked toward thee, nor seen thee.' Plain it is, that the Prophet was a subject in the kingdom of Israel, and yet how little reverence he gives to the King, we hear. Jeremiah the Prophet was commanded to cry to the King and to the Queen, and to say, 'Behave yourselves lowly; execute justice and judgment; or else your carcasses shall be cast to the heat of the day, and unto the frost of the night.' Unto Coniah, Shallum and Zedekiah, he speaks in special, and shows unto them in his public sermons their miserable ends; and therefore ye ought not to think it strange, my Lord (said he), that the servants of God mark the vice of kings and queens, even as well as of other offenders, and that because their sins be more noisome to the Commonwealth than are the sins of inferior persons."

The most part of this reasoning, Secretary Lethington leaned upon the Master of Maxwell's breast, who said, "I am almost weary: I would that some other would reason in the chief head, which is not touched."

Then the Earl of Morton, Chancellor,[1] commanded Mr. George Hay to reason against John Knox, in the head of Obedience due unto Magistrates; who began so to do. Unto whom John Knox said, "Brother, that ye shall reason in my contrary I am well content,

[1] James, fourth Earl of Morton. He appears as Chancellor in January 1563. (*Register Privy Council of Scotland*, i, 228)

because I know you both a man of learning and of modesty: but that ye shall oppose yourself in the truth whereof, I suppose, your own conscience is no less persuaded than is mine, I cannot well approve; for I would be sorry that I and ye should be reputed to reason as two scholars of Pythagoras, to show the quickness of our engine,[1] as it were to reason on both the parts. I protest here before God, that whatsoever I sustain, I do the same of conscience; yea, I dare no more sustain a proposition known unto myself untrue, than that I dare teach false doctrine in the public place. And therefore Brother, if conscience move you to oppose yourself to that doctrine, which ye have heard of my mouth in that matter, do it boldly: it shall never offend me. But that ye shall be found to oppose yourself unto me, ye being persuaded in the same truth, I say yet again, it pleases me not; for therein may be greater inconvenience than either ye or I do consider for the present."

The said Mr. George answered, "That I would oppose myself unto you as willing to impugn or confute that head of doctrine which not only ye, but many others, yea, and I myself have affirmed, far be it from me; for so should I be found contrarious to myself. For my Lord Secretary knows my judgment in that head."

"Marry!" said the Secretary, "ye are well the worst of the two; for I remember well your reasoning when the Queen was in Carrick."

"Well," said John Knox, "seeing, Brother, that God has made you to occupy the chair of verity, wherein, I am sure, we will agree in all principal heads of doctrine, let it never be said that we disagree in disputation." John Knox was moved thus to speak, because he understood more of the craft than the other did.

"Well," said Lethington, "I am somewhat better provided in this last head than I was in the other two. Mr. Knox (said he), yesterday[2] we heard your judgment upon the 13th [chapter of the Epistle] to the Romans; we heard the mind of the Apostle well opened; we heard the causes why God has established Powers upon the earth; we heard the necessity that mankind has of the same; and we heard the duty of Magistrates sufficiently declared. But in two things I was offended, and I think some more of my Lords that then were present. The one was, ye made difference betwix the ordinance of God and the persons that were placed in authority; and ye affirmed that men might refuse[3] the persons and yet not offend

[1] *genius*

[2] Probably the "exhortation and prayer" of 25 June 1564. (*Booke of the Universall Kirk*, i, 46)

[3] ? *lege* resist

against God's ordinance. This is the one ; the other ye had no time to explain ; but this, methought, ye meant, that subjects were not bound to obey their princes if they commanded unlawful things ; but that they might resist their princes, and were not ever bound to suffer."

" In very deed," said the other, " ye have rightly both marked my words, and understood my mind ; for of that same judgment I have long been, and so yet I remain."

" How will ye prove your division and difference," said Lethington, " and that the person placed in authority may be resisted, and God's ordinance not transgressed, seeing that the Apostle says, ' He that resists [the power], resisteth the ordinance of God.' "

" My Lord," said he, " the plain words of the Apostle make the difference ; and the facts [1] of many approved by God prove my affirmative. First, The Apostle affirms, that the powers are ordained of God, for the preservation of quiet and peaceable men, and for the punishment of malefactors ; whereof it is plain, That the ordinance of God, and the power given unto man, is one thing, and the person clad with the power or with the authority, is another ; for God's ordinance is the conservation of mankind, the punishment of vice, the maintaining of virtue, which is in itself holy, just, constant, stable, and perpetual. But men clad with the authority, are commonly profane and unjust ; yea, they are mutable and transitory, and subject to corruption, as God threateneth them by his Prophet David, saying, ' I have said, Ye are gods, and every one of you the sons of the Most Highest ; but ye shall die as men, and the Princes shall fall like others.' Here I am assured, that persons, the soul and body of wicked princes, are threatened with death. I think that such ye will not affirm is the authority, the ordinance and the power, wherewith God has endued such persons ; for as I have said, as it is holy, so it is the permanent will of God. And now, my Lord, that the Prince may be resisted, and yet the ordinance of God not violated, it is evident ; for the people resisted Saul, when he had sworn by the living God that Jonathan should die. The people (I say), swore in the contrary, and delivered Jonathan, so that one hair of his head fell not. Now, Saul was the anointed King, and they were his subjects, and yet they so resisted him that they made him no better than mansworn."

" I doubt," said Lethington, " if in so doing the people did well."

" The Spirit of God," said the other, " accuses them not of any

[1] *deeds* ; *actions*

crime, but rather praises them, and damns the King, as well for his foolish vow and law made without God, as for his cruel mind that so severely would have punished an innocent man. But herein I shall not stand: this that follows shall confirm the former. This same Saul commanded Ahimelech and the Priests of the Lord to be slain, because they had committed treason, as he alleged, for intercommuning with David. His guard and principal servants would not obey his unjust commandment; but Doeg the flatterer put the King's cruelty to execution. I will not ask your judgment, Whether that the servants of the King, in not obeying his commandment, resisted God or not? Or whether Doeg, in murdering the Priests, gave obedience to a just authority? For I have the Spirit of God, speaking by the mouth of David, to assure me of the one as well as of the other; for he, in his 52nd Psalm, damns that fact as a most cruel murder, and affirms that God would punish, not only the commander, but the merciless executor. And therefore, I conclude, that they who gainstood his commandment, resisted not the ordinance of God.

"And now, my Lord, to answer to the place of the Apostle who affirms, 'That such as resists the power, resists the ordinance of God'; I say, that the power in that place is not to be understood of the unjust commandment of men, but of the just power wherewith God has armed his Magistrates and Lieutenants to punish sin and maintain virtue. As if any man should enterprise to take from the hands of a lawful judge a murderer, an adulterer, or any other malefactor that by God's law deserved death, this same man resisted God's ordinance, and procured to himself vengeance and damnation, because that he stayed God's sword to strike. But so it is not, if that men in the fear of God oppose themselves to the fury and blind rage of princes; for so they resist not God, but the Devil, who abuses the sword and authority of God."

"I understand sufficiently," said Lethington, "what ye mean; and to the one part I will not oppose myself. But I doubt of the other. For if the Queen would command me [to] slay John Knox, because she is offended at him, I would not obey her. But, and she would command others to do it, or yet by a colour of justice take his life from him, I cannot tell if I [would] be found to defend him against the Queen and against her officers."

"Under protestation," said the other, "that the auditure [1] think not that I seek favours to myself, I say, my Lord, that if ye be persuaded of my innocence, and if God has given unto you such a

[1] *audience*

power and credit as might deliver me, and yet suffered me to perish, that in so doing ye should be criminal and guilty of my blood."

"Prove that, and win the play," said Lethington.

"Well, my Lord," said the other, "remember your promise, and I shall be short of my probation. The Prophet Jeremiah was apprehended by Priests and Prophets (who were a part of the authority within Jerusalem), and by the multitude of the people, and this sentence was pronounced against him, 'Thou shalt die the death; for thou hast said, This house shall be like Shiloh, and this city shall be desolate without an habitant.' The Princes hearing the uproar, came from the King's house and sat down in judgment in the entry of the new gate of the Lord's house, and there the Priests and the Prophets before the Princes, and before all the people, intended [1] their accusation in these words, 'This man is worthy to die, for he has prophesied against this city, as your ears have heard.' Jeremiah answered, 'That whatsoever he had spoken proceeded from God; and therefore (said he), as for me, I am in your hands: do with me as ye think good and right: But know ye for certain, that if ye put me to death, ye shall surely bring innocent blood upon your souls, and upon this city, and upon the habitations thereof; for of truth, the Lord has sent me unto you, to speak all these words.' Now, my Lord, if the Princes and the whole people should have been guilty of the Prophet's blood, how shall ye or others be judged innocent before God, if ye shall suffer the blood of such as have not deserved death to be shed, when that ye may save it?"

"The cases are nothing like," said Lethington.

"And I would learn," said the other, "wherein the dissimilitude stands."

"First," said Lethington, "the King had not condemned him to the death. And next, the false Prophets and the Priests and the people accused him without a cause, and therefore they could not but be guilty of his blood."

"Neither of these," said John Knox, "fights against my argument; for albeit the King was neither present, nor yet had condemned him, yet were the Princes and chief Councillors there sitting in judgment, who represented the King's person and authority, hearing the accusation laid unto the charge of the Prophet; and therefore he forewarns them of the danger, as before I said, to wit, that in case he should be condemned, and so put to death, that the King, the Council, and the whole city of Jersualem, should be guilty

[1] *directed*

of his blood, because he had committed no crime worthy of death. And if ye think that they should have been all criminal only because that they all accused him, the plain text witnesses the contrary; for the Princes defended him, and so no doubt did a great part of the people; and yet he boldly affirms, that they should be all guilty of his blood if that he should be put to death. And the prophet Ezekiel gives the reason why all are guilty of a common corruption, 'Because,' says he, 'I sought one man amongst them that should make up the hedge, and stand in the gap before me for the land, that I should not destroy it, but I found none; therefore, have I poured my indignation upon them.' Hereof, my Lord (said he), it is plain, that God craves not only that a man do no iniquity in his own person, but also that he oppose himself to all iniquity, so far forth as into him lies."

"Then will ye," said Lethington, "make subjects to control their princes and rulers?"

"And what harm," said the other, "should the commonwealth receive, if that the corrupt affections of ignorant rulers were moderated, and so bridled by the wisdom and discretion of godly subjects, that they should do wrong nor violence to no man?"

"All this reasoning," said Lethington, "is not of the purpose; for we reason as if the Queen should become such an enemy to our religion, that she should persecute it, and put innocent men to death; which I am assured she never thought, nor never will do. For if I should see her begin at that end, yea, if I should suspect any such thing in her, I should be as far forward in that argument as ye or any other within this Realm. But there is not such a thing. Our question is, Whether that we may and ought to suppress the Queen's Mass? Or whether her idolatry shall be laid to our charge?"

"What ye may [do]," said the other, "by force, I dispute not; but what ye may and ought to do by God's express commandment, that I can tell. Idolatry ought not only to be suppressed, but the idolater ought to die the death, unless that we will accuse God."

"I know," said Lethington, "the idolater is commanded to die the death; but by whom?"

"By the people of God," said the other; "for the commandment was given to Israel, as ye may read, 'Hear, Israel,' says the Lord, 'the statutes and the ordinances of the Lord thy God,' &c. Yea, a commandment was given, That if it be heard that idolatry is committed in any one city, inquisition shall be taken; and if it be found true, that then the whole body of the people shall arise and destroy that city, sparing in it neither man, woman, nor child."

"But there is no commandment given to the people," said the Secretary, "to punish their King if he be an idolater."

"I find no more privilege granted unto kings," said the other, "by God, more than unto the people, to offend God's majesty."

"I grant," said Lethington; "but yet the people may not be judges unto their King to punish him, albeit he be an idolater."

"God," said the other, "is the Universal Judge, as well unto the King as to the people; so that what his word commands to be punished in the one, is not to be absolved in the other."

"We agree in that," said Lethington; "but the people may not execute God's judgment, but must leave it unto Himself, who will either punish it by death, by war, by imprisonment, or by some other plagues."

"I know the last part of your reason," said John Knox, "to be true; but for the first, to wit, that the people, yea, or a part of the people may not execute God's judgments against their King, being an offender, I am assured ye have no other warrant except your own imagination, and the opinion of such as more fear to offend princes than God."

"Why say ye so?" said Lethington, "I have the judgments of the most famous men within Europe, and of such as ye yourself will confess both godly and learned."

And with that he called for his papers, which produced by Mr. Robert Maitland, he began to read with great gravity the judgments of Luther, Melanchthon, [and] the minds of Bucer, Musculus,[1] and Calvin, how Christians should behave themselves in time of persecution; yea, the Book of Baruch[2] was not omitted with this conclusion. "The gathering of these things," said he, "has cost more travail than I took these seven years in reading of any commentaries."

"The more pity," said the other, "and yet, what ye have profited your own cause, let others judge. But as for my argument, I am assured, ye have infirmed it nothing; for your first two witnesses speak against the Anabaptists, who deny that Christians should be subject to magistrates, or yet that [it] is lawful for a Christian to be a magistrate; which opinion I no less abhor than ye do, or any other that lives do. The others speak of Christians, subject unto tyrants and infidels, so dispersed that they have no other force but only to

[1] Andreas Musculus, the German divine

[2] In the Apocrypha

sob to God for deliverance. That such indeed should hazard any further than these godly men will them, I cannot hastily be of counsel. But my argument has another ground; for I speak of the people assembled together in one body of a Commonwealth, unto whom God has given sufficient force, not only to resist, but also to suppress all kind of open idolatry: and such a people yet again I affirm, are bound to keep their land clean and unpolluted. And that this my division shall not appear strange unto you, ye shall understand that God required one thing of Abraham and of his seed when he and they were strangers and pilgrims in Egypt and Canaan; and another thing required he of them when they were delivered from the bondage of Egypt, and the possession of the land of Canaan [was] granted unto them. At the first, and during all the time of their bondage, God craved no more but that Abraham should not defile himself with idolatry. Neither was he, nor yet his posterity commanded to destroy the idols that were in Canaan or in Egypt. But when God gave unto them the possession of the land, he gave unto them this strait commandment, 'Beware that you make league or confederacy with the inhabitants of this land: give not thy sons unto their daughters, nor yet give thy daughters unto their sons. But this shall ye do unto them, cut down their groves, destroy their images, break down their altars, and leave thou no kind of remembrance of those abominations which the inhabitants of the land used before: for thou art an holy people unto the Lord thy God. Defile not thyself, therefore, with their gods.'

"To this same commandment, I say, are ye, my Lords, and all such as have professed the Lord Jesus within this Realm bound. For God has wrought no less miracle upon you, both spiritual and corporal, than he did unto the carnal seed of Abraham. For in what estate your bodies and this poor Realm were, within these seven years, yourselves cannot be ignorant. You and it were both in bondage of a strange nation; and what tyrants rang[1] over your conscience, God perchance may let you feel, because that ye do not rightly acknowledge the benefit received. When our poor Brethren before us gave their bodies to the flames of fire, for the testimony of the truth, and when scarcely could ten be found into a country, that rightly knew God, it had been foolishness to have craved either of the Nobility, or of the mean subjects, the suppressing of idolatry; for that had been nothing but to have exposed the simple sheep in a prey to the wolves. But since that God has multiplied knowledge,

[1] *reigned*

yea, and has given the victory to his truth, even in the hands of his servants, if ye suffer the land again to be defiled, ye and your Princess shall both drink the cup of God's indignation, she for her obstinate abiding in manifest idolatry in this great light of the Evangel of Jesus Christ, and ye for your permission and maintaining her in the same."

Lethington said, " In that point we will never agree ; and where find ye, I pray you, that ever any of the Prophets or of the Apostles taught such a doctrine that the people should be plagued for the idolatry of the Prince ; or yet, that the subjects might suppress the idolatry of their rulers, or punish them for the same ? "

" What was the commission given to the Apostles," said he, " my Lord, we know : it was to preach and plant the Evangel of Jesus Christ, where darkness afore had dominion ; and therefore it behoved them, first to let them see the light before that they should will them to put to their hands to suppress idolatry. What precepts the Apostles gave unto the faithful in particular, other than that they commanded all to flee from idolatry, I will not affirm : But I find two things which the faithful did ; the one was, they assisted their preachers, even against the rulers and magistrates ; the other was, they suppressed idolatry wheresoever God gave unto them force, asking no leave at the Emperor, nor of his deputes. Read the ecclesiastical history, and ye shall find example sufficient. And as to the doctrine of the Prophets, we know they were interpreters of the law of God ; and we know they spake as well to the kings as to the people. I read that neither of both would hear them ; and therefore came the plague of God upon both. But that they more flattered kings than that they did the people, I cannot be persuaded. Now, God's laws pronounce death, as before I have said, to idolaters without exception of any person. Now, how the Prophets could rightly interpret the law, and show the causes of God's judgments, which ever they threatened should follow idolatry, and [the] rest of [the] abominations that accompany it (for it is never alone ; but still corrupt religion brings with it a filthy and corrupt life), how, I say, the Prophets could reprove the vices, and not show the people their duty, I understand not. And therefore I constantly believe that the doctrine of the Prophets was so sensible,[1] that the kings understood their own abominations, and the people understood what they ought to have done, in punishing and repressing them. But because that the most part of the people were no less rebellious unto God than were their princes, therefore the one and the other convened against God and

[1] *evident ; easy to be perceived*

against his servants. And yet, my Lord, the facts of some Prophets are so evident, that thereof we may collect what doctrine they taught; for it were no small absurdity to affirm that their facts should repugn to their doctrine."

"I think," said Lethington, "ye mean of the history of Jehu. What will ye prove thereby?"

"The chief head," said John Knox, "that ye deny, to wit, That the Prophets never taught that it appertained to the people to punish the idolatry of their kings; the contrary whereof I affirm: And for the probation, I am ready to produce the fact of one Prophet; for ye know, my Lord, said he, that Elisha sent one of the children of the Prophets to anoint Jehu, who gave him in commandment to destroy the house of his master Ahab for the idolatry committed by him, and for the innocent blood that Jezebel his wicked wife had shed. Which he obeyed, and put in full execution; for the which God promised unto him the stability of the kingdom to the fourth generation. Now," said he, "here is the fact of one Prophet, that proves that subjects were commanded to execute judgments upon their King and Prince."

"There is enough," said Lethington, "to be answered thereto; for Jehu was a King before he put anything in execution; and besides this, the fact is extraordinary, and ought not to be imitated."

"My Lord," said the other, "he was a mere subject, and no King when the Prophet's servant came unto him; yea, and albeit that his fellow captains, hearing of the message, blew the trumpet, and said, 'Jehu is King'; yet I doubt not, but Jezebel both thought and said, 'He was a traitor'; and so did many others that were in Israel and in Samaria. And as touching that ye allege, that the fact was extraordinary, and is not to be imitated, I say, that it had ground of God's ordinary judgment, which commands the idolater to die the death; and, therefore, I yet again affirm, that it is to be imitated of all those that prefer the true honour, the true worship and glory of God, to the affections of flesh, and of wicked princes."

"We are not bound to imitate extraordinary examples," said Lethington, "unless we have the like commandment and assurance."

"I grant," said the other, "if the example repugn to the law; as if avaricious and deceitful men would borrow gold, silver, raiment, or any other necessaries from their neighbour, and withhold the same, alleging that so they might do, and not offend God, because that the Israelites did so to the Egyptians at their departure forth of Egypt. [There] the example served to no purpose unless that they could produce the like cause, and the like commandment that the Israelites had; and that because their fact repugned to this commandment of God, 'Thou shalt not steal.' But where the example agrees with the law, and is, as it were, the execution of God's judgments expressed in the same, I say that the example approved of God stands to us in place of a commandment. For, as God of his nature is constant, immutable, so can he not damn in the ages subsequent that which he has approved in his servants before us. But in his servants before us, He by his own commandment has approved that subjects have not only destroyed their kings for idolatry, but also have rooted out their whole posterity, so that none of that race was left after to empire above the people of God."

"Whatsoever they did," said Lethington, "was done at God's commandment."

"That fortifies my argument," said the other; "for by God's commandment He approved that subjects punish their princes for idolatry and wickedness by them committed."

"We have not the like commandment," said Lethington.

"That I deny," said the other; "for the commandment, 'The idolater shall die the death,' is perpetual, as [ye] yourself have granted. You doubted only who should be executors against the King; and I said the people of God, and have sufficiently proved, as I think, that God has raised up the people, and by his Prophet has anointed a King to take vengeance upon the King, and upon his posterity. Which fact, God since that time has never retreated [1]; and, therefore, to me it remains for a constant and clean commandment to all the people professing God, and having the power to punish vice, what they ought to do in the like case. If the people had enterprised anything without God's commandment, we might have doubted whether they had done well or evil; but seeing that God did bring the execution of his law again in practice, after that it was come in oblivion and contempt, what reasonable man can doubt now of God's will, unless we will doubt of all things which God renews not unto us by miracles, as it were from age to age? But I am assured, that the answer of Abraham unto the rich man who, being into hell, desired that Lazarus, or some of the dead, should be sent unto his brethren and friends, to forewarn them of his incredible pain and torments, and that they should behave themselves so that they should not come in that place of torment: the answer, I say, given unto him, shall confound such as crave further approbation of God's

[1] *withdrawn*

will than is already expressed within his holy Scriptures; for Abraham said, 'They have Moses and the Prophets, whom if they will not believe, neither will they believe albeit that one of the dead should rise.' Even so, I say, my Lord, that such as will not be taught what they ought to do, by commandment of God once given, and once put in practice, will not believe nor obey, albeit that God should send angels from heaven to instruct that doctrine."

"Ye have but produced one example," said Lethington.

"One sufficeth," said the other; "but yet, God be praised, we lack not others; for the whole people conspired against Amaziah, King of Judah, after that he had turned away from the Lord, followed him to Lachish and slew him, and took Uzziah and anointed him King instead of his father. The people had not altogether forgotten the league and covenant which was made betwix their King and them, at the inauguration of Joash, his father, to wit, 'That the King and the people should be the people of the Lord,' and then should they be his faithful subjects. From the which covenant, when that first the father, and after the son declined, they were both punished to the death, Joash by his own servants, and Amaziah by the whole people."

2 Chron. 2

"I doubt," said Lethington, "whether they did well or not."

"It shall be free for you," said the other, "to doubt as ye please, but where I find execution according to God's laws, and God himself not to accuse the doers, I dare not doubt of the equity of their cause. And further, it appears unto me that God gave sufficient approbation and allowance to their fact; for he blessed them with victory, peace, and prosperity, the space of fifty-two years thereafter."

"But prosperity," said Lethington, "does not always prove that God approves the facts of men."

"Yes," said the other; "when the facts of men agree with the law of God, and are rewarded according to God's own promise, expressed in his law, I say, that the prosperity succeeding the fact is most infallible assurance that God has approved that fact. Now so it is, that God has promised in his law, that when his people shall exterminate and destroy such as decline from Him, that He will bless them, and multiply them, as He has promised unto their fathers. But so it is, that Amaziah turned from God; for so the texts do witness; and plain it is the people slew their King; and like plain it is, that God blessed them: Therefore, yet again conclude I, that God approved their fact, in so far as it was done according to his commandment, [and] was blessed according to his promise."

"Well," said Lethington, "I think not the ground so sure as I durst build my conscience thereupon."

"I pray God," said the other, "that your conscience have no worse ground than is this, whensoever ye shall begin that like work which God in your own eyes has already blessed. And now, my Lord (said he), I have but one example to produce, and then I will put an end to my reasoning, because I weary longer to stand." (Commandment was given that he should sit down; but he refused it, and said, "Melancholious reasons would have some mirth intermixed.") "My last example (said he), my Lord, is this: Uzziah the King, not content of his royal estate, malapertly took upon him to enter within the temple of the Lord, to burn incense upon the altar of incense; 'And Azariah the priest went in after him, and with him fourscore priests of the Lord, valiant men, and they withstood Uzziah the King, and said unto him, It pertaineth [to] thee not, Uzziah, to burn incense unto the Lord, but to the priests, the sons of Aaron, that are consecrated to offer incense: Go forth of the sanctuary, for thou hast transgressed, and you shall have no honour of the Lord God.' Hereof, my Lord, I conclude, that subjects not only may, but also ought to withstand and resist their princes, whensoever they do anything that expressly repugns to God, his law, or holy ordinance."

"They that withstood the King," said Lethington, "were not simple subjects, but were the priests of the Lord, and figures of Christ, and such priests have we none this day, to withstand kings if they do wrong."

"That the High Priest was the figure of Christ," said the other, "I grant: but that he was not a subject, that I deny. For I am assured, that he in his priesthood had no prerogative above those that had passed before him. Now, so it is, that Aaron was subject unto Moses, and called him his Lord. Samuel, being both prophet and priest, subjected himself to Saul, after he was inaugurated of the people. Zadok bowed before David; and Abiathar was deposed from the priesthood by Solomon: which all confessed themselves subjects to the kings, albeit that therewith they ceased not to be the figures of Christ. And whereas ye say, that we have no such priests this day, I might answer, that neither have we such kings this day as then were anointed at God's commandment, and sat upon the seat of David, and were no less the figure of Christ Jesus in their just administration, than were the priests in their appointed office: and such kings, I am assured, we have not now more than that we have such priests: for Christ Jesus being anointed in our nature, of God his Father, both King, Priest, and Prophet, has put an end to all external unction.[1] And yet, I think, ye will not say that God has now diminished his graces for those whom He appoints ambassadors betwix Him and his people, more than that He does from kings and princes; and therefore, why that the servants of Jesus Christ may not as justly withstand kings and princes, that this day no less offends God's majesty than Uzziah did, I see not, unless that ye will say that we, in the brightness of the Evangel, are not so straitly bound to regard God's glory, nor yet his commandments, as were the fathers that lived under the dark shadows of the Law."

"Well," said Lethington, "I will dip no further in that head. But how resisted the Priests the King? They only spake unto him without further violence intended."

"That they withstood him," said the other, "the text assures me; but that they did nothing but speak, I cannot understand; for the plain text affirms the contrary, to wit, that they caused him hastily to depart from the sanctuary, yea, and that he was compelled to depart: which manner of speaking, I am assured in the Hebrew tongue imports other thing than exhorting, or commanding by word."

"They did that," said Lethington, "after that he was espied leprous."

"They withstood him before," said the other; "but yet their last fact confirms my proposition so evidently, that such as will oppose them unto it, must needs oppose them unto God; for my assertion is, that kings have no privilege more than has the people to offend God's majesty; and if that so they do, they are no more exempted from the punishment of the law than is any other subject; yea, and that subjects may not only lawfully oppose themselves to their kings, whensoever they do anything that expressedly repugns to God's commandment, but also that they may execute judgment upon them according to God's law; so that if the king be a murderer, adulterer, or idolater, he should suffer according to God's law, not as a king, but as an offender; and that the people may put God's laws in execution, this history clearly proves. For how soon that the leprosy appeared in his forehead, he was not only compelled to depart out of the sanctuary, but also he was removed from all public society

[1] Calderwood tells us that at the coronation of James VI, "Mr. Knox and other preachers repyned at the ceremonie of anointing, yitt was he anointed." (*History of the Kirk of Scotland*, ii, 384)

and administration of the kingdom, and was compelled to dwell in a house apart, even as the law commanded, and got no greater privilege in that case than any other of the people should have done; and this was executed by the people; for it is no doubt more were witnesses of his leprosy than the priests alone. But we find none oppose themselves to the sentence of God pronounced in his law against the leprous; and therefore, yet again say I, that the people ought to execute God's law even against their princes, when that their open crimes by God's law deserve death, but especially when they are such as may infect the rest of the multitude. And now, my Lords (said he), I will reason no longer, for I have spoken more than I intended."

"And yet," said Lethington, "I cannot tell what can be concluded."

"Albeit ye cannot," said the other, "yet I am assured what I have proven, to wit:

"1. That subjects have delivered an innocent from the hands of their king, and therein offended not God.

"2. That subjects have refused to strike innocents when a king commanded, and in so doing denied no just obedience.

"3. That such as struck at the commandment of the king, before God were reputed murderers.

"4. That God has not only of a subject made a king, but also has armed subjects against their natural kings, and commanded them to take vengeance upon them according to his law.

"And, last, That God's people have executed God's law against their king, having no further regard to him in that behalf than if he had been the most simple subject within this Realm.

"And therefore, albeit ye will not understand what should be concluded, yet I am assured that not only God's people may, but also that they are bound to do the same where the like crimes are committed, and when he gives unto them the like power."

"Well," said Lethington, "I think ye shall not have many learned men of your opinion."

"My lord," said the other, "the truth ceases not to be the truth, howsoever it be that men either misknow it, or yet gainstand it. And yet (said he), I praise my God, I lack not the consent of God's servants in that head." And with that he presented unto the Secretary the Apology of Magdeburg; and willed him to read the names of the ministers who had subscribed the defence of the town to be a most just defence; and therewith added, "That to resist a tyrant, is not to resist God, nor yet his ordinance." [1]

Which when he had read, he scripped [2] and said, "*Homines obscuri*." [3] The other answered, "*Dei tamen servi*." [4]

And so Lethington arose and said, "My Lords, ye have heard the reasons upon both parts: it becomes you now to decide, and to put an order unto preachers, that they may be uniform in doctrine. May we, think ye, take the Queen's Mass from her?"

While that some began to give their votes, for some were appointed, as it were, leaders to the rest, John Knox said, "My Lords, I suppose that ye will not do contrary to your Lordships' promise made to the whole Assembly, which was, That nothing should be voted in secret, till that the first all matters should be debated in public, and that then the votes of the whole Assembly should put an end to the controversy.[5] Now have I only sustained the argument, and have rather shown my conscience in most simple manner, than that I have insisted upon the force and vehemence of any one argument: And therefore I, for my part, utterly disassent from all voting, till that the whole Assembly have heard the propositions and the reasons of both parties. For I unfeignedly acknowledge that many in this company are more able to sustain the argument than I am."

"Think ye it reasonable," said Lethington, "that such a multitude as are now convened, should reason and vote in these heads and matters that concern the Queen's Majesty's own person and affairs?"

"I think," said the other, "that whatsoever should bind, the multitude should hear, unless that they have resigned their power unto their Commissioners, which they have not done, so far as I understand; for my Lord Justice-Clerk [6] heard them with one voice say, That in no way would they consent that anything should either here be voted or concluded."

"I cannot tell," said Lethington, "if that my Lords that be here present, and that bear the burden of such matters, should be

[1] The city of Magdeburg had joined the Schmalkaldic League of Mutual Defence against attacks made on any member on account of the Protestant religion. It held out against the Emperor Charles V, and for long successfully withstood a siege by Maurice of Saxony. Its resistance to Charles V and his religious measures, and its "Apology" for its resistance, roused a fever of enthusiasm in Lutheran Germany. Although it capitulated in November 1551 (after being under the ban of the Empire for more than a year) the terms of the capitulation guaranteed to the citizens the religion they desired.

[2] *mocked, derided* [3] That is, "Men of no note"

[4] That is, "Yet servants of God" [5] *Cf. supra*, 108

[6] Sir John Bellenden

bound to their will. What say ye (said he), my Lords? Will ye vote in this matter, or will ye not vote?"

After long reasoning, some that were made for the purpose said, "Why may not the Lords vote, and then show unto the Kirk whatsoever is done?"

"That appears to me," said John Knox, "not only a backward order, but also a tyranny usurped upon the Kirk. But for me, do as ye list (said he), for as I reason, so I vote, yet protesting as before, that I dissent from all voting till that the whole Assembly understand as well the questions as the reasonings."

"Well," said Lethington, "that cannot be done now, for the time is spent; and therefore, my Lord Chancellor (said he), ask ye the votes, and take, by course,[1] every one of the Ministers, and [every] one of us."

Mr. John Douglas, rector

And so was the Rector of Saint Andrews[2] commanded first to speak his conscience; who said, "I refer to the Superintendent of Fife,[3] for I think we are both in one judgment; and yet (said he), if ye will that I speak first, my conscience is this, That if the Queen oppose herself to our religion, which is the only true religion, that in that case the Nobility and Estates of this Realm, professors of the true doctrine, may justly oppose themselves unto her. But as concerning her own Mass, I know it is idolatry, but yet I am not yet resolved whether that by violence we may take it from her or not." The Superintendent of Fife said, "That same is my conscience." And so affirmed some of the Nobility. But others voted frankly, and said, "That as the Mass was abomination, so was it just and right that it should be suppressed; and that in so doing, men did no more wrong to the Queen's Majesty than they that should by force take from her a poison cup when she was going to drink it."

Mr. John Craig

At last, Mr. John Craig, fellow-minister with John Knox in the Kirk of Edinburgh, was required to give his judgment and vote, who said, "I will gladly show unto your Honours what I understand; but I greatly doubt whether my knowledge and conscience shall satisfy you, seeing that ye have heard so many reasons and are so little moved by them. But yet I shall not conceal from you my judgment, adhering first to the protestation of my Brother, to wit, That our voting prejudge not the liberty of the General Assembly. I was (said he), in the University of Bononia,[4] in the year of God 1554, where, in the place of the Black-Friars of the same town, I saw in the time of their General Assembly this Conclusion set forth: This same I heard reasoned, determined, and concluded:

[1] *in turn* [2] Mr. John Douglas [3] Mr. John Winram [4] Bologna

CONCLUSIO

"PRINCIPES omnes, tam supremi, quam inferiores, possunt et debent reformari, vel deponi per eos, per quos eliguntur, confirmantur, vel admittuntur ad officium, quoties a fide præstita subditis per juramentum deficiunt: Quoniam relatio juramenti subditorum et principum mutua est, et utriusque æquo jure servanda et reformanda, juxta legem et conditionem juramenti ab utraque parte facti."

"That is, All Rulers, be they supreme or be they inferior, may and ought to be reformed or deposed by them by whom they are chosen, confirmed, or admitted to their office, as oft as they break that promise made by the oath to their subjects: Because that their Prince is no less bound by oath to the subjects, than are the subjects to their Prince, and therefore ought to be kept and reformed equally, according to the law and condition of the oath that is made of either party."

"This Conclusion, my Lords, I heard sustained and concluded, as I have said, in a most notable auditure. The sustainer was a learned man, Magister Thomas de Finola, the Rector of the University, a man famous in that country. Magister Vincentius de Placentia affirmed the Conclusion to be most true and certain, agreeable both with the law of God and man. The occasion of this disputation and conclusion, was a certain disorder and tyranny that was attempted by the Pope's governors, who began to make innovations in the country against the laws that were before established, alleging themselves not to be subject to such laws, by reason that they were not instituted by the people, but by the Pope, who was King of that country; and therefore they, having full commission and authority of the Pope, might alter and change statutes and ordinances of the country, without all consent of the people. Against this their usurped tyranny, the learned and the people opposed themselves openly: and when that all reasons which the Pope's governors could allege were heard and confuted, the Pope himself was feign to take up the matter, and to promise to keep not only the liberty of the people, but also that he should neither abrogate any law or statute, neither yet make any new law without their own consent. And, therefore, my Lord (said he), my vote and conscience is, that princes are not only bound to keep laws and promises to their subjects, but also, that in case they fail, they justly may be deposed; for the band betwix the Prince and the people is reciprocal."

Then started up a claw-back [1] of that corrupt Court, and said, "Ye wat not what ye say; for ye tell us what was done in Bononia; we are a kingdom, and they are but a commonwealth."

"My Lord," said he, "my judgment is, that every kingdom is, or at least, should be a commonwealth, albeit that every commonwealth be not a kingdom; and, therefore, I think, that in a kingdom no less diligence ought to be taken, that laws be not violated, than is in a commonwealth; because that the tyranny of princes who continually ring [2] in a kingdom, is more hurtful to the subjects, than is the misgovernment of those that from year to year are changed in free commonwealths. But yet, my Lords, to assure you and all others further, that head was disputed to the uttermost; and then, in the end, it was concluded that they spake not of such things as were done in divers kingdoms and nations by tyranny and negligence of people. 'But we conclude,' said they, 'what ought to be done in all kingdoms and commonwealths, according to the law of God, and unto the just laws of man. And if by the negligence of the people, or by tyranny of princes, contrary laws have been made, yet may that same people, or their posterity, justly crave all things to be reformed, according to the original institution of kings and commonwealths: and such as will not do so, deserve to eat the fruit of their own foolishness.'"

Master James M'Gill, then Clerk of Register, perceiving the votes to be different, and hearing the bold plainness of the foresaid servant of God, said, "I remember that this same question was long debated once before this in my house, and there, by reason that we were not all of one mind, it was concluded that Mr. Knox should in all our names have written to Mr. Calvin for his judgment in the controversy." [3]

"Nay," said Mr. Knox, "my Lord Secretary would not consent that I should write, alleging that the greatest weight of the answer stood in the narrative,[4] and therefore promised that he would write, and I should see it. But when (said he), that divers times I required him to remember his promise, I found nothing but delay."

Whereto the Secretary did answer, "True it is I promised to write, and true it is that divers times Mr. Knox required me so to do. But when I had more deeply considered the weight of the matter, I began to find more doubts than that I did before, and this one

[1] *sycophant*; *flatterer*; *toady* [2] *reign* [3] See *supra*, 23

[4] That is, that the answer largely depended upon the way in which the question was put. (See *supra*, 24, *note* 1)

amongst others, How I durst, I being a subject, and the Queen's Majesty's Secretary, take upon me to seek resolution of controversies depending betwix her Highness and her subjects, without her own knowledge and consent." Then was there an acclamation of the claw-backs of the Court, as if Apollo had given his response: "It was wisely and faithfully done."

"Well," said John Knox, "let worldly men praise worldly wisdom so highly as they please, I am assured that by such shifts idolatry is maintained, and the truth of Jesus Christ is betrayed, whereof God one day will be revenged." [1] At this, and the like sharpness, many offended, the voting ceased, and every faction began plainly to speak as affection moved them.

John Knox in the end was commanded yet to write to Mr. Calvin, and to the learned in other Kirks, to know their judgments in that question; which he refused,[2] showing his reason, "I myself am not only fully resolved in conscience, but also I have heard the judgments in this, and all other things that I have affirmed within this Realm, of the most godly and most learned that be known in Europe. I came not to this Realm without their resolution; and for my assurance I have the handwritings of many; and, therefore, if I should now move the same question again, what should I do other, but either show my own ignorance and forgetfulness, or else inconstancy: And, therefore, it may please you to pardon me, albeit I write not. But I will teach you the surer way, which is this, that ye write and complain upon me, that I teach publicly and affirm constantly such doctrine as offends you, and so shall ye know their plain minds, and whether that I and they agree in judgment or not."

The end of the reasoning betwix John Knox and the Secretary in June 1564

Divers said the offer was good; but no man was found that would be the secretary. And so did that Assembly in long reasoning break up. After the which time, the ministers that were called precise were held of all the courtiers as monsters.

[3] In all that time the Earl of Moray was so formed [4] to John Knox, that neither by word nor write was there any communication betwix them.

[1] For Knox's previous prophecies against Lethington, see *supra*, i, 335; ii, 65, 106; for their supposed fulfilment, see the note in Robertson's *Inventaires de la Royne Descosse* (Bannatyne Club), Preface, l.

[2] Again Knox conceals the fact that *he had already written to Calvin* (see *supra*, 23, *note* 6).

[3] In the manuscript (folio 387 *recto*) this final short paragraph has been added in a hand that looks like that of Knox.

[4] This word is clearly written *formed*, but is equally intended to be *fremmed*, that is, *strange*, *foreign*, or *alien*. For the beginning of this coolness between Knox and Moray, see *supra*, 78–79.

THE FIFTH BOOK
OF THE HISTORY OF THE REFORMATION OF RELIGION WITHIN THE REALM OF SCOTLAND

(BY KNOX'S CONTINUATOR)

IN the next month, which was July, the Queen went into Atholl to the hunting ; and from thence she made her progress into Moray, and returned to Fife in September.[1] All this while there was appearance of love and tender friendship betwix the two Queens ; for there were many letters full of civility and compliments sent from either of them to the other in sign of amity ; besides costly presents for tokens. And in the meantime the Earl of Lennox [2] laboured to come home forth of England ; and in the month of October he arrived at Holyrood-House,[3] where he was graciously received by the Queen's Majesty ; namely, when he had presented the Queen of England's letters, written in his favour. And because he could not be restored to his lands without Act of Parliament, therefore there was a Parliament procured to be held at Edinburgh, the 13 day of December.[5] But before the Queen would cause to proclaim a Parliament, she desired the Earl of Moray, by whose means chiefly the said Earl of Lennox came into Scotland, that there should no word be spoken, or at least concluded, that concerned Religion in the Parliament. But he answered, that he could not promise it. In the meantime, the Hamiltons and the Earl of Lennox were agreed.[6]

There be two Epigrams extant, written by George Buchanan, of a rich diamond sent from Queen Mary to Queen Elizabeth[4]

At the day appointed, the Parliament was held at Edinburgh, where the said Earl of Lennox was restored, after two and twenty years exile : he was banished, and forfeited by the Hamiltons, when they had the rule.[7] There were some Articles given in by the Church,

[1] For the Queen's itinerary in July, August, and September 1564, see Hay Fleming, *Mary Queen of Scots*, 529. The Queen returned to Edinburgh on 15 September. (*Foreign Calendar, Elizabeth*, vii, Nos. 681, 682)

[2] Matthew Stewart, fourth Earl of Lennox

[3] Lennox apparently arrived on 23 September 1564. (*Calendar of Scottish Papers*, ii, No. 97)

[4] The marginal notes in this book were probably added by David Buchanan by whom it was printed.

[5] The restitution of Lennox was "proclaimed" at the Market Cross of Edinburgh on 16 October 1564 (*Calendar of Scottish Papers*, ii, No. 108), and the Earl was restored by a Parliament which was called mainly for that purpose and which, summoned for 4 December, apparently sat from 11 to 16 December 1564. (*Ibid.*, Nos. 108, 124 ; *Acts Parl. Scot.*, ii, 545)

[6] *reconciled*

[7] Lennox had been pronounced guilty of treason in 1545, during the regency of Arran (a Hamilton) ; and it must not be forgotten that then, and until the birth of James [VI] in 1566, Lennox was next in succession to the Crown *if* the divorce of the first Earl of Arran was invalid. (See *Scots Peerage*, iv, 358–360 ; *Two Missions of Jacques de la Brosse*, Scot. Hist. Soc., 18–19, 26–29 ; and the genealogical table given *infra*, 351)

especially for the abolishing of the Mass universally, and for punishment of vice ; but there was little thing granted, save that it was statute that scandalous livers should be punished first by prison, and then publicly shown unto the people with ignominy [1] ; but the same was not put in execution.

In the end of this month of December, the General Assembly of the Church was held at Edinburgh : many things were ordained for settling of the affairs of the Church.[2]

In the end of January the Queen passed to Fife,[3] and visiting the gentlemen's houses, was magnificently banqueted everywhere, so that such superfluity was never seen before within this Realm ; which caused the wild fowl to be so dear, that partridges were sold for a crown a piece. At this time was granted by an Act of Parliament, the confirmation of the feus of Church Lands,[4] at the desire of divers Lords, whereof the Earl of Moray was chief. During the Queen's absence the Papists of Edinburgh went down to the Chapel [5] to hear Mass ; and seeing there was no punishment, they waxed more bold, some of them thinking thereby to please the Queen. Upon a certain Sunday in February, they made an Even-song of their own, setting two Priests on the one side of the choir, and one or two on the other side, with Sandy Steven, minstrel (baptizing their children, and making marriages), who, within eight days after, [was] convicted of blasphemy, [for] alleging that he would give no more credit to the New Testament than to a tale of Robin Hood, except it were confirmed by the Doctors of the Church. The said superstitious Even-song was the occasion of a great slander, for many were offended with it ; which being by the Brethren declared to the Lords of the Privy Council, especially to the Earl of Moray, he lamented the cause to the Queen's Majesty, showing her what inconvenience should come if such things were suffered unpunished. And, after sharp reasoning, it was promised that the like should not be done hereafter. The Queen also alleged that they were a great number ; and that she could not trouble their conscience.

About the 20 of this month, arrived at Edinburgh, Henry Stewart, Lord Darnley. From thence he passed to Fife : and in

[1] The records of this Parliament are sadly incomplete, but Randolph gives an account of the statutes passed against adulterers and fornicators. (*Calendar of Scottish Papers*, ii, No. 124)

[2] The records of the General Assembly of 25–27 December 1564 will be found in the *Booke of the Universall Kirk*, i, 52–56.

[3] Details of the Queen's movements are given in Hay Fleming, *Mary Queen of Scots*, 531 and *note*.

[4] See *Acts Parl. Scot.*, ii, 545, c. 2

[5] Of Holyrood

the place of Wemyss he was admitted to kiss the Queen's hand [1]; whom she liked so well that she preferred him before all others, as shall hereafter, God willing, be declared. Soon after, in the month of March, the Earl Bothwell arrived out of France; whereat the Earl of Moray was highly offended, because of the evil report made to him of the Lord Bothwell [2]; and passing immediately to the Queen's Majesty, demanded of her if it was her will, or by her advice, that he was come home; and seeing he was his deadly enemy, either he or the other should leave the country, and therefore desired that he might have justice. Her answer was that seeing the Earl Bothwell was a nobleman, and had done her service, she could not hate him. Nevertheless she would do nothing that might be prejudicial to the Earl of Moray, but desired that the matter might be taken away. Within few days she caused summon the Earl Bothwell to answer to the course of law the 2nd of May, for the conspiracy which the Earl of Arran had alleged two years before, and for the breaking of the ward of the Castle.[3] In the meanwhile there was nothing in the Court but banqueting, balling, and dancing, and other such pleasures as were meet to provoke the disordered appetite; and all for the entertainment of the Queen's cousin from England, the Lord Darnley, to whom she did show all the expressions imaginable of love and kindness.

Within few days, the Queen being at Stirling, order was given to Secretary Lethington to pass to the Queen of England. The chief point of his message was, to declare to the Queen of England that the Queen was minded to marry her cousin the Lord Darnley [4] and the rather, because he was so near of blood to both Queens, for by his mother he was cousin-german to the Queen of Scotland, also of near kindred, and of the same name by his father; his mother was cousin-german to the Queen of England. Here mark God's providence: King James the Fifth having lost his two sons, did declare his resolution to make the Earl of Lennox his heir of the Crown; but

[1] Darnley reached Edinburgh on Tuesday 13 February 1565, tarried there three nights, and on Friday 16 February passed over to Fife to Wemyss where he was "admitted" to the Queen on Saturday 17 February. (*Calendar of Scottish Papers*, ii, Nos. 147, 148)

[2] Randolph, writing to Cecil on 15 March 1565, refers to Bothwell's arrival and adds that Bothwell has been accused by Moray of speaking dishonourable words against the Queen and of threatening Moray and Lethington that he would be the death of both of them. (*Ibid.*, ii, No. 157)

[3] See *supra*, 42, 54, 64. Randolph reports a "day of law" against Bothwell on 2 May 1565 when judgment was given against him in his absence. (*Calendar of Scottish Papers*, ii, Nos. 171, 174)

[4] For Lethington's embassy, see Hay Fleming, *Mary Queen of Scots*, 335, *note* 88.

he [being] prevented by sudden death, that design ceased. Then came the Earl of Lennox from France, with intention to marry King James's widow; but that failed also. He marries Margaret Douglas, and his son marrieth Mary, King James the Fifth's daughter.[1] And so the King's desire is fulfilled, to wit, the Crown continueth in the name and in the family. The Queen of England, nevertheless, shewed herself nothing pleased therewith, but rather declared, That she would in nowise suffer her subjects to make such contracts or alliance that might be prejudicial to her ; and for the same purpose sent a post to the Queen with letters, wherein she complained greatly of the mind of our Mistress, seeing the great affection she bore to her, intending to declare her heritrix of her Realm of England, providing only that she would use her counsel in marriage ; but she could not approve her marriage with the Lord Darnley, although he was their near cousin by birth, since he was below the rank of the Queen by condition, being but a private subject.[2] At the same time she wrote to the Earl of Lennox, and to his son, commanding them to repair both into England.[3] Some write that all this was but counterfeit by the Queen of England, and from her heart she was glad of the marriage, for by that means the succession of the Crown of England was secured, the Lord Darnley being the right heir after the Queen of Scotland : and Queen Elizabeth was not angry to see her married to one of inferior rank, for by that means she thought the Scots Queen would be less proud.[4]

During this time there were certain letters directed to the Brethren of Edinburgh, to Dundee, Fife, Angus, and Mearns, and other places, from the Brethren of Kyle and other places in the West Country, desiring the professors of the Evangel in all places to remember what the Eternal God had wrought, and how potently he had abolished all kind of idolatry and superstition, and placed his word in this Realm so that no man could say otherwise but it was the work of God, who also had delivered this country from the bondage and tyranny of strangers. Nevertheless by our slothfulness, we have suffered that idol the Mass not only to be planted again,

[1] See the genealogical table *infra*, 351

[2] See the instructions given to Throckmorton (*Foreign Calendar, Elizabeth*, vii, Nos. 1118, 1135) and his report to Elizabeth of his interview with Mary on 15 May (*Calendar of Scottish Papers*, ii, No. 183). Knox's continuator gives fuller details, *infra*, 145–146

[3] See Randolph's account in his letter of 2 July 1565. (Keith, *History of Affairs of Church and State in Scotland*, ii, 296–309)

[4] This reasoning is repeated *infra*, 146

but to increase, so that the maintainers thereof are like, by all appearance, to get the upper hand, which would be the occasion of our destruction. And for that the Papists purposed to set up their idol at Easter following, in all places, which was to be imputed to the slothfulness and want of godly zeal of the professors; therefore they admonished the Brethren to strive to avert the evil in time, and not to suffer such wickedness to continue and increase, lest God's heavy wrath come upon us unawares like a consuming fire. By these letters many Brethren were animated, and their spirits wakened, minding to provide as God should give them grace. And first of all, by the advice of the most learned in Edinburgh, there was a Supplication made, and given to the Queen's Majesty by the Superintendent of Lothian, containing, in effect, that the Church in general of the Realm had divers times most humbly craved of her Majesty that committers of adultery should be punished according to the law of God and the Acts of Parliament; nevertheless they continued in their wickedness; and the Papists, of obstinate malice, pretended nothing else but to erect and set up their idolatry and superstition; and especially at Easter day following they intended to put the same in practice, which the Brethren and Professors of the Evangel could not suffer; therefore wished her Majesty to take heed of the matter.

At this time an Italian, named Davie, entered in great familiarity with the Queen, so that there was nothing done without him [1]

This Supplication the Secretary received of the hands of the Superintendents of Lothian and Glasgow, and told them, in the Queen's name, that there should be such provision made as should serve to their contentment. And for the same purpose, the Queen's Majesty wrote to all such places as were suspected, especially to the Bishops of Saint Andrews [2] and Aberdeen [3] (as was said) not to use any Mass, and that they should not do any such thing as was feared by the Protestants, or convene any Council; and thereto commanded them. Now the Communion was administered in Edinburgh, the 1st day of April 1565. At which time, because it was near Easter, the Papists used to meet at their Mass; and as some of the Brethren were diligent to search such things, they having with them one of the Bailies, took one sir James Carvet, riding hard, as he had now ended the saying of the Mass, and conveyed him, together with the master of the house, and one or two more of the assistants, to the Tolbooth, and immediately revested [4] him with all his garments upon him, and so carried him to the Market-Cross, where they set him on high, binding the chalice in his hand,

[1] *Cf. supra*, 106. See also Calderwood's *History*, ii, 285–286.
[2] John Hamilton [3] William Gordon [4] *re-attired*

and himself fast tied to the said Cross, where he tarried the space of one hour ; during which time the boys served him with his Easter eggs. The next day following, the said Carvet, with his assistants, were accused and convicted by an assize, according to the Act of Parliament. And albeit for the same offence he deserved death, yet for all punishment he was set upon the Market-Cross for the space of three or four hours, the hangman standing by, and keeping him, the boys and others were busy with eggs casting ; and some Papists there were that stopped [it] as far as they could : and as the press of people increased about the Cross, there appeared to have been some tumult. The Provost, Archibald Douglas,[1] came with some halberdiers, and carried the priest safe again to the Tolbooth. The Queen being advertised, and having received sinister information that the priest was dead, suddenly thought to have used and inflicted some extreme punishment ; for she thought that all this was done in contempt of her, and of her religion. And it was affirmed that the Town should have been sacked, and a great number executed to death. She sent to such as she pleased, commanding them to come to her at Edinburgh suddenly with their whole forces ; and in the meantime she sent her Advocate, Master Spens of Condie, to Edinburgh, to take a sure trial of the matter. The Provost and Council wrote to the Queen the truth of the matter as it was, desiring her Majesty to take the same in good part, and not to give credit to false reports, and therewith sent to her Majesty the process and enrolment of the Court of the priest convicted.[2] Thus the Queen's Majesty being informed of the truth by her said Advocate, sent again, and stayed the said meeting of men, and sent to the Town a grave Letter, whereof the copy followeth :

The Queen's Letter to the Provost, Bailies, and Council of Edinburgh.

"Provost, Bailies, and Council of our City of Edinburgh, We received your letter from our Advocate, and understand by this report what diligence you took to stay the tumult in the late disorder attempted at Edinburgh ; wherein, as you did your duty in suppress-

[1] Archibald Douglas of Kilspindie

[2] In the burgh records this priest is called "sir James Tarbot," and he is so called, *infra*, 143. The Provost, with two of the Bailies, and other neighbours to the number of forty persons, are to ride to the Queen at Stirling "for mitigating of her Majesty" who had been "highly moved . . . upon the unjust report made to her Highness of the striking and casting of eggs" at him. (*Edinburgh Burgh Recs.*, Burgh Rec. Soc., iii, 195–196). Further details may be read in *Calendar of Scottish Papers*, ii, Nos. 169, 171 (enclosure), where "10,000 eggs" is either an exaggeration or an illuminating commentary upon the ample supplies then available.

ing the tumult, so can We not take in good part, nor think our self satisfied of so notorious a thing, without certain seditious persons, who were pleased to do justice perforce and without the Magistrates' authority, be condignly and really punished for their rashness and misbehaviour. For if all private persons should usurp to take vengeance at their own hands, what lies in ours? And to what purpose hath good laws and statutes been established? Since, therefore, We have never been obstinate to the due punishment of any offenders, prescribed by the laws, but have always maintained justice in that case without respect of persons, it is our will, and We command you, as you will answer to us upon your obedience and allegiance, that you will take before you certain of the most responsible persons which are declared authors of the said sedition, and usurpers of our authority, and to administer justice upon them, in such sort as We may know a sincerity on your part, and our authority no ways slighted. But if you fail, persuade yourselves (and that shortly), We will not oversee it, but will account this contempt not only to be in the committers thereof, but in yourselves, who ought to punish it, and relieve us on our part, remitting the rest to your diligence and execution, which We look for so soon as reason will permit.

"Subscribed with our hand at Stirling, this 24 of April, Anno 1565."

By this manner of writing and high threatening, may be perceived how grievously the Queen's Majesty would have been offended if the said Tarbot and mass-monger had been handled according to his demerit, being not only a Papist idolater, but a manifest whoremaster, and a common fighter and blasphemer; nevertheless, within few days the Queen charged the Provost and Bailies to set him at liberty, commanding them further, that no man should trouble nor molest him in any sort for whatsoever cause; and soon after rewarded him with a benefice, and likewise his assisters, John Low [1] and John Kennedy, set at liberty in the same manner. At this Easter-tide, in Stirling, the Queen made her domestic servants use Papistical rites and ceremonies, and more, she persuaded others by fair means to do the same, and threatened those that were most constant at the Earl of Cassillis' house.[2]

Upon the second day of May 1565, convened at Edinburgh the Earl of Moray with his friends in great numbers, to keep the day

[1] He is called John Loich in *Calendar of Scottish Papers*, ii, No. 171 (enclosure).
[2] Gilbert, fourth Earl of Cassillis

of law against the Earl of Bothwell [1]; who, being called, appeared not, only the Laird of Riccarton [2] protested that the personal absence of the Earl Bothwell should not be prejudicial to him by reason that, for just fear, which might happen in the heart of any man, since he had so potent an enemy as the Lord of Moray who, next the Queen's Majesty, was of greatest estimation and authority of any man within this Realm, to whom assisted at this present day of law, seven or eight hundred men,[3] which force he could not resist, therefore had absented himself; which protestation being made, those that had been sureties for his appearance were outlawed. The said Earl Bothwell, a few days after, passed into France, after he had been in Liddesdale, where, suspecting almost every man, he was not in great assurance of his life, notwithstanding he was not put to the horn; for the Queen continually bore a great favour towards him,[4] and kept him to be a soldier, as appeared within less than half a year; for she would not suffer the Lord Morton,[5] nor my Lord Erskine,[6] my Lord of Moray's great friends, to keep the day. There assisted my Lord of Moray, the Earls of Argyll,[7] Glencairn,[8] and Crawford,[9] with great numbers, and many Lords and Barons, who for the most part convened the same afternoon to treat and consult for the maintaining of Religion; where some articles were devised, and delivered to the Lord of Moray to be presented to the Queen's Majesty and Privy Council; which articles were enlarged at the General Assembly following, as shall be declared.[10]

In the meantime, as they were informed in Court of this great Assembly of people in Edinburgh, they were afraid, for naturally the Queen hated and suspected all such Conventions as were not in her own presence and devised by herself. The chief Councillors in the Court were the Earls of Lennox [11] and Atholl.[12] The Queen wrote incontinent for all the Lords to come to Stirling, so soon as she was advertised that they had treated in Edinburgh of Religion.

[1] See *supra*, 139 and *note* 3; Pitcairn's *Criminal Trials*, i, 462*-464*
[2] Alexander Hepburn of Whitsome and Riccarton
[3] Randolph, writing to Cecil, says that "the company that came in favour of Moray are estimated at 5,000 or 6,000." (*Calendar of Scottish Papers*, ii, No. 174)
[4] See Randolph's account, *ibid.*
[5] James, fourth Earl of Morton; then Chancellor
[6] John, sixth Lord Erskine, becoming, in the following month, Earl of Mar
[7] Archibald, fifth Earl of Argyll
[8] Alexander, fourth Earl of Glencairn
[9] David, tenth Earl of Crawford
[10] *Infra*, 148-150
[11] Matthew, fourth Earl of Lennox, and father of Henry, Lord Darnley
[12] John, fourth Earl of Atholl

She wrote likewise for the Superintendents and other learned men ; who went thither, and, being there, they caused to keep the ports or gates, and make good watch about the town. The special cause of this Convention was to give to the Lord Darnley title of honour, openly and solemnly, with consent of the Nobles, before the marriage.

The fourth day of May the Earl of Moray came to Stirling, where he was well received by the Queen's Majesty, as appeared. And immediately, as he passed with her to my Lord Darnley's chamber, they presented to him a contract, containing in effect, That forasmuch as, or since, the Queen had contracted marriage with the Lord Darnley, that therefore sundry Lords of the Nobility had under-written, ratified, and approved the same, and obliged themselves to grant unto him in full Parliament the Crown Matrimonial (by a new Court solecism in policy, the Crown for the second time is surnamed Matrimonial ; before, when the Queen was first married, it was so called also [1]), to serve and obey him and her as their lawful Sovereigns. The Queen desired my Lord Moray to subscribe, as many others had done before ; which he refused to do, "Because (said he), it is required necessarily that the whole Nobility be present, at least the principal, and such as he himself was posterior unto, before that so grave a matter should be advised and concluded." [2]

The Queen's Majesty no ways content with this answer, insisted still upon him, saying the greatest part of the Nobility were there present and content with the matter, wished him to be so much a Stewart as to consent to the keeping of the Crown in the family, and the surname, according to their father's will and desire, as was said of him a little before his death.[3] But he still refused for the causes above written.

Now as the Lords were assembled, an Ambassador from England, named Sir Nicholas Throckmorton, arrived at Stirling, and in his company the Laird of Lethington. The Ambassador was at the Castle gate before they were aware ; and as he stood there in the entry, he was desired to pass to his lodgings. The next day he had audience of the Queen, and was graciously received according to the dignity of his message. The whole sum of this his message was, to show and declare to the Queen, how highly the Queen his mistress

[1] *Supra*, i, 140–141

[2] Randolph gives a slightly different account in his letter to Cecil of 8 May 1565. (*Calendar of Scottish Papers*, ii, No. 175)

[3] *Cf. supra*, 139–140

was offended with this precipitated marriage, and wondered what had moved her to take a man of inferior rank and condition to herself: and therefore dissuaded her therefrom. And specially desiring her most earnestly to send home her subjects, the Earl of Lennox and the Lord Darnley: but all in vain; for the matter was well far proceeded.[1] In her heart Queen Elizabeth was not angry at this marriage[2]; first, because if Queen Mary had married a foreign Prince, it had been an access to her greatness, and consequently she had been more redoubted by the other; next, both Harry[3] and Mary were alike and in equal degree of consanguinity unto her, the father of Mary and the mother of Harry being children to her father's sister.[4]

With many fair words the Queen let the Ambassador depart, promising to do all she could to satisfy the Queen of England; and for the same purpose she would send an Ambassador to her.

The Earl of Moray seeing the other Nobles consent gave his, which before he refused

In the meantime the Queen's marriage with the Lord Darnley was prepared and propounded in Council; and the chief of the Nobility, such as the Duke,[5] the Earls of Argyll, Moray, [and] Glencairn, with the rest, granted freely to the same providing that they might have the Religion established in Parliament, by the Queen, and the idolatrous Mass and superstition abolished.[6] Shortly it was concluded, that they should convene again to Saint Johnston, where the Queen promised to take a final order for Religion. The day was appointed, to wit, the last of May, at Perth: My Lord of Argyll came too late. The Queen's Majesty communed with the Lords, who were very plain with her, saying, except the Mass were abolished, there should be no quietness in the country. The twelfth day of May the Lord Darnley was belted (that is, created) Earl of Ross, with great solemnity, a belt or girdle being tied about his waist or middle; and albeit all kind of provision was made to make him Duke of Rothesay, yet at that time it came not to effect, albeit the crown and robe-royal were prepared to him for the same. For the entertainment of this triumph there were many Knights made, to the number

[1] See Throckmorton's own account in his letter to Elizabeth of 21 May 1565. (*Calendar of Scottish Papers*, ii, No. 183) [2] *Cf. supra*, 140

[3] Henry, Lord Darnley

[4] Mary's father was James V, son of James IV and Margaret Tudor, daughter of Henry VII and sister to Henry VIII, the father of Elizabeth; Darnley's mother was Margaret Douglas, daughter of Margaret Tudor by her second marriage to Archibald, sixth Earl of Angus. See genealogical tables *infra*, 351, 352.

[5] The Duke of Châtelherault

[6] See Throckmorton's letters in *Calendar of Scottish Papers*, ii, Nos. 178, 180; and the account in Aikman's *Buchanan*, ii, 469.

of fourteen.[1] The next day, which was the thirteenth of May, the Queen called for the Superintendents, by name John Willock, John Winram, and John Spottiswoode, whom she cherished with fair words, assuring them that she desired nothing more earnestly than the glory of God and satisfying of men's consciences, and the good of the commonwealth ; and albeit she was not persuaded in any Religion but in that wherein she was brought up, yet she promised to them that she would hear conference and disputation in the Scriptures : And likewise she would be content to hear public preaching, but always out of the mouth of such as pleased her Majesty ; and above all others, she said, she would gladly hear the Superintendent of Angus (for he was a mild and sweet-natured man), with true honesty and uprightness, John Erskine of Dun.

Soon after the Queen passed to Saint Johnston, after that she had directed Master John Hay, Prior of Monymusk, to pass to England, who sped at the Queen of England's hand, even as Sir Nicholas Throckmorton did in Scotland.[2]

Before the day which was appointed for the meeting at Saint Johnston,[3] my Lord of Moray, most careful of the maintenance of Religion, sent to all the principal Churches, advertising them of the matter, and desiring them to advise, and send the most able men in learning and reputation, to keep the day ; but their craft and dissimulation appeared, for the Dean of Restalrig, who lately arrived out of France,[4] with others, such as Mr John Lesley, Parson of Oyne, afterward Bishop of Ross, caused the Queen to understand that thing whereof she was easily persuaded, to wit, that there ought to be given to all men liberty of conscience,[5] and for this purpose to shun or put off the first day appointed. The Queen wrote to the Nobility, that because she was informed that there were great meetings out of every shire and town in great number ; and then the other party (so termed she the Papists) were minded to gather to the said

[1] Darnley was created Earl of Ross on 15 May 1565. (*Calendar of Scottish Papers*, ii, No. 183) The names and designations of the fourteen knights are given in a memorial of the same date (*ibid.*, ii, No. 181).

[2] See *Calendar of Scottish Papers*, ii, Nos. 183 (*in fin.*), 198, 200, 202. In Mary's letter he is called " Commendator of Balmerino " (*ibid.*, ii, No. 198).

[3] The Lords of Secret Council were to convene at Perth on 10 June 1565 (*Reg. Privy Council of Scotland*, i, 335–336 ; see also Randolph's account in his letter of 3 June 1565 to Cecil, *Calendar of Scottish Papers*, ii, No. 192) ; but the convention " held not " (*ibid.*, ii, No. 193). Neither was the later convention of 22 June held. (See Keith, *History*, ii, 300)

[4] John Sinclair. On 18 September 1564 Mary had applied to Elizabeth for a safe conduct for Master John Sinclair, Dean of Restalrig, with eight companions, to return from France to Scotland through her realm. (*Calendar of Scottish Papers*, ii, No. 91)

[5] An argument that had been advanced as early as 1561 (*supra*, 12)

Convention, which should apparently make trouble or sedition, rather than any other thing; therefore she thought it expedient, and willed them to stay the said meetings, and to defer the same till such a day that she should appoint with advice of her Council. At this time there was a Parliament proclaimed to be held at Edinburgh the twentieth day of July.[1] By this Letter some of the Protestants, having best judgment, thought themselves sufficiently warned of the inconveniences and troubles to come. Now her Council at this time was only the Earls of Lennox and Atholl, [and] the Lord Ruthven; but chiefly David Riccio the Italian ruled all [2]; yet the Earl of Ross [3] was already in greatest credit and familiarity.

These Letters were sent out to the Lords about the eight and twentieth day of May; and within twelve days thereafter, she directed new missives to the chief of the Nobility, desiring or commanding them to come to Saint Johnston the three and twentieth day of June following, to consult upon such things as concerned Religion, and other things, as her Majesty should propose. Which day was even the day before that the General Assembly should have been held in Edinburgh. This last Letter uttered the effect of the former; so that the Protestants thought themselves sufficiently warned. Always as the Earl of Moray was passing to Saint Johnston to have kept the said day, he chanced to fall sick of the fluxes in Lochleven,[4] where he remained till the Queen came forth of Saint Johnston to Edinburgh, where the General Assembly of the whole Church of Scotland was held the four and twentieth day of June.[5] The Earls of Argyll and Glencairn assisted the Church, with a great company of Lords, Barons, and others. It was there ordered and concluded, That certain Gentlemen, as Commissioners from the Church National, should pass to the Queen's Majesty with certain Articles, to the number of six, desiring her most humbly to ratify and approve the same in Parliament.

And because the said ARTICLES are of great weight, and worthy of memory, I thought good to insert the same word by word.[6]

Imprimis, That the Papistical and blasphemous Mass, with all Papistical idolatry, and Papal jurisdiction, be universally suppressed

[1] See *Reg. Privy Council of Scotland*, i, 335

[2] See Randolph's graphic account in his letter to Leicester of 3 June 1565. (*Calendar of Scottish Papers*, ii, No. 191)

[3] Darnley

[4] For differing versions of Moray's "illness" see Calderwood, *History*, ii, 286; Keith, *History*, ii, 311–314; Aikman's *Buchanan*, ii, 468–469. See also Hay Fleming, *Mary Queen of Scots*, 354, *note* 16.

[5] The General Assembly met in Edinburgh on 25 June 1565

[6] See *Booke of the Universall Kirk*, i, 59–60

and abolished throughout this Realm, not only in the subjects, but also in the Queen's own person, with punishment against all persons that should be deprehended to transgress and offend in the same: And that the sincere word of God and Christ's true Religion, now at this present received, be established, approved, and ratified,[1] throughout the whole Realm, as well in the Queen's own person as in the subjects. And that the people be astricted to resort upon the Sundays at the least to the prayers and preaching of God's word, even as they were before to the idolatrous Mass: And these Heads to be provided by Act of Parliament, and ratified by the Queen's Majesty.

Secondly, That sure provision be made for sustentation of the Ministry, as well for the time present, as the time to come: And that such persons as are presently admitted to the Ministry, may have their livings assigned unto them in places where they travail in their calling, or at least next adjacent thereto: And that the Benefices now vacant, or hath been vacant since the month of March 1558,[2] or that hereafter shall happen to be vacant, be disponed to qualified and learned persons, able to preach God's Word and discharge the vocation concerning the Ministry, by trial and admission of the Superintendents and Overseers: And that no Benefice or Living, having many churches annexed thereunto, be disponed altogether in any time to come, to any one man, but at the least the churches thereof be severally disponed, and that to several persons; so that every man having charge may serve at his own church according to his vocation: And to that effect, likewise the glebes and the manses be given to the Ministers, that they may make residence at their churches, whereby they may discharge their consciences according to their vocation; and also, that the kirks may be repaired accordingly; and that a law be made and established hereupon by Act of Parliament, as said is.

Thirdly, That none be permitted to have charge of Schools, Colleges, or Universities, neither privately nor publicly to teach and instruct the youth, but such as shall be tried by the Superintendents or Visitors of churches, and found sound and able in doctrine, and admitted by them to their charges.

Fourthly, For the Sustentation of the Poor, That all lands founded for hospitality of old, be restored again to the same use; and that

[1] The Acts of the Reformation Parliament of 1560 had never been ratified by the Queen, and were never to be ratified by her. See also on this point, *supra*, 78, *note* 4.

[2] That is, 1559

all lands, annual rents, or any other emoluments, pertaining any ways sometime to the Friars, of whatsoever Order they had been of, as likewise the annuities, altarages, obits, and other duties pertaining to priests, to be applied to the sustentation of the poor, and uphold of the town schools in towns, and other places where they lie.

Fifthly, That such horrible crimes as now abound within this Realm, without any correction, to the great contempt of God and his Word; such as idolatry, blasphemy of God's name, manifest breaking of the Sabbath-day, witchcraft, sorcery, enchantment, adultery, manifest whoredom, maintenance of brothels, murder, slaughter, oppression, with many other detestable crimes, may be severely punished; and Judges appointed in every province and diocese, for execution thereof, with power to do the same, and that by Act of Parliament.

Lastly, That some order be devised and established for ease of the poor labourers of the ground, concerning the unreasonable payment of the tithes, who are oppressed by the leasers of the tithes set over their heads, without their own consent and advice.

The persons who were appointed by the Church to carry these Articles, and present them to the Queen's Majesty, were the Lairds of Cunninghamhead, Lundie, Spott, and Grange in Angus, and James Barron for the Burghs.[1] These five passed from Edinburgh to Saint Johnston, where they presented the said Articles to the Queen's Majesty, desiring and requiring her Highness most humbly to advise therewith, and to give them answer. The next day, ere they were aware, the Queen departed to Dunkeld,[2] and immediately they followed; and after they had got audience, they desired the Queen's Majesty most humbly to give their dispatch. She answered that her Council was not there present, but she intended to be in Edinburgh within eight days, and there they should receive their answer.

At the same time as the General Assembly was held in Edinburgh, the Brethren perceiving the Papists to brag, and trouble like to be, they assembled themselves at Saint Leonard's

[1] That is, William Cunningham of Cunninghamhead; Walter Lundie of that Ilk; George Hume of Spott; William Durham of Grange; and James Barron, burgess of Edinburgh.

[2] According to Randolph, Mary was "now in suspicion of all men" and at night, after supper, on 26 June, rode from Ruthven to Dunkeld with only a small retinue. (Keith, *History*, ii, 301–304)

Craig,[1] where they concluded they would defend themselves; and for the same purpose, elected eight persons of the most able, two of every quarter, to see that [the] Brethren should be ready armed.

And when the five Commissioners above named had waited upon the Court four or five days after her Majesty's coming to Edinburgh,[2] there the matter was proponed in Council. And after long and earnest reasoning upon these Articles, at length it was answered to the Commissioners by the Secretary, that the Queen's Majesty's command was, that the matter should be reasoned in her presence; which, for the gravity of the same, there could nothing be concluded at that time, albeit the Queen's Majesty had heard more in that matter than ever she did before: But within eight days thereafter, she understood that a great part of the Nobility should be present in Edinburgh, where they should have a final answer.[3]

At length, the one and twentieth of August,[4] they received the answer in writing in her presence, according to the tenor hereof, as followeth:

The Queen's Majesty's Answer to the Articles presented to Her Highness, by certain Gentlemen, in the Name of the whole Assembly of the Church.[5]

To the first, Desiring the Mass to be suppressed and abolished, as well in the head as in the members, with punishment against the contraveners; as also, the Religion professed to be established by Act of Parliament[6]: It was answered first, for her Majesty's part, That her Highness is no way yet persuaded in the said Religion, nor

[1] The Crags in the lands of St. Leonard's. The lands of St. Leonard's were added to the King's Park by James V in 1540. 'Saint Leonard's Craig' for the Salisbury Crags would be unusual; it may be that the reference is to the rising ground in St. Leonard's *opposite* the Salisbury Crags.

[2] The Queen returned to Edinburgh on 4 July 1565. (Keith, *History*, ii, 321)

[3] On 12 July, "eight days" after Mary's return to Edinburgh, and following a meeting of the Privy Council, an "assurance touart the state of religion" was issued, certifying the Queen's good subjects that they would not be "molestit" in the "quiet using of thair religioun and conscience" (*Reg. Privy Council of Scotland*, i, 338); but, three days later, since a great number of her lieges had taken to arms owing to "untrew report" of her intentions, it was thought necessary to renew the assurance *and also* to charge all her subjects to come to her, in Edinburgh, all well armed, and to remain with her for fifteen days. (*Ibid.*, i, 339) See also *infra*, 155–156, and Keith, *History*, ii, 326–328.

[4] On 29 July, according to the copy in *Calendar of Scottish Papers*, ii, No. 217

[5] These answers were presented by the Commissioners at the meeting of the General Assembly on 25 December 1565. They were declared to be unsatisfactory, and Mr. John Row was directed to draw up in writing the Assembly's "Answers to the Answers." For the Queen's Answers, the Assembly's Answers, and the Assembly's Supplication, see *Booke of the Universall Kirk*, i, 67–71.

[6] See *supra*, 149, *note* 1

yet that any impiety is in the Mass; and therefore believeth that her loving subjects will not press her to receive any Religion against her conscience, which should be unto her a continual trouble by remorse of conscience, and therewith a perpetual unquietness. And to deal plainly with her subjects, her Majesty neither will nor may leave the Religion wherein she hath been nourished and brought up, and believeth the same to be well-grounded; knowing, besides the grudge of conscience that she should receive upon the change of her own Religion, that she should lose the friendship of the King of France, the married allia[1] of this Realm, and of other great Princes her friends and confederates, who would take the same in evil part, and of whom she may look for their great support in all her necessities. And having no assured consideration that may countervail[2] the same, she will be loth to put in hazard [the loss of] all her friends at an instant; praying all her loving subjects, seeing they have had experience of her goodness, that she hath neither in times past, nor yet intends hereafter, to press the conscience of any man, but that they may worship God in such sort as they are persuaded in their conscience to be best,[3] that they will also not press her conscience.

As to the establishing of Religion in the body of the Realm, they themselves know, as appears by their Articles, that the same cannot be done only by consent of her Majesty, but requires necessarily the consent of the three States in Parliament[4]; and therefore so soon as the Parliament holds, those things which the three States agree upon amongst themselves, her Majesty shall consent unto the same; and in the meantime shall make sure, that no men be troubled for using themselves in religion according to conscience; so that no man shall have cause to doubt, that for religion's sake men's lives and heritage shall be in any hazard.

To the second Article, it is answered that her Majesty thinks it no ways reasonable that she should defraud herself of so great a part of the patrimony of the Crown, as to put the Patronage of Benefices forth of her own hands; for her own necessity in bearing of her port[5] and common charges will require the retention thereof, and that in a good part, in her own hands. Nevertheless her Majesty

[1] *ally by marriage*. In the *Booke of the Universall Kirk* the words are "ancient allya."

[2] *counterbalance*

[3] But it now appears that in seeking a dispensation Mary and Darnley had promised to "defend the Catholic religion to the utmost of their power" (Robertson, *Statuta Ecclesiæ Scoticanæ*, i, Preface, clxviii–clxix; Hay Fleming, *Mary Queen of Scots*, 122–124 and supporting notes). [4] See *supra*, 149, *note* 1

[5] That is, her royal living and retinue

is well pleased that, consideration being had of her own necessity, and what may be sufficient for her, and for the reasonable sustentation of the Ministers, a special assignation be made to them in places most commodious and meet: with which her Majesty shall not meddle, but suffer the same to come to them.

To the third Article, it is answered that her Majesty shall do therein as shall be agreed by the States in Parliament.

To the fourth Article, Her Majesty's liberality towards the poor shall always be so far extended as can be reasonably required at her hands.

To the fifth and sixth Articles, Her Majesty will refer the taking order therein unto the States assembled in Parliament.

As the Queen's Majesty came from Saint Johnston, over Forth to the Callendar,[1] she was conveyed to the waterside of Forth with two hundred spears. For at that time it was bruited, that there were some lying in wait at the Path of Dron.[2] In the meantime the Earl of Moray was in Lochleven, and the Earl of Argyll with him. Now in the Callendar the Lord Livingston [3] had desired the Queen's Majesty to be witness to the christening of a child; for his Lady was lately delivered and brought to bed: And when the Minister made the sermon and exhortation concerning baptism, the Queen's Majesty came in the end, and said to the Lord Livingston, "That she would shew him that favour that she had not done to any other before"; that is, that she would give her presence to the Protestant sermon, which was reckoned a great matter.

The Queen being in the Callendar, was informed both by word and letters by false brethren, That a great part of the Protestants of Edinburgh had lately convened upon Saint Leonard's Craigs, and there made a conspiration against her; and had chosen for the same purpose certain Captains to govern the rest. And without any trial, or perfect notice taken in the case, she sent to the Provost and Bailies of Edinburgh, commanding them to take and apprehend Alexander Guthrie, Alexander Clerk, Gilbert Lauder, and Andrew Slater, and put them in prison in the Castle.[4]

This new and unaccustomed fashion of proceeding seemed to be very strange: And because the said four persons were not apprehended, she sent the next day a charge to the Provost and Bailies,

[1] Callendar House, near Falkirk

[2] About six miles south-east of Perth. For an analysis of this incident, see Hay Fleming, *Mary Queen of Scots*, 354, *note* 16.

[3] William, sixth Lord Livingston

[4] See *Accounts Lord High Treasurer*, xi, 376, 380

and to her own great Treasurer, to pass to the houses of the said four men, and likewise to their booths or shops, and there to take inventory of all their goods and chattels ; and commanded the said Treasurer to take the keys of the said houses and booths, together with the said inventory ; which was executed in effect, especially upon the said Alexander Guthrie's wife, he being then common clerk,[1] and one of the greatest in estimation within the town : his wife and children were shut out of their house, and compelled to seek some other lodging in the town.

By this manner of proceeding, the hearts of all men of spirit and judgment were wonderfully abashed and wounded, seeing and perceiving these things so furiously handled upon sinister and wrong information, men never called to their answer, nor heard, nor any trial taken therein. Immediately thereafter, as she came to Edinburgh, she called to council such as pleased her Majesty, and there complained of the said matter, alleging it to be a conspiracy and manifest treason. And another matter likewise was complained upon, that the Earl of Argyll (as the Queen was surely informed) was riding with a great army to invade the Earl of Atholl and his lands.[2] For the first matter it was concluded by the Council that diligent inquisition should be made in the matter, and to that purpose appointed the Queen's Advocates, Master John Spens of Condie and Master Robert Crichton, to examine such as they would ; and when the said Advocates had called before them and examined a sufficient number, and their depositions subscribed and delivered to the Queen, there was nothing found worthy of death nor treason : At length the said four persons were summoned to answer at law.[3] For the other matter, that the Queen's Majesty should send to the Earls of Argyll and Atholl some of her Council or familiar servants to take order touching it. And when the Secretary, the Justice-Clerk, and Lord of Saint Colm [4] had passed to the said Earl of Argyll, they found no such thing [5] ; but in Atholl there was great fear come of a sudden fray ; for after many proclamations, the fire-cross (which they made use of in lieu of beacons) was raised in Atholl.

Now as the day of Parliament approached, the Lords pretend-

[1] Town Clerk of Edinburgh

[2] This is also reported by Randolph in a letter to Cecil of 6 July 1565. (*Calendar of Scottish Papers*, ii, No. 204)

[3] To the 26 July, according to a letter from Randolph to Cecil, printed in Keith, *History*, ii, 330–331.

[4] Sir James Stewart, Commendator of Inchcolm

[5] See also *Calendar of Scottish Papers*, ii, Nos. 204, 205 ; *Accounts Lord High Treasurer*, xi, 375

ing to consult before what should be done, as well in Religion, as for the Commonwealth, the fifteenth day of July [1] there convened at Stirling the Duke, the Earls of Argyll and Moray, Rothes, and other Lords and Barons ; and as they were devising and consulting, the Queen's Majesty taking their meeting in evil part, sent her Advocates, Master John Spens and Master [Robert] Crichton, to them at Stirling, requiring the cause of their meeting. They answered, That the special occasion of their meeting was for the cause of Religion and the assurance thereof, according as they had lately written to the Queen's Majesty in Seaton from the town of Edinburgh, they desiring then to prorogate the day.

Finally, when the said Advocates could by no means persuade them to come to Edinburgh, they returned again to Edinburgh, and declared to the Queen's Majesty according as they had found.

In the meantime the Parliament was prorogated at the Queen's Majesty's command to the first of September next after following [2] ; for it was thought that, the best part and principal of the chief Nobility being absent, there could no Parliament be held : at the same time the Queen's Majesty perceiving that the matter was already come to a maturity and ripeness, so that the minds and secrecy of men's hearts must needs be disclosed, she wrote to a great number of Lords, Barons, Gentlemen, and others that were nearest in Fife, Angus, Lothian, Merse, Teviotdale, Perth, Linlithgow, Clydesdale, and others to resort to her, in this form of words hereafter following [3] :

The Queen's Letter

" TRUSTY FRIEND, We greet you well : We are grieved indeed by the evil bruit spread amongst our lieges, as that we should have molested any man in the using of his Religion and conscience freely, a thing which never entered into our mind [4] ; yet since we perceive the too easy believing such reports hath made them careless, and so we think it becomes us to be careful for the safety and preservation of our State ; wherefore we pray you most affectionately, that with all possible haste (after the receipt of this our letter) you with your kindred, friends, and whole force, well furnished with arms for war, provided for fifteen days after your coming, address you to come to us, to wait and attend upon us, according to our expectation and

[1] On 18 July 1565, according to Drury (*Foreign Calendar, Elizabeth*, vii, No. 1305). See also *Calendar of Scottish Papers*, ii, Nos. 210, 211.

[2] *Reg. Privy Council of Scotland*, i, 335, 338

[3] *Cf.* Keith, *History*, ii, 326–328 ; *Calendar of Scottish Papers*, ii, No. 209. See also *supra*, 151, *note* 3.

[4] But see *supra*, 152, *note* 3.

trust in you, as you will thereby declare the good affection you bear to the maintenance of our authority, and will do us therein acceptable service.

Subscribed with our hand at Edinburgh, the seventeenth day of July, 1565."

There was likewise Proclamation made in Edinburgh, that the Queen minded not to trouble nor alter the Religion; and also Proclamations made in the shires above mentioned, for the same purpose,[1] that all freeholders and other gentlemen should resort (in the aforesaid manner) to Edinburgh, where the Earl of Ross was made Duke of Rothesay, with great triumph, the 23rd day of July.[2] The same afternoon the Queen complained grievously upon the Earl of Moray, in open audience of all the Lords and Barons; and the same day the banns of the Earl of Ross and Duke of Rothesay and the Queen's marriage were proclaimed.[3] About this time the Lord Erskine was made Earl of Mar.[4] In the meantime there were divers messages sent from the Queen's Majesty to the Lord of Moray, first, Master Robert Crichton, to persuade him by all means possible to come and resort to the Queen's Majesty. His answer was, that he would be glad to come to herself, according to his bounden duty; yet for as much as such persons as were most privy in her company were his capital enemies, who also had conspired his death, he could no ways come so long as they were in Court.

Soon after, my Lord Erskine[5] and the Master [of] Maxwell[6] passed to him to St. Andrews, rather suffered and permitted by the Queen, than sent by her Highness; after them the Laird of Dun, who was sent by the means of the Earl of Mar; but all this did not prevail with him; and when all hope of his coming was past, an herald was sent to him, charging him to come to the Queen's Majesty, and answer to such things as should be laid to his charge, within eight and forty hours next after the charge, under pain of rebellion; and because he appeared not the next day after the eight and forty

[1] See *Reg. Privy Council of Scotland*, i, 338–339

[2] On Sunday 22 July Darnley, who had previously been made Earl of Ross (*supra*, 146) was raised to the Dukedom of Albany. (*Foreign Calendar, Elizabeth*, vii, No. 1312; Hay Fleming, *Mary Queen of Scots*, 105) See also *infra*, 157, *note* 9.

[3] The banns were proclaimed on Sunday 22 July.

[4] The grant of the Earldom of Mar to John, sixth Lord Erskine, was made on 23 June 1565 and infeftment was given on 24 July. (*Scots Peerage*, v, 613)

[5] The Earl of Mar

[6] John, second son of Robert, fifth Lord Maxwell; later Lord Herries. (See *Scots Peerage*, vi, 481; iv, 409–411)

hours, he was denounced rebel, and put to the horn.[1] The same order they used against the Earl of Argyll ; for the Queen said she would serve him and the rest with the same measure they had meted to others, meaning the said Argyll.[2]

In the meanwhile, as the fire was well kindled and enflamed, all means and ways were sought to stir up enemies against the chief Protestants that had been lately at Stirling ; for the Earl of Atholl [3] was ready bent against the Earl of Argyll : the Lord Lindsay [4] against the Earl Rothes [5] in Fife, they both being Protestants ; for they had contended now a long time for the sheriffship [6] of Fife. And that no such thing should be left undone, the Lord Gordon, who now had remained near three years in prison in Dunbar, was, after some little travail of his friends, received by the Queen ; and being thus received into favour, was restored first to the Lordship of Gordon, and soon after to the Earldom of Huntly, and to all his lands, honours, and dignities, that he might be a bar and a party in the North to the Earl of Moray.[8]

The Dispensation being come from Rome for the marriage.[7] *Before which, according to the Romish Law, it was unlawful to marry, being cousins-german, brother and sister's children, and so the degree of consanguinity forbidden*

The 28th of July, late in the evening, near an hour after the sun's going down, there was a proclamation made at the Market-Cross of Edinburgh, containing in effect :

" THAT forasmuch as at the will and pleasure of Almighty God, the Queen had taken to her husband a right excellent and illustrious Prince, Harry Duke of Rothesay, Earl of Ross, Lord Darnley, Therefore it was her will, that he should be held and obeyed, and reverenced as King : Commanding all letters and proclamations to be made in the names of Henry and Mary in times coming." [9]

[1] Moray was denounced as an outlaw on 6 August (*Reg. Privy Council of Scotland*, i, 349–350). See also Hay Fleming, *op. cit.*, 111 and supporting notes.

[2] Archibald, fifth Earl of Argyll. (See Hay Fleming, *op. cit.*, 358, *note* 24)

[3] John, fourth Earl of Atholl

[4] Patrick, sixth Lord Lindsay of the Byres

[5] Andrew, fifth Earl of Rothes

[6] In Laing's reprint (*Knox*, ii, 495), the erroneous word " heir-ship " has been retained. For this dispute, see Leslie, *Historical Records of the Family of Leslie*, ii, 76–77 and *Hist. MSS. Commission*, 4th Report, 500–502.

[7] Robertson (*Statuta Ecclesiæ Scoticanæ*, i, clxix, *note*) states that the Papal dispensation arrived in Edinburgh on 22 July, the day on which the banns were proclaimed ; but Pollen has shown that the dispensation did not reach Scotland until some time *after* the marriage had taken place, and that it was ante-dated to 25 May. (*Scottish Historical Review*, iv 241–248) For the dispensation, see Pollen, *Papal Negotiations with Mary Queen of Scots*, Scot. Hist. Soc., 218–220.

[8] George, Lord Gordon, fifth Earl of Huntly. Lord Gordon was apparently received by the Queen on 3 August 1565 (*Diurnal of Occurrents*, 80). See *infra*, 171, *note* 6.

[9] See *Reg. Privy Council of Scotland*, i, 345–346 ; *National MSS. of Scotland*, iii, No. 48, (where the transcript gives the month, erroneously, as *January*). For " Rothesay " in the text here (and elsewhere) read " Albany."

The next day following, at six hours in the morning, they were married in the Chapel Royal of Holyrood-House, by the Dean of Restalrig,[1] the Queen being all clothed in mourning. But immediately, as the Queen went to Mass, the King went not with her, but to his pastime.[2] During the space of three or four days, there was nothing but balling, and dancing, and banqueting.

In the meantime, the Earl Rothes, the Laird of Grange,[3] the Tutor of Pitcur,[4] with some gentlemen of Fife, were put to the horn for non-appearance; and immediately the swash,[5] tabor, and drums were stricken or beaten for men of war to serve the King and Queen's Majesty, and to take their pay.[6] This sudden alteration and hasty creation of Kings, moved the hearts of a great number.

Now, amongst the people there were divers bruits: for some alleged that the cause of this alteration was not for Religion, but rather for hatred, envy of sudden promotion or dignity, or such worldly causes; but they that considered the progress of the matter, according as is heretofore declared, thought the principal cause to be only for Religion.

In this meantime, the Lords passed to Argyll, taking, apparently, little care of the trouble that was to come. Howbeit they sent into England Master Nicolas Elphinstone [7] for support, who brought some moneys in this country, to the sum of ten thousand pounds sterling. There came one forth of England to the Queen, who got presence the seventh of August in Holyrood-House. He was not well [received] &c.[8]

About the fifteenth of August, the Lords met at Ayr, to wit, the Duke of Hamilton,[9] the Earls Argyll, Moray, Glencairn, Rothes, the

[1] John Sinclair, Bishop of Brechin

[2] 29 July 1565. See Hay Fleming, *Mary Queen of Scots*, 347–348, *notes* 113, 114

[3] Sir William Kirkcaldy of Grange

[4] James Haliburton, Tutor of Pitcur, and Provost of Dundee. This was on 7 August 1565. (*Diurnal of Occurrents*, 81) On 2 August they had been charged to enter themselves in ward in the Castles of Dumbarton and Dunbar within five days. (*Reg. Privy Council of Scotland*, i, 348)

[5] *drum*; later mistakenly used for *trumpet*

[6] See *Reg. Privy Council of Scotland*, i, 348–349 (4 August 1565), and *Diurnal of Occurrents*, 80 (6 August 1565)

[7] Moray writes to Bedford, on 2 August 1565, requesting him to assist his servant "Maistre Nychol Elphistoun" on his way from Berwick to Newcastle (*Calendar of Scottish Papers*, ii, No. 223); on 13 August the Privy Council issue letters for Nichol Elphingstoun to be sought and charged to surrender himself under pain of rebellion. (*Reg. Privy Council of Scotland*, i, 352)

[8] This was John Thomworth, sent by Elizabeth at the end of July, but who, received by Mary on 7 August, found the Scottish Queen "marvellously stout." (See *Calendar of Scottish Papers*, ii, Nos. 220, 225, 226–229; Hay Fleming, *Mary Queen of Scots*, 110–112 and supporting notes)

[9] That is, Châtelherault

Lords Boyd and Ochiltree, with divers Barons and Gentlemen of Fife and Kyle, where they concluded to be in readiness with their whole forces the four and twentieth day of August.[1] But the King and Queen with great celerity prevented them ; for their Majesties sent through Lothian, Fife, Angus, Strathearn, Teviotdale, and Clydesdale, and other shires, making their proclamations in this manner, " That forasmuch as certain Rebels, who (under colour of Religion) intended nothing but the trouble and subversion of the Commonwealth, were to convene with such as they might persuade to assist them ; therefore they charged all manner of men, under pain of life, lands, and goods, to resort and meet their Majesties at Linlithgow, the 24 day of August." [2]

Note this for our time

This Proclamation was made in Lothian the third day of the said month. Upon Sunday the nineteenth of August the King came to the High Kirk of Edinburgh, where John Knox made the sermon : his text was taken out of the six and twentieth chapter of Isaiah his Prophecy, about the thirteenth verse, where, in the words of the Prophet, he said, " O Lord our God, other lords than thou have ruled over us." Whereupon he took occasion to speak of the government of wicked princes who, for the sins of the people, are sent as tyrants and scourges to plague them. And amongst other things, he said, " That God sets in that room (for the offences and ingratitude of the people) boys and women." And some other words which appeared bitter in the King's ears as, " That God justly punished Ahab and his posterity, because he would not take order with that harlot Jezebel." And because he had tarried an hour and more longer than the time appointed, the King (sitting in a throne made for that purpose), was so moved at this sermon that he would not dine ; and being troubled, with great fury he passed in the afternoon to the hawking.[4]

The King, to make himself more popular, and to take from the Lords of the Congregation the pretext of Religion, he went to Kirk to hear John Knox preach[3]

Immediately John Knox was commanded to come to the Council, where, in the Secretary's chamber, were convened the Earl of Atholl,

[1] Moray was on his way to Ayr on 18 August, and on 27 August Randolph reported that the Protestant Lords were " now at Ayr ". (*Calendar of Scottish Papers*, ii, Nos. 232, 237)

[2] *Cf. Reg. Privy Council of Scotland*, i, 355 (22 August 1565)

[3] This marginal rubric seems to have been taken from Spottiswoode. (See *History of the Church of Scotland*, Spottiswoode Society, ii, 31)

[4] This is reported in the *Diurnal of Occurrents* (81), the writer adding that the King " was crabbit, and causit discharge the said Johne of his preitching." The sermon was subsequently published by Knox, written out " indigestly, but yet truly so far as memory would serve " on 31 August 1565 amid " the terrible roaring of guns and the noise of armour " (*cf. infra*, 161). The date added to the Preface is 19 September 1565. (Laing's *Knox*, vi, 223–273)

the Lord Ruthven, the Secretary, the Justice-Clerk,[1] with the Advocate.[2] There passed along with the Minister a great number of the most apparent men of the Town. When he was called, the Secretary declared, " That the King's Majesty was offended with some words spoken in the sermon (especially such as are above rehearsed), desiring him to abstain from preaching for fifteen or twenty days, and let Master Craig [3] supply the place." [4]

He answered, " That he had spoken nothing but according to his text ; and if the Church would command him either to speak or abstain, he would obey, so far as the Word of God would permit him." [5]

Within four days after, the King and Queen sent to the Council of Edinburgh, commanding them to depose Archibald Douglas, and to receive the Laird [of] Craigmillar [6] for their Provost, which was presently obeyed.[7]

The five and twentieth of August,[8] the King's and Queen's Majesties passed from Edinburgh to Linlithgow, and from thence to Stirling, and from Stirling to Glasgow. At their [first] arrival, their whole people were not come. The next day after their arrival to Glasgow, the Lords came to Paisley, where they remained that night, being in company about one thousand horse. On the morrow they came to Hamilton, keeping the high passage from Paisley hard by Glasgow, where the King and Queen easily might behold them. The night following, which was the penult of August, they remained in Hamilton with their company ; but for divers respects moving them, they thought it not expedient to tarry ; especially because the Earl of Argyll was not come : for his diet was not afore the second of September following, to have been at Hamilton.

[1] Sir John Bellenden of Auchinoul [2] John Spens of Condie

[3] Mr. John Craig, Knox's fellow-preacher in Edinburgh

[4] *Cf.* Laing's *Knox*, vi, 230–31

[5] And the Council, Bailies, and Deacons of Crafts of the Burgh, on the afternoon of 23 August, unanimously concluded and delivered " that thai will na maner of way consent or grant that his mouth be closit or he dischargeit in preiching the trew word." (*Edinburgh Burgh Records*, Burgh Rec. Soc., iii, 200) The editor of the Fifth Book again adds a long marginal rubric—" In answering he said more than he had preached, for he added, That as the King had (to pleasure the Queen) gone to Mass, and dishonoured the Lord God, so should God in his justice make her an instrument of his ruin ; and so it fell out in a very short time ; but the Queen being incensed with these words, fell out in tears, and to please her, John Knox must abstain from preaching for a time"—which again seems to be derived from Spottiswoode (*op. cit.*, ii, 31).

[6] Sir Simon Preston [7] See *Edinburgh Burgh Records*, iii, 199, 200, 201.

[8] On Sunday 26 August, according to Randolph (*Calendar of Scottish Papers*, ii, No. 237) and the *Diurnal of Occurrents* (82)

Finally, They took purpose to come to Edinburgh, the which they did the next day.[1] And albeit Alexander Erskine, Captain under the Lord his brother,[2] caused to shoot forth of the Castle two shot of cannon, they being near the town; and likewise that the Laird [of] Craigmillar, Provost, did his endeavour to hold the Lords forth of the town, in causing the common bells to be rung, for the convening of the town to the effect aforesaid; yet they entered easily at the West Port or Gate, without any molestation or impediment, being in number, as they esteemed themselves, one thousand three hundred horse. Immediately they dispatched messengers southward and northward to assist them; but all in vain. And immediately after they were in their lodgings, they caused to strike or beat the drum, desiring all such men as would receive wages for the defence of the glory of God, that they should resort the day following to the Church, where they should receive good pay. But they profited little that way; neither could they in Edinburgh get any comfort or support, for none or few resorted unto them [3]; yet they got more rest and sleep when they were at Edinburgh than they had done in five or six nights before.

The Noblemen of this company were the Duke, the Earls Moray, Glencairn, and Rothes; the Lords Boyd and Ochiltree; the Lairds of Grange, Cunninghamhead, Balcomie, and Lawers [4]; the Tutor of Pitcur [5]; the Lairds of Barr, Carnell, and Dreghorn [6]; and the Laird of Pittarrow, Comptroller,[7] went with them. Some said merrily that they were come to keep the Parliament; for the Parliament was continued till the first day of September. Upon the which day they wrote to the King's and Queen's Majesties a letter, containing in effect that, albeit they were persecuted most unjustly, which they understood proceeded not of the King's and Queen's Majesties own nature, but only by evil counsel, yet notwithstanding, they were willing and content to suffer according to the laws of the Realm, providing that the true Religion of God might be established, and the dependants thereupon be likewise reformed: beseeching

[1] Friday 31 August. (See *Diurnal of Occurrents*, 82; *Calendar of Scottish Papers*, ii, Nos. 239, 241)

[2] Sir Alexander Erskine of Gogar, second surviving son of John, fifth Lord Erskine, and brother to John, sixth Lord Erskine, now Earl of Mar

[3] See also *Calendar of Scottish Papers*, ii, No. 245; *Edinburgh Burgh Records*, iii, 203–205

[4] These lairds were: Sir William Kirkcaldy of Grange; William Cunningham of Cunninghamhead; George Learmonth of Balcomie, and John Campbell of Lawers.

[5] James Haliburton, Provost of Dundee

[6] These lairds were: John Lockhart of Barr, Hugh Wallace of Carnell, and John Fullerton of Dreghorn.

[7] Sir John Wishart of Pittarrow

their Majesties most humbly to grant these things ; but otherwise, if their enemies would seek their blood, they should understand it should be dear bought. They had written twice, almost to the same effect, to the King's and Queen's Majesties, after their passing from Edinburgh ; for the Laird of Preston [1] presented a letter to the King's and Queen's Majesties, and was therefor imprisoned, but soon after released ; nevertheless they got no answer.

The same day that they departed out of Hamilton, the King's and Queen's Majesties issued out of Glasgow in the morning betimes, and passing towards Hamilton, the army met their Majesties near the Bridge of Cadder.[2] As they mustered, the Master of Maxwell sat down upon his knees, and made a long oration to the Queen, declaring what pleasure she had done to them, and ever laid the whole burden upon the Earl of Moray. Soon after, they marched forward in battle array. The Earl of Lennox took the vanguard, the Earl of Morton the middle battle, and the King and Queen the rear. The whole number were about five thousand men, whereof the greatest part were in the vanguard.

As the King's and Queen's Majesties were within three miles of Hamilton, they were advertised that the Lords were departed in the morning ; but where they pretended to be that night, it was uncertain. Always, soon after their return to Glasgow, the King and Queen were certainly advertised that they were passed to Edinburgh ; and therefore caused immediately to warn the whole army to pass with them to Edinburgh the next day, who, early in the morning, long before the sun was risen, began to march. But there arose such a vehement tempest of wind and rain from the west, as the like had not been seen before in a long time ; so that a little brook turned incontinent into a great river ; and the raging storm being in their faces, with great difficulty went they forward. And albeit the most part waxed weary, yet the Queen's courage increased man-like, so much that she was ever with the foremost.[3] There were divers persons drowned that day in the water of Carron ; and amongst others, the King's master, a notable Papist, who, for the zeal he bore to the Mass, carried about his neck a round god of bread, well closed in a case, which always could not save him.

Before the end of August, there came a post to the Queen's

[1] Sir David Hamilton of Singleton. (See *Reg. Privy Council of Scotland*, i, 363)

[2] About two miles south-west of Kirkintilloch

[3] These details are confirmed in a letter from Randolph to Cecil, of 4 September 1565. (*Calendar of Scottish Papers*, ii, No. 246) The storm of wind and rain was on Saturday, 1 September.

Majesty, sent by Alexander Erskine, who declared that the Lords were in the town of Edinburgh, where there was a multitude of innocent persons, and therefore desired to know if he should shoot. She commanded incontinent that he should return again to the said Alexander, and command him, in her name, that he should shoot so long as he had either powder or bullet, and not spare for anybody.

At night, the King and Queen came well wet to the Callendar,[1] where they remained that night. And about eight hours at night, the first of September, the post came again to the Castle, and reported the Queen's command to Alexander Erskine, who incontinently caused to shoot six or seven shot of cannon, whereof the marks appeared, having respect to no reason, but only to the Queen's command.

The Lords perceiving that they could get no support in Edinburgh, nor soldiers for money, albeit they had travailed all that they could; and being advertised of the Queen's returning with her whole company, they took purpose to depart. And so the next day betimes, long before day, they departed with their whole company, and came to Lanark[2] and from thence to Hamilton, where the Master of Maxwell came to them, with his uncle, the Laird of Drumlanrig.[3] And after consultation, the said Master wrote to the Queen's Majesty, that being required by the Lords as he was passing homeward, he could not refuse to come to them; and after that he had given them counsel to disperse their army, they thought it expedient to pass to Dumfries[4] to repose them, where they would consult and make their offers, and send to their Majesties; and thus beseeching their Majesties to take this in good part. The town of Edinburgh sent two of the Council of the town to make their excuse.

The next day the King and Queen passed to Stirling, and sent to Edinburgh, and caused a proclamation to be made, commanding all men to return to Glasgow[5] where, having remained three or four days, and understanding that the Lords were passed to Dumfries, they returned to Stirling, and from thence to Fife[6]; and in their

[1] That is, Callendar House, near Falkirk

[2] Randolph reports them as retiring at 3 a.m. on the morning of Sunday 2 September. (*Calendar of Scottish Papers*, ii, No. 245) The *Diurnal of Occurrents* (82) says they departed " at 12 houris at evin or thairby " of 1 September, " and raid to Lanerk."

[3] Sir James Douglas of Drumlanrig. His sister, Janet, had married Robert, fifth Lord Maxwell.

[4] They arrived at Dumfries on 5 September. (*Foreign Calendar, Elizabeth*, vii, No. 1464)

[5] Kilsyth, in *Reg. Privy Council of Scotland*, i, 361

[6] The Queen left Stirling for St. Andrews on 9 September. (*Calendar of Scottish Papers*, ii, No. 251)

passage, caused to take in Castle Campbell, which was delivered without impediment to the Lord of Sanquhar.[1]

Before the King and Queen went out of Stirling, there came from Edinburgh two ensigns of footmen, to convey them into Fife. In the meantime, the Burghs were taxed in great sums unaccustomed, for the payment of the soldiers.[2] Further, there were raised divers troops of horsemen, to the number of five or six hundred horse. The soldiers had taken two poor men that had received the Lords' wages; which two men being accused and convicted, at the Queen's command, were hanged at Edinburgh, the third day after the Lords departing.[3] At this time, Master James Balfour, Parson of Flisk,[4] had got all the guiding in the court.

The third day after the Queen's coming to Fife, the whole Barons and Lairds of Fife convoyed her Majesty till she came to Saint Andrews, where the said Lairds and Barons, especially the Protestants, were commanded to subscribe to a Band, containing in effect, that they obliged themselves to defend the King's and Queen's persons against Englishmen and rebels: and in case they should come to Fife, they should resist them to their utmost power; which charge every man obeyed.[5]

The second night after the Queen's coming to Saint Andrews, she sent a band, or troop of horsemen, and another of foot, to Lundie, and at midnight took out the Laird, being a man of eighty years old,[6] then they passed to Falside, and took likewise Thomas Scott,[7] and brought him to Saint Andrews; where they, with the Laird of Balvaird,[8] and some others, were commanded to prison.[9] This manner of handling and usage, being unkend[10] and strange, was heavily spoken of, and a great terror to others, who thought themselves warned of greater severity to come.

In the meantime the houses of the Earls of Moray [and] Rothes, and the houses of divers gentlemen, were given in keeping to such as

[1] Edward, seventh Lord Crichton of Sanquhar

[2] Randolph speaks of the Queen having taken a "benevolence" from the burghs of St. Andrews, Dundee, and Perth, which was given with as evil a will as ever money was paid. (*Calendar of Scottish Papers*, ii, No. 261)

[3] See *Edinburgh Burgh Records*, iii, 206

[4] Later, Sir James Balfour of Pittendreich. On 19 September Bedford, writing to Cecil, says that Riccio, Fowler, "and one Balfour" rule all. (*Foreign Calendar, Elizabeth*, vii, No. 1510)

[5] See the "Band in Fyffe" in *Reg. Privy Council of Scotland*, i, 367. (12 September 1565)

[6] Walter Lundie of that Ilk

[7] Thomas Scott of Pitgorno and Abbotshall

[8] Andrew Murray of Balvaird

[9] See *Reg. Privy Council of Scotland*, i, 369

[10] *unknown*

the Queen pleased, after that their children and servants had been cast out.

At the same time the Duke, the Earls of Glencairn and Argyll, the Lords Boyd and Ochiltree, with the Laird of Cunninghamhead, and the rest, were charged to come and present themselves in Saint Andrews, before the King's and Queen's Majesties, to answer to such things as should be laid to their charge, within six days, under the pain of rebellion.[1] And the day being expired, and they not appearing, were denounced rebels, and put to the horn.

As the Queen remained in Saint Andrews, the inhabitants of Dundee were sore afraid, because of some evil report made of them to the Queen, as if they had troubled the Queen in seeking men-of-war and suffering some to be raised in their town for the Lords; for there was nothing done in Dundee, but it was revealed to the Queen; especially that the Minister[2] had received a letter from the Lords, and delivered the same to the Brethren, persuading them to assist the Lords; which being granted by the Minister, the Queen remitted it for trial. After great travail and supplication made by some Noblemen, at length, the King and Queen being in the town, they agreed for two thousand marks, five or six of the principal left out, with some others, that were put to their shift.[3] After the King and Queen had remained two nights in the town of Dundee, they came to Saint Andrews[4]; and soon after they came over Forth, and so to Edinburgh. During this time the Master of Maxwell wrote to the King and Queen, making offers for, and in the name of the Lords.

The next day after the King's and Queen's coming to Edinburgh, there was a Proclamation made at the Market Cross: And because the same is very notable, I thought good to insert it here word by word, albeit it be somewhat long.[5]

> "HENRY and MARY, by the Grace of God, King and Queen of Scots; To all and sundry, our Lieges and Subjects whom it may concern, and to whose knowledge these letters shall come, greeting.

[1] *Reg. Privy Council of Scotland*, i, 365 [2] William Christison

[3] That is, the town "compounded" for a remission, certain persons being excepted and left "to make what shift they could." Bedford reports that Mary thought to have sacked Dundee, but the town bought its "quietness" for two thousand pounds Scots. (*Foreign Calendar, Elizabeth*, vii, No. 1510)

[4] Mary apparently spent three nights in Dundee and returned to Edinburgh (on 17 September), not by way of St. Andrews, but by Perth and Dunfermline. (Hay Fleming, *Mary Queen of Scots*, 534)

[5] See *Reg. Privy Council of Scotland*, i, 369–371

"Forasmuch as in this uproar lately raised up against us, by certain rebels and their assistants, the authors thereof (to blind the eyes of the simple people) have given them to understand that the quarrel they have in hand is only Religion, thinking with that cloak to cover their ungodly designs, and so, under that plausible argument, to draw after them a large train of ignorant persons, easy to be seduced: Now, for the preservation of our good subjects, whose case were to be pitied, if they blindly should suffer themselves to be induced and trapped in so dangerous a snare, it hath pleased the goodness of God, by the utterance of their own mouths and writings to us, to discover the poison that before lay hid in their hearts, albeit to all persons of clear judgment the same was evident enough before: For what other thing might move the principal raisers of this tumult to put themselves in arms against us so unnaturally, upon whom We had bestowed so many benefits, but that the great honour We did them, they being thereof unworthy, made them misknow themselves; and their ambition could not be satisfied with heaping riches upon riches, and honour upon honour, unless they retain in their hands us and our whole Realm, to be led, used, and disposed at their pleasure. But this could not the multitude have perceived, if God (for disclosing their hypocrisy) had not compelled them to utter their unreasonable desire to govern; for now by letters, sent from themselves to us, they make plain profession that the establishing of Religion will not content them, but We must be forced to govern by such Council as it shall please them to appoint us; a thing so far beyond all measure, that We think the only mention of so unreasonable a demand is sufficient to make their nearest kinsfolk their most mortal enemies, and all men to run on them [1] without further scruple, that are zealous to have their native country to remain still in the state of a kingdom. For what other thing is this, but to dissolve the whole policy; and (in a manner), to invert the very order of nature, to make the Prince obey, and subjects command. The like was never demanded of any of our most noble progenitors heretofore, yea, not of Governors and Regents; but the Princes, and such as have filled their places, chose their Council of such as they thought most fit for the purpose. When We ourselves were of less age, and at our first returning into this our Realm, We had free choice of our Council at our pleasure, and now when We are at our full maturity, shall We be brought back to the state of pupils, and be put under tutory? So long as some

Note how this agrees with our times

Let this be conferred with our times

[1] *to oppose them*

of them bore the whole sway with us, this matter was never called in question ; but now when they cannot be longer permitted to do and undo all at their pleasure, they will put a bridle into our mouths, and give us a Council chosen after their fantasy. This is the quarrel of Religion they made you believe they had in hand. This is the quarrel for which they would have you hazard your lands, lives, and goods, in the company of a certain number of rebels against your natural Princes. To speak in good language, they would be Kings themselves, or at least the leaving to us the bare name and title, and take to themselves the credit and whole administration of the kingdom.

Note diligently

" We have thought good to make publication hereof to show that you suffer not yourselves to be deceived, under pretence of Religion, to follow them who, preferring their particular advancement to the public tranquillity, and having no care of you, in respect of themselves would (if you would hearken to their voice) draw you after them, to your utter destruction. Assuring you, that [as] you have heretofore good experience of our clemency, and under our wings enjoyed in peace the possession of your goods, and lived at liberty of your conscience, so may you be in full assurance of the like hereafter, and have us always your good and loving Princes, to so many as shall continue yourselves in due obedience, and do the office of faithful and natural subjects.

" Given under our Signet at Saint Andrews, the tenth [1] of September, and of our Reigns the first and twentie three years, 1565."

Now, the Lords desired, next the establishing of Religion, that the Queen's Majesty, in all the affairs of the Realm and Commonwealth, should use the council and advice of the Nobility, and ancient blood of the same ; whereas in the meantime the council of David, and Francisco, the Italians,[2] with Fowler the Englishman,[3] and Master James Balfour, parson of Flisk, was preferred before all others,[4] save only the Earl of Atholl, who was thought to be a man of gross judgment, but nevertheless in all things given to please the Queen. It

[1] In the Register the date is given as the " third day of September," presumably the clerk's error for " thirteenth ".

[2] That is, David Riccio, and Francis de Busso, who was Mary's Master of Works

[3] Fowler, the Englishman, was Lennox's servant.

[4] This charge is included in the " information" sent to Elizabeth. (*Calendar of Scottish Papers*, ii, No. 264) See also *supra*, 164, *note* 4.

was now finally come to this point that, instead of law, justice, and equity, only will ruled in all things.

There was throughout all the country set out a proclamation in the King's and Queen's names, commanding all persons to come and meet them at Stirling, the first day of October following, with twenty days provision, under pain of life, lands, and goods.[1] It was uncertain whether their Majesties intended to pass from Stirling or not, and I believe the principal men knew not well at that time; for a report was, that by reason the Castles of Hamilton and Draffen were kept fortified and victualled at the Duke's command, that they would pass to siege the said houses, and give them some shot of a cannon[2]: others said they would pass towards my Lord of Argyll, who had his people always armed, whereof his neighbours were afraid, especially the inhabitants of Atholl and Lennox; but at length it was concluded that they should pass to Dumfries, as shall be declared.

During this time there were propositions made continually to the King and Queen by the Lords, desiring always their Majesties most humbly to receive them into their hands. Their Articles tended continually to these two heads, viz., To abolish the Mass, root out idolatry, and establish the true Religion: And that they and the affairs of the Realm should be governed by the advice and council of the true Nobility of the same; offering themselves, and their cause, to be tried by the laws of the country. Yet nothing could be accepted nor taken in good part, albeit the Master of Maxwell laboured by all means to redress the matter, who also entertained the Lords most honourably in Dumfries, for he had the government of all that country. But he himself incurred the Queen's wrath,[3] so that he was summoned to present himself, and appear before the King's and Queen's Majesties, after the same form that the rest of the Lords were charged with; and also commanded to give over the house of Lochmaben, and the Castle, which he had in keeping for the Queen. And albeit he obeyed not, yet was he not put to the horn, as the rest. Nevertheless there was no man that doubted of his good will and partaking with the Lords,[4] who in the meantime

[1] See *Calendar of Scottish Papers*, ii, No. 258; *Diurnal of Occurrents*, 83

[2] See *Calendar of Scottish Papers*, ii, No. 259

[3] *Ibid.*, ii, No. 236

[4] Later Randolph spoke of him as one who laboured "tooth and nail" for reconciliation. (*Ibid.*, ii, No. 293) For a subsequent vindication of his actions, registered in "the Books of Council," see *Reg. Privy Council of Scotland*, i, 414–415.

sent Robert Melville to the Queen of England, and declared their state to her Majesty, desiring support.[1]

Now, the chief care and solicitude that was in the Court was by what means they might come to have money ; for notwithstanding this great preparation for war, and eminent appearance of trouble, yet were they destitute of the sinews of war.[2] Albeit the Treasurer,[3] and the Comptroller, to wit, the Laird of Tullibardine,[4] had disbursed many thousands ; yet there was no appearance of payment of soldiers, nor scarcely how the King's and Queen's houses and pompous trains should be upheld : there were about 600 horsemen, besides the guard and three ensigns of footmen. The charge of the whole would amount to £1000 sterling every month, a thing surpassing the usual manner of Scotland.

At this time arrived the Earl of Bothwell,[5] who was welcome, and graciously received by the Queen, and immediately placed in Council, and made Lieutenant of the West and Middle Marches.[6] Now as every one of the burghs compounded to be exempted from this meeting, the Earl of Atholl demanded of Edinburgh £200 sterling ; but they refused to pay it : notwithstanding, 27 September, there was a certain number of the principal and rich persons of the town warned by a macer to pass to the Palace of Holyroodhouse to the King and Queen, who declared to them by their own mouths' speaking that they had use for money, and therefore knowing them to be honest men, and the inhabitants of the best city in their country, they must needs charge them ; and for security they should have other men bound for pledges, or any hand therefor. The sum that they desired was £1000 sterling and no less. They being astonished, made no answer ; but Parson Flisk,[7] standing by, said, that seeing the King's and Queen's Majesties desired them so civilly, in a thing most lawful in their necessity, they did show themselves not honest to keep silence and give no answer to their Majesties, for that must needs be had of them which was required ; and if they

[1] See *Calendar of Scottish Papers*, ii, Nos. 255–257 ; *Foreign Calendar, Elizabeth*, vii, No. 1493. See also Hay Fleming, *Mary Queen of Scots*, 116 and supporting notes.

[2] See Hay Fleming, *op. cit.*, 115–116 and supporting notes.

[3] Robert Richardson

[4] William Murray of Tullibardine

[5] Randolph, on 19 September, says he has been told of Bothwell's return ; and he adds a brief and devastating character sketch. (*Calendar of Scottish Papers*, ii, No. 261) The *Diurnal of Occurrents* (83) says he arrived in Scotland, out of France, on 17 September. He had apparently landed at Eyemouth on 17 September. (*Foreign Calendar, Elizabeth*, vii, No. 1509)

[6] See *Reg. Privy Council of Scotland*, i, 378, 383. His name occurs in a sederunt of the Privy Council on 10 October (*ibid.*, i, 379).

[7] James Balfour

would not, they should be constrained by the laws, which they would not abide; for some of them had deserved hanging (said he), because they had lent large sums of money to the King's and Queen's enemies and rebels; and therefore they must shortly suffer great punishment.

So was the City of London, for war against Scotland, vexed for levy money[2]

Soon after they were called in one by one, and demanded how much they would lend. Some made this excuse, and some that; by reason there were [those] that offered to lend money. Amongst whom there was one offered to lend £20; to him the Earl of Atholl[1] said, thou art worthy to be hanged that speakest of £20, seeing the Princes charge thee so easily. Finally, they were all imprisoned, and soldiers set over them, having their muskets ready charged, and their match lighted, even in the house with them, where they remained all that night, and the next day till night; and then being changed from one prison to another, there were six chosen out and sent in the night to the Castle of Edinburgh, convoyed with musketeers round about them, as if they had been murderers or most vile persons.[3] At length (the third day), by means of the Laird of Craigmillar, Provost, and some others, the sum was made more easy, to wit, 1000 marks sterling, to be paid immediately, and to have the superiority of Leith in pledge (to wit), upon condition of redemption.[4] And besides the said sum of 1000 marks sterling, they paid £1000 sterling for the meeting at Dumfries.[5] At the day appointed for electing the officers, the Queen sent, in a ticket, such as she would have them choose for Provost, Bailies, and Council, whereof there

[1] John, fourth Earl of Atholl

[2] This must be David Buchanan's own marginal note for his edition of 1644. The reference is to the forced loan of 1640 levied on the City of London for Charles I's war against the Scots (the Second Bishops' War).

[3] According to the *Diurnal of Occurrents* (83, 84) the principal burgesses of Edinburgh were summoned to Holyroodhouse on 27 September, when they refused to lend money to the Queen and were commanded to enter themselves in ward; on 29 September, six of them were transferred to the Castle, there "to thole the lawis for certane crymes; and becaus thaj appoyntit with our soueranis, thaj wer put to libertie."

[4] But, according to the Burgh Records, Edinburgh was asked to lend the King and Queen £5,000; after "lang avisement" the sum was increased to 10,000 marks (£6,666, 13s. 4d.), the security for repayment of the loan being the grant to Edinburgh of the superiority of Leith. (*Edinburgh Burgh Records*, Burgh Rec. Soc., iii, 207–208, 213, 224–225, 227, 228–229) The sum was advanced by way of loan by 381 persons, whose names, and the amount of their contributions, appear in the Records—some of the larger sums being furnished by twenty-five persons, "men of law"; and the Town of Edinburgh received a charter of the Superiority of Leith, dated 4 October 1565 and presented to the Council on 14 November.

[5] The burgh paid £1000 to "remane and abide at hame" from the hosting at Dumfries, on 17 September, 1565. (*Edinburgh Burgh Records*, iii, 206–207)

was a number of Papists, the rest not worthy.[1] Of the number given in by the Queen, they named such as should rule for that year; notwithstanding, without free election, the Laird of Craigmillar remained Provost,[2] who showed himself most willing to set forward Religion, to punish vice, and to maintain the Commonwealth. All this time the Ministers cried out against the Mass, and such idolatry; for it was more advanced by the Queen than before.

The first day of October, met in Edinburgh the Superintendent of Lothian,[3] with all the Ministers under his charge, according to their ordinary custom—for every Superintendent used to convene the whole Ministry—and there it was complained on, that they could get no payment of their stipends, not only about the city, but throughout the whole Realm. Therefore, after reasoning and consultation taken, they framed a supplication, directed to the King and Queen, and immediately presented the same to their Majesties, by Master John Spottiswoode, Superintendent of Lothian, and Master David Lindsay, Minister of Leith. It contained in effect, that forasmuch as it had pleased the King's and Queen's Majesties (with advice of the Privy Council) to grant unto the Ministers of the Word their stipends, to be taken of the Thirds of the Benefices,[4] which stipends are now detained from the said Ministers by reason of the troubles, and changing of the Comptroller,[5] whereby they are not able to live; and therefore most humbly craved the King's and Queen's Majesty to cause them to be paid. Their answer was that they would cause order to be taken therein to their contentment.

Soon after the Lord Gordon came to Edinburgh, and left the most part of his people at Stirling with his carriage; the King and Queen, for hope of his good service to be done, restored him to his father's place, to the Earldom of Huntly, the lands and heritage thereof.[6]

October 8 the King and Queen marched forth of Edinburgh

[1] *Ibid.*, iii, 207 (26 September 1565)

[2] Sir Simon Preston of Craigmillar. He had superseded Archibald Douglas of Kilspindie (*supra* 160; *Diurnal of Occurrents*, 81). Preston of Craigmillar remained in office as Provost until 1568. [3] Mr. John Spottiswoode

[4] See *infra*, Appendix IX

[5] Sir John Wishart of Pittarrow had been replaced by Sir William Murray of Tullibardine.

[6] *Supra*, 157. By proclamation on 25 August 1565 he was restored "to his fame, honour, and dignitie, and to the lordschipe of Gordoun" (*Diurnal of Occurrents*, 81; *Calendar of Scottish Papers*, ii, No. 237). On 6 October he was restored to the Earldom of Huntly (*Diurnal*, 84; *Calendar of Scottish Papers*, ii, No. 278) and on 10 October he appears in the sederunt of the Privy Council as Earl of Huntly. (*Reg. Privy Council of Scotland*, i, 379)

towards Dumfries,[1] and as they passed from the Palace of Holyroodhouse, all men were warned with jack and spear. The first night they came to Stirling, and the next to Crawford. The day after, the Lairds of Drumlanrig and Lochinvar [2] met the Queen, albeit they had been with the Lords familiar enough.

The Lords perceiving that all hope of reconciliation was past, they rode to Annan, where they remained till the Queen came to Dumfries, and then they passed to Carlisle. Now the Master of Maxwell had entertained the Lords familiarly, and subscribed with them, and had spoken as highly against their enemies as any of themselves, and had received large money by that means, to wit, £1000, to raise a band or troop of horsemen; and that the same day the King and Queen came to Dumfries; [yet] the third day after their coming, he came to them, conveyed by the Earl Bothwell, with divers other Noblemen. At length the Earls of Atholl and Huntly were sureties for him, and all things past remitted, upon condition that he should be a faithful and obedient subject hereafter.[3] The same day they made musters; the next day the army was dispersed, being about 18,000 men: the King and Queen passed to Lochmaben, where the Master of Maxwell gave a banquet, and then forthwith marched to Tweeddale, so to Peebles, and then to Edinburgh.[4]

The best and chief part of the Nobility of this Realm, who also were the principal instruments of the Reformation of Religion, and therefore were called the Lords of the Congregation, in manner above rehearsed, were banished and chased into England: they were courteously received and entertained by the Earl of Bedford, Lieutenant, upon the Borders of England. Soon after, the Earl of Moray took post towards London, leaving the rest of the Lords at Newcastle; every man supposed that the Earl of Moray should have been graciously received of the Queen of England, and that he should have got support according to his heart's desire. But far beyond his expectation, he could get no audience of the Queen of England; but by means of the French Ambassador, called Monsieur de Four,[5] his true friend, he obtained audience. The Queen, with a fair countenance, demanded, "How he, being a rebel

Note diligently

[1] *Calendar of Scottish Papers*, ii, No. 278

[2] Sir James Douglas and Sir John Gordon

[3] These comments upon the part played by the Master of Maxwell are also to be found in Buchanan (*ed.* Aikman, ii, 473–474)

[4] See Hay Fleming, *Mary Queen of Scots*, 117 and supporting notes

[5] Paul de Foix

to her Sister of Scotland, durst take the boldness upon him to come within her Realm?" These, and the like words got he, instead of the good and courteous entertainment expected. Finally, after private discourse, the Ambassador being absent, she refused to give the Lords any support, denying plainly that ever she had promised any such thing as to support them, saying, "She never meant any such thing in that way"; albeit her greatest familiars knew the contrary. In the end, the Earl of Moray said to her, "Madam, whatsoever thing your Majesty meant in your heart, we are thereof ignorant; but thus much we know assuredly, that we had lately faithful promises of aid and support by your Ambassador, and familiar servants, in your name: and further, we have your own handwriting, confirming the said promises." And afterward he took his leave, and came northward from London, towards Newcastle. After the Earl of Moray's departure from the Court, the Queen sent them some aid, and wrote unto the Queen of Scotland in their favour: Whether [it was] she had promised it in private to the Earl of Moray, or whether she repented her of the harsh reception of the Earl of Moray, [we know not].[1]

Note diligently: Queen Elizabeth

Here mark either deep dissimulation, or a great inconstancy

At this time David Riccio, Italian, began to be higher exalted, insomuch as there was no matter or thing of importance done without his advice.[2] And during this time the faithful within this Realm were in great fear, looking for nothing but great trouble and persecution to be shortly. Yet supplications and intercessions were made throughout all the congregations, especially for such as were afflicted and banished, that it would please God to give them patience, comfort, and constancy; and this especially was done at Edinburgh, where John Knox used to call them that were banished, the best part of the Nobility, chief members of the Congregation. Whereof the Courtiers being advertised, they took occasion to revile and bewray[3] his sayings, alleging he prayed for the rebels, and desired the people to pray for them likewise. The Laird of Lethington, chief Secretary, in presence of the King's and Queen's Majesties and Council, confessed that he heard the sermons, and said there was nothing at that time spoken by the Minister whereat any man need be offended: and further, declared plainly that by the Scripture it was lawful to pray for all men.

In the end of November, the Lords, with their complices, were

[1] For the flight of the Protestant Lords to England and Moray's chilly reception from Elizabeth, see the analysis in Hay Fleming, *Mary Queen of Scots*, 117–118 and supporting notes. [2] *Supra*, 106, 148, 167 and supporting notes [3] *distort*

summoned to appear the fourth day of February, for treason, and *Læse-majestie*.[1] But in the meantime, such of the Nobility as had professed the Evangel of Christ, and had communicated with the Brethren at the Lord's Table, were ever longer the more suspected by the Queen, who began to declare herself, in the months of November and December, to be [a] maintainer of the Papists [2]; for at her pleasure the Earls of Lennox, Atholl, and Cassillis,[3] with divers others, without any dissimulation known, went to the Mass openly in her chapel. Yet, nevertheless, the Earls of Huntly and Bothwell went not to Mass, albeit they were in great favour with the Queen. As for the King, he passed his time in hunting and hawking, and such other pleasures as were agreeable to his appetite, having in his company gentlemen willing to satisfy his will and affections.

About this time, in the beginning of [the year 1566] as the Court remained at Edinburgh, the banished Lords, by all means possible, by writings and their friends, made suit and means to the King's and Queen's Majesties, to be received into favour.

At this time the Abbot of Kilwinning [4] came from Newcastle to Edinburgh, and after he had got audience of the King and Queen, with great difficulty he got pardon for the Duke [5] and his friends and servants, upon this condition, that he should pass into France; which he did soon after.[6]

The five and twentieth of December [1565] convened in Edinburgh the Commissioners of the churches within this Realm, for the General Assembly. There assisted to them the Earls of Morton and Mar, the Lord Lindsay, and Secretary Lethington, with some Barons and gentlemen. The principal things that were agreed and concluded, were that forasmuch as the Mass, with such idolatry and Papistical ceremonies, were still maintained expressly against the Act of Parliament, and the proclamations made at the Queen's arrival; and that the Queen had promised that she would hear conference and disputation; that the Church therefore offered to prove, by the Word of God, that the doctrine preached within this Realm was according to the Scriptures; and that the Mass, with

[1] *Reg. of the Privy Council of Scotland*, i, 409 (1 December 1565); *Diurnal of Occurrents*, 85–86. (Proclamations at the Market Cross of Edinburgh on 18 and 19 December)

[2] See Randolph's reports in *Calendar of Scottish Papers*, ii, Nos. 313, 319

[3] Gilbert, fourth Earl of Cassillis

[4] Gavin Hamilton

[5] Châtelherault

[6] *Diurnal of Occurrents*, 86; Hay Fleming, *Mary Queen of Scots*, 369, *note* 85

all the Papistical doctrine, was but the invention of men, and mere idolatry. Secondly, that by reason of the change of the Comptroller,[1] who had put in new collectors, forbidding them to deliver anything to the Ministry, by these means the Ministry was like to decay and fail, contrary to the ordinance made in the year of God 1562,[2] in favour and support of the Ministry.[3]

During this time, as the Papists flocked to Edinburgh for making court, some of them that had been Friars, as Black [Friars] Abercromby and Roger, presented supplication to the Queen's Majesty, desiring in effect, that they might be permitted to preach ; which was easily granted. The noise was further, that they offered disputation. For as the Court stood, they thought they had a great advantage already, by reason they knew the King to be of their Religion, as well as the Queen, with some part of the Nobility who, with the King, after declared themselves openly. And especially the Queen was governed by the Earls of Lennox and Atholl ; but in matters most weighty and of greatest importance, by David Riccio, the Italian afore-mentioned, who went under the name of the French Secretary ; by whose means, all grave matters, of what weight soever, must pass ; providing always, that his hands were anointed. In the meantime he was a manifest enemy to the Evangel, and therefore a greater enemy to the banished Lords.[4] And at this time, the principal Lords that waited at Court were divided in opinions ; for the Earl of Morton, Chancellor, with the Earl of Mar, and Secretary Lethington, were on the one part ; and the Earls of Huntly and Bothwell on the other part, so that a certain dryness was amongst them ; nevertheless, by means of the Earl of Atholl, they were reconciled. Now, as there was preparation made by the Papists for Christmas, the Queen being then at Mass, the King came publicly, and bore company ; and the Friars preached the days following, always using another style than they had done seven years before, during which time they had not preached publicly. They were so little esteemed, that they continued not long in preaching.

At the same time, convened in Edinburgh the General Assembly of the Ministers, and Commissioners of the Churches Reformed

[1] Sir John Wishart of Pittarrow, a Reformer, had been succeeded as Comptroller in 1565 by Sir William Murray of Tullibardine, and by an Act of Privy Council of 22 December 1565 the Queen had ordered certain Thirds to be set apart entirely for the royal expenses. (*Reg. Privy Council of Scotland*, i, 412–413) [2] *Infra*, Appendix IX

[3] See *Booke of the Universall Kirk*, i, 65–76 ; Calderwood, *History*, ii, 294–310 ; *infra*, 176–177 [4] See Hay Fleming, *Mary Queen of Scots*, 373, *note* 15

within this Realm [1]: There assisted them of the Nobility, the Earls of Morton and Mar, the Lord Lindsay, and Secretary Lethington, with others. The chief things that were concluded in this Assembly, were, that for the avoiding of the plagues and scourges of God, which appeared to come upon the people for their sins and ingratitude, there should be proclaimed by the Ministers a Public Fast, to be universally observed throughout all the Reformed Churches; which manner of Fasting was soon after devised by John Knox, at the command of the Church, and put in print, wherefore needs not here to be recited in this place.[2] What followed upon the said Fast, shall be plainly, God willing, declared. The second thing that was ordained in this Assembly, was, concerning the Ministers, who, for want of payment of their stipends, were like to perish, or else to leave their Ministry; wherefore it was found necessary that supplication should be made to the King's and Queen's Majesties: And for the same purpose, a certain number of the most able men were elected to go to their Majesties aforesaid, to lament and bemoan their case; which persons had commission to propone some other things, as shall be declared.

At the end of this Book you shall find this [3]

The names of them that passed from the Church to the King's and Queen's Majesties, were, Master John Spottiswoode, Superintendent of Lothian; John Winram, Superintendent of Fife; Master John Row, Minister of Perth; Master David Lindsay, Minister of Leith. Who easily obtained audience of the King's and Queen's Majesties; and after their reverence done, Master John Row, in name of the rest, opened the matter, lamenting and bewailing the miserable state of the poor Ministers, who by public command had been reasonably satisfied three years or more, by virtue of the Act made with advice of the Honourable Privy Council, for the taking up of the Thirds of the Benefices, which was especially made in their favours. Nevertheless the Laird of Tullibardine, new Comptroller, would answer them nothing; wherefore, they besought their Majesties for relief.

Secondly, Seeing that in all supplications made to the King's and Queen's Majesties by the Church at all times, they desired most earnestly that all idolatry and superstition, and especially the Mass,

[1] Part of what follows is a repetition of the account given *supra*, 174–175. The repetitions in, and the loose arrangement of Book V suggest that it is an unrevised draft written from notes.

[2] On 28 December 1565 the Assembly "ordained Mr. Knox and Mr. Craig ministers at Edinburgh, to set out the form" of a Public Fast, "with the exercise to be used in the same, and to cause Robert Likprevick print it." (*Booke of the Universall Kirk*, i, 76; Calderwood's *History*, ii, 303–306) *The Ordour and Doctrine of the Generall Faste* has been reprinted by Laing. (Laing's *Knox*, vi, 391ff)

[3] This promise is unfulfilled.

should be rooted out and abolished quite out of this Realm ; and that in the last General Assembly of the Church, by their Commissioners, they had most earnestly desired the same ; and that their answer was then, that they knew no impediment in the Mass ; therefore, the Assembly desired that it might please their Highnesses to hear disputation, to the end that such as now pretend to preach in the Chapel Royal, and maintain such errors, the truth being tried by disputation, that they might be known to be abusers ; submitting themselves always to the word of God written in the Scriptures.

To this it was answered by the Queen that she was always minded that the Ministers should be paid their stipends ; and if there was any fault therein, the same came by some of their own sort, meaning the Comptroller Pittarrow,[1] who had the handling of the Thirds. Always by the advice of her Council she should cause such order to be taken therein, that none should have occasion to complain. As to the second, She would not jeopard her Religion upon such as were there present ; for she knew well enough that the Protestants were more learned.

The Ministers and Commissioners of Churches perceiving nothing but delay, and driving of time in the old manner, went home every one to their own churches, waiting upon the good providence of God, continually making supplication unto Almighty God that it would please Him of his mercy to remove the apparent plague. And in the meantime the Queen was busied with banqueting about with some of the Lords of the Session of Edinburgh, and after with all men of law, having continually in her company David Riccio, who sat at table near to herself, sometimes more privately than became a man of his condition, for his over-great familiarity was already suspected ; and it was thought that by his advice alone the Queen's sharpness and extremity towards the [Protestant] Lords was maintained.

In the end of January, arrived an Ambassador from France, named M. Rambouillet,[2] having with him about forty horse in train, who came through England. He brought with him the Order of the Cockle from the King of France, to the King, who received the same at the Mass, in the Chapel of the Palace of Holyroodhouse.

[1] *Cf. supra*, 175, *note* 1

[2] Jacques d'Angennes, Sieur de Rambouillet. He arrived in Edinburgh on Monday 4 February 1566, and on 10 February invested Darnley with the Order of St. Michael, commonly called the "Order of the Cockle" (*Diurnal of Occurrents*, 87 ; *Calendar of Scottish Papers*, ii, No. 335. And see *supra*, i, 102, *note* 13).

There assisted the Earls of Lennox, Atholl, and Eglinton,[1] with divers such other Papists as would please the Queen; who, three days after, caused the herald to convene in Council, and reasoned what Arms should be given to the King. Some thought he should have the Arms of Scotland; some others said, Seeing it was not concluded in Parliament that he should have the Crown Matrimonial, he could have arms but only as Duke of Rothesay, Earl of Ross, &c. The Queen bade give him only his due; whereby it was perceived her love waxed cold towards him. Finally, his Arms were left blank; and the Queen caused put her own name before her husband's in all writs; and thereafter she caused to leave out his name wholly. And because formerly he had signed everything of any moment, she caused to make a seal like the King's, and gave it to David Riccio, who made use of it by the Queen's command, alleging that the King being at his pastime, could not always be present.[2]

About the same time, the Earl of Glencairn came from Berwick to his own country. Soon after the Earl of Bothwell was married unto the Earl of Huntly's sister.[3] The Queen desired that the marriage might be made in the Chapel at the Mass; which the Earl Bothwell would in no wise grant.[4] Upon Sunday, the third day of March, began the fasting at Edinburgh.[5] The seventh day of March, the Queen came from the Palace of Holyroodhouse to the Town, in wondrous gorgeous apparel, albeit the number of Lords and train was not very great.[6] In the meantime the King, accompanied with seven or eight horse, went to Leith to pass his time there, for he was not like to get the Crown Matrimonial.

In the Tolbooth were devised and named the heads of the Articles that were drawn against the banished Lords. Upon the morrow,

[1] Hugh, third Earl of Eglinton

[2] See Aikman's *Buchanan*, ii, 475. Already on 25 December 1565, Randolph had written, "A while there was nothing but 'King and Queen, his Majesty and hers'; now, the 'Queen's husband' is most common. He was wont to be first named in all writings, but now is placed second. Certain pieces of money lately coined 'with both their faces *Hen. et Maria*' are called in, and others 'framed'." (*Calendar of Scottish Papers*, ii, No. 319)

[3] James Hepburn, fourth Earl of Bothwell, married Lady Jane Gordon, daughter of (the then deceased) George, fourth Earl of Huntly, on 24 February 1566. (*Scots Peerage*, ii, 165; *Calendar of Scottish Papers*, ii, No. 346)

[4] See the many details in Robertson's *Inventaires de la Royne Descosse*, Preface, xcii–xciv and supporting notes.

[5] The fast was appointed for eight days from the eve of the last Sunday in February 1566 (24 February) to the first Sunday in March (3 March). (*Supra* 176; Laing's *Knox*, vi, 393, 416, 417; and see the extracts from the *Register of the Canongate Kirk Session* printed in Hay Fleming, *op. cit.*, 495) But the *Diurnal of Occurrents* (88) supports Knox's continuator in putting the fast a week later. Even Calderwood later confused the dates. (Laing's *Knox*, vi, 389)

[6] See *Diurnal of Occurrents*, 89

and Saturday following, there was great reasoning concerning the Attainder. Some alleged that the summons was not well libelled or dressed ; others thought the matter of treason was not sufficiently proved ; and indeed they were still seeking proof, for there was no other way but the Queen would have them all attainted, albeit the time was very short ; the twelfth day of March should have been the day, which was the Tuesday following.[1]

Now, the matter was stayed by a marvellous tragedy, for by the Lords (upon the Saturday before, which was the ninth of March, about supper-time), David Riccio, the Italian, named the French Secretary, was slain in the gallery, below stairs (the King, staying in the room with the Queen, told her that the design was only to take order with that villain), after that he had been taken violently from the Queen's presence, who requested most earnestly for the saving of his life : which act was done by the Earl of Morton, the Lord Ruthven, the Lord Lindsay, the Master of Ruthven, with divers other Gentlemen. They first purposed to have hanged him, and had provided cords for the same purpose ; but the great haste which they had, moved them to dispatch him with whingers or daggers, wherewith they gave him three and fifty strokes. They sent away and put forth all such persons as they suspected.

The Earls Bothwell and Huntly hearing the noise and clamour, came suddenly to the Close, intending to have made work, if they had had a party strong enough ; but the Earl Morton commanded them to pass to their chamber, or else they should do worse. At the which words they retired immediately, and so passed forth at a back window, they two alone, and with great fear came forth of the town to Edmondstone [2] on foot, and from thence to Crichton.[3]

This David Riccio [4] was so foolish, that not only he had drawn unto him the managing of all affairs, the King set aside, but also his equipage and train did surpass the King's ; and at the Parliament that was to be, he was ordained to be Chancellor [5] ; which made the Lords conspire against him. They made a bond to stand to the religion and liberties of the country, and to free themselves of the slavery of the villain David Riccio. The King and his father sub-

[1] *Ibid.*, 85–86 [2] Then about four miles south-east of Edinburgh

[3] About five miles south-east of Dalkeith

[4] For an analysis of the various accounts of the murder of Riccio, see Hay Fleming, *Mary Queen of Scots*, 387–390, *notes* 49, 50.

[5] Randolph, writing to Cecil on 6 March 1566, reports that the Seal is to be taken from Morton 'and as some say, shall be given to keep to David' (*Calendar of Scottish Papers*, ii, No. 352 *in fin.*). See also Spottiswoode's *History*, ii, 35–36.

scribed to the bond, for they durst not trust the King's word without his signet.[1]

There was a French priest (called John Daniot) who advised David Riccio to make his fortune, and be gone,[2] for the Scots would not suffer him long. His answer was that the Scots would brag but not fight. Then he advised him to beware of the bastard. To this he answered that the bastard should never live in Scotland in his time (he meant the Earl Moray); but it happened that one George Douglas, bastard son to the Earl of Angus, gave him the first stroke. The Queen, when she heard he was dead, left weeping, and declared she would study revenge, which she did.[3]

Immediately it was noised in the town of Edinburgh that there was murder committed within the King's Palace; wherefore the Provost [4] caused to ring the common bell, or, *Sonner le toksain* (as the French speaks), and straightway passed to the Palace, having about four or five hundred men in warlike manner; and as they stood in the outer court, the King called to the Provost, commanding him to pass home with his company, saying the Queen and he were merry. But the Provost desired to hear the Queen speak herself; whereunto it was answered by the King, "Provost, know you not that I am King? I command you to pass home to your houses"; and immediately they retired.[5]

The next day (which was the second Sunday of our Fast in Edinburgh) [6] there was a proclamation made in the King's name, subscribed with his hand, that all Bishops, Abbots, and other Papists should avoid and depart the town; which proclamation was indeed observed, for they had "a flea in their hose."[7] There were letters sent forth in the King's name, and subscribed with his hand, to the Provost and Bailies of Edinburgh, the Bailies of Leith and Canongate, commanding them to be ready in armour to assist the King

[1] See Hay Fleming, *Mary Queen of Scots*, 384, *note* 44; 387, *notes* 48, 49.

[2] See Aikman's *Buchanan*, ii, 481

[3] See Hay Fleming, *op. cit.*, 127 and *note* 51

[4] Sir Simon Preston of Craigmillar

[5] See *Diurnal of Occurrents*, 90–91. Later the Town Council paid £4, 7s. 6d. for thirty-five torches furnished to pass to the Abbey to vise the Queen's Grace immediately after the slaughter of umquhile Seigneur David Riccio. (*Edinburgh Burgh Records*, iii, 214) The number of torches would be about the number of the members of the Council.

[6] But see *supra*, 178, *note* 5

[7] But the *Diurnal of Occurrents* (91) says that the Proclamation charged all the earls, lords, barons, and bishops that had come to Edinburgh for the Parliament to depart within three hours under pain of treason. A second Proclamation forbade the wearing of weapons on the street. It is significant that these proclamations ran in the King's name. (See *supra*, 178 and *note* 2)

and his company, and likewise other private writings directed to divers Lords and gentlemen, to come with all expedition. In the meantime, the Queen, being above measure enraged, offended, and troubled, as the issue of the matter declared, sometime railing upon the King, and sometime crying out at the windows, desired her servants to set her at liberty ; for she was highly offended and troubled.

This same tenth of March, the Earl of Moray, with the rest of the Lords and Noblemen that were with him, having received the King's letter (for after the bond, above named, was subscribed, the King wrote unto the banished Lords to return into their country, being one of the articles of the said bond),[1] came at night to the Abbey, being also convoyed by the Lord Home, and a great company of the Borderers, to the number of 1,000 horses. And first, after he had presented himself to the King, the Queen was informed of his sudden coming, and therefore sent unto him, commanding him to come to her ; and he obeying, went to her who, with a singular gravity received him, after that he had made his purgation, and declared the over-great affection which he bore continually to her Majesty. The Earls of Atholl, Caithness,[2] and Sutherland,[3] departed out of the town, with the Bishops, upon the Monday, the third day after the slaughter of David Riccio. The Earls of Lennox, Moray, Morton, and Rothes, Lords Ruthven, Lindsay, Boyd, and Ochiltree, sitting in Council, desired the Queen, that forasmuch as the thing which was done could not be undone, that she would (for avoiding of greater inconveniences) forget the same, and take it as good service, seeing there were so many Noblemen restored. The Queen dissembling her displeasure and indignation, gave good words ; nevertheless she desired that all persons armed or otherwise (being within the Palace at that time), should remove, leaving the Palace void of all, saving only her domestic servants. The Lords being persuaded by the uxorious King, and the facile Earl of Moray, condescended to her desire, who finally, the next morning, two hours before day, passed to Seton, and then to Dunbar, having in her company the simple King, who was allured by her sugared words. From Dunbar immediately were sent pursuivants with letters throughout the country ; and especially letters to the Noblemen and Barons, commanding them to come to Dunbar, to assist the King and Queen

[1] See Hay Fleming, *op. cit.*, 387, *note* 48 ; and, for an analysis of the subsequent events to the "dolorous" departure of the Protestant Lords from Edinburgh on Sunday 17 March, and Mary's triumphant return the day following, see *ibid.*, 127–128, and supporting notes.

[2] George, fourth Earl of Caithness

[3] John, tenth Earl of Sutherland

within five days.[1] In the meantime the Lords being informed of the [Queen's] sudden departure, they were astonished, and knew not what were best for them to do. But because it was the self-same day (to wit, the twelfth day of March) that they were summoned unto; therefore, having good opportunity, they passed to the Tolbooth, which was richly hung with tapestry, and adorned (but not for them), and set themselves making protestations,[2] the Earl of Glencairn, and some others being present. The Earl of Argyll, who was written for by the King, came to Linlithgow; and being informed of the matter, he remained there.

After this manner above specified, to wit, by the death of David Riccio, the Noblemen were relieved of their trouble, and restored to their places and rooms. And likewise the Church Reformed, and all that professed the Evangel within this Realm, after fasting and prayer, were delivered and freed from the apparent dangers which were like to have fallen upon them; for if the Parliament had taken effect, and proceeded, it was thought by all men of the best judgment that the true Protestant Religion should have been wrecked, and Popery erected; and for the same purpose, there were certain wooden altars made, to the number of twelve, found ready in the Chapel of the Palace of Holyrood-house, which should have been erected in Saint Giles's Church.

The Earls Bothwell and Huntly, being informed of the King and Queen's sudden departure forth of Edinburgh, came to Dunbar, where they were most graciously received by the Queen's Majesty; who consulting with them and the Master of Maxwell, together with Parson Oyne [3] and Parson Flisk,[4] chief Councillors, what was best to be done, and how she should be revenged upon the murderers, at first they did intend to go forward, leaving no manner of cruelty unpractised, and putting to death all such as were suspected. This was the opinion of such as would obey their Queen's rage and fury for their own advantage; but in the end they concluded that she should come to Edinburgh with all the force and power she could make, and there proceed to justice. And for the same purpose, she caused to summon, by open proclamation, all persons of defence,

[1] The summons was at first to Haddington and Musselburgh for 17 to 19 March. (*Diurnal of Occurrents*, 93–94; *Reg. Privy Council of Scotland*, i, 436)

[2] See *Diurnal of Occurrents*, 93

[3] John Lesley, Parson of Oyne, later Bishop of Ross

[4] James Balfour, Parson of Flisk, shortly to be appointed Clerk Register in place of Mr. James M'Gill, one of the conspirators in the murder of Riccio; later to be Lord President as Sir James Balfour of Pittendreich

and all Noblemen and Gentlemen, to come to her in Dunbar incontinent. In the meantime, the Captains laboured by all means to take up and enrol men and women. The Earls of Morton, Moray, Glencairn, [and] Rothes, with the rest that were in Edinburgh, being informed of the Queen's fury and anger towards the committers of the slaughter, and perceiving they were not able to make any party, thought it best to give place to her fury for a time; for they were divided in opinions, and finally departed out of Edinburgh, upon Sunday the seventeenth of March, every one a several way; for the Queen's Majesty was now bent only against the slayers of David Riccio; and to the purpose she might be the better revenged upon them, she intended to give pardon to all such as before had been attainted for whatsoever crime.

The eighteenth day of March, the King and Queen came to Edinburgh, having in their company horse and foot to the number of 8000 men; whereof there were four companies of foot-men of war. The Town of Edinburgh went out to meet them, for fear of war. And finally, coming within the town, in most awful manner they caused to place their men of war within the town, and likewise certain field-pieces against their lodging, which was in the middle of the town, over against the Salt Tron.[1] Now, a little before the Queen's entrance into the town, all that knew of her cruel pretence and hatred towards them, fled here and there, and amongst others, Master James M'Gill, the Clerk Register, the Justice-Clerk, and the common clerk of the town.[2] The chief Secretary Lethington was gone before; likewise John Knox passed west to Kyle.[3] The men of war likewise kept the ports or gates. Within five days after their entry, there was a proclamation made at the Market-Cross, for the purgation of the King from the aforesaid slaughter[4]; which

[1] See Randolph's account in *Calendar of Scottish Papers*, ii, No. 363. According to the *Diurnal of Occurrents* (93–94), Mary had 2,000 horsemen "and lugeit not in thair palice of Halyrudhous, bot lugeit in my lord Homes lugeing, callit the auld bischope of Dunkell his lugeing, [for]anent the salt trone in Edinburgh." The 'Bishop of Dunkeld's lodging' lay on the north side of the High Street, on the opposite side to the Tron, a little to the west of Halkerston's Wynd—now lost through the cutting of Cockburn Street.

[2] That is, Mr. James M'Gill, Sir John Bellenden, and Alexander Guthrie. David Chalmers of Ormond received the gift from the Queen of the common clerkship of Edinburgh. (*Edinburgh Burgh Records*, iii, 212–213) For Mr. James M'Gill, see also Pollen, *Papal Negotiations with Mary Queen of Scots*, Scot. Hist. Soc., 273, *note*.

[3] According to the *Diurnal of Occurrents* (94), at two o'clock on the afternoon of Sunday 17 March, "with ane greit murnyng of the godlie of religioun." Although Knox thoroughly approved of the murder of Riccio (*supra*, i, 44, 112), it cannot be shown that he knew of the murder beforehand (see the analysis of the evidence in Hay Fleming, *Mary Queen of Scots*, 395, *note* 58).

[4] See also *Diurnal of Occurrents*, 96

made all understanding men laugh at the passage of things, since the King not only had given his consent, but also had subscribed the bond afore-named [1]; and the business was done in his name, and for his honour, if he had had wisdom to know it.

After this proclamation, the King lost his credit among all men, and also his friends, by this his inconstancy and weakness. And in the meantime, the men of war committed great outrages in breaking up doors, thrusting themselves into every house; and albeit the number of them was not great, yet the whole town was too little for them. Soon after, the King and Queen passed to the Castle, and caused to warn all such as had absented themselves, by open proclamation, to appear before their Majesties and the Privy Council within six days, under pain of rebellion [2]; which practice was devised in the Earl of Huntly's case, before the battle of Corrichie. And because they appeared not, they were denounced rebels, and put to the horn, and immediately thereafter, their escheats given or taken up by the Treasurer. There was a certain number of the townsmen charged to enter themselves prisoners in the Tolbooth,[3] and with them were put in certain gentlemen: where, after they had remained eight days, they were convoyed down to the Palace by the men of war, and then kept by them eight days more. And of that number was Thomas Scott, sheriff-depute of Saint Johnston, who was condemned to death, and executed cruelly, to wit, hanged and quartered, for keeping the Queen in prison, as was alleged, although it was by the King's command. And two men likewise were condemned to death, and carried likewise to the ladder foot; but the Earl Bothwell presented the Queen's ring to the Provost, who then was justice,[4] for safety of their life. The names of those two were John Mowbray, merchant, and William Harlaw, saddler.[5] About the same time, notwithstanding all this hurlyburly, the Ministers of the Church and professors of Religion ceased not; as for the people, they convened to public prayers and preaching with boldness; yea, a great number of Noblemen assisted likewise. The Earl Bothwell had now, of all men, greatest access and familiarity with the Queen, so that nothing of any great importance was done without him; for he showed favour to such as liked him; and amongst others, to the Lairds of

[1] *Supra*, 179–180
[2] *Reg. Privy Council of Scotland*, i, 436–437; *Diurnal of Occurrents*, 95
[3] *Diurnal of Occurrents*, 96–97; *Reg. Privy Council of Scotland*, i, 442
[4] That is, holding a commission of justiciary
[5] Further details will be found in Pitcairn's *Criminal Trials*, i, 480*, and *Diurnal of Occurrents*, 97–98.

Ormiston, Halton, and Calder,[1] who were so reconciled unto him that by his favour they were relieved of great trouble.

The Earls of Argyll and Moray, at the Queen's command, passed to Argyll, where, after they had remained about a month, they were sent for by the Queen; and, coming to Edinburgh, they were received by the Queen into the Castle, and banqueted, the Earls of Huntly and Bothwell being present. At this time the King grew to be contemned and disesteemed, so that scarcely any honour was done to him, and his father likewise.

About Easter the King passed to Stirling, where he was shriven after the Papist manner: and in the meantime, at the Palace of Holyrood-house, in the Chapel, there resorted a great number to the Mass, albeit the Queen remained still in the Castle, with her priests of the Chapel Royal, where they used ceremonies after the Popish manner.

At the same time departed this life Master John Sinclair, Bishop of Brechin and Dean of Restalrig, of whom hath been oft mention, President of the College of Justice, called the Session[2]; who succeeded in the said office and dignity after the decease of his brother, Master Henry Sinclair, Bishop of Ross, Dean of Glasgow, who departed this life at Paris, about a year before.[3] They were both learned in the laws, and given to maintain the Popish religion, and therefore great enemies to the Protestants. A little before died Master Abraham Crichton, who had been President likewise.[4] Now, in their rooms, the Queen placed such as she pleased, and had done her service (always very unfit). The patrimony of the Kirk, Bishoprics, Abbeys, and such other Benefices, was disponed by the Queen to courtiers, dancers, and flatterers. The Earl Bothwell, whom the Queen preferred above all others, after the decease of David Riccio, had for his part Melrose, Haddington, and Newbattle; likewise the Castle of Dunbar was given to him, with the principal lands of the Earldom of March, which were of the patrimony of the Crown.[5]

[1] That is, John Cockburn of Ormiston, William Lauder of Halton, and James Sandilands of Calder

[2] He died in April 1566. (*Diurnal of Occurrents*, 98; Dowden's *Bishops*, 191–192)

[3] He had died in January 1565. (*Diurnal of Occurrents*, 79; Dowden's *Bishops*, 228–229)

[4] Abraham Crichton, Provost of Dunglass, Official of Lothian, an ordinary Senator, was never President of the College of Justice. He had died before 15 November 1565. (Brunton and Haig, *Senators of the College of Justice*, 1836, 92–93)

[5] Apart from Dunbar there appears to be no official record of these grants, and, again apart from Dunbar, they are not mentioned in the ratification of 19 April 1567. (*Acts Parl. Scot.*, ii, 550, c. 6) Randolph reports on 7 June 1566 that "Bothwell has the whole inheritance of Dunbar given him, the castle reserved to the Queen." (*Calendar of Scottish Papers*, ii, No. 393)

At the same time, the Superintendents, with the other ministers of the Churches, perceiving the Ministry like to decay for lack of payment of stipends to Ministers, they gave this supplication at Edinburgh :

The Supplication of the Ministers to the Queen

" UNTO your Majesty, and your most honourable Council, most humbly and lamentably complain your Highness's poor Orators, the Superintendents, and other Ministers of the Reformed Church of God, travailing throughout all your Highness's Realm in teaching and instructing your lieges in all quarters in the knowledge of God, and Christ Jesus his Son : That where your Majesty, with the advice of the Council and Nobility aforesaid, moved by godly zeal, concluded and determined that the travailing ministry through this Realm, should be maintained upon the rents of the Benefices of this Realm of Scotland ; and for that cause your Majesty, with the advice of the Council and Nobility aforesaid, upon the 15 day of December 1562, in like manner concluded and determined that if the said part of the rents of the whole Benefices Ecclesiastical within this Realm would be sufficient to maintain the Ministers throughout the whole Realm, and to support your Majesty in the setting forward of your common affairs, [it] should be employed accordingly : Failing thereof, the Third part of the said fruits, or more, to be taken up yearly in time coming, until a general order be taken therein ; as the act made thereupon at more length bears. Which being afterward considered by your Majesty, the whole Thirds of the fruits aforesaid were propounded to the uses aforesaid, by Act of Council.[1] And we your Majesty's poor Orators [were] put in peaceable possession of the part assigned by your Majesty to us, by the space of three years or thereabouts, which we did enjoy without interruption. Notwithstanding all this, now of late we, your Majesty's poor Orators aforesaid, are put wrongfully and unjustly from our aforesaid part of the above specified Thirds, by your Majesty's officers, and thereby brought to such extreme penury and extreme distress as we are not able any longer to maintain ourselves. And albeit we have given in divers and sundry complaints to your Majesty herein, and have received divers promises of redress, yet have we found no relief. Therefore, we most humbly beseech your Majesty to consider our most grievous complaint, together with the right above specified, whereon the same is grounded. And if

[1] See *infra*, Appendix IX. The date, 15 December 1562, given in the text above, is incorrect.

your Majesty, with the advice of your Council aforesaid, finds our right sufficient to continue us in possession of our part assigned to us, while and until a general order be taken (which possession was ratified by the yearly allowance of your Majesty's Exchequer's account), that your Majesty would grant us letters upon the aforesaid Act, and Ordinance passed thereupon, against all intromettors and meddlers with the aforesaid Thirds, to answer and obey, according to the aforesaid Act and Ordinance of our possession proceeding thereupon. And likewise, that we may have letters, if need be, to arrest and stay the aforesaid Thirds in the possessor's hands, while and until sufficient caution be found to us for our part aforesaid. And your Answer most humbly we beseech."

This Supplication being presented by the Superintendent of Lothian,[1] and Master John Craig, in the Castle of Edinburgh, was graciously received by the Queen, who promised that she would take sufficient order therein, so soon as the Nobility and Council might convene.

The 19 of June, the Queen was delivered of a man-child, the Prince (in the aforesaid Castle), and immediately sent into France and England her posts, to advertise the neighbour Princes, and to desire them to send gossips[2] or witnesses to the Prince's baptism. In the meantime, there was joy and triumph made in Edinburgh,[3] and such other places where it was known, after thanks and praises given unto God, with supplications for the godly education of the Prince; and principally, wishing that he should be baptized according to the manner and form observed in the Reformed Churches within this Realm.

About the same time, to wit, the 25 of June, the General Assembly of the whole Church convened at Edinburgh.[4] The Earls of Argyll and Moray assisted at the Assembly. Paul Methven, who before, as we heard, was excommunicated,[5] gave in his Supplication, and desired to be heard, as he had done divers times; for the said Paul had written oft times out of England to the Laird of Dun, and to divers others, most earnestly desiring to be received again into the fellowship of the Church. After reasoning of the matter, it was finally granted that he should be heard. And so, being before the Assembly, and falling upon his knees, burst out with tears, and said, he was not worthy to appear in their presence; always he desired

The order of Paul Methven's repentance

[1] Mr. John Spottiswoode
[2] *god-parents* or *sponsors*
[3] See *Diurnal of Occurrents,* 100
[4] See *Booke of the Universall Kirk,* i, 77–81
[5] *Supra,* 66–67

them, for the love of God, to receive him to the open expression of his repentance. Shortly after, they appointed certain of the ministers to prescribe to him the form of his declaration of repentance, which was thus in effect: First, that he should present himself bare-foot and bare-head, arrayed in sack-cloth, at the principal entry of Saint Giles's Kirk in Edinburgh, at seven hours in the morning, upon the next Wednesday, and there to remain the space of an hour, the whole people beholding him, till the prayer was made, psalms sung, and [the] text of Scripture was read, and then to come into the place appointed for expression of repentance, and tarry the time of sermon; and to do so likewise the next Friday following, and also upon the Sunday; and then, in the face of the whole church, to declare his repentance with his own mouth. The same form and manner he should use in Jedburgh and Dundee; and that being done, to present himself again at the next General Assembly following in winter, where he should be received to the communion of the Church. When the said Paul had received the said Ordinance, he took it very grievously, alleging they had used over-great severity. Nevertheless, being counselled and persuaded by divers notable personages, he began well in Edinburgh to proceed, whereby a great number were moved with compassion of his state; and likewise in Jedburgh; but he left his duty in Dundee, and passing again into England, the matter, not without offence to many, ceased.

The Ministers complaining that they could not be paid their stipends, were licensed by the Assembly to pass to other churches to preach, but in no wise to leave the ministry. And because that the Queen's Majesty had promised often before to provide remedy, it was thought expedient that supplication should be yet made, as before, that the Queen's Majesty should cause such order to be taken that the poor ministers might be paid their stipends. The Bishop of Galloway, who was brother to the Earl of Huntly,[1] and now a great man in the court, travailed much with the Queen's Majesty in that matter, and got of her a good answer, and fair promises. A few years before, the said Bishop of Galloway desired of the General Assembly to be made Superintendent of Galloway [2]; but now being

[1] Alexander Gordon, Bishop of the Isles (*c.* 1553), of Galloway (1559), and titular Archbishop of Athens, was the brother of George, fourth Earl of Huntly.

[2] Alexander Gordon had early joined the Reformers (*supra*, i, 310, 315, 335), but in certain quarters was not over-trusted (*cf. supra*, 73, and *Booke of the Universall Kirk*, i, 15, 39–40). For an analysis of his work in the Reformed Church, however, see Gordon Donaldson, 'Alexander Gordon, Bishop of Galloway, 1559–1575', in *Trans. Dumfries-shire and Galloway Nat. Hist. and Antiquarian Soc.*, vol. xxiv.

promoted to great dignity, as to be of the number of the Lords of the Privy Council, and likewise one of the Session,[1] he would no more be called Over-looker, or Over-seer of Galloway, but Bishop. Always truth it is, that he laboured much for his nephew the Earl of Huntly, that he might be restored to his lands and honours; for the said Earl was now Chancellor, since the slaughter of David Riccio,[2] and had for his clawback [3] the Bishop of Ross, Master John Lesley, one of the chief Councillors to the Queen. But of all men the Earl Bothwell was most in the Queen's favour, so far that all things passed by him; yea, by his means the most part of all those that were partakers in the slaughter of David Riccio, got remission and relief. But from that day he was not present at any sermon, albeit before he professed the Evangel by outward speaking, yet he never joined to the Congregation. About this time the Earl of Cassillis was contracted with the Lord of Glamis's sister,[4] by whose persuasion he became a Protestant, and caused in the month of August to reform his churches in Carrick, and promised to maintain the doctrine of the Evangel.

See in what sense proud ambitious men take the name of Bishop

As is said before

The Queen, not yet satisfied with the death of her man David, caused in August to be apprehended a man called Harry, who sometime had been of her Chapel-Royal, but afterward became an Exhorter in a Reformed Church; and for want of stipend, or other necessaries, passed in service to my Lord Ruthven, and chanced that night to be present when the said David was slain; and so, finally, he was condemned, and hanged, and quartered.[5]

The King being now contemned of all men, because the Queen cared not for him, he went sometime to the Lennox to his father, and sometime to Stirling, whither the Prince was carried a little before. Always he was destitute of such things as were necessary for him, having scarcely six horses in train. And being thus desolate, and half desperate, he sought means to go out of the country: and,

This inconstant young man sometimes declared himself for the Protestants; witness

[1] He was appointed an Extraordinary Lord of Session on 26 November 1565. (Brunton and Haig, *Senators of the College of Justice*, 129)

[2] George, fifth Earl of Huntly, was appointed Chancellor in March 1566 in place of the Earl of Morton, who had fled after Riccio's murder. (*Diurnal of Occurrents*, 95–96)

[3] a *flattering supporter*; *toady*

[4] Gilbert, fourth Earl of Cassillis, married (contract 30 September 1566) Margaret Lyon, daughter of John, seventh Lord Glamis, and sister of John, eighth Lord Glamis.

[5] This was Henry Yair, sometime a priest, and afterwards a retainer of Lord Ruthven. He was "delattit of treason" on 1 April 1566, for accession to Riccio's murder, and was sentenced to be hanged and quartered, and his goods forfeited. (Pitcairn's *Criminal Trials*, i, 481*–482*)

his last band. And now for the Papists. And as he left God, so he was left by Him

about the same time, by the advice of foolish cagots,[1] he wrote to the Pope, to the King of Spain, and to the King of France, complaining of the state of the country, which was all out of order, all because that Mass and Popery were not again erected, giving the whole blame thereof to the Queen, as not managing the Catholic cause aright. By some knave, this poor Prince was betrayed, and the Queen got a copy of these letters into her hands, and therefore threatened him sore ; and there was never after that any appearance of love betwixt them.[2]

The Churches of Geneva, Berne, and Basle, with other Reformed Churches of Germany and France, sent to the whole Church of Scotland the sum of the Confession of their Faith, desiring to know if they agreed in uniformity of doctrine, alleging that the Church of Scotland was dissonant in some Articles from them. Wherefore the Superintendents, with a great part of the other most qualified Ministers, convened in September in Saint Andrews, and reading the said letters, made answer, and sent word again, that they agreed in all points with those Churches, and differed in nothing from them ; albeit in the keeping of some Festival days our Church assented not, for only the Sabbath-day was kept in Scotland.[3]

In the end of this month, the Earl Bothwell, riding in pursuit of the thieves in Liddesdale, was ill hurt, and worse terrified by a thief; for he believed surely to have departed forth of this life, and sent word thereof to the Queen's Majesty, who soon after passed forth of Jedburgh to the Hermitage to visit him, and give him comfort.[4] And within a few days after, she took sickness in a most extreme manner, for she lay two hours long cold dead, as it were without breath, or any sign of life : at length she revived, by reason they had

[1] *hypocrites.* The entry in the *Oxford English Dictionary* is hopelessly incorrect. See Littré, *Dictionnaire de la Langue Française* s.v. *cagot,* and the quotation there given from Pasquier's *Recherches.* The meaning given in Craigie's *Dictionary of the Older Scottish Tongue,* s.v. *cagot,* " an affectedly pious person," is equivalent to Molière's use of the word in *Tartuffe* to mean " an excessive outward show of religion ".

[2] For an analysis of these statements see Hay Fleming, *Mary Queen of Scots,* 415, *note* 63.

[3] The Helvetian Confession was drawn up by the Pastors of Zürich in 1566. It was approved by the General Assembly of the Church of Scotland, and the translation made by Mr. Robert Pont was ordered to be printed ; but no copy of this translation is known to be extant. In the " epistle " to be sent to Zürich a marginal note was to be added regarding " the remembrance of some holy days." (*Booke of the Universall Kirk,* i, 90 ; Calderwood, *History of the Kirk of Scotland,* ii, 331–332) The letter, addressed to Beza, dated from St. Andrews, 4 September 1566, and signed by forty-one Ministers, is printed in *Zürich Letters,* Second Series (Parker Society), 362–365.

[4] For an analysis of this well-known incident see Hay Fleming, *op. cit.,* 415, *notes* 64, 65.

bound small cords about her shackle bones,[1] her knees, and great toes, and speaking very softly, she desired the Lords to pray for her to God. She said the creed in English, and desired my Lord of Moray, if she should chance to depart, that he would not be over extreme to such as were of her Religion ; the Duke [2] and he should have been Regents. The bruit went from Jedburgh in the month of October 1566, that the Queen was departed this life, or, at least, she could not live any time,[3] wherefore there were continually prayers publicly made at the Church of Edinburgh, and divers other places, for her conversion towards God and amendment.[4] Many were of opinion that she should come to the preaching and renounce Popery ; but all in vain, for God had some other thing to do by her. The King being advertised, rode post from Stirling to Jedburgh,[5] where he found the Queen somewhat convalesced, but she would scarce speak to him, and hardly give him presence or a good word ; wherefore he returned immediately to Stirling, where the Prince was, and after to Glasgow to his father.[6]

There appeared great trouble over the whole Realm, and especially in the countries near the Borders, if the Queen had departed at that time. As she began to recover, the Earl Bothwell was brought in a chariot [7] from the Hermitage to Jedburgh, where he was cured of his wounds ; in whose presence the Queen took more pleasure than in all the rest of the world. Always, by his means, most part of all that were outlawed for the slaughter of David Riccio got relief ; for there was no other means, but all things must needs pass by him. Wherefore every man sought to him, where immediately favour was to be had, as before to David Riccio.

Soon after, the Queen passing along the Borders, she came within the bounds of Berwick, where she viewed the town at her pleasure afar off, being within half a mile and less. All the ordnance within Berwick were discharged ; the Captain came forth, with fourscore horses bravely arrayed, to do her honour, and offer her

[1] *wrists.* For fuller details of Mary's illness see the letter written to James Beaton, Archbishop of Glasgow, by John Lesley, Bishop of Ross, from Jedburgh, 26, 27 October 1566, and printed in Keith's *History*, iii, 286–289.

[2] Châtelherault

[3] Lethington, writing to Cecil on 26 October 1566, says "for the space off half an hour, we wer all desperate off her lyfe." (*Calendar of Scottish Papers*, ii, No. 435)

[4] See *Birrel's Diary* (in Dalyell, *Fragments of Scotish History*, 6) ; *Diurnal of Occurrents*, 101

[5] But see Hay Fleming, *op. cit.*, 418, *note* 73

[6] See *Diurnal of Occurrents*, 101–102 ; *Historie of King James the Sext* (Bannatyne Club), 4

[7] a *horse-litter*

lawful service.[1] Then she came to Craigmillar, where she remained in November, till she was advertised of the coming of the Ambassadors to the baptism of the Prince. And for that purpose there was great preparation made, not without the trouble of such as were supposed to have money in store, especially of Edinburgh; for there was borrowed a good round sum of money for the same business.[2] All her care and solicitude was for that triumph. At the same time arrived the Count de Briance,[3] Ambassador of the King of France, who had a great train. Soon after the Earl of Bedford [4] went forth of England, with a very gorgeous company, to the number of fourscore horses, and passing to Stirling, he was humanely received of the Queen's Majesty, and every day banqueted. The excessive expenses, and superfluous apparel, which was prepared at that time, exceeded far all the preparation that ever had been devised or set forth afore that time in this country.

The 17 of December 1566, in the great hall [5] of the Castle of Stirling, was the Prince baptized by the Bishop of Saint Andrews,[6] at five a clock at even, with great pomp, albeit with great pain could they find men to bear the torches, wherefore they took boys. The Queen laboured much with the Noblemen to bear the salt, grease, and candle, and such other things, but all refused; she found at last the Earls of Eglinton, Atholl, and the Lord Seton,[7] who assisted at the baptism, and brought in the said trash.[8] The Count de Briance (being the French Ambassador), assisted likewise. The Earl of Bedford brought for a present from the Queen of England a font of gold, valued to be worth three thousand crowns.[9] Soon after the said baptism, as the Earl was in communing with the Queen, who entertained him most reverently, he began to say merrily to her, amongst other talking, "Madam, I rejoice very greatly at this time, seeing your Majesty hath here to serve you so many Noblemen, especially twelve Earls, whereof two only assist at this baptism to

[1] See the account by Lethington, printed in Keith's *History*, ii, 469–471

[2] See the arrangements for the taxation of £12,000 for the expenses of the baptism of the Prince (*Reg. Privy Council of Scotland*, i, 485–487)

[3] Jean de Luxembourg, Comte de Brienne et de Ligny, a favourite of Henry III of France. Melville's comment is that he was "na courteour, bot a semple man." (*Memoirs*, Bannatyne Club, 171)

[4] Francis Russell, Earl of Bedford

[5] In the chapel. The subsequent banquet was held in the great hall.

[6] John Hamilton

[7] George, fifth Lord Seton; but possibly a mistake for Robert, third Lord Sempill

[8] See the details given in *Diurnal of Occurrents*, 103–104

[9] It is said to have weighed three hundred and thirty-three ounces. (Hay Fleming, *op. cit.*, 426, *note* 99)

the superstition of Popery." [1] At the which saying the Queen kept good countenance. Soon after they banqueted in the said great hall, where they wanted no prodigality. During the time of the Earl of Bedford's remaining at Stirling, the Lords, for the most part, waited upon him, and conveyed him every day to the sermon, and after to banqueting.

The King, who remained at Stirling all that time (never being present), kept his chamber. His father hearing how he was used, wrote to him to repair unto him; who soon after went (without good-night) toward Glasgow, to his father. He was hardly a mile out of Stirling, when the poison (which had been given him) wrought so upon him, that he had very great pain and dolour in every part of his body. At length, being arrived at Glasgow, the blisters broke out, of a bluish colour; so the physicians presently knew the disease to come by poison. He was brought so low, that nothing but death was expected; yet the strength of his youth at last did surmount the poison.[2]

During the time of this triumph, the Queen was most liberal in all things that were demanded of her. Amongst other things, she subscribed a writing for the maintenance of the Ministers in a reasonable proportion,[3] which was to be taken up of the Thirds of Benefices; which writing, being purchased by the Bishop of Galloway, was presented at the General Assembly of the Church at Edinburgh, the five and twentieth day of December 1566, where were convened the Superintendents and other Ministers in reasonable number, but very few Commissioners.[4] The first matter that was there proponed, was concerning the said writing lately obtained; and the most part of the Ministers being demanded their opinions in the matter, after advice, and passing a little aside, they answered very gravely that it was their duty to preach to the people the word of God truly and sincerely, and to crave of the auditors the things that were necessary for their sustentation, as of duty the Pastors might justly crave of their flocks; and, further, it became them not to have any care. Nevertheless, the Assembly taking into consideration that the said gift granted by the Queen's Majesty was not to be refused, they

[1] Huntly, Moray, and Bothwell—as well as the Earl of Bedford—had stood outside the chapel, because the baptism had been according to the rites of the Roman Church. (*Ibid.*, 144; *Diurnal of Occurrents*, 104)

[2] But the disease may have been small-pox, or perhaps syphilis. (See the analysis of the evidence in Hay Fleming, *Mary Queen of Scots*, 430, *notes* 114, 115; and the article by Karl Pearson in *Biometrika*, 1928, xx^{B}, 1–104)

[3] *Reg. Privy Council of Scotland*, i, 494–495

[4] See *Booke of the Universall Kirk*, i, 83

ordained that certain faithful men of every shire should meet, and do their utmost diligence for gathering and receiving the said corn and money ; and likewise appointed the Superintendent of Lothian,[1] and Master John Row, to wait upon the Bishop of Galloway, and concur and assist him for further expedition in the Court, that the said gift might be despatched through the Seals.

In the same Assembly there was presented a remonstrance by writ, by some gentlemen of Kyle, containing in effect that inasmuch as the tithes ought to be given only to the Ministers of the Word, and Schools, and for maintenance of the poor, that therefore the Assembly would statute and ordain that all the Professors of the Evangel should keep the same in their own hands, to the effects aforesaid, and no way permit the Papists to meddle therewith. This writing took no effect at that time, for there was none else but the gentlemen of Kyle of that opinion.[2] It was statute in the said Assembly that such public fornicators and scandalous livers as would not confess their offences, nor come to declare their repentance, should be declared by the Minister to be out of the Church, and not of the body thereof, and their names to be declared publicly upon the Sunday.

The Queen intending vengeance upon the poor King, and being in love with the Earl Bothwell, grants to the Protestants their petitions, that they may be quiet and not trouble her plots

After this Assembly, the Bishop of Galloway (with the Superintendent of Lothian and Master John Row) passing to Stirling, obtained their demands in an ample manner at the Queen's Majesty's hand, according to their desire ; and likewise, they obtained for every burgh, a gift or donation of the altarages, annuals, and obits, which before were given to the Papists, now to be disponed for the maintenance of the Ministers and Schools within the burghs, and the rest to the poor or hospitals.[3]

[4] It was ordained that humble supplication should be made to the Lords of Secret Council concerning the Commission of Jurisdiction supposed to be granted to the Bishop of Saint Andrews,[5] to the effect their honours might stay the same, in respect that the causes for the most part judged by his usurped authority pertain to the true Kirk ; and also, because in respect of that coloured Commis-

[1] Mr. John Spottiswoode [2] But see *Booke of the Universall Kirk*, i, 83–84

[3] See *Reg. Privy Council of Scotland*, i, 497–498

[4] This paragraph, together with the Supplication of the Assembly and Knox's Letter to the Professors, appear in the Edinburgh (1644) edition of the *History*, but not in the London edition of that same year. It may be surmised with some probability that the additions were supplied by Calderwood. (*Cf.* Calderwood's *History*, ii, 335–340)

[5] By a grant under the Privy Seal, of 23 December 1566, proceeding upon the Queen's signature, Mary had restored Archbishop Hamilton to all his former consistorial jurisdiction. (See Hay Fleming, *op. cit.*, 145–146 and supporting notes)

sion, he might assume again his old usurped authority, and the same might be a means to oppress the whole Kirk. The tenor of the Supplication followeth [1]:

"THE GENERAL ASSEMBLY OF THE KIRK OF SCOTLAND CONVENED AT EDINBURGH THE 25 OF DECEMBER 1566, TO THE NOBILITY OF THIS REALM THAT PROFESS THE LORD JESUS WITH THEM, AND HAVE RENOUNCED THAT ROMAN ANTICHRIST, DESIRES CONSTANCY IN FAITH, AND THE SPIRIT OF RIGHTEOUS JUDGMENT.

John Knox's supplication to the Council to recall the commission granted to the Archbishop of St. Andrews

"SEEING that Satan, by all our negligences (Right Honourable), hath so far prevailed within this Realm of late days that we do stand in extreme danger, not only to lose our temporal possessions, but also to be deprived of the glorious Evangel of Jesus Christ, and so we and our posterity to be left in damnable darkness; We could no longer contain ourselves, nor keep silence, lest by so doing we might be accused as guilty of the blood of such as shall perish for lack of admonition, as the Prophet threateneth. We, therefore, in the fear of our God, and with grief and anguish of our heart, complain unto your Honours (yea, we must complain unto God, and to all his obedient creatures), that that conjured enemy of Jesus Christ, and cruel murderer of our dear brethren, most falsely styled Archbishop of Saint Andrews, is reponed and restored, by signature passed, to his former tyranny: For not only are his ancient jurisdictions (as they are termed) of the whole Bishopric of Saint Andrews granted unto him, but also the execution of judgment, confirmation of testaments, and donation of benefices, as more amply in his signature is expressed. If this be not to cure [2] the head of that venomous beast, which once within this Realm by the potent hand of God was so broken down and banished, that by tyranny it could not have hurt the faithful, judge ye. His ancient jurisdiction was, that he with certain colleagues collaterals, might have damned of heresy upon probation as pleased him, and then to take all that were suspected of heresy. What they have judged to be heresy heretofore, ye cannot be ignorant of; and whether they remain in their former malice or not, their fruits and travails openly declare. The danger may be feared, say ye. But what remedy? It is easy, and at hand (Right Honourable), if ye will not betray the cause of God, and leave your brethren, who will never more be subject to that usurped tyranny than they will be to the Devil himself. Our Queen belike is not well informed. She ought not, nor justly may not break the laws

[1] *Booke of the Universall Kirk,* i, 88–90

[2] *restore*

of this Realm; and so consequently she may not set up against us, without our consent, that Roman Antichrist again. For in a lawful and the most free Parliament that ever was in this Realm before, was that odious beast deprived of all jurisdiction, office and authority within the Realm.[1] Her Majesty at her first arrival, and by divers proclamations since, hath expressly forbidden any other form and face of Religion, than that which she found publicly established at her arrival. Therefore she may not bring us (the greatest part of the subjects of this Realm) back again to bondage, till that as lawful and as free a Parliament as justly damned that Antichrist and his usurped tyranny, hath given decision betwixt us and him. If hereof, and of other things which no less concern yourselves than us, ye plainly and boldly admonish our Sovereign, and without tumult only crave justice, the tyrants dare no more be seen in lawful judgment, than dare the owls in daylight. Weigh this matter as it is, and ye will find it more weighty than it appeareth to many. Further at this present we complain not, but humbly crave of your Honours a reasonable answer what ye will do, in case such tyrants and devouring wolves begin to invade the flock of Jesus Christ within this Realm, under what title soever it be. For this we boldly profess, that we will never acknowledge such either pastors to our souls, or yet judges to our causes. And if, for denial thereof, we suffer either in body or in goods, we doubt not but we have not only a judge to punish them that unjustly trouble us, but also an advocate and strong champion in Heaven to recompense them who, for his name's sake, suffer persecution: Whose Holy Spirit rule your hearts in his true fear to the end.

"Given in the General Assembly and third Session thereof, at Edinburgh, the 27 of December, 1566."

Besides this Supplication of the Assembly to the Nobility penned (as appeareth by the style) by John Knox, a letter was written by John Knox in particular to the Professors, to advertise them of the danger of this commission or power granted to the said bastard, Bishop of Saint Andrews, the tenor whereof doth follow[2]:

"*The Lord cometh, and shall not tarry. Blessed shall he be whom He shall find fighting against impiety.*

"To deplore the miseries of these our most wicked days (Beloved Brethren) can neither greatly profit us, neither yet relieve us of our

[1] *Supra*, i, 340–341

[2] Calderwood, *History of the Kirk of Scotland*, ii, 337–340

John Knox's Letter to the Professors

present calamities ; and yet utterly to keep silence, cannot lack the suspicion of apostasy, and plain defection from God, and from his truth, once by us publicly professed. For now are matters (that in years bypast have been denied) so far discovered, that he who seeth not the plain subversion of all true Religion within this Realm to be concluded, and decreed in the hearts of some, must either confess himself blind, or else an enemy to the Religion which we profess. For besides the open erecting of idolatry in divers parts of this Realm, and besides the extreme poverty wherein our Ministers are brought (by reason that idle bellies are fed upon that which justly appertaineth to such as truly preach Jesus Christ, and rightly and by order minister his blessed Sacraments), that cruel murderer of our brethren, falsely called Archbishop of Saint Andrews, most unjustly, and against all law, hath presumed to his former tyranny, as a signature passed for his restitution to his ancient jurisdiction (as it is termed) more fully doth proport. What end may be looked for of such beginnings, the half-blind may see, as we suppose. And yet we have heard that a certain sum of money and victuals should be assigned by the Queen's Majesty for sustentation of our Ministry. But how that any such assignation, or any promise made thereof, can stand in any stable assurance, when that Roman Antichrist (by just laws once banished from this Realm) shall be intruded above us, we can no wise understand. Yea, farther, we cannot see what assurance any within this Realm that have professed the Lord Jesus can have of life or inheritance, if the head of that odious beast be cured [1] amongst us. And therefore we yet again, in the bowels of Christ Jesus, crave of you to look into this matter, and to advertise us again, with reasonable expedition of your judgments, that in the fear of God, and with unity of minds, we may proceed to crave justice, and oppose ourselves to such tyranny, as most unjustly is intended against us. For, if we think not that this last erecting of that wicked man is the very setting up again of that Roman Antichrist within this Realm, we are deprived of all right judgment. And what is that else, but to separate us and our posterity from God ; yea, and to cut ourselves from the freedom of this Realm. We desire therefore that the wisest amongst you may consider the weight of this cause, which long hath been neglected, partly by our sloth, and partly by believing fair promises, by which to this hour we have been deceived. And therefore we ought to be the more vigilant and circumspect, especially seeing a Parliament is proclaimed.

[1] *restored*

"We have sent to you the form of a Supplication and Articles, which we would have presented to the Queen's Majesty. If it please you, we would ye should approve it by your subscriptions; or if you would alter it, we desire you so to do, and we shall allow whatsoever you shall propound, not repugnant to God. If it shall be thought expedient that Commissioners of Counties shall convene, to reason upon the most weighty matters that now occur, the time and place being appointed by you, and due advertisement being given to us, by God's grace, there shall no fault be found in us; but as from the beginning we have neither spared substance nor life, so mind we not to faint unto the end, to maintain the same, so long as we can find the concurrence of brethren; of whom (as God forbid) if we be destitute, yet are we determined never to be subject to that Roman Antichrist, neither yet to his usurped tyranny. But when we can do no further to suppress that odious beast, we mind to seal with our blood, to our posterity, that the bright knowledge of Jesus Christ hath banished that man of sin, and his venomous doctrine, from our hearts and consciences. Let this our letter and request bear witness before God, before his angels, before the world, and before our own consciences, that we require you that have professed the Lord Jesus within this Realm, as well Nobility, as Gentlemen, Burgesses, and Commons, to deliberate upon the estate of things present; and specially whether that this usurped tyranny of that Roman Antichrist shall be any longer suffered within this Realm, seeing that by just law it is already abolished. Secondly, Whether that we shall be bound to feed idle bellies upon the patrimony of the Kirk, which justly appertaineth unto Ministers. Thirdly, Whether that idolatry, and other abominations, which now are more than evident, shall any longer by us be maintained and defended. Answer us as ye will answer to God, in whose fear we send these letters unto you, lest that our silence should be counted for consent unto such impiety. God take from our hearts the blind love of ourselves, and all ungodly fear. Amen. Let us know your minds with expedition."

Notwithstanding the domestic troubles that the Church of God had in Scotland in this turbulent time within the kingdom, yet they were not unmindful of the affliction of Jacob everywhere upon the face of the earth; namely, they had before their eyes the state and condition of the Church of God in England: Witness this Letter from the General Assembly to the Rulers of the Church of God in England; [wherein they entreat them to deal gently with the preachers their brethren about the surplice and other apparel. John Knox formed the Letter in name of the Assembly, as follows] [1]:

"THE SUPERINTENDENTS, WITH OTHER MINISTERS AND COMMISSIONERS OF THE CHURCH OF GOD IN THE KINGDOM OF SCOTLAND, TO THEIR BRETHREN, THE BISHOPS AND PASTORS OF GOD'S CHURCH IN ENGLAND, WHO PROFESS WITH US IN SCOTLAND THE TRUTH OF JESUS CHRIST.

"BY word and letters it is come to our knowledge (Reverend Brethren, Pastors of God's word in the Church of England), that divers of our Brethren (of whom some be of the most learned in England) are deprived from all ecclesiastical function, namely, are forbidden to preach, and so by you are stopped to promote the Kingdom of God, because they have a scruple of conscience to use at the command of Authority such garments as idolaters in time of greatest darkness did use in their superstitious and idolatrous service; which report cannot but be very grievous to our hearts, considering the sentence of the Apostle, 'If ye bite and devour one another, take heed ye be not consumed one of another.' We intend not at this present to enter into the question, which we hear is agitated and handled with greater vehemency by either party than well liketh us, to wit, Whether such apparel be accounted amongst things indifferent or not; wherefore (through the bowels of Jesus Christ) we crave that Christian charity may so far prevail with you, who are the pastors and guides of Christ's flock in England, that ye do one to another as ye desire others to do to you. You cannot be ignorant what tenderness is in a scrupulous conscience, and all that have knowledge are not alike persuaded. The consciences of some of you stir not with the wearing of such things; on the other side, many thousands (both godly and learned) are otherways persuaded, whose consciences are continually stricken with these sentences, 'What hath Christ to do with Belial?' 'What fellowship is there betwixt light and darkness?' If surplice, corner-cap and tippet have been the badges of idolaters in the very act of their idolatry, what hath the preachers of Christian liberty, and the rebukers of superstition to do with the dregs of that Romish Beast? Yea, what is he that ought not to fear, either to take in his hand, or on his forehead, the prints and mark of that odious Beast? The brethren

[1] See *Booke of the Universall Kirk*, i, 85–88; Calderwood's *History*, ii, 332–335. Again, the words in square brackets, which are added to the Edinburgh edition of 1644, appear to have been supplied by Calderwood. (*Cf.* Calderwood's *History*, ii, 332)

that refuse such unprofitable apparel, do neither condemn nor molest you who use such trifles. On the other side, if ye that use these things will do the like to your brethren, we doubt not but therein you shall please God, and comfort the hearts of many, which are wounded to see extremity used against these godly brethren. Humane arguments or coloured rhetoric we use none to persuade you, only in charity we desire you to mind the sentence of Peter, 'Feed the flock of Christ which is committed to your charge, caring for it, not by constraint, but willingly; not being as lords of God's heritages, but being examples to the flock.' We further desire you to meditate upon that sentence of Paul, 'Give no offence, neither to Jews, nor Gentiles, nor to the church of God.' In what condition of time you and we both travail for the promoting of Christ's kingdom, you are not ignorant; therefore we are the more bold to exhort you to deal more wisely than to trouble the godly for such vanities; for all things which seem lawful, edify not. If Authority urge you further than your consciences can bear, we pray you remember, that the Ministers of the Church are called the 'Light of the world,' and 'Salt of the earth'; all civil authority hath not always the light of God shining before their eyes, in statutes and commands, for their affections savour too much of the earth and worldly wisdom. Therefore we tell you, that ye ought to oppose yourselves boldly, not only to all power that dare extol itself against God, but also against all such as dare burden the consciences of the faithful further than God chargeth them in his own word. But we hope you will excuse our freedom in that we have entered in reasoning further than we intended in the beginning. Now, again we return to our former request, which is, That the brethren among you, who refuse the Romish rags, may find of you, who use and urge them, such favour as our Head and Master commandeth each one of his members to show to another, which we look to receive of your courtesy, not only because you will not offend God in troubling your brethren for such vain trifles, but also because you will not refuse the earnest request of us your Brethren, and fellow Ministers; in whom, although there appear no worldly pomp, yet we are assured, you will esteem us as God's servants, travailing to set forth his glory against the Roman Antichrist. The days are evil, iniquity aboundeth, and charity (alas) waxeth cold; wherefore we ought to walk diligently, for the hour is uncertain when the Lord shall come, before whom we must all give an account of our administration. In conclusion, yet once more we desire you to be favourable one to another. The

Lord Jesus rule your hearts in his fear unto the end, and give to you and us victory over that conjured enemy of true Religion (the Pope), whose wounded head Sathan by all means strives to cure again ; but to destruction shall he go, and all his maintainers, by the power of our Lord Jesus, to whose mighty protection we commit you.

"From our General Assembly, December 27, 1566."

[1] At the same time the Bishop of Saint Andrews, by means of the Earl Bothwell, procured a writing from the Queen's Majesty, to be obeyed within the diocese of his jurisdiction, in all such causes as before in time of Popery were used in the Consistory, and therefore to discharge the new Commissioners [2] ; and for the same purpose came to Edinburgh in January, having a company of one hundred horses, or more, intending to take possession, according to his gift lately obtained. The Provost being advertised thereof by the Earl of Moray, they sent to the Bishop three or four of the Council, desiring him to desist from the said matter, for fear of trouble and sedition that might rise thereupon ; whereby he was persuaded to desist at that time.

Soon after, the Queen came to Edinburgh, where she remained a few days. In the month of January she was informed that the King was recovered of the poison given him at Stirling, and therefore she passed to Glasgow to visit him, and there tarried with him six days, using him wonderfully kindly, with many gracious and good words ; and likewise his father, the Earl of Lennox, insomuch that all men marvelled whereto it should turn, considering the great contempt and dryness that had been before so long together. The Queen, notwithstanding all the contempt that was given him, with a known design to take away his life, yet by her sweet words gains so far upon the uxorious husband, and his facile father, that he went in company with her to Edinburgh, where she had caused to lodge him at the Kirk of Field, in a lodging, lately bought by Master James Balfour, Clerk Register, truly very unmeet for a King. The

[1] An interpolated paragraph is here omitted, and at the head of the present paragraph appears the following long marginal note : As she had lately gratified the Protestants by granting their Petition, so at this time she yields unto the Papists their demands also, that she might be stopped by neither of them in her design of vengeance and new love.

[2] By a writ of 8 February 1564, the Queen had appointed four Commissaries, sitting at Edinburgh, to exercise the jurisdiction formerly exercised by the Officials of the Roman Church ; but with Mary's restoration of consistorial jurisdiction to the Archbishop of St. Andrews, the newly appointed Commissaries were discharged of all office within the diocese of St. Andrews. (Robertson, *Concilia Scotiæ*, i, Preface, clxxv–clxxviii)

Queen resorted often to visit him, and lay in the house two nights by him (although her lodging was in the Palace of Holyroodhouse). Every man marvelled at this reconciliation and sudden change. The ninth of February, the King was murdered, and the house where he lay burned with powder, about twelve of the clock in the night [1]: his body was cast forth in a yard, without the town wall, adjoining close by. There was a servant likewise murdered beside him, who had been also in the chamber with him. The people ran to behold this spectacle; and wondering thereat some judged one thing, some another.

Shortly thereafter, Bothwell came from the Abbey with a company of men of war, and caused the body of the King to be carried to the next house. Where, after a little, the surgeons being convened at the Queen's command to view and consider the manner of his death, most part gave out, to please the Queen, that he was blown in the air, albeit he had no mark of fire; and truly he was strangled. Soon after, he was carried to the Abbey, and there buried.[2]

[When many of the common people had gazed long upon the King's corpse, the Queen caused it to be brought down to the Palace by some pioneers. She beheld the corpse without any outward show or sign of joy or sorrow. When the Lords had concluded amongst themselves that he should be honourably buried, the Queen caused his corpse to be carried by some pioneers in the night without solemnity, and to be laid beside the sepulchre of David Riccio.[3] If there had been any solemn burial, Buchanan had wanted wit to relate otherwise, seeing there would have been so many witnesses to testify the contrary. Therefore the contriver of the late History of Queen Mary [4] wanted policy here to convey a lie.

The Queen, according to the ancient custom, should have kept herself forty days within, and the doors and windows should have been closed in token of mourning; but the windows were opened, to let

[1] About two o'clock in the morning of 10 February

[2] In place of these words "Soon after, he was carried to the Abbey, and there buried," the Edinburgh (1644) edition contains the two following paragraphs, enclosed within square brackets. Both appear to come direct from Calderwood's *History* (ii, 346, 347).

[3] See Hay Fleming, *Mary Queen of Scots*, 441, *note* 34. For a critical examination of the tragedy of Kirk o' Field, see *ibid.*, 148–152 and supporting notes.

[4] Laing suggests that this is probably a reference to [W. Udall], *The Historie of the Life and Death of Mary Stuart, Queene of Scotland*, published in London in 1636. (Laing's *Knox*, ii, 550, *note*) In the *Detectio* Buchanan stated that Darnley's corpse was carried and buried hard by Riccio, "without any funeral honour, upon a vile bier, and in the night time by the common carriers of dead bodies"; and certainly the author of the *Historie* refers to the *Detectio* as "of small credit," Buchanan being an adversary of the Queen who had been "wonne by money to write." (*Historie, etc.*, 115)

in light, the fourth day. Before the twelfth day, she went out to Seton, Bothwell never parting from her side. There she went out to the fields to behold games and pastimes.[1] The King's armour, horse, and household stuff were bestowed upon the murderers. A certain tailor, when he was to reform the King's apparel to Bothwell, said jestingly, He acknowledged here the custom of the country, by which the clothes of the dead fall to the hangman. [2]]

This tragical end had Henry Stewart, after he had been King eighteen months. A Prince of great lineage, both by mother and father. He was of a comely stature, and none was like unto him within this island. He died under the age of one and twenty years [3]; prompt and ready for all games and sports; much given to hawking and hunting, and running of horses, and likewise to playing on the lute, and also to Venus chamber. He was liberal enough. He could write and dictate well; but he was somewhat given to wine, and much feeding, and likewise to inconstancy; and proud beyond measure, and therefore contemned all others. He had learned to dissemble well enough, being from his youth misled up in Popery. Thus, within two years after his arriving in this Realm, he was highly by the Queen alone extolled; and, finally, had this unfortunate end by her procurement and consent. To lay all other proofs aside, her marriage with Bothwell, who was the main executioner of the King, notwithstanding all the advices and counsels that the King of France, and the Queen of England, did earnestly and carefully give her, as other friends did likewise,[4] witness anent their guilt. Those that laid hands on the King to kill him, by Bothwell's direction, were Sir James Balfour, Gilbert Balfour, David Chalmers, black John Spens, Francis, Sebastien, John de Bordeaux, and Joseph, the brother of David Riccio.[5] These last four were the Queen's domestics, and strangers. The reason why the King's death was so hastened, was because the affection or passion of the Earl Bothwell could not bear so long a delay as the procurement of a bill of divorce required, although the Romish clergy offered their service willingly to the business, namely, Bishop Hamilton, and so he became great again at court. And he for the advancement of the business, did good offices to increase the hatred betwixt the King and Queen; yea, some that had been the chief instruments of the marriage of the King and

[1] See Hay Fleming, *op. cit.*, 152, 442, *notes* 35, 36

[2] See Aikman's *Buchanan*, ii, 499

[3] See Hay Fleming, *op. cit.*, 437, *note* 20

[4] See Hay Fleming, *op. cit.*, 456, *note* 1; *Calendar of Scottish Papers*, ii, No. 477

[5] These were the "suspected murderers" named by the Earl of Lennox, Darnley's father. (*Calendar of Scottish Papers*, ii, No. 488; Keith's *History*, ii, 529–531)

Queen, offered their service for the divorce, seeing how the Queen's inclination lay. So unhappy are Princes, that men, for their own ends, further them in all their inclinations and undertakings, be they never so bad or destructive to themselves.

The Earl of Lennox, in the meantime, wrote to the Queen, to cause punish Bothwell, with his other complices, for murdering the King.[1] The Queen, not daring openly to reject the Earl of Lennox's solicitation, did appoint a day for the trial of Bothwell, by an assize[2]; the members whereof were the Earl of Caithness, President,[3] the Earl of Cassillis[4] (who at the first refused, but thereafter, being threatened to be put in prison, and under the pain of treason, was present by the Queen's command), John Hamilton, Commendator of Arbroath,[5] Lord Ross,[6] Lord Sempill,[7] Lord Boyd,[8] Lord Herries,[9] Lord Oliphant[10]; the Master of Forbes,[11] the Lairds of Lochinvar,[12] Langton,[13] Cambusnethan,[14] Barnbougle,[15] and Boyne.[16] They, to please the Queen, and for fear, did pronounce Bothwell not guilty, notwithstanding the manifest evidences of the cruel fact committed by Bothwell who, before the trial, did make himself strong by divers means; namely, by the possession of the Castle of Edinburgh,[17] so that the accusers durst not appear, not being strong enough. The Earl of Mar did retire to Stirling, and had committed to his charge the young Prince. All this was done in February.

[1] Keith's *History*, ii, 529–530

[2] A copy of the proceedings of 12 April 1567, before the Court of Justiciary in the Tolbooth of Edinburgh, attested by Sir John Bellenden, the Justice-Clerk, is printed in J. Anderson, *Collections relating to the History of Mary Queen of Scotland*, ii, 97–114. See also *Calendar of Scottish Papers*, ii, No. 488 (abridging a "Copy of the processe . . . subscrivit be the Justice-Clerk"), and Keith's *History*, ii, 539–548. Knox's continuator has omitted Andrew, fifth Earl of Rothes, from the assize.

[3] George, fourth Earl of Caithness, was chancellor or foreman of the jury.

[4] Gilbert, fourth Earl of Cassillis

[5] John Hamilton, third son of the Duke of Châtelherault; later (1599) Marquess of Hamilton

[6] James, fourth Lord Ross

[7] Robert, third Lord Sempill

[8] Robert, fifth Lord Boyd

[9] John, second son of Robert, fifth Lord Maxwell, usually called "The Master of Maxwell." He assumed the title of Lord Herries as the husband of Agnes, eldest daughter of William, third Lord Herries, and, *suo jure*, Lady Herries.

[10] Laurence, fourth Lord Oliphant

[11] John, son of William, seventh Lord Forbes; later eighth Lord Forbes

[12] Sir John Gordon of Lochinvar

[13] James Cockburn of Langton (Berwickshire)

[14] James Somerville of Cambusnethan (Lanarkshire)

[15] Sir John Mowbray of Barnbougle (West Lothian)

[16] Alexander Ogilvy of Boyne (Banffshire)

[17] See Hay Fleming, *op. cit.*, 443, *note* 45

In April, Bothwell called together sundry of the Lords, who had come to Edinburgh, to a meeting that was there ; and having gained some before, made them all, what by fear, what by fair promises, first of their private state, and then of advancing the Papist's Religion, to consent by their subscriptions to the marriage with the Queen.[1] Then the Queen goes to Stirling, to see her son. Bothwell makes a show as if he were going to the Borders to suppress robbers, and so he raiseth some men of war ; which, when he had done, he turneth towards the way to Stirling, where he meets the Queen, according to appointment betwixt them, and carrieth her to Dunbar, as it had been by force, although every one knew it was with the Queen's liking.[2] The prime Nobility convened at Stirling, and from thence sent to her, to know whether or not she was taken against her will. She answered that it was true she was taken against her will but, since her taking, she had no occasion to complain ; yea, the courteous entertainment she had, made her forget and forgive all former offences. These expressions were used by way of preface to the pardon which was granted immediately thereafter to Bothwell ; for, by Letters Patent, he was pardoned by the Queen for laying violently hands upon her Majesty, and for all other crimes. So by these [means] the murder of the King was pardoned. During the Queen's abode in Dunbar, there were letters of divorce demanded and granted unto Bothwell from his Lady (who afterward was married to the Earl Sutherland [3]), she was sister to the Earl of Huntly. The ground of divorce was, the parties, being within the degrees prohibited, could not be lawfully joined ; next, because Bothwell was an adulterer, the marriage was void. The bill of divorce was granted by the Papistical Court of the Archbishop of Saint Andrews.[4] And here mark how they juggle in sacred things ; for when it pleaseth them, they untie the bond of marriage, as now, and as we have seen in the First Book of this History. When the Queen fell in distaste of the late King her husband, it was proposed

[1] See *ibid.*, 446, *note* 60. The bond, commonly known as that of " Ainslie's Supper," is printed in Keith's *History*, ii, 562–569.

[2] See Hay Fleming, *Mary Queen of Scots*, 156 and supporting notes

[3] Alexander, eleventh Earl of Sutherland. After his death (1594), Lady Jean Gordon married, thirdly (1599), Alexander Ogilvy of Boyne.

[4] There was a double process for divorce. Lady Bothwell received a divorce from the Commissary Court of Edinburgh ; Bothwell received a decision from the newly re-instituted Consistorial Court of St. Andrews (*supra*, 194, *note* 5) that his marriage had been null for lack of a dispensation. (But a dispensation *had* been granted. See Hay Fleming, *op. cit.*, 157 ; 453, *note* 76.) The sederunt in each of the two courts is given in Spottiswoode's *History*, ii, 52.

unto her to have divorce upon the same ground from the King. To which, at first ear was given, but after second thoughts, a bill of divorce was too tedious (as we have now said) and could not be stayed for [1]; therefore the King must be despatched.

The Queen, when Bothwell had obtained by the Archbishop a letter of divorce from his lawful wife, sent a letter signed with her own hand to Master John Craig, minister of Edinburgh, commanding him to publish the band of matrimony betwixt her and Bothwell. Master John Craig, the next sermon day thereafter, declared in full congregation, that he had received such a command, but in conscience he could not obey it; the marriage was altogether unlawful; and of that he would declare the reasons to the parties, if he had audience of them, otherwise he would make known his just reasons in the hearing of the people. Immediately thereafter, Bothwell sends for Master Craig to the Council, where Master Craig told, first, that by an Act of the Assembly, it was forbidden to allow the marriage of any divorced for adultery; the divorce of Bothwell from his lawful wife was by collusion, witness the quick dispatch thereof,[2] for it was sought and had within ten days, and his contracting with the Queen instantly thereafter; then his rape of the Queen, and the guilt of the King's death, which was confirmed by this marriage. Withal, he desired the Lords to stop the Queen from that infamous marriage. The Sunday after, he told publicly to the people what he had said to the Council; and he took heaven and earth to witness that he detested that scandalous and infamous marriage; and that he discharged his conscience unto the Lords, who seemed unto him as so many slaves, what by flattery, what by silence, to give way to that abomination. Upon this, he was called to the Council again, and was reproved, as if he had exceeded the bounds of his calling. Whereunto he answered, That the bounds of his commission were the word of God, right reason, and good laws, against which he had said nothing; and by all these, offered to prove this marriage to be scandalous and infamous. At this he was stopped by Bothwell, and sent from the Council.[3] Notwithstanding all this done and said by Master Craig, and the opposition of many that wished well to the Queen, and were jealous of her honour, the marriage went on, and

[1] But there was also the important consideration that a divorce would affect the legitimacy of the infant Prince James, for, in the Roman Church, a divorce could proceed only upon the ground that the marriage had been, from the first, null and void.

[2] See Spottiswoode's *History*, ii, 52

[3] See Mr. John Craig's "purgation" registered in the Records of the General Assembly (*Booke of the Universall Kirk*, i, 115–116)

they were married the 15 of May. This makes good the Latin proverb, *Mala nubunt mense Maio.*[1] And a Bishop must bless the marriage. The good Prelate was Bishop of Orkney.[2] If there be a good work to be done, a Bishop must do it. Here mark the difference betwixt this worthy minister, Master Craig, and this base bishop. *Note*

The Earl of Atholl, immediately after the murder of the King, had retired home, waiting for the occasion to revenge the King's death. But, seeing this abominable marriage, he went to Stirling, where other honest Lords with him had a meeting, and made a bond, to defend the young Prince from the murderers of his father[3]; as already they had had one plot to cut him off, which God in his mercy did prevent. The Nobles that entered in this bond, were the Earls of Argyll,[4] Atholl,[5] Morton,[6] Mar,[7] and Glencairn[8]; the Lords Lindsay[9] and Boyd.[10] Argyll thereafter, seduced by some fair words, fell off; and Boyd became a great factionary for Bothwell in all things. The Queen, soon after the marriage, was advised to send abroad an Ambassador to acquaint her foreign friends and kindred; and this must be a Bishop. It is pity that any good work should be done without a Bishop: was not this a worthy employment for a pastor in God's Church?[11]

Bothwell, seeing the bond made at Stirling, caused the Queen to write to sundry of the Nobility. Divers repaired unto her, where they found a bond tendered unto them, by which they were to bind themselves to defend the Queen and Bothwell. Some that were

[1] The correct form is, *Mense malas Maio nubere vulgus ait.* Keith (*History*, ii, 586), says this Latin phrase was found affixed to the gate of the Palace of Holyrood on the night of the marriage. And on Sunday, 15 June 1567, exactly a month after the fateful wedding, Mary was to persuade Bothwell "to loup on horsebak and ryd away," never again to see one another.

[2] Adam Bothwell, successor to Bishop Reid. He had joined the Reformers, and the marriage of Mary and Bothwell was solemnized "not with the Mass, but with preaching." Later, December 1567, he was delated before the General Assembly for various offences including "Because he solemnized the marriage of the Queen and the Earl of Bothwell, which was altogether wicked, and contrary to God's law and statutes of the Kirk." (*Booke of the Universall Kirk*, i, 112, 131)

[3] See *Calendar of Scottish Papers*, ii, No. 501; Hay Fleming, *op. cit.*, 463, *note* 25

[4] Archibald, fifth Earl of Argyll

[5] John, fourth Earl of Atholl

[6] James, fourth Earl of Morton

[7] John, sixth Lord Erskine, Earl of Mar

[8] Alexander, fourth Earl of Glencairn

[9] Patrick, sixth Lord Lindsay of the Byres

[10] Robert, fifth Lord Boyd

[11] This was William Chisholm [II], Bishop of Dunblane. His instructions for his embassy to France, and also the instructions for Sir Robert Melville for England, are printed in Keith's *History*, ii, 592–606.

corrupt, did willingly subscribe; others for fear did the same. And there was not one that went to Court that did refuse but the Earl of Moray, who, refusing absolutely to enter into a bond with Bothwell, said it was not the part of a good subject; yet since he had been made friends with him some time before, he would keep his promise unto the Queen; and to enter into a bond with the Queen, it was needless and unfit, since he was to obey her in all lawful and just things. Upon this, he got leave, although with great difficulty, to go into France.

The Queen receives now Hamilton, Archbishop of Saint Andrews, into favour since these changes; who was no less a faithful councillor to her, than he was a good pastor of Christ's flock; that is, he betrayed her, and disobeyed God. With this a proclamation comes out in favour of the poor Protestants, whereby the Queen declares that she will keep and confirm all that she had promised at her arrival into Scotland.[1] This was done to stop the people's mouths; but all in vain, for the people were universally against the abomination of the court.

Within few days, Bothwell and the Queen were raising men, under pretext to go to the Borders to repress the robbers there[2]; but in effect to go to Stirling, to have the Prince in their custody, that they might dispose of him according to their mind. Then a new proclamation came out that the Queen hereafter would rule only by the advice of the Nobles of the land, as her best predecessors had done. The Lords at Stirling, hearing of this plot, strive to prevent it, and to this purpose they appointed with the Lord Home[3] to besiege the Castle of Borthwick, where the Queen and Bothwell were. But because the Earl of Atholl did not come at the hour appointed, they had not men enough to environ and compass the Castle; so that Bothwell, having notice given him of the business, escaped to Dunbar, and the Queen after him, in man's clothes.[4] The Lords, failing of their design at Borthwick Castle, went to Edinburgh, whereof they made themselves masters easily, having the affections of the people, notwithstanding the Earl Huntly's and the Archbishop of Saint Andrews' persuasion to the contrary. These two, with their associates, were constrained to retire to the Castle,

[1] See the Queen's declaration of 23 May 1567 (*Reg. Privy Council of Scotland*, i, 513–514)

[2] See the proclamations of 28 May 1567. (*Ibid.*, i, 516–517)

[3] Alexander, fifth Lord Home

[4] Bothwell slipped out of Borthwick Castle probably on the night of 10 June, and Mary, in male attire, on the night of 11 June. (Birrel, *Diary*, in Dalyell, *Fragments of Scotish History*, 9; *Diurnal of Occurrents*, 112–113)

where they were received by Sir James Balfour, left there by Bothwell.[1]

The twelfth of June, which was the next day following, the Lords at Edinburgh caused to publish a proclamation, whereby they declared that the Earl Bothwell, who had been the principal author, deviser, and actor of the cruel murder of the late King, had since laid hand upon the Queen's person, and had her for the present in Dunbar in his power; and, finding her utterly destitute of all good counsel, had seduced her to a dishonest and unlawful marriage with himself; yea, that now he was gathering forces, and stirring himself to get the young Prince in his hands, that he might murder the child as he had murdered the father. This wicked man the Nobles of the land resolved to withstand, and deliver the Queen out of his bondage; wherefore they did charge all lieges within the kingdom that could come to them, to be in readiness at three hours' warning to assist them (the Nobles) for the freeing of the Queen from captivity, and bringing the said Earl Bothwell to a legal trial and condign punishment for the aforesaid murder and other crimes. All such that would not side with the Lords were by this proclamation commanded to depart from Edinburgh within four hours, under the pain of being accounted enemies, &c.[2]

Notwithstanding this proclamation, the people did not join unto these Lords as was expected, for sundry of the Nobles were adversaries to the business, others stood as neutrals; and withal, those that were convened together were not well provided of arms and munition for exploits of war; so that they were even thinking to dissolve and leave off their enterprise till another time, and had absolutely done so, but God had ordained other ways, as the event did show (if the Queen and Bothwell could have had patience to stay at Dunbar for three or four days without any stir).[3] But the Queen and Bothwell, having gathered together about four or five thousand men, trusting in their force (the Queen being puffed up by flatterers), set forth and marched towards Leith. Being come forward as far as Gladsmuir, she caused public proclamation against the aforesaid Lords, calling them a number of conspirators, and that she now discerned their inward malice against her and her husband, the Duke of Orkney (for so now they called Bothwell).[4] They had endeavoured to appre-

[1] *Diurnal of Occurrents*, 113. Sir James Balfour of Pittendriech, the Clerk-Register, had been made Captain of Edinburgh Castle on 8 May. (*Ibid.*, 111)

[2] See the proclamation in *Reg. Privy Council of Scotland*, i, 520–521

[3] See the comment by Lord Herries, *Memoirs* (Abbotsford Club), 93

[4] Mary had created Bothwell Duke of Orkney on 12 May. (*Diurnal of Occurrents*, 111)

hend her and her husband at Borthwick, and had made a seditious proclamation, under pretence of seeking the revenge of the King her late husband, and to free her from captivity; giving out, that the Duke her husband had a mind to invade the Prince her son; all which was false, for the Duke her husband had used all means to clear himself, both by a legal way and by the offer of a combat to any that did accuse him, as they knew well enough. As touching her captivity, she was in none, but was in company with her husband, unto whom she was publicly married in the view of the world, and many of the Nobles had given their consent unto this her marriage. As for the Prince her son, it was but a specious pretence to the treason and rebellion against her their natural Sovereign and her posterity, which they intended to overthrow; wherefore she declared herself necessitated to take arms, hoping that all her faithful subjects would adhere unto her, and that those who were already assembled with her, would with good hearts and hands stand to her defence; and for the recompense of their valour they should have the lands and goods of these unnatural rebels.[1] After this proclamation, the army went on, and the Queen that night came to Seton, where she lay.

About midnight the Lords of Edinburgh were advertised of the Queen's approach; presently they took arms, and at the sun-rising they were at Musselburgh, where they refreshed themselves with meat and rest. The Queen's camp was not yet stirring. About mid-day the scouts that the Lords had sent out brought word that the enemy was marching towards them; presently they put themselves in two battles; the first was conducted by the Earl Morton and the Lord Home; the second by the Earls Atholl, Glencairn, the Lords Lindsay, Ruthven, Sempill, and Sanquhar,[2] with the Lairds Drumlanrig,[3] Tullibardine,[4] Cessford,[5] and Grange,[6] with divers others. Their number was almost as great as the Queen's, their men better, being many of them expert men—I say nothing of the cause. The Queen had gained a hill called Carberry, which the Lords (by reason of the steepness of the ascent) could not well come at; wherefore they wheeled about to get a more convenient place to go to the hill, where the enemy was, and to have the sun behind them in the time of the fight. At first the Queen, seeing their thus going about,

[1] So also in Spottiswoode's *History*, ii, 59. Specific rewards for the slaying of those who opposed her are stated in *Diurnal of Occurrents*, 115; *Historie of King James the Sext* (Bannatyne Club), 12; and Calderwood, *History*, ii, 362.

[2] Edward, seventh Lord Crichton of Sanquhar

[3] Sir James Douglas of Drumlanrig

[4] Sir William Murray of Tullibardine

[5] Sir Walter Ker of Cessford

[6] Sir William Kirkcaldy of Grange

did imagine they were fleeing away to Dalkeith, but when she saw them come directly towards her, she found herself deceived.

The French Ambassador,[1] seeing them ready to fight, strove to take up the business, and having spoken with the Queen, went to the Lords, telling them, that the Queen was disposed to peace, and to forgive and pardon this insurrection: wherefore it was very fit to spare blood and to agree in a peaceable way. The Earl of Morton (in the name of all the rest) answered that they had taken up arms, not against the Queen, but against the murderer of the King whom, if she would deliver to be punished, or at least put from her company, she should find a continuation of dutiful obedience by them, and all other good subjects; otherwise no peace: besides, we are not to ask pardon for any offence done by us. The Ambassador, seeing their resolution to stand to the right of their cause, withdrew, and went to Edinburgh.

While the French Ambassador was thus labouring for accommodation, Bothwell came out of the camp (which was in the trench that the Englishmen had left at their last being in these places, as we have said in the former Books [2]), well mounted, with a defiance to any that would fight with him. James Murray, brother to the Laird of Tullibardine, who before had accepted of Bothwell's challenge, when he made the rhodomontade at Edinburgh, immediately after the King's death (but then James Murray did not make known his name), [accepted the challenge]. Bothwell refused to fight with James Murray, alleging he was not his equal. Upon this the elder brother, William Murray, Laird of Tullibardine, answered that he would fight with him, as being his better in estate, and in antiquity of house many degrees above him. Yet Bothwell refused him, saying that he was not a Peer of the Kingdom, as he was. Then sundry Lords would have gone to fight with Bothwell; but the Lord Lindsay said to the rest of the Lords and Gentlemen that he would take it as a singular favour of them, and as a recompense of his service done to the State, if they would suffer him to fight with the braggadocio.[3] Bothwell seeing that there was no more subterfuge nor excuse, under-hand made the Queen to forbid him. After this

[1] Philibert du Croe, Sieur du Croc, ambassador 1565–67. Sir James Melville speaks of him as "a graif agit and discret gentilman, advancit be the house of Guise." (*Memoirs*, Bannatyne Club, 181)

[2] The site was that of the Battle of Pinkie (*supra*, i, 98–101).

[3] There are various accounts of this challenge to single combat. (See Sir James Melville's *Memoirs*, Bannatyne Club, 183; Calderwood's *History*, ii, 363–364; George Neilson, *Trial by Combat*, 299–301)

challenge and answers, Bothwell's accomplices and followers were very earnest to fight, but others that had come only for the Queen's sake, became [a] little cold, saying that Bothwell would do well to fight himself, and spare the blood of divers gentlemen that were there. Some counselled to delay the battle till the Hamiltons came, whom they did expect. All this the Queen heard with anger ; and riding up and down, burst out in tears, and said they were all cowards and traitors that would not fight. Immediately after thus vapouring, the Queen, perceiving sundry to leave her, she advised Bothwell to look unto himself, for she said to him, she would render herself unto the Noblemen. Upon this she sent for James Kirkcaldy of Grange, with whom she kept discourse for a while, till that she was assured that Bothwell was out of danger. Then she went to the Lords, whom she did entertain with many fair words, telling them that it was neither fear, nor want of hope of victory, that made her come unto them, but a mere desire to spare shedding of innocent blood : withal she promised to be ruled and advised by them. With this she was received with all respect. But shortly after, declaring that she would go to the Hamiltons, with promise to return, they restrained her liberty, and brought her along with them to Edinburgh at night. She was very slow in marching, looking to be rescued by the Hamiltons ; but in vain. She lay that night in the Provost's house. The next day, the Lords sent the Queen to the Castle that is within an isle of Lochleven.[1] Sir James Balfour, seeing the Queen committed, and Bothwell consequently defeated, he capitulated with the Lords for the delivery of the Castle. Bothwell, finding himself thus in disorder, sent a servant to Sir James Balfour, to save a little silver cabinet which the Queen had given him. Sir James Balfour delivers the cabinet to the messenger, and under-hand giveth advice of it to the Lords. In this cabinet had Bothwell kept the letters of privacy he had from the Queen. Thus he kept her letters, to be an awe-bond upon her, in case her affection should change. By the taking of this cabinet, many particulars betwixt the Queen and Bothwell were clearly discovered. These letters were after printed. They were in French, with some sonnets of her own making.[2]

Note how God changeth things in a moment

[1] Mary surrendered to the Confederate Lords on Sunday 15 June, and was imprisoned in Lochleven on Tuesday 17 June. (See Hay Fleming, *op. cit.*, 164–165 and supporting notes)

[2] For an examination of the whole of the difficult problem of the "Casket Letters," see T. F. Henderson, *Mary Queen of Scots*, and *The Casket Letters and Mary Queen of Scots* ; Andrew Lang, *The Mystery of Mary Stuart* ; and the discussion between those two writers in *Scottish Historical Review*, v, 1–12 ; 160–174

[About this time the Earl Bothwell was declared by open proclamation not only the murderer of the King, but also the committer of it with his own hand ; and a thousand crowns were offered to any man that would bring him in.[1]]

Few days after the commitment of the Queen, the Earl of Glencairn with his domestics went to the Chapel of Holyroodhouse, where he broke down the altars and the images : which fact, as it did content the zealous Protestants, so it did highly offend the Popishly affected.[2] The Nobles, who had so proceeded against Bothwell, and dealt so with the Queen, hearing that the Hamiltons had a great number of men, and had drawn the Earls of Argyll and Huntly to their side, sent to Hamilton, desiring those that were there to join with them, for the redress of the disorders of the Kirk and State. But the Hamiltons, thinking now they had a fair occasion fallen unto them to have all again in their hands, and to dispose of all according to their own mind, did refuse audience to the message sent by the Lords.[3]

Upon this, the Lords moved the General Assembly, then met in Edinburgh, in the month of June, to write to the Lords that either were actually declared for the Hamiltons or were neutrals : and so several letters were directed to the Earls of Argyll, Huntly, Caithness, Rothes, Crawford, and Menteith ; to the Lords Boyd, Drummond, Graham, Cathcart, Yester, Fleming, Livingston, Seton, Glamis, Ochiltree, Gray, Oliphant, Methven, Innermeath, and Somerville, as also to divers other men of note. Besides the letters of the Assembly, commissioners were sent from the Assembly to the Lords abovenamed, to wit, John Knox, John Douglas, John Row, and John Craig, who had instructions conform to the tenor of the letters, to desire these Lords and others, to come to Edinburgh, and join with the Lords there, for the settling of God's true worship in the Church, and Policy reformed according to God's Word, a maintenance for the

[1] *Diurnal of Occurrents*, 116. This paragraph appears in the Edinburgh (1644) edition of the *History*, but not in the London edition of that same year. It may well have been supplied by Calderwood. (*Cf.* Calderwood's *History*, ii, 367)

[2] So also in Spottiswoode's *History*, ii, 62–63. And see Hay Fleming, *The Reformation in Scotland*, 446, *note*

[3] For the Hamiltons were still next in succession to the Crown. On 18 July 1567 Throckmorton wrote to Elizabeth that the Hamiltons would concur with the Confederate Lords " in anye extremytie agaynst the Quene " on the understanding that Darnley's brother would not inherit the Crown should the infant Prince die without issue. (*Calendar of Scottish Papers*, ii, No. 563) And on 20 August, in a letter to Cecil, Throckmorton does not spare his words in his opinion of the Hamiltons. (*Ibid.*, ii, No. 605)

Ministers, and support for the poor.[1] But neither the commissioners nor the letters did prevail with these men ; they excused [themselves], that they could not repair to Edinburgh with freedom, where there were so many armed men, and a garrison so strong.[2] But for the Church affairs they would not be any ways wanting, to do what lay in them.

The Lords at Edinburgh, seeing this, joined absolutely with the Assembly (which had been prorogated to the 20 of July, upon the occasion of these letters and commissioners aforesaid), and promised to make good all the Articles they thought fit to resolve upon in the Assembly. But how they performed their promises, God knows. Always the Articles they agreed upon were these [3] :

1. That the Acts of [the] Parliament held at Edinburgh the 24 of August 1560, touching Religion, and abolishing the Pope's authority, should have the force of a public law ; and consequently this Parliament defended as a lawful Parliament, and confirmed by the first Parliament that should be kept next.[4]

2. That the Thirds of the Tithes, or any more reasonable proportion of Benefices, should be allowed towards the maintenance of the Ministry ; and that there should be a charitable course taken concerning the exacting of the tithes of the poor labourers.

3. That none should be received in the Universities, Colleges, or Schools, for instruction of the youth, but after due trial both of capacity and probity.

4. That all crimes and offences against God should be punished according to God's word ; and that there should be a law made thereanent, at the first Parliament to be held.

5. As for the horrible murder of the late King, husband to the Queen, which was so heinous before God and man, all true professors, in whatsoever rank or condition, did promise to strive that all persons should be brought to condign punishment who are found guilty of the same crime.

6. They all promised to protect the young Prince against all

[1] The General Assembly had met on 25 June 1567, and on 26 June it was "thought good by all the brethren" that a further Assembly should convene on 20 July "for the setting forward of such things as shall at that time be proponed." The Letters sent out to the Earls, Lords, and Barons, and the names of those to whom they were addressed are printed in *Booke of the Universall Kirk*, i, 94–96.

[2] See the "Letters of Excusation" of the Earl of Argyll, of the Commendators of Arbroath and Kilwinning (Lord John Hamilton and Gavin Hamilton), and of Lord Boyd, in *Booke of the Universall Kirk*, i, 101, 102.

[3] The Articles are here given in an abridged form. They are printed in full, together with the names of those who subscribed to them, in *Booke of the Universall Kirk*, i, 106–110.

[4] See *supra*, i, 340–343

violence, lest he should be murdered as his father was ; and that the Prince should be committed to the care of four wise and godly men, that by a good education he might be fitted for that high calling he was to execute one day.

7. The Nobles, Barons, and others, doth promise to beat down and abolish Popery, idolatry, and superstition, with anything that may contribute unto it ; as also to set up and further the true worship of God, his government, the Church, and all that may concern the purity of Religion and life ; and for this to convene and take arms, if need require.

8. That all princes and kings hereafter in this Realm, before their coronation, shall take oath to maintain the true Religion now professed in the Church of Scotland, and suppress all things contrary to it, and that are not agreeing with it.

To these Articles subscribed the Earls of Morton, Glencairn, and Mar, the Lords Home, Ruthven, Sanquhar, Lindsay, Graham, Innermeath, and Ochiltree, with many other Barons, besides the Commissioners of the Burghs.[1]

This being agreed upon, the Assembly dissolved. Thereafter the Lords Lindsay and Ruthven were sent to Lochleven to the Queen, to present unto her two writs. The one contained a renunciation of the Crown and royal dignity in favour of the Prince her son ; with a Commission to invest him into the Kingdom, according to the manner accustomed. Which, after some reluctance, with tears, she subscribed by the advice of the Earl of Atholl, who had sent to her, and of Secretary Lethington, who had sent to her Robert Melville for that purpose. So there was a procuration given to the Lords Lindsay and Ruthven by the Queen, to give up and resign the rule of the Realm, in presence of the States.

The second writ was, to ordain the Earl of Moray Regent during the Prince's minority, if he would accept the charge. And in case he refused, the Duke [of] Châtelherault, the Earls of Lennox, Argyll, Atholl, Morton, Glencairn, and Mar should govern conjunctly.[2]

[1] See the names of the subscribers, numbering in all seventy-seven, printed in *Booke of the Universall Kirk*, i, 110.

[2] Actually there were three writs. The second writ appointed Moray to act as Regent until the Prince was seventeen ; and the third writ appointed Châtelherault, Lennox, Argyll, Atholl, Morton, Glencairn, and Mar to act as Regents until Moray's return, or to act in case of his death, or to act with him if he refused to accept the office of Regent singly. All three documents are dated 24 July 1567, the date of Mary's signature at Lochleven, under her Privy Seal. All three are printed in *Reg. Privy Council of Scotland*, i, 531–533, 539–541. For an analysis of the evidence relating to the pressure brought to bear upon the Queen and of the conditions under which she signed, see Hay Fleming, *Mary Queen of Scots*, 474, *note* 68.

These writs were published the 29 of July 1567, at the Market Cross of Edinburgh. Then at Stirling was the Prince crowned King, where John Knox made the sermon. The Earl Morton and the Lord Home took the oath for the King, that he should constantly live in the profession of the true Religion, and maintain it; and that he should govern the Kingdom according to [the] law thereof, and do justice equally to all.[1]

In the beginning of August the Earl Moray, being sent for, cometh home. In all haste he visits the Queen at Lochleven, and strives to draw the Lords that had taken part with the Hamiltons, or were neutrals, to join with those that had bound themselves to stand for the King's authority. He was very earnest with divers, by reason of their old friendship, but to little purpose. The twentieth of August, he received his Regency, after mature and ripe deliberation, at the desire of the Queen, and Lords that were for the King, and so was publicly proclaimed Regent, and obedience showed unto him by all that stood for the young King.[2]

[1] See *Reg. Privy Council of Scotland*, i, 537–542, where only the Earl of Morton takes the oath in name and upon the behalf of the infant King.

[2] Moray, after an absence of four months, reached Edinburgh 11 August 1567; on 15 and 16 August he had long interviews with Mary at Lochleven; and on 22 August he was proclaimed Regent. In the Parliament which met in December 1567, Mary's demission of the Government was declared "lawful and perfect"; the Prince's coronation and investiture were held to be as valid as those of any of his predecessors; Moray's appointment as Regent was confirmed; and the Acts of the "Reformation Parliament" of 1560 were ratified and approved together with the "Confession of the Faith and Doctrine believed and professed by the Protestants of the Realm of Scotland".

THE END OF THE HISTORY OF THE CHURCH OF SCOTLAND, TILL THE YEAR 1567, AND MONTH OF AUGUST

APPENDICES

APPENDIX I

"PATRICK'S PLACES"[1]

Now that all men may understand what was the singular erudition and godly knowledge of the said Mr. Patrick, we have inserted this little pithy work containing his Assertions and Determinations concerning the Law, and the Office of the same; concerning Faith, and the fruits thereof—first by the foresaid Master Patrick collected in Latin, and after translated in English.

A BRIEF TREATISE OF MR. PATRICK HAMILTON, CALLED PATRICK'S PLACES, TRANSLATED INTO ENGLISH BY JOHN FRITH; WITH THE EPISTLE OF THE SAID FRITH PREFIXED BEFORE THE SAME, AS FOLLOWETH:[2]

JOHN FRITH UNTO THE CHRISTIAN READER[3]

Blessed be God, the Father of our Lord Jesus Christ, which in these last and perilous times, hath stirred up, in all countries, witnesses unto his Son, to testify the truth unto the unfaithful, to save at the least some from the snares of Antichrist, which lead unto perdition, as ye may here perceive by that excellent and well-learned young man, Patrick [Hamilton], born in Scotland of a noble progeny; who, to testify the truth, sought all means, and took upon him priesthood (even as Paul circumcised Timothy to win the weak Jews), that he might be admitted to preach the pure word of God. Notwithstanding, as soon as the Chamberlain [Chancellor[4]], and other Bishops of Scotland, had perceived that the light began to spring which disclosed their falsehood that they convey in darkness, they laid hands on him, and because he would not deny his Saviour Christ, at their instance, they burnt him to ashes. Nevertheless, God of his bounteous mercy (to publish unto the whole world what a man the monsters have murdered), hath reserved a little Treatise, made by this Patrick, which, if ye list, ye may call PATRICK'S PLACES (for it entreateth exactly of certain common places); which known, ye have the pith of all Divinity. This Treatise have I turned into the English tongue, to the profit of my nation; to whom I beseech God give light, that they may espy the deceitful paths of perdition, and return to the right way which leadeth unto life everlasting. Amen.

[1] In the manuscript this treatise follows immediately upon the description of the martyrdom of Patrick Hamilton (*supra*, i, 14).

[2] This title, and Frith's Preface, are not given by Knox, but are here given for clarity. The title has been taken from Foxe's *Acts and Monuments* (London, 1631), ii, 229*a*.

[3] Frith's Preface has been taken from the original work in *Dyvers Frutful Gatheringes of Scrypture concernyng Fayth and Workes* (London, ? 1532)

[4] Evidently James Beaton, Archbishop of St. Andrews

PATRICK'S PLACES

[The Doctrine] [1] of the Law

The Law is a doctrine that biddeth good, and forbiddeth evil, as the Commandments here contained do specify :

The Ten Commandments

1 Thou shalt worship but one God. 2 Thou shalt make thee none image to worship it. 3 Thou shalt not swear by his name in vain. 4 Hold the Sabbath day holy. 5 Honour thy father and mother. 6 Thou shalt not kill. 7 Thou shalt not commit adultery. 8 Thou shalt not steal. 9 Thou shalt bear no false witness. 10 Thou shalt not desire aught that belongeth unto thy neighbour.

[All these Commandments are briefly comprised in these two hereunder ensuing] :—" Love the Lord thy God with all thine heart, with all thy soul, and with all thy mind " (Deut 6.).—" This is the first and great commandment. The second is like unto this, Love thy neighbour as thy self. On these two commandments hang all the Law and the Prophets " (Matt. 12.).

[Certain General Propositions proved by the Scripture]

I He that loveth God, loveth his neighbour.—" If any man say, I love God, and yet hateth his neighbour, he is a liar : He that loveth not his brother whom he hath seen, how can he love God whom he hath not seen ? " (1 John 4).

II He that loveth his neighbour as himself, keepeth the whole commandments of God.—" Whatsoever ye would that men should do unto you, even so do unto them : for this is the law and the prophets " (Matt. 7). He that loveth his neighbour fulfilleth the law. " Thou shalt not commit adultery : Thou shalt not kill : Thou shalt not steal : Thou shalt not bear false witness against thy neighbour : Thou shalt not desire ; and so forth. And if there be any other commandment, all are comprehended under this saying, Love thy neighbour as thyself." [All the Law is fulfilled in one word ; that is, love thy neighbour as thyself.] (Rom. 13 ; Gal. 5).

" He that loveth his neighbour, keepeth all the commandments of God." "He that loveth God, loveth his neighbour" (Rom. 13; 1 John 4). Ergo, he that loveth God, keepeth all his commandments.

[1] In all cases the words included within brackets have been supplied from Foxe's *Acts and Monuments* (London, 1631), ii, 229–233. Minor variations in phraseology have not been indicated.

III He that hath the faith, loveth God.—" My father loveth you, because ye love me, and believe that I came of God " (John 19). He that hath the faith keepeth all the commandments of God. He that hath the faith, loveth God ; and he that loveth God, keepeth all the commandments of God.—Ergo, he that hath faith, keepeth all the commandments of God.

IV He that keepeth one commandment, keepeth them all.—" For without faith it is impossible to keep any of the commandments of God." —And he that hath the faith, keepeth all the commandments of God.— Ergo, he that keepeth one commandment of God, keepeth them all.

V He that keepeth not all the commandments of God, he keepeth none of them.—He that keepeth one of the commandments, he keepeth all.—Ergo, he that keepeth not all the commandments, he keepeth none of them.

VI It is not in our power, without grace, to keep any of God's commandments.—Without grace it is impossible to keep one of God's commandments ; and grace is not in our power.—Ergo, it is not in our power to keep any of the commandments of God.

Even so may ye reason concerning the Holy Ghost, and faith : [Forsomuch as neither without them we are able to keep any of the commandments of God, neither yet be they in our power to have.]

VII The law was given to show us our sin.—" By the law cometh the knowledge of the sin. I knew not what sin meant, but through the law. I knew not what lust had meant, except the law had said, Thou shalt not lust. Without the law, sin was dead " : that is, It moved me not, neither wist I that it was sin, which notwithstanding was sin, and forbidden by the law.

VIII The law biddeth us do that which is impossible for us.—For it biddeth us keep all the commandments of God : yet it is not in our power to keep any of them.—Ergo, it biddeth us do that which is impossible for us.

Thou wilt say, " Wherefore doth God command us that which is impossible for us." I answer, " To make thee know that thou art but evil, and that there is no remedy to save thee in thine own hand, and that thou mayest seek remedy at some other ; for the law doeth nothing but command thee."

[The Doctrine] of the Gospel

The Gospel is as much to say, in our tongue, as Good Tidings : like as every one of these sentences be—

Christ is the Saviour of the world.
Christ is our Saviour.
Christ died for us.
Christ died for our sins.
Christ offered himself for us.
Christ bore our sins upon his back.
Christ bought us with his blood.
Christ washed us with his blood.

Christ came in the world to save sinners.
Christ came in the world to take away our sins.
Christ was the price that was given for us and for our sins.
Christ was made debtor for our sins.
Christ hath paid our debt, for He died for us.
Christ hath made satisfaction for us and for our sin.
Christ is our righteousness.
Christ is our wisdom.
Christ is our sanctification.
Christ is our redemption.
Christ is our satisfaction.
[Christ is our peace.]
Christ is our goodness.
Christ hath pacified the Father of Heaven.
Christ is ours, and all his.
Christ hath delivered us from the law, from the devil, and hell.
The Father of Heaven hath forgiven us for Christ's sake. Or any such other, as declare unto us the mercies of God.

The Nature [and Office] of the Law, and of the Gospel

The Law showeth us,
Our sin.
Our condemnation:
Is the word of ire.
Is the word of despair.
Is the word of displeasure.

The Gospel showeth us,
A remedy for it.
Our redemption:
Is the word of grace.
Is the word of comfort.
Is the word of peace.

A Disputation betwixt the Law and the Gospel; [Where is showed the Difference or Contrariety between them Both]

The Law sayeth,
Pay thy debt.
Thou art a sinner desperate.
And thou shalt die.

The Gospel sayeth,
Christ hath paid it.
Thy sins are forgiven thee.
Be of good comfort, thou shalt be saved.

The Law sayeth,
Make amends for thy sin.
The Father of Heaven is wrath with thee.
Where is thy righteousness, goodness, and satisfaction ?
Thou art bound and obligate unto me, [to] the devil, and [to] hell.

The Gospel sayeth,
Christ hath made it for thee.
Christ hath pacified Him with his blood.
Christ is thy righteousness, thy goodness, and satisfaction.
Christ hath delivered thee from them all.

[The Doctrine] of Faith

Faith is to believe God ; " Like as Abraham believed God, and it was accounted unto him for righteousness " (Gen. 15). " He that believed God, believed his word " (John 5). To believe in Him, is to believe his word, and account it true that He speaketh. He that believeth not God's word, believeth not Himself. He that believeth not God's word, he accounteth Him false, and a liar, and believeth not that He may and will fulfil his word ; and so he denieth both the might of God and [God] himself.

IX Faith is the gift of God.—" Every good thing is the gift of God " (James 1). Faith is good.—Ergo, faith is the gift of God.

X [Faith is not in our power.]—The gift of God is not in our power.—" Faith is the gift of God."—Ergo, faith is not in our power.

XI [He that lacketh faith cannot please God.]—" Without faith it is impossible to please God " (Heb. 11). All that cometh not of faith, is sin ; for without faith can no man please God.—Besides that, he that lacketh faith, he trusteth not God. He that trusteth not God, trusteth not in his word. He that trusteth not in his word, holdeth Him false, and a liar. He that holdeth Him false and a liar, he believeth not that He may do that He promiseth, and so denieth he that He is God. And how can a man, being of this fashion, please Him ? No manner of way. Yea, suppose he did all the works of man and angel.

XII All that is done in faith, pleaseth God.—" Right is the word of God, and all his works in faith." " Lord, thine eyes look to faith." That is as much to say as, Lord, Thou delightest in faith. God loveth him that believeth in Him. How can they then displease Him ?

XIII He that hath the faith, is just and good.—And a good tree bringeth forth good fruit.—Ergo, all that is in faith done pleaseth God.[1]

XIV [He that hath faith, and believeth God, cannot displease him.] —Moreover, he that hath the faith believeth God.—He that believeth God, believeth his word. He that believeth his word, woteth [2] well that He is true and faithful, and may not lie : But knoweth well that He may

[1] In Foxe, this argument runs : He that is a good tree bringing forth good fruit, is just and good.—He that hath faith is a good tree bringing forth good fruit.—Ergo, he that hath faith is just and good.

[2] *knoweth*

and will both fulfil his word. How can he then displease Him? For thou canst not do a greater honour unto God, than to count Him true. Thou wilt then say, that theft, murder, adultery, and all vices, please God? None, verily; for they cannot be done in faith: " For a good tree beareth good fruit." He that hath the faith, woteth [1] well that he pleaseth God; for all that is done in faith pleaseth God (Heb. 11).

XV Faith is a sureness.—" Faith is a sure confidence of things which are hoped for, and a certainty of things which are not seen" (Heb. 11). " The same spirit certifieth our spirit that we are the children of God" (Rom. 8). Moreover, he that hath the faith, woteth well that God will fulfil his word.—Ergo, faith is a sureness.

A Man is Justified by Faith

" Abraham believeth God, and it was imputed unto him for righteousness." " We suppose therefore that a man is justified (saith the Apostle) without the works of law" (Rom. 4). " He that worketh not, but believeth in him that justifieth the ungodly, his faith is accounted unto him for righteousness." "The just man liveth by faith" (Habak. 2; Rom. 1). " We wote, that a man that is justified, is not justified by the works of the law, but by the faith of Jesus Christ [and we believe in Jesus Christ that we may be justified by the faith of Christ], and not by the deeds of the law."

Of the Faith of Christ

The faith of Christ is, to believe in Him; that is, to believe his word, and to believe that He will help thee in all thy need, and deliver thee from evil. Thou wilt ask me, What word? I answer, The Gospel. " He that believeth on Christ shall be saved." " He that believeth the Son hath eternal life." " Verily, verily, I say unto you, he that believeth on me hath everlasting life" (John 6). " This I write unto you, that believing in the name of the Son of God, ye may know that ye have eternal life" (1 John 5). " Thomas, because thou hast seen me thou believest; but happy are they that have not seen, and yet believe in me." " All the Prophets to him bare witness that whosoever believeth in Him shall have remission of their sins" (Acts 10). " What must I do that I may be saved?" The Apostle answered, " Believe in the Lord Jesus Christ, and thou shalt be saved." " If thou acknowledge with the mouth, that Jesus is the Lord, and believe in thine heart that God raised Him up from the death, thou shalt be saved" (Rom. 10). " He that believeth not in Christ shall be condemned." " He that believeth not the Son shall never see life; but the ire of God abideth upon him" (John 3). " The Holy Ghost shall reprove the world of sin, because they believe not in me." " They that believe in Jesus Christ are the sons of God." Ye are all the sons of God, because ye believe in Jesus Christ.

He that believeth in Christ the Son of God is saved (Gal. 3). " Peter said, Thou art Christ, the Son of the living God. Jesus answered and said

[1] *knoweth*

unto him, Happy art thou, Simon, the son of Jonas; for flesh and blood hath not opened unto thee that, but my Father which is in heaven" (Matt. 16). "We have believed and know that thou art Christ the Son of the living God." "I believe that thou art Christ the Son of the living God, which should come into the world." "These things are written that ye might believe that Jesus Christ is the Son of God, and that in believing ye might have life. I believe that Jesus is the Son of the living God" (John 9).

XVI He that believeth God, believeth the Gospel.[1]—He that believeth God, believeth his Word:—And the Gospel is his Word. Therefore he that believeth God, believeth his Gospel. As Christ is the Saviour of the world, Christ is our Saviour. Christ bought us with his blood. Christ washed us with his blood. Christ offered himself for us. Christ bore our sins upon his back.

XVII He that believeth not the Gospel, believeth not God.—He that believeth not God's Word believeth not [God] himself:—And the Gospel is God's Word.—Ergo, he that believeth not the Gospel believeth not God himself; and consequently they that believe not as is above written, and such other, believe not God.

XVIII He that believeth the Gospel, shall be saved.—"Go ye into all the world and preach the Gospel unto every creature: He that believeth and is baptised shall be saved; but he that believeth not shall be condemned."

A Comparison Betwix Faith and Incredulity

Faith is the root of all good:—
Maketh God and man friends.
Bringeth God and man together.

Incredulity is the root of all evil:—
Maketh them deadly foes.
Bringeth them sunder.

All that proceeds from Faith pleaseth God.
All that proceedeth from Incredulity displeaseth God.

Faith only maketh a man good and righteous.
Incredulity maketh him unjust and evil.

Faith only maketh a man,
The member of Christ;
The inheritor of heaven;
The servant of God.
Faith showeth God to be a sweet Father.
Faith holdeth stiff by the Word of God: Counteth God to be true.
Faith knoweth God: Loveth God and his neighbour.
Faith only saveth: Extolleth God and his works.

[1] In Foxe, this proposition is inverted: He that believeth the Gospel, believeth God.

Incredulity maketh him,

The member of the devil;

The inheritor of hell;

The servant of the devil.

Incredulity maketh God a terrible Judge: It causeth man wander here and there: Maketh him false and a liar.

Incredulity knoweth Him not.

Incredulity loveth neither God nor neighbour: Only condemneth: Extolleth flesh and her own deeds.

Of Hope

Hope is a trusty looking for of things that are promised to come unto us: as we hope the everlasting joy which Christ hath promised unto all that believe on Him. We should put our hope and trust in God only, and no other thing. "It is good to trust in God, and not in man." "He that trusteth in his own heart, he is a fool." "It is good to trust in God, and not in princes" (Ps. 117). "They shall be like unto images that make them, and all that trust in them." He that trusteth in his own thoughts doeth ungodly. "Cursed be he that trusteth in man." "Bid the rich men of this world, that they trust not in their unstable riches, but that they trust in the living God." "It is hard for them that trust in money to enter in the kingdom of God." Moreover, we should trust in him only, that may help us: [God only may help us.]—Ergo, we should trust in Him only. Well is them that trust in God: and woe to them that trust Him not. "Well is the man that trusts in God; for God shall be his trust." He that trusteth in Him shall understand the truth. "They shall all rejoice that trust in Thee: they shall all ever be glad; and Thou wilt defend them."

Of Charity

Charity is the love of thy neighbour. The rule of charity is to do as thou wouldst were done unto thee: for charity [1] esteemeth all alike; the rich and the poor; the friend and the foe; the thankful and the unthankful; the kinsman and stranger.

A Comparison Betwix Faith, Hope, and Charity

Faith cometh of the word of God: Hope cometh of faith; and Charity springs of them both.

Faith believes the word: Hope trusteth after that which is promised by the word: and Charity doeth good unto her neighbour, through the love that she hath to God, and gladness that is within herself.

Faith looketh to God and his word: Hope looketh unto his gift and reward: Charity looketh unto her neighbours' profit.

Faith receiveth God: Hope receiveth his reward: Charity looketh

[1] In Foxe, *for Christ*

to her neighbour with a glad heart, and that without any respect of reward.

Faith pertaineth to God only : Hope to his reward, and Charity to her neighbour.

[The Doctrine] of Good Works

No manner of works make us righteous.—" We believe that a man shall be justified without works " (Gal. 3). " No man is justified by the deeds of the law ; but by the faith of Jesus Christ. And we believe in Jesus Christ, that we may be justified by the faith of Christ, and not by the deeds of the law. If righteousness came by the law, then Christ died in vain." That no man is justified by the law, it is manifest : for a righteous man liveth by his faith ; but the law is not of faith. Moreover, since Christ, the maker of heaven and earth, and all that therein is, behoved to die for us, we are compelled to grant, that we were so far drowned in sin, that neither our deeds, nor all the treasures that ever God made, or might make, might have helped us out of it : Ergo, no deeds nor works may make us righteous.

No works make us unrighteous.—For if any [evil] works made us unrighteous, then the contrary works would make us righteous. But it is proven, that no works can make us righteous : Ergo, no works make us unrighteous.

Works Make Us neither Good nor Evil

It is proven, that works neither make us righteous nor unrighteous : Ergo, no works neither make us good nor evil. For righteous and good are one thing, and unrighteous and evil, one. Good works make not a good man, nor evil works an evil man : But a good man maketh good works, and an evil man evil works. Good fruit maketh not the tree good, nor evil fruit the tree evil : But a good tree beareth good fruit, and an evil tree evil fruit. A good man cannot do evil works, nor an evil man good works ; for an evil tree cannot bear good fruit, nor a good tree evil fruit. A man is good before he do good works, and an evil man is evil before he do evil works ; for the tree is good before it bear good fruit, and evil before it bear evil fruit. Every man is either good or evil. [Every tree, and the fruits thereof, are either good or evil.] Either make the tree good, and the fruit gòod also, or else make the tree evil, and the fruit likewise evil. Every man's works are either good or evil : for all fruits are either good or evil. " Either make the tree good and the fruit also, or else make the tree evil and the fruit of it likewise evil " (Matt. 13). A good man is known by his works ; for a good man doeth good works, and an evil, evil works. " Ye shall know them by their fruit ; for a good tree bringeth forth good fruit, and an evil tree evil fruit " (Matt. 7). A man is likened to the tree, and his works to the fruit of the tree. " Beware of the false prophets, which come unto you in sheep's clothing ; but inwardly they are ravening wolves. Ye shall know them by their fruits."

None of Our Works neither Save Us, nor Condemn Us

It is proven, that no works make us either righteous or unrighteous, good nor evil : but first we are good before that we do good works, and evil before we do evil works : Ergo, no works neither save us nor condemn us. Thou wilt say then, Maketh it no matter what we do ? I answer thee, Yes ; for if thou doest evil, it is a sure argument that thou art evil, and wantest faith. If thou do good, it is an argument that thou art good and hast faith ; for a good tree beareth good fruit, and an evil tree evil fruit. Yet good fruit maketh not the tree good, nor evil fruit the tree evil. So that man is good before he do good works, and evil before he do evil works.

The man is the tree : the works are the fruit. Faith maketh the good tree : Incredulity the evil tree. Such a tree, such a fruit : such man, such works. For all that is done in faith pleaseth God, and are good works ; and all that is done without faith displeaseth God, and are evil works. Whosoever thinketh to be saved by his works, denieth Christ is our Saviour, that Christ died for him, and, finally, all things that belongeth to Christ. For how is He thy Saviour, if thou mightest save thy self by thy works ? Or to what end should He have died for thee, if any works of thine might have saved thee ? What is this to say, Christ died for thee ? It is that thou shouldest have died perpetually, and that Christ, to deliver thee from death, died for thee, and changed thy perpetual death in his own death. For thou made the fault, and He suffered the pain, and that for the love He had to thee, before ever thou wert born, when thou hadst done neither good nor evil. Now, since He hath paid thy debt, thou diest not : no, thou canst not, but shouldst have been damned, if his death were not.[1] But since He was punished for thee, thou shalt not be punished. Finally, He hath delivered thee from thy condemnation, and desireth nought of thee, but that thou shouldst acknowledge what He hath done for thee, and bear it in mind ; and that thou wouldst help others for his sake, both in word and deed, even as He hath helped thee for nought, and without reward. O how ready would we be to help others, if we knew his goodness and gentleness towards us ! He is a good and a gentle Lord, and He doeth all things for nought. Let us, I beseech you, follow his footsteps, whom all the world ought to praise and worship. Amen.

He that Thinketh to be Saved by His Works, Calleth Himself Christ

For he calleth himself a Saviour, which appertaineth to Christ only. What is a Saviour, but he that saveth ? And thou sayest, I save myself ; which is as much to say as, I am Christ ; for Christ is only the Saviour of the world.

We should do no good works for that intent to get the inheritance of

[1] Foxe gives this sentence : " Now, seeing He hath paid thy debt, thou needest not, neither canst thou pay it, but shouldst be damned, if his blood were not."

heaven, or remission of sins through them. For whosoever believeth to get the inheritance of heaven or remission of sins, through works, he believeth not to get that for Christ's sake. And they that believe not, that their sins are forgiven them, and that they shall be saved for Christ's sake, they believe not the Gospel ; for the Gospel sayeth, You shall be saved for Christ's sake : sins are forgiven you, for Christ's sake.

He that believeth not the Gospel, believeth not God. And consequently, they which believe to be saved by their works, or to get remission of sins by their own deeds, believe not God, but account Him a liar, and so utterly deny Him to be God. Thou wilt say, Shall we then do no good works ? I say not so, but I say, We should do no good works for that intent to get the kingdom of heaven, or remission of sins. For if we believe to get the inheritance of heaven through good works, then we believe not to get it through the promise of God. Or, if we think to get remission of our sins, as said is, we believe not that they are forgiven us by Christ, and so we account God a liar. For God sayeth, Thou shalt have the inheritance of heaven for my Son's sake. You say, It is not so ; but I will win it through my own works. So, I condemn not good works ; but I condemn the false trust in any works ; for all the works that a man putteth confidence in, are therewith intoxicate or empoisoned, and become evil. Wherefore, do good works ; but beware thou do them to get any good through them ; for if thou do, thou receivest the good, not as the gift of God, but as debt unto thee, and makest thyself fellow with God, because thou wilt take nothing from Him for nought. What needeth He anything of thine, who giveth all things, and is not the poorer ? Therefore do nothing to Him but take of Him ; for He is a gentle Lord, and with a gladder heart will give us all things that we need, than we take it of Him. So that if we want anything, let us wit [1] ourselves. Press not then to the inheritance of heaven, through presumption of thy good works ; for if thou do, thou accountest thyself holy and equal unto Him, because thou wilt take nothing of Him for nought ; and so shalt thou fall as Lucifer fell from heaven for his pride.

Thus ends the said Master Patrick's Articles. And so we return to our History.[2]

[1] *wite*, that is, *blame* [2] That is, *supra*, i, 15

APPENDIX II

ALEXANDER SETON'S LETTER TO KING JAMES V[1]

Most Gracious and Sovereign Lord under the Lord and King of all ; of whom only thy Highness and Majesty has power and authority to exercise justice within this thy Realm, under God, who is King and Lord of all thy realms, and thy Grace and all mortal kings are but only servants unto that only immortal Prince Christ Jesus, etc. It is not (I wate [2]) unknown to thy gracious Highness, how that thy Grace's umquhile servant and orator [3] (and ever shall be to my life's end), is departed out of thy Realm unto the next adjacent of England. None the less I believe the cause of my departing is unknown to thy gracious Majesty : which only is, because the Bishops and Kirkmen of thy Realm has had heretofore such authority upon thy subjects, that apparently they were rather King, and thou the subject (which unjust regiment is of the self false, and contrary to holy Scripture and law of God), than thou their King and master, and they thy subjects (which is very true, and testified expressly by the Word of God). And also, because they will give no man of any degree or state (whom they oft falsely call Heretics) audience, time, nor place to speak and have defence ; which is against all law, both the Old law, called the Law of Moses, and the New law of the Evangel. So that, if I might have had audience and place to speak, and have shown my just defence, conform to the law of God, I should never have fled to any other realm, suppose it should have cost me my life. But because I believed that I should have had no audience nor place to answer (they are so great with thy Grace), I departed, not doubting, but moved of God, unto a better time that God illuminate thy Grace's eyn [4] to give every man audience (as thou should and may, and is bound of the law of God), who are accused to the death. And to certify thy Highness that these are no vain words, but of deed and effect, here I offer me to thy Grace to come in thy realm again, so that thy Grace will give me audience, and hear what I have for me of the law of God : and cause any Bishop or Abbot, Friar or Secular, which is most cunning [5] (some of them can not read their matins who are made judges in heresy !) to impugn me by the law of God ; and if my part be found wrong, thy Grace being present and judge, I refuse no pain worthy or condign for my fault. And if that I convict them by the law of God, and that they have nothing to lay to my charge, but the law of man, and their own inventions to uphold their vain glory and prideful life, and daily scourging of thy poor lieges ; I report me to thy Grace, as judge, Whether he has the victory that holds him at the law of

[1] From *supra*, i, 21 [2] *know*
[3] Probably here used in the sense of *petitioner* [4] *eyes*
[5] *knowledgeable*

God, which cannot fail nor be false, or they that holds them at the law of man, which is right oft plain contrary and against the law of God, and therefore of necessity false, and full of lesings [1]? For all thing that is contrary to the verity (which is Christ and his law), is of necessity lesing.

And to witness that this comes of all my heart, I shall remain in Berwick while I get thy Grace's answer, and shall without fail return, having thy hand writ that I may have audience, and place to speak. No more I desire of thee ; whereof if I had been sure, I should never have departed. And that thou may know the truth thereof : if fear of the justness of my cause, or dredour of persecution for the same, had moved me to depart, I would not so pleasingly revert [2] ; only distrust therefore was the cause of my departing. Pardon me to say that which lies to thy Grace's charge. Thou art bound by the law of God (suppose they falsely lie, saying it pertains not to thy Grace to intromett [3] with such matters), to cause every man, in any case, accused of his life, to have his just defence, and his accusers produced conform to their own law. They blind thy Grace's eyn, that knows nothing of their law : but if I prove not this out of their own law, I offer me to the death. Thy Grace, therefore, by experience may daily learn (seeing they neither fear the King of Heaven, as their lives testify, neither thee their natural Prince, as their usurped power in thy actions shows), why thy Highness should lie no longer blinded. Thou may consider, that they pretend nothing else but only the maintenance and upholding of their barded mulls,[4] augmenting of their insatiable avarice, and continual down-thringing [5] and swallowing up thy poor lieges ; neither preaching nor teaching out of the law of God, (as they should), to the rude, ignorant people, but aye contending who may be most high, most rich, and nearest thy Grace, to put the temporal Lords and lieges out of thy council and favour, who should be, and are, most tender servants to thy Grace in all time of need, to the defence of thee and thy crown.

And where they desire thy Grace to put at [6] thy temporal Lords and lieges, because they despise their vicious lives, what else intend they but only thy death and destruction ? As thou may easily perceive, suppose they colour [7] their false intent and mind with the pursuit of heresy. For when thy barons are put down, what art thou but the King of Bean [8] ? And then of necessity must [thou] be guided by them : and there (no doubt), where a blind man is guide, must [there] be a fall in the mire. Therefore let thy Grace take hardiment [9] and authority, which thou has of God, and suffer not their cruel persecution to proceed, without audience giving to him that is accused, and just place of defence. And then (no doubt), thou shalt have thy lieges' hearts, and all that they can or may do in time of need ; tranquillity, justice, and policy in thy realm, and finally,

[1] *lies* ; *falsehoods* [2] *willingly return* [3] *to intermeddle*

[4] Probably *richly caparisoned mules*. The *bardit* horse was armoured—see the interesting letter in *Letters and Papers, Henry VIII*, xix, i, No. 713. [5] *destruction* ; *downcasting*

[6] *to exert his power against* [7] *camouflage*

[8] *King of the Bean* : a mock-king, chosen on the Vigil of the Epiphany (which is sometimes called the King's Even, as *supra*, i, 110) ; similar to the *Lord of Misrule*, etc. (See the explanation in Jamieson's *Scottish Dictionary*, s.v. *Bane*) [9] *boldness*

the kingdom of the heavens. Please to gar [1] have this, or the copy, to the clergy and kirkmen, and keep the principal, and thy Grace shall have experience if I go against one word that I have hecht.[2] I shall daily make my heartly devotion for thy Grace, and for the prosperity and welfare of thy body and soul. I doubt not but thy gracious Highness will give answer to these presents unto the presenter of this to thy Highness. Of Berwick, by thy Highness's servant and orator,

(*Sic subscribitur*)
ALEXANDER SETON.

This letter was delivered to the King's own hands, and of many read. But what could greatly [3] admonitions avail, where the pride and corruption of prelates commanded what they pleased, and the flattery of courtiers fostered the insolent Prince in all impiety.

[1] *cause* [2] *promised* [3] *weighty*

APPENDIX III

THE CONDEMNATION AND MARTYRDOM OF GEORGE WISHART [1]

UPON the last of February, was sent to the prison, where the servant of God lay, the Dean of the town, by the commandment of the Cardinal and his wicked council, and they summoned the said Master George that he should, upon the morn following, appear before the Judge then and there to give account of his seditious and heretical doctrine. To whom the said Master George answered, "What needeth (said he), my Lord Cardinal to summon me to answer for my doctrine openly before him, under whose power and dominion I am thus straitly bound in irons? May not my Lord compel me to answer to his extorte [2] power? Or believeth he that I am unprovided to render account of my doctrine? To manifest yourselves what men ye are, it is well done that ye keep your old ceremonies and constitutions made by men."

Upon the next morn, my Lord Cardinal caused his servants to dress themselves in their most warlike array, with jack, knapscall,[3] splint,[4] spear, and axe, more seeming for the war than for the preaching of the true word of God. And when these armed champions, marching in warlike order, had conveyed the Bishops unto the Abbey Church, incontinently they sent for Master George, who was conveyed unto the said Church by the Captain of the Castle, and the number of an hundred men, dressed in manner foresaid, like a lamb led they him to sacrifice. As he entered in at the Abbey Church door, there was a poor man lying vexed with great infirmities, asking of his almous,[5] to whom he flung his purse. And when he came before the Cardinal, by and by the Subprior of the Abbey, called Dean John Winram, stood up in the pulpit, and made a sermon to all the congregation there then assembled, taking his matter out of the xiii chapter of Matthew; whose sermon was divided into four principal parts. The First, was a short and brief declaration of the Evangelist. The Second, of the interpretation of the good seed; and because he called the Word of God the good seed, and Heresy the evil seed, he declared what Heresy was, and how it should be known. He defined it on this manner: "Heresy is a false opinion, defended with pertinacity, clearly repugning to the word of God." The Third part of his sermon was, the cause of Heresy within that realm, and all other realms. "The cause of Heresy (quod he), is the ignorance of them which have the cure of men's souls, to whom it necessarily belongeth to have the true understanding of the word of God, that they may be able to win against the false doctors of heresies, with the sword of the Spirit, which is the word

Bona hæresoes definitio

[1] See *supra*, i, 74, *note* 6
[2] *extortionate*
[3] *headpiece*
[4] *leg-armour*
[5] *alms*

of God ; and not only to win against, but also to overcome :—as saith Paul, ' A bishop must be faultless, as becometh the minister of God, not stubborn, not angry, no drunkard, no fighter, not given to filthy lucre ; but harberous,[1] one that loveth goodness, sober minded, righteous, holy, temperate, and such as cleaveth unto the true word of the doctrine, that he may be able to exhort with wholesome learning, and to improve that which they say against him.' " The Fourth part of his sermon was, how Heresies should be known. " Heresies (quod he) be known on this manner : As the goldsmith knoweth the fine gold from the imperfect, by the touchstone, so likewise may we know heresy by the undoubted touchstone, that is, the true, sincere, and undefiled word of God." At the last, he added, " That heretics should be put down in this present life : To the which proposition the Gospel appeared to repugn which he entreated of, ' Let them both grow unto the harvest ' : The harvest is the end of the world ; nevertheless, he affirmed that they should be put down by the Civil Magistrate and law."

And when he ended his Sermon, incontinent they caused Master George to ascend into the pulpit, there to hear his Accusation and Articles. For right against him stood up one of the fed flock,[2] a monster, John Lauder,[3] laden full of cursings, written in paper, of the which he took out a roll both long and also full of cursings, threatenings, maledictions, and words of devilish spite and malice, saying to the innocent Master George so many cruel and abominable words, and hit him so spitefully with the Pope's thunder, that the ignorant people dreaded lest the earth then would have swallowed him up quick. Notwithstanding, he stood still with great patience hearing their sayings, not once moving or changing his countenance. When that this fed sow had read throughout all his lying menacings, his face running down with sweat, and frothing at the mouth like a bear, he spat at Master George's face, saying, " What answerest thou to these sayings, thou runagate, traitor, thief, which we have duly proved by sufficient witness against thee ? " Master George hearing this, sat down upon his knees in the pulpit, making his prayer to God. When he had ended his prayer, sweetly and Christianly he answered to them all in this manner :

Master George's Oration

" Many and horrible sayings unto me, a Christian man, many words abominable for to hear, ye have spoken here this day, which not only to teach, but also to think, I thought it ever great abomination. Wherefore, I pray your discretions quietly to hear me, that ye may know what were my sayings, and the manner of my doctrine. This my petition, my Lords,

[1] *providing shelter or protection* ; ' given to hospitality '

[2] It has been observed that Foxe drew his account of the martyrdom of Wishart from an earlier black-letter tract, printed by Day and Seres (M'Crie, *Life of John Knox*, 5th. edn., i, 382–383), and Andrew Lang regarded that tract as Knox's first printed work (*John Knox and the Reformation*, 20–21). Certainly, phrases such as " the fed flock," " the fed sow," and " two false fiends (I should say, Friars)" ring remarkably like Knox.

[3] For details of Lauder's career, see *St. Andrews Formulare* (Stair Soc.), i, vii–ix ; ii, ix–xvii.

I desire to be heard for three causes: The First is, Because through preaching of the word of God his glory is made manifest: it is reasonable therefore, for the advancing of the glory of God, that ye hear me teaching truly the pure and sincere word of God, without any dissimulation. The Second reason is, Because that your health springeth of the word of God, for he worketh all things by his word: it were therefore an unrighteous thing if ye should stop your ears from me teaching truly the word of God. The Third reason is, Because your doctrine speaketh forth many pestilentious, blasphemous, and abominable words, not coming by the inspiration of God, but of the devil, on no less peril than my life. It is just therefore, and reasonable, [for] your discretions to know what my words and doctrine are, and what I have ever taught in my time in this realm, that I perish not unjustly, to the great peril of your souls. Wherefore, both for the glory and honour of God, your own health, and safeguard of my life, I beseech your discretions to hear me, and in the meantime I shall recite my doctrine without any colour.

First and chiefly, since the time I came into this realm, I taught nothing but the Ten Commandments of God, the Twelve Articles of the Faith, and the Prayer of the Lord, in the mother tongue. Moreover, in Dundee, I taught the Epistle of Saint Paul to the Romans; and I shall show your discretions faithfully what fashion and manner I used when I taught, without any human dread, so that your discretions give me your ears benevolent and attent."

Suddenly then, with an high voice, cried the Accuser, the fed sow, "Thou heretic, runagate, traitor, and thief, it was not lawful for thee to preach. Thou hast taken the power at thine own hand, without any authority of the Church. We forethink that thou hast been a preacher so long." Then said all the whole congregation of the Prelates, with their complices, these words, "If we give him licence to preach, he is so crafty, and in Holy Scriptures so exercised, that he will persuade the people to his opinion, and raise them against us."

Master George, seeing their malicious and wicked intent, appealed [from the Lord Cardinal to the Lord Governor, as [1]] to an indifferent [2] and equal judge. To whom the Accuser, John Lauder foresaid, with hoggish voice answered, "Is not my Lord Cardinal the second person within this realm, Chancellor of Scotland, Archbishop of Saint Andrews, Bishop of Mirepoix, Commendator of Arbroath, *Legatus Natus*, *Legatus a Latere*?" [3] And so reciting as many titles of his unworthy honours as would have laden a ship, much sooner an ass. "Is not he (quod John Lauder) an equal judge apparently to thee? Whom other desirest thou to be thy judge?"

To whom this humble man answered, saying, "I refuse not my Lord Cardinal, but I desire the word of God to be my judge, and the Temporal Estate, with some of your Lordships, mine auditors; because I am here

[1] The words within brackets are supplied from Foxe. [2] *impartial*

[3] Beaton was Chancellor, Cardinal Priest of St. Stephen-on-the-Caelian, Archbishop of St. Andrews, Primate of Scotland, *Legatus Natus*, Legate *a latere*, Bishop (administrator) of Mirepoix, and Abbot (Commendator) of Arbroath.

my Lord Governor's prisoner." Whereupon the prideful and scornful people that stood by, mocked him, saying, "Such man, such judge," speaking seditious and reproachful words against the Governor, and other the Nobles, meaning them also to be Heretics. And incontinent, without all delay, they would have given sentence upon Master George, and that without further process, had not certain men there counselled my Lord Cardinal to read again the Articles, and to hear his answers thereupon, that the people might not complain of his wrongful condemnation.

And shortly for to declare, these were the Articles following, with his Answers, as far as they would give him leave to speak ; for when he intended to mitigate their lesings,[1] and show the manner of his doctrine, by and by they stopped his mouth with another Article.

The First Article

Thou false Heretic, runagate, traitor, and thief, deceiver of the people, despisest the Holy Church, and in like case contemnest my Lord Governor's authority. And this we know for surety, that when thou preached in Dundee, and was charged by my Lord Governor's authority to desist, nevertheless thou wouldst not obey, but persevered in the same.[2] And therefore the Bishop of Brechin[3] cursed thee, and delivered thee into the Devil's hands, and gave thee in commandment that thou shouldst preach no more. Yet notwithstanding, thou didst continue obstinately.

The Answer

My Lords, I have read in the Acts of the Apostles that it is not lawful for the threats and menacings of men to desist from the preaching of the Evangel. Therefore it is written, "We shall rather obey God than men." I have also read [in] the Prophet Malachi, "I shall curse your blessings, and bless your cursings, says the Lord" : believing firmly, that he would turn your cursings into blessings.

The Second Article

Thou false Heretic did say that a priest standing at the altar saying Mass was like a fox wagging his tail in July.

The Answer

My Lords, I said not so. These were my sayings : The moving of the body outward, without the inward moving of the heart, is nothing else but the playing of an ape, and not the true serving of God ; for God is a secret searcher of men's hearts : Therefore, who will truly adorn and honour God, he must in spirit and verity honour him.

Then the Accusator stopped his mouth with another Article.

[1] *lies* [2] But see *supra*, i, 60–61

[3] John Hepburn. But apparently this was in 1538. (See Laing's *Knox*, i, 535)

THE THIRD ARTICLE

Thou false Heretic preachest against the Sacraments, saying, That there are not seven Sacraments.

THE ANSWER

My Lords, if it be your pleasure, I taught never of the number of the Sacraments, whether they were seven, or an eleven. So many as are instituted by Christ, and are shown to us by the Evangel, I profess openly. Except it be the word of God, I dare affirm nothing.

THE FOURTH ARTICLE

Thou false Heretic hast openly taught that Auricular Confession is not a blessed Sacrament; and thou sayest that we should only confess us to God, and to no priest.

THE ANSWER

My Lords, I say that Auricular Confession, seeing that it hath no promise of the Evangel, therefore it can not be a Sacrament. Of the Confession to be made to God, there are many testimonies in Scripture; as when David sayeth, "I thought that I would acknowledge my iniquity against myself unto the Lord; and he forgave the trespasses of my sins." Here, Confession signifieth the secret knowledge of our sins before God: when I exhorted the people on this manner, I reproved no manner of Confession. And further, Saint James sayeth, "Acknowledge your sins one to another, and so let you to have peace among yourselves." Here the Apostle meaneth nothing of Auricular Confession, but that we should acknowledge and confess ourselves to be sinners before our brethren, and before the world, and not to esteem ourselves as the Grey Friars do, thinking themselves already purged.

When that he had said these words, the horned Bishops and their complices cried, and girned [1] with their teeth, saying, "See ye not what colours he hath in his speech, that he may beguile us, and seduce us to his opinion."

THE FIFTH ARTICLE

Thou Heretic didst say openly that it was necessary to every man to know and understand his Baptism, and that it [2] was contrary to General Councils, and the Estates of Holy Church.

THE ANSWER

My Lords, I believe there be none so unwise here, that will make merchandise with a Frenchman, or any other unknown stranger, except

[1] To *girn* is to distort the countenance. Thus, *girned* may mean *grinned*; but also it may mean, as here, *snarled* and showed their teeth.

[2] That is, infant baptism, where the infant could not know the promise made unto God.

he know and understand first the condition or promise made by the Frenchman or stranger. So likewise I would that we understood what thing we promise in the name of the infant unto God in Baptism. For this cause, I believe, ye have Confirmation.

Then said Master Bleiter,[1] chaplain, that he had the Devil within him, and the spirit of error. Then answered him a child, saying, " The Devil can not speak such words as yonder man doth speak."

The Sixth Article

Thou false Heretic, traitor, and thief, thou saidst that the Sacrament of the Altar was but a piece of bread, baked upon the ashes, and no other thing else ; and all that is there done is but a superstitious rite against the commandment of God.

The Answer

Oh Lord God ! so manifest lies and blasphemies the Scripture doth not so teach you. As concerning the Sacrament of the Altar (my Lords), I never taught any thing against the Scripture, the which I shall (by God's grace) make manifest this day, I being ready therefor to suffer death.

The lawful use of the Sacrament is most acceptable unto God : but the great abuse of it is very detestable unto Him. But what occasion they have to say such words of me, I shall shortly show your Lordships. I once chanced to meet with a Jew, when I was sailing upon the water of Rhine.[2] I did inquire of him, what was the cause of his pertinacity, that he did not believe that the true Messiah was come, considering that they had seen all the prophecies, which were spoken of Him, to be fulfilled : moreover, the prophecies taken away, and the Sceptre of Judah. By many other testimonies of the Scripture, I vanquished him, and proved that Messiah was come, the which they called Jesus of Nazareth. This Jew answered again unto me, " When Messiah cometh, He shall restore all things, and He shall not abrogate the Law, which was given to our fathers, as ye do. For why ? We see the poor almost perish through hunger among you, yet you are not moved with pity towards them ; but among us Jews, though we be poor, there are no beggars found. Secondly, It is forbidden by the Law to feign any kind of imagery of things in heaven above, or in the earth beneath, or in the sea under the earth ; but one God only to honour ; but your sanctuaries and churches are full of idols. Thirdly, A piece of bread baked upon the ashes, ye adore and worship, and say that it is your God." I have rehearsed here but the sayings of the Jew, which I never affirmed to be true.

Then the Bishops shook their heads and spat into the earth. And what he meant in this matter, further they would not hear.

[1] Perhaps *Mr. Nonsense*, for the word may be taken from " blether " or from " bleat."

[2] Leslie says Wishart "had remaned long in Germanie." (*History*, Bannatyne Club, 191)

The Seventh Article

Thou false Heretic did say that Extreme Unction was not a Sacrament.

The Answer

My Lord, forsooth, I never taught any thing of Extreme Unction in my doctrine, whether it were a Sacrament or not.

The Eighth Article

Thou false Heretic saidst that the Holy Water is not so good as wash, and such like. Thou contemnest conjuring,[1] and sayest that Holy Church's cursing availed not.

The Answer

My Lords, as for Holy Water, what strength it is of, I taught never in my doctrine. Conjurings and exorcisms, if they were conformable to the word of God, I would commend them. But in so far as they are not conformable to the commandment and word of God, I reprove them.

The Ninth Article

Thou false Heretic and runagate hast said that every layman is a Priest ; and such like thou sayest, that the Pope hath no more power than any other man.

The Answer

My Lords, I taught nothing but the word of God. I remember that I have read in some places in Saint John and Saint Peter, of the which one sayeth, " He hath made us kings and priests " ; the other sayeth, " He hath made us the kingly priesthood " : Wherefore, I have affirmed any man being cunning [2] and perfect in the word of God, and the true faith of Jesus Christ, to have his power given him from God, and not by the power or violence of men, but by the virtue of the word of God, the which word is called the power of God, as witnesseth Saint Paul evidently enough. And again, I say, any unlearned man, and not exercised in the word of God, nor yet constant in his faith, whatsoever estate or order he be of, I say, he hath no power to bind or loose, seeing he wanteth the instrument by the which he bindeth or looseth, that is to say, the word of God.

After that he had said these words, all the Bishops laughed, and mocked him. When that he beheld their laughing, " Laugh ye (sayeth he), my Lords ? Though that these my sayings appear scornful and worthy of derision to your Lordships, nevertheless they are very weighty to me, and of a great value ; because that they stand not only upon my life, but also the honour and glory of God." In the meantime many godly men, beholding the wodness [3] and great cruelty of the Bishops, and the in-

[1] The invocation of relics or saints [2] *wise* [3] *rage*

vincible patience of the said Master George, did greatly mourn and lament.

The Tenth Article

Thou false Heretic saidst that a man hath no Free Will ; but is like to the Stoics, which say, That it is not in man's will to do any thing, but that all concupiscence and desire cometh of God, of whatsoever kind it be of.

The Answer

My Lords, I said not so, truly. I say, that as many as believe in Christ firmly, unto them is given liberty, conformable to the saying of Saint John, " If the Son make you free, then shall ye verily be free." Of the contrary, as many as believe not in Christ Jesus, they are bound servants of sin : " He that sinneth is bound to sin."

The Eleventh Article

Thou false Heretic sayest, It is as lawful to eat flesh upon Friday, as on Sunday.

The Answer

Pleaseth it your Lordships, I have read in the Epistles of Saint Paul, " They who are clean, unto them all things are clean." Of the contrary, " To the filthy man, all things are unclean." A faithful man, clean and holy, sanctifieth by the word the creature of God ; but the creature maketh no man acceptable unto God : so that a creature may not sanctify any impure and unfaithful man. But to the faithful man, all things are sanctified, by the prayer of the word of God.

After these sayings of Master George, then said all the Bishops, with their complices, " What needeth us any witness against him : hath he not openly here spoken blasphemy ? "

The Twelfth Article

Thou false Heretic dost say, That we should not pray to Saints, but to God only : Say whether thou hast said this or not, say shortly.

The Answer

For the weakness and the infirmity of the hearers he said, without doubt plainly, that Saints should not be honoured nor called upon. My Lords (said he), there are two things worthy of note : the one is certain, and the other uncertain. It is found plainly and certain in Scriptures that we should worship and honour one God, according to the saying of the first Commandment, " Thou shalt only worship and honour thy Lord God with all thy heart." But as for praying to and honouring of Saints, there is great doubt among many, whether they hear or not invocation made unto them. Therefore, I exhorted all men equally in my doctrine, that they should leave the unsure way, and follow the way which was taught us by our Master Christ :

He is our only Mediator, and maketh intercession for us to God his Father :

He is the door, by which we must enter in :

He that entereth not in by this door, but climbeth another way, is a thief and a murderer :

He is the Verity and Life :

He that goeth out of this way, there is no doubt but he shall fall into the mire ; yea, verily, he is fallen into it already. This is the fashion of my doctrine, the which I have ever followed. Verily that which I have heard and read in the word of God, I taught openly and in no corners, and now ye shall witness the same, if your Lordships will hear me : Except it stand by the word of God, I dare not be so bold to affirm anything. These sayings he rehearsed divers times.

The Thirteenth Article

Thou false Heretic hast preached plainly, saying, That there is no Purgatory ; and that it is a feigned thing, any man, after this life, to be punished in Purgatory.

The Answer

My Lords, as I have oftentimes said heretofore, without express witness and testimony of Scripture I dare affirm nothing. I have oft and divers times read over the Bible, and yet such a term found I never, nor yet any place of Scripture applicable thereunto. Therefore, I was ashamed ever to teach of that thing, which I could not find in Scripture.

Then said he to Master John Lauder, his accuser, " If you have any testimony of the Scripture, by the which ye may prove any such place, show it now before this auditure [1]." But that dolt had not a word to say for himself, but was as dumb as a beetle [2] in that matter.

The Fourteenth Article

Thou false Heretic hast taught plainly against the vows of Monks, Friars, Nuns, and Priests, saying, That whosoever was bound to such like vows, they vowed themselves to the estate of damnation : Moreover, that it was lawful for Priests to marry wives, and not to live sole.

The Answer

Of sooth, my Lords, I have read in the Evangel that there are three kinds of chaste men : some are gelded from their mother's womb ; some are gelded by men ; and some have gelded themselves for the kingdom of heaven's sake. Verily, I say, these men are blessed by the Scripture of

[1] *audience* [2] a heavy wooden mallet used for beating (*e.g.* clothes)

God. But as many as have not the gift of Chastity, nor yet for the Evangel have not overcome the concupiscence of the flesh, and [yet] have vowed chastity, ye have experience ; although I should hold my tongue, to what inconvenience they have vowed themselves.

When he had said these words, they were all dumb, thinking better to have ten concubines, than one married wife.

The Fifteenth Article

Thou false Heretic and runagate sayest, That thou wilt not obey our General nor Provincial Councils.

The Answer

My Lords, what your General Councils are, I know not. I was never exercised in them ; but to the pure word of God I gave my labours. Read here your General Councils, or else give me a book, wherein they are contained, that I may read them : If that they agree with the word of God, I will not disagree.

Then the ravening wolves turned into madness, and said, " Whereunto let we him speak any further ? Read forth the rest of the Articles, and stay not upon them." Amongst these cruel tigers, there was one false hypocrite, a seducer of the people, called John [1] Scott, standing behind John Lauder's back, hastening him to read the rest of the Articles, and not to tarry upon his witty [2] and godly answers ; " For we may not abide them (quod he), no more than the Devil may abide the sign of the cross, when it is named."

This was Friar Scott

The Sixteenth Article

Thou Heretic sayest, That it is vain to build to the honour of God costly churches, seeing that God remaineth not in churches made by men's hands, nor yet can God be in so little space, as betwix the Priest's hands.

The Answer

My Lords, Solomon sayeth, " If that the heaven of heavens cannot comprehend thee, how much less this house that I have built." And Job consenteth to the same sentence, saying, " Seeing that he is higher than the heavens, therefore what can thou build unto him ? He is deeper than the hell, then how shalt thou know him ? He is longer than the earth, and broader than the sea." So that God cannot be comprehended into one space, because that He is infinite. These sayings notwithstanding, I said never that churches should be destroyed ; but of the contrary, I affirmed ever that churches should be sustained and upheld, that the people should be congregate in them to hear the word of God preached. Moreover, wheresoever is the true preaching of the word of God, and the

[1] In the manuscript (folio 55 *recto*) there is a space between *Johnne* and *Scot*. Perhaps the copyist could not read the missing word *Gray-finde* (*Grey-fiend*, that is, Grey Friar) which occurs in Foxe. [2] *wise*

lawful use of the Sacraments, undoubtedly there is God Himself. So that both these sayings are true together : God cannot be comprehended into any one place : And, " Wheresoever there are two or three gathered in his name, there is He present in the midst of them." Then said he to his Accuser, " If thou thinkest any otherwise than I say, show forth thy reasons before this auditory." Then, he, without all reason, was dumb[1], and could not answer a word.

The Seventeenth Article

Thou false Heretic contemnest Fasting, and sayest, Thou shouldst not fast.

The Answer

My Lords, I find that Fasting is commended in the Scripture ; therefore I were a slanderer of the Gospel, if I contemned fasting. And not so only, but I have learned by experience that fasting is good for the health and conservation of the body. But God knoweth only who fasteth the true fast.

The Eighteenth Article

Thou false Heretic hast preached openly, saying, That the souls of men shall sleep to the latter day of judgment, and shall not obtain life immortal until that day.

The Answer

God, full of mercy and goodness, forgive them that sayeth such things of me. I know surely by the word of God, that he which hath begun to have the faith of Jesus Christ, and believeth firmly in Him, I know surely that the soul of that man shall never sleep, but ever shall live an immortal life ; the which life, from day to day, is renewed in grace and augmented ; nor yet shall ever perish, or have an end, but shall ever live immortal with Christ their head : To the which life all that believe in Him shall come, and rest in eternal glory. Amen.

When that the Bishops, with their complices, had accused this innocent man, in manner and form aforesaid, incontinently they condemned him to be burnt as an Heretic, not having respect to his godly answers and true reasons which he alleged, nor yet to their own consciences, thinking verily that they should do to God good sacrifice, conformable to the sayings of Jesus Christ in the Gospel of Saint John, chapter 16 : " They shall excommunicate you ; yea, and the time shall come, that he which killeth you shall think that he hath done to God good service."

The Prayer of Master George

" O immortal God ! how long shalt Thou suffer the woodness[2] and great cruelty of the ungodly to exercise their fury upon thy servants,

[1] *having no reason to offer, was dumb* [2] *rage*

which do further thy word in this world, seeing they desire to do the contrary, that is, to choke and destroy thy true doctrine and verity, by the which Thou hast showed Thee unto the world, which was all drowned in blindness and misknowledge of thy name. O Lord, we know surely, that thy true servants must needs suffer, for thy name's sake, persecution, affliction, and troubles in this present life, which is but a shadow, as Thou has showed to us, by thy Prophets and Apostles. But yet we desire Thee (Merciful Father), that Thou conserve, defend, and help thy Congregation, which Thou hast chosen before the beginning of the world, and give them thy grace to hear thy word, and to be thy true servants in this present life."

Then, by and by, they caused the common people to remove,[1] whose desire was always to hear that innocent speak. And the sons of darkness pronounced their sentence definitive, not having respect to the judgment of God. When all this was done and said, my Lord Cardinal caused his tormentors to pass again with the meek lamb unto the Castle, until such time [as] the fire was made ready. When he was come into the Castle, then there came two Grey fiends, Friar Scott and his mate, saying, "Sir, ye must make your confession unto us." He answered, and said, "I will make no confession unto you. Go fetch me yonder man that preached this day, and I will make my confession unto him." Then they sent for the Subprior of the Abbey,[2] who came to him with all diligence; but what he said in this confession, I cannot show.

When the fire was made ready, and the gallows, at the West [3] part of the Castle, near to the Priory, my Lord Cardinal, dreading that Master George should have been taken away by his friends, therefore he commanded to bend all the ordnance of the Castle right against the place of execution, and commanded all his gunners to be ready, and stand beside their guns, unto such time as he were burned.[4] All this being done, they bound Master George's hands behind his back and led him forth with their soldiers, from the Castle, to the place of their cruel and wicked execution. As he came forth of the Castle gate, there met him certain beggars, asking of his alms, for God's sake. To whom he answered, "I want[5] my hands, wherewith I [was] wont to give[6] you alms. But the merciful Lord, of his benignity and abundant grace, that feedeth all men, vouchsafe to give you necessaries, both unto your bodies and souls." Then afterward met him two false fiends (I should say, Friars), saying, "Master George, pray to our Lady, that she may be a mediatrix for you to her Son." To whom he answered meekly, "Cease: tempt me not, my brethren." After this, he was led to the fire, with a rope about his neck, and a chain of iron about his middle.

When that he came to the fire, he sat down upon his knees, and rose

[1] *remove themselves* [2] John Winram (see *supra*, 233)

[3] This is clearly a mistake for *East*

[4] *Cf. supra*, i, 74 [5] *lack*

[6] In the manuscript (folio 56 *verso*), originally "I should yow almes"; *should* has been scored through, and *wont to geve* added above the line.

again; and thrice he said these words, "O Thou Saviour of the world, have mercy upon me: Father of Heaven, I commend my spirit into thy holy hands." When he had made this prayer, he turned him to the people, and said these words: "I beseech you, Christian brethren and sisters, that ye be not offended at the word of God for the affliction and torments which ye see already prepared for me. But I exhort you, that ye love the word of God, your salvation, and suffer patiently, and with a comfortable heart, for the word's sake, which is your undoubted salvation and everlasting comfort. Moreover, I pray you, show my brethren and sisters, which have heard me oft before, that they cease not nor leave off to learn the word of God, which I taught unto them, after the grace given unto me, for no persecutions nor troubles in this world, which lasteth not. And show unto them that my doctrine was no wives' fables, after the constitutions made by men; and if I had taught men's doctrine, I had got greater thanks by men. But for the word's sake, and true Evangel, which was given to me by the grace of God, I suffer this day by men, not sorrowfully, but with a glad heart and mind. For this cause I was sent, that I should suffer this fire for Christ's sake. Consider and behold my visage, ye shall not see me change my colour. This grim fire I fear not; and so I pray you for to do, if that any persecution come unto you for the word's sake; and not to fear them that slay the body, and afterward have no power to slay the soul. Some have said of me, that I taught that the soul of man should sleep until the last day; but I know surely, and my faith is such, that my soul shall sup with my Saviour this night, or it be six hours, for whom I suffer this." Then he prayed for them which accused him, saying, "I beseech the Father of Heaven to forgive them that have of any ignorance, or else of any evil mind, forged lies upon me; I forgive them with all mine heart: I beseech Christ to forgive them that have condemned me to death this day ignorantly." And last of all, he said to the people on this manner, "I beseech you, brethren and sisters, to exhort your Prelates to the learning of the word of God, that they at the last may be ashamed to do evil, and learn to do good; and if they will not convert themselves from their wicked error, there shall hastily come upon them the wrath of God, which they shall not eschew."

Many faithful words said he in the meantime, taking no heed or care of the cruel torments which were then prepared for him. Then, last of all, the hangman, that was his tormentor, sat down upon his knees and said, "Sir, I pray you, forgive me, for I am not guilty of your death." To whom he answered, "Come hither to me." When he was come to him he kissed his cheek and said, "Lo! Here is a token that I forgive thee. My heart, do thine office." And then, by and by, he was put upon the gibbet, and hanged, and there burnt to powder. When that the people beheld the great tormenting of that innocent, they might not withhold from piteous mourning and complaining of the innocent lamb's slaughter.[1]

[1] A fuller account of Wishart's martyrdom is given by Pitscottie (*Chronicles*, Scot. Text Soc., ii, 76–82). Pitscottie, living near to St. Andrews in the next generation, probably wrote part of his narrative from the accounts of eye-witnesses.

APPENDIX IV

THE LETTER OF JOHN HAMILTON, ARCHBISHOP OF ST. ANDREWS, TO ARCHIBALD, EARL OF ARGYLL; AND ARGYLL'S ANSWERS THERETO [1]

THE BISHOP'S LETTER TO THE OLD EARL OF ARGYLL

MY LORD, After most heartly commendation: This is to advertise your Lordship, we have directed this bearer, our cousin, toward your Lordship, in such business and affairs as concerns your Lordship's honour, profit, and great weal; like as the said bearer will declare [to] your Lordship at more length. Praying your Lordship effectuously [2] to advert thereto, and give attendance to us, your Lordship's friends, that aye has willed the honour, profit, and utter wealth of your Lordship's house, as of our own; and credit to the bearer. And Jesu have your Lordship in everlasting keeping.

Of Edinburgh, the xxv day of March, Anno 1558.

(*Sic subscribitur*)

Your Lordship's at all power,

J. SAINT ANDREWS [3]

FOLLOWS THE CREDIT—MEMORANDUM TO SIR DAVID HAMILTON, TO MY LORD EARL OF ARGYLL, IN MY BEHALF, AND LET HIM SEE AND HEAR EVERY ARTICLE.

In primis, To repeat the ancient blood of his house, how long it has stood, how notable it has been, and so many noble men have been earls, lords, and knights thereof; how long they have reigned in those parts, ever true and obedient both to God and the Prince without any smote [4] to these days in any manner of sort: and to remember how many notable men are come of his house.

Secondly, To show him the great affection I bear towards him, his blood, house, and friends, and of the ardent desire I have of the perpetual standing of it in honour and fame, with all them that are come of it: which is my part for many and divers causes, as ye shall show.

Thirdly, To show my Lord, how heavy and displeasing it is to me now to hear that he, who is and has been so noble a man, should be seduced and abused by the flattery of such an infamed person of the law [5] and mensworn apostate that, under the pretence that he gives himself forth

[1] See *supra*, i, 138 [2] *affectionately*; though the word may also mean *efficaciously*
[3] John Hamilton, Archbishop of St. Andrews [4] *stain*
[5] That is, a person whom the law had made infamous. The reference is to John Douglas (see *supra*, i, 138; *infra*, 247, 251–252).

as a preacher of the Evangel and verity, under that colour sets forth schisms and divisions in the Holy Kirk of God, with heretical propositions, thinking under his maintenance and defence to infect this country with heresy, persuading my said Lord and others his bairns and friends that all that he speaks is Scripture, and conform thereto, albeit that many of his propositions are many years past condemned by General Councils and the whole estate of Christian people.

4 To show to my Lord how perilous this is to his Lordship and his house, and decay thereof, in case the Authority would be sharp, and would use [itself] conform both to civil and canon [law], and also your own municipal law of this Realm.

5 To show his Lordship, how wa [1] I would be either to hear, see, or know any displeasure that might come to him, his son, or any of his house, or friends, and especially in his own time and days ; and also how great displeasure I have else to hear great and evil bruit of him, that should now, in his age, in a manner vary in his faith ; and to be altered therein, when the time is that he should be most sure and firm therein.

6 To show his Lordship, that there is delation [2] of that man, called Douglas or Grant, of sundry Articles of heresy, which lies to my charge and conscience to put remedy to, or else all the pestilentious doctrine he sows, and suchlike all that are corrupted by his doctrine, and all that he draws from our faith and Christian religion, will lie to my charge before God, and I to be accused before God for over seeing [3] of him, if I put not remedy thereto, and correct him for such things he is delated of. And therefore that my Lord consider, and weigh it well, how highly it lies both to my honour and conscience : for if I thole [4] him, I will be accused for all them that he infects and corrupts in heresy.

[7] Herefore, I pray My Lord, in my most heartly manner, to take this matter in the best part, for his own conscience, honour, weal of himself, house, friends, and servants. And suchlike for my part, and for my conscience and honour, that considering that there are divers Articles of heresy to be laid to him that he is delated of, and that he is presently in my Lord's company, that my Lord would, by some honest way, depart with this man, and put him from him and from his son's company ; for I would be right sorry that any being in any of their companies should be called for such causes, or that any of them should be bruited to hold any such men. And this I would advertise my Lord, and have his Lordship's answer and resolution, ere any summons passed upon him, together with my Lord's answer.

Item [8] If my Lord would have a man to instruct him truly in the faith, and preach to him, I would provide a cunning man to him, wherefore I shall answer for his true doctrine, and shall put my soul therefor, that he shall teach nothing but truly according to our Catholic faith.

Of Edinburgh, this last of March, 1558.

(*Sic subscribitur*),

J. Saint Andrews

[1] *unhappy* [2] *formal accusation*
[3] *overlooking*, in the sense of *not seeing* [4] *suffer*

Item [9] Attour, your Lordship shall draw to good remembrance, and weigh the great and heavy murmur against me, both by the Queen's Grace, the Kirkmen, Spiritual and Temporal Estates, and well given [1] people, meaning [2], crying, and murmuring me greatly, that I do not my office to thole such infamous persons with such perverse doctrine within my Diocese and this Realm, by reason of my Legacy and Primacy.[3] Which I have rather sustained and long suffered, for the great love that I had to your Lordship and posterity, and your friends, and your house ; also believing surely your Lordship's wisdom should not have maintained and melled [4] with such things that might do me dishonour or displeasure, considering I being ready to have put good order thereto always ; but has allanerly [5] abstained, for the love of your Lordship and house foresaid, that I bear truly, knowing and seeing the great scathe and dishonour and lack apparently that might come therethrough, in case your Lordship remedy not the same hastily, whereby we might both be quiet of all danger, which doubtless will come upon us both, if I use not my office,[6] ere that he [7] be called, the time that he is now with your Lordship, and under your Lordship's protection.

Flesh and blood is preferred to God with the Bishop

(*Subscribed again*)

J. Saint Andrews

By these former Instructions, thou may perceive, Gentle Reader, what was the care that this pastor, with his complices, took to feed the flock committed to their charge (as they allege), and to gainstand [8] false teachers. Here is oft mention of conscience, of heresy, and such other terms that may fray [9] the ignorant, and deceive the simple. But we hear no crime in particular laid to the charge of the accused ; and yet is he damned as a mensworn apostate. This was my Lord's conscience, which he learned of his fathers, the Pharisees, old enemies to Christ Jesus, who damned Him before they heard Him. But who ruled my Lord's conscience when he took his eme's [10] wife, Lady Gilton ? [11] Consider thou the rest of his persuasion, and thou shalt clearly see that honour, estimation, love to house and friends, is the best ground that my Lord Bishop has, why he should persecute Jesus Christ in his members.

We thought good to insert the Answers of the said Earl, which follow :

Memorandum—This Present Writing is to make Answer particularly to everilk [12] Article, directed by my Lord of Saint Andrews to me, with Sir David Hamilton ; which Articles are in number nine, and here repeated and answered as I trust to his Lordship's contentment

[1] *well-affected* [2] *complaining*

[3] By Bull of Pope Innocent VIII (of 27 March 1487) St. Andrews was erected into a Primatial Church, and the Archbishop of St. Andrews was made Primate of all Scotland and *Legatus Natus* of the Apostolic See. (Robertson, *Concilia Scotiæ*, i, cxviii)

[4] *meddled* [5] *only*

[6] In the manuscript (folio 96 *verso*) the words (*of cruel butcher*) originally followed the word *office*, and were then scored through. [7] That is, John Douglas

[8] *oppose* [9] *frighten* [10] *kinsman's* [11] *Cf. supra*, i, 59 [12] *each and every*

1 The First Article puts me in remembrance of the ancianity of the blood of my house, how many earls, lords, and knights have been thereof; how many Noble men descended of the same house, how long it continued true to God and the Prince, without smot [1] in their days, in any manner of sort.

[Answer]

True it is, my Lord, that there is well long continuance of my house, by God's providence and benevolence of our Princes, whom we have served, and shall serve truly next to God: And the like obedience towards God and our Princes remains with us yet, or rather better (praised be the Lord's name), neither know we any spot towards our Princess and her due obedience. And if there be offence towards God, He is merciful to remit our offences; for "He will not the death of a sinner". Like as, it stands in his Omnipotent power to make up houses, to continue the same, to alter them, to make them small or great, or to extinguish them, according to his own inscrutable wisdom; for in exalting, depressing, and changing of houses, the laud and praise must be given to that one eternal God, in whose hand the same stands.

2 The Second Article bears the great affection and love your Lordship bears towards me and my house; and of the ardent desire ye have of the perpetual standing thereof in honour and fame, with all them that come of it.

[Answer]

Forsooth it is your duty to wish good unto my house, and unto them that come of the same, not allanerly for the faithfulness, amity, and society, that has been betwix our forebears, but also for the late conjunction of blood that is betwix our said houses,[2] if it be God's pleasure that it have success; which should give sufficient occasion to your Lordship to wish good to my house, and perpetuity with God's glory, without which nothing is perpetual, unto whom be praise and worship for ever and ever. Amen.

3 Thirdly, your Lordship declares how displeasing it is to you, that I should be seduced by an infamed person of the law,[3] and by the flattery of a mensworn apostate that, under pretence of his forth giving, makes us to understand that he is a preacher of the Evangel, and therewith raises schisms and divisions in the whole Kirk of God; and by our maintenance and defence, would infect this country with heresy; alleging that to be Scripture which, these many years bygone, has been condemned as heresy by the General Councils and whole estate of Christian people.

[1] *stain*

[2] Archibald, fourth Earl of Argyll, had married as his first wife Helen, eldest daughter of James Hamilton, first Earl of Arran; and the Archbishop of St. Andrews, John Hamilton, was her half-brother.

[3] John Douglas (*supra*, 246 and *note* 5)

ANSWER

The God that created heaven and earth, and all that therein is, preserve me from seducing ; and I dread many others under the colour of godliness are seduced, and think that they do God a pleasure, when they persecute one of them that professes his name. What that man is of the law we know not : we hear none of his flattery : his mensworn oath of apostasy is ignorant to us. But if he had made an unlawful oath, contrary to God's command, it were better to violate it than to observe it. He preaches nothing to us but the Evangel. If he would otherwise do, we would not believe him, nor yet an angel of heaven. We hear him sow no schisms nor divisions, but such as may stand with God's word, which we shall cause him confess in presence of your Lordship and the Clergy, when ye require us thereto. And as to it that has been condemned by the General Councils, we trust ye know well that all the General Councils have been at diversity amongst themselves, and never two of them universally agreeing in all points, in samekle as [1] they are of men. But the Spirit of verity that bears testimony of our Lord Jesus has not, neither cannot, err ; "for heaven and earth shall perish or a jot of it perish". By [2] this, my Lord, neither teaches he, neither will we accept of him, but that which agrees with God's sincere word, set forth by Patriarchs, Prophets, Apostles, and Evangelists, left to our salvation in his express word. And so, my Lord, to condemn the doctrine not examined is not required ; for when your Lordship pleases to hear the confession of that man's faith, [and] the manner of his doctrine, which agrees with the Evangel of Jesus Christ, I will cause him to assist to [3] judgment, and shall be present thereat with God's pleasure, that he may render reckoning of his belief and our doctrine, to the superior powers, according to the prescription of that blood of the eternal Testament, sealed by the immaculate Lamb, to whom, with the Father, and the Holy Spirit, be all honour and glory, for ever and ever. Amen.

4 The Fourth Article puts me in remembrance how dangerous it is if the authority would put at [4] me and my house, according to civil and canon laws, and our own municipal laws of this Realm, and how it appeareth to the decay of our house.

ANSWER

All laws are (or at the least should be) subject to God's law, which law should be first placed and planted in every man's heart ; it should have no impediment : men should not abrogate it for the defence and upsetting [5] of their own advantage. If it would please Authorities to put at our house, for confessing of God's word, or for maintenance of his law, God is mighty enough in his own cause. He should be rather obeyed nor man. I will serve my Princess with body, heart, goods, strength, and

[1] *insomuch as* [2] *Apart from* [3] *to stand to*
[4] *exert itself against* [5] *setting up*

all that is in my power, except that which is God's duty, which I will reserve to himself alone: That is, to worship him in truth and verity and, as near as I can, conform to his prescribed word, to his own honour and obedience of my Princess.

5 The Fifth Article puts me in remembrance how wa [1] your Lordship would be to hear, see, or know any displeasure that might come to me, my son, or any of my house, and specially in my time and days, and also to hear the great and evil bruit of me that should now in my age in a manner begin to vary from my faith, and to be altered therein, when the time is that I should be most sure and firm therein.

ANSWER

Your Lordship's goodwill is ever made manifest to me in all your Articles, that would not hear, see, or know my displeasure, for the which I am bound to render your Lordship thanks, and shall do the same assuredly. But as for wavering in my faith, God forbid that I should so do; for I believe in God the Father Almighty, maker of heaven and earth, and in Jesus Christ his only Son our Saviour. My Lord, I vary not in my faith; but I praise God that of his goodness now in my latter days [He] has of his infinite mercy opened his bosom of grace to me, to acknowledge him the Eternal Wisdom, his Son Jesus Christ, my omnisufficient satisfaction, to refuse all manner of idolatry, superstition, and ignorance, wherewith I have been blinded in times bygone, and now believe that God will be merciful to me, for now he has declared his blessed will clearly to me, before my departing of this transitory life.

6 The Sixth Article declared that there are delations [2] of sundry points of heresy upon that man, called Douglas or Grant, which lies to your charge and conscience to put remedy to, or else that all the pestilentious doctrine he sows, and all whom he corrupts with his seed, will be required at your hands, and all whom he draws from your Christian faith. And if ye should thole him, that ye will be accused for all them whom he infects with heresy; and therefore to regard your Lordship's honour and conscience hereinto.

ANSWER

What is his surname I know not, but he calls himself Douglas; for I know neither his father nor his mother. I have heard him teach no Articles of heresy; but that which agrees with God's word; for I would maintain no man in heresy or error. Your Lordship regards your conscience in the punishment thereof. I pray God that ye so do, and examine well your conscience. He preaches against idolatry: I remit to your Lordship's conscience if it be heresy or not. He preaches against adultery and fornication: I refer that to your Lordship's conscience. He preaches against hypocrisy: I refer that to your Lordship's conscience. He

[1] *unhappy* [2] *formal accusations*

preaches against all manner of abuses and corruption of Christ's sincere religion : I refer that to your Lordship's conscience. My Lord, I exhort you, in Christ's name, to weigh all these affairs in your conscience, and consider if it be your duty also, not only to thole this, but in like manner to do the same. This is all, my Lord, that I vary in my age, and no other thing, but that I knew not before these offences to be abominable to God, and now knowing his will by manifestation of his word, abhors them.

7 The Seventh Article desires me to weigh these matters in most heartly manner, and to take them in best part, for the weal of both our consciences, my house, friends, and servants, and to put such a man out of my company, for fear of the cummer [1] and bruit that should follow thereupon, by reason he is delated of sundry heresies : and that your Lordship would be sorry to hear any of our servants delated or bruited for such causes, or for holding of any such men ; and that your Lordship would understand my answer hereinto, ere any summons passed thereupon.

Answer

I thank your Lordship greatly that ye are so solist [2] for the weal of me and my house, and are so humane as to make me the advertisement before ye have summoned, of your own good will and benevolence ; and have weighed these matters, as highly as my judgment can serve me, both for your Lordship's honour and mine. And when I have reasoned all that I can do with myself in it, I think it aye best to serve God, and obey his manifest word, and not be obstinate in his contrary : syne [3] to give their due obedience to our Princes, rulers, and magistrates, and to hear the voice of God's prophets, declaring his good promises to them that repent, and threatening to obstinate wicked doers, everlasting destruction. Your Lordship knows well the man : he has spoken with your Lordship : I thought you content with him. I heard no occasion of offence in him. I cannot well want [4] him, or some preacher. I cannot put away such a man, without I knew him an offender, as I know not ; for I hear nothing of him, but such as your Lordship's self heard of him, and such as he yet will profess in your presence, whenever your Lordship requires. Such a man that is ready to assist himself to judgment, should not be expelled without cognition of the cause. For like as I answered before in another Article, when your Lordship pleases that all the spiritual and temporal men of estate in Scotland be convened, I shall cause him render an account of his belief and doctrine in your presences. Then if he deserves punishment and correction, let him so suffer ; if he be found faithful, let him live in his faith.

8 The Eighth Article propones to me that your Lordship would take the labour to get me a man to instruct me in your Catholic faith, and to be my preacher, for whose doctrine ye would lay your soul that he would teach nothing but truly conform to your faith.

[1] *trouble* [2] *solicitous* [3] *afterwards* [4] *do without*

ANSWER

God Almighty send us many of that sort, that will preach truly, and nothing but one Catholic universal Christian faith ; and we Highland rude people has mister [1] of them. And if your Lordship would get and provide me such a man, I should provide him a corporal living, as to myself, with great thanks to your Lordship ; for truly, I and many more has great mister of such men. And because I am able to sustain more than one of them, I will request your Lordship earnestly to provide me such a man as ye wrote ; " for the harvest is great, and there are few labourers."

9 The Last and Ninth Article puts me in remembrance to consider what murmur your Lordship tholes, and great bruit, at many men's hands, both Spiritual and Temporal, and at the Queen's Grace's hand, and other well given people, for not putting of order to these affairs ; and that your Lordship has abstained from execution hereof, for love of my house and posterity, to the effect that myself should remedy it, for fear of the dishonour might come upon us both for the same ; which being remedied, might bring us out of all danger.

ANSWER

My Lord, I know well what murmur and indignation your Lordship tholes at [your] enemies' hands of all estates, for non-pursuing of poor simple Christians ; and I know, that if your Lordship would use their counsel, that would be blood-shedding and burning of poor men, to make your Lordship serve their wicked appetites. Yet your Lordship knows your own duty, and should not fear the danger of men, as of Him whom ye profess. And verily, my Lord, there is nothing that may be to your Lordship's relief in this behalf, but I will use your Lordship's counsel therein, and further the same, God's honour being first provided, and the truth of his eternal word having liberty. And to abstain, for my love, from pursuit, as your Lordship has signified, I am indebted to your Lordship, as I have written divers times before. But there is one above, for whose fear ye must abstain from blood-shedding, or else, my Lord, knock on your conscience. Last of all, your Lordship, please to consider, how desirous some are to have sedition amongst friends ; how mighty the Devil is to sow discord ; how that many would desire no better game but to hunt us at other.[2] I pray your Lordship beguile them : we will agree upon all purposes, with God's pleasure, standing to his honour. There are divers houses in Scotland by us,[3] that profess the same God secretly. They desire but that ye begin the bargain at [4] us ; and when it begins at us, God knows the end thereof, and who shall bide the next put. My Lord, consider this : make no preparative of us. Let not the vain exhortation of them that regard little of the weal and strength of both our

[1] *need* [2] *to put us in opposite camps* [3] *apart from us*
[4] *open the question with*

houses, stir up your Lordship, as they would to do against God, your own conscience, and the weal of your posterity for ever. And therefore now, in the end, I pray your Lordship weigh these things wisely ; and if ye do otherwise, God is God, was, and shall be God, when all is wrought that man can work.

APPENDIX V

"THE BEGGARS' SUMMONDS"[1]

"THE BLYND, CRUKED, BEDDRELLES,[2] WEDOWIS, ORPHELINGIS,[3] AND ALL UTHER PURE, SA VISEIT BE THE HAND OF GOD, AS MAY NOT WORKE,

TO THE FLOCKES OF ALL FREIRES WITHIN THIS REALME, WE WISCHE RESTITUTIOUN OF WRANGES BYPAST, AND REFORMATIOUN IN TYME CUMING, FOR SALUTATIOUN.

"YE your selfes ar not ignorant (and thocht ye wald be) it is now (thankes to God) knawen to the haill warlde, be his maist infallible worde, that the benignitie or almes of all Christian people perteynis to us allanerly[4]; quhilk ye, being hale of bodye, stark, sturdye, and abill to wyrk, quhat under pretence of poverty (and neverles possessing maist easelie all abundance), quhat throw cloiket and huded[5] simplicitie (thoght your proudnes is knawen) and quhat be feynzeit[6] halynes, quhilk now is declared superstitioun and idolatrie, hes thire[7] many yeiris, exprese aganis Godis word, and the practeis[8] of his holie Apostles, to our great torment (allace!) maist falslie stowin[9] fra ws. And als ye have, be your fals doctryne and wresting of Godis worde (lerned of your father Sathan), induced the hale people, hie and law,[10] in seure hoip and beleif, that to cleith, feid [   ][11] and nurreis[12] yow, is the onlie maist acceptable almouss allowit before God; and to gif ane penny, or ane peice of breade anis in the oulk[13] is aneuch[14] for ws. Even swa ye have perswaded thame to bigge[15] yow great Hospitalis, and manteyne yow thairin [   ][11] force, quhilk onlye pertenis now to ws be all law, as biggit and dotat[16] to the pure[17] of whois number ye are not, nor can be repute, nether be the law of God, nor yit be na uther law proceding of nature, reasoun, or civile policie. Quhairfore seing our number is sa greate, sa indigent, and sa heavelie oppressed be your false meanes, that nane takes cair of owre miserie; and that it is better for ws to provyde thire our impotent members, quhilkis God hes geven ws, to oppone to yow in plaine controversie, than to see yow heirefter (as ye have done afore) steill fra ws our lodgeings, and our selfis, in the meanetyme, to perreis and die for want of the same. WE have thocht gude therfore, or we enter with yow in conflict, to warne yow, in the name

[1] See *supra*, I, 139, *note* 2; and the description of folio 112 *verso* of the manuscript. given *supra*, i, xcviii
[2] *Bed-ridden*
[3] *Orphans*
[4] *only*
[5] *cloaked and hooded*
[6] *feigned*
[7] *these*
[8] *practice*
[9] *stolen*
[10] *high and low*
[11] This page at the end of the manuscript is badly torn down the right-hand side.
[12] *nourish*
[13] *once a week*
[14] *enough*
[15] *build*
[16] *endowed; mortified*
[17] *poor*

of the grit God, be this publick wryting, affixt on your yettis quhair ye now dwell, that ye remove fourth of oure saidis Hospitales, betuix this and the Feist of Witsunday next,[1] sua[2] that we the onlie lauchfull proprietares thairof may enter thairto, and efterward injoye thai[3] commodities of the Kyrk, quhilkis ye haif heirunto wranguslie halden fra us. Certefying yow, gif ye failye, we will at the said terme, in hale nummer (with the help of God, and assistance of his sanctis in erthe, of quhais reddie support we dout not), enter and tak posessioun of our saide patrimony, and eject yow utterlie fourth of the same.

" *Lat hym therfore that before hes stollin, steill na mare ; but rather lat him wyrk wyth his handes, that he may be helpefull to the pure.*

" FRA THE HALE CITEIS, TOWNES, AND VILLAGES OF SCOTLAND, THE FYRST DAY OF JANUARE 1558." [4]

[1] Whitsunday was the term of entry and removing of tenants, the Act of 1555 having laid down that no removing could be made unless forty days of warning had been given before the term of Whitsunday. (*Acts Parl. Scot.*, ii, 494, c. 12)

[2] *So* [3] *those*

[4] That is, 1st January, 1559. The " Historie of the Estate of Scotland " says that " in the end of October preceeding [*i.e.* 1558], there wes ticketts of warning, at the instance of the whole poore people of this realme, affixt upon the doores of everie place of Friers within this countrey." (*Wodrow Miscellany*, i, 57–58 ; and see *Extracts from the Council Register of Aberdeen*, Spalding Club, i, 315–316) As part of the background to this 'summonds,' it should be noted that, in the first half of the sixteenth century, many endowments of hospitals and almshouses had been transferred to the Friars.

APPENDIX VI

THE CONFESSION OF FAITH[1]

THE CONFESSION OF FAITH PROFESSED AND BELIEVED BY THE PROTESTANTS WITHIN THE REALM OF SCOTLAND, PUBLISHED BY THEM IN PARLIAMENT, AND BY THE ESTATES THEREOF RATIFIED AND APPROVED, AS WHOLESOME AND SOUND DOCTRINE, GROUNDED UPON THE INFALLIBLE TRUTH OF GOD'S WORD

MATTHEW 24

And these glad tidings of the Kingdom shall be preached through the whole world, for a Witness unto all Nations, and then shall the end come

THE PREFACE

THE ESTATES OF SCOTLAND, with the inhabitants of the same, professing Christ Jesus his Holy Evangel, To their natural countrymen, and to all other Realms and Nations, professing the same Lord Jesus with them, wish grace, peace, and mercy from God the Father of our Lord Jesus Christ, with the spirit of righteous judgment, for Salutation.

LONG have we thirsted, dear Brethren, to have notified unto the world the sum of that doctrine which we profess, and for the which we have sustained infamy and danger. But such has been the rage of Sathan against us, and against Christ Jesus his eternal verity, lately born amongst us, that to this day no time has been granted unto us to clear our consciences, as most gladly we would have done; for how we have been tossed a whole year past, the most part of Europe (as we suppose) does understand. But seeing that of the infinite goodness of our God (who never suffers his afflicted to be utterly confounded) above expectation we have obtained some rest and liberty, we could not but set forth this brief and plain Confession of such doctrine as is proponed unto us, and as we believe and profess, partly for satisfaction of our Brethren, whose hearts we doubt not have been and yet are wounded by the despiteful railing of such as yet have not learned to speak well; and partly for stopping of the mouths of impudent blasphemers, who boldly condemn that which they have neither heard nor yet understand. Not that we judge that the cankered malice of such is able to be cured by this simple Confession: No, we know that the sweet savour of the Evangel is, and shall be, death to the sons of perdition. But we have chief respect to our weak and infirm brethren, to whom we would communicate the bottom of our hearts, lest that they

[1] See *supra*, i, 338, *note* 2

be troubled or carried away by the diversities of rumours, which Sathan sparsis [1] contrary us, to the defecting of this our most godly enterprise; Protesting, that if any man will note in this our Confession any article or sentence repugning to God's holy word,[2] that it would please him of his gentleness, and for Christian charity's sake, to admonish us of the same in writ; and We of our honour and fidelity do promise unto him satisfaction from the mouth of God (that is, from his holy Scriptures), or else reformation of that which he shall prove to be amiss. For God we take to record in our consciences, that from our hearts we abhor all sects of heresy, and all teachers of erroneous doctrine; and that with all humility we embrace the purity of Christ's Evangel, which is the only food of our souls; and therefore so precious unto us, that we are determined to suffer the extremity of worldly danger, rather than that we will suffer ourselves to be defrauded of the same. For hereof we are most certainly persuaded, "That whosoever denies Christ Jesus, or is ashamed of him, in presence of men, shall be denied before the Father, and before his holy angels." And therefore by the assistance of the mighty Spirit of the same, our Lord Jesus, we firmly purpose to abide to the end in the Confession of this our Faith [as by the articles followeth].

Cap. i.[3]—Of God

We confess and acknowledge one only God, to whom only we must cleave [whom only we must serve [4]], whom only we must worship, and in whom only we must put our trust; who is eternal, infinite, unmeasurable, incomprehensible, omnipotent, invisible: one in substance, and yet distinct in three persons, the Father, the Son, and the Holy Ghost: By whom we confess and believe all things in heaven and in earth, as well visible as invisible, to have been created, to be retained in their being, and to be ruled and guided by his inscrutable Providence, to such end as his eternal wisdom, goodness, and justice has appointed them, to the manifestation of his own glory.

Cap. ii.—Of the Creation of Man

We confess and acknowledge this our God to have created Man (to wit, our first father Adam), of whom also God formed the Woman to his own image and similitude; to whom he gave wisdom, lordship, justice, free-will, and clear knowledge of himself; so that in the whole nature of man there could be no imperfection: From which honour and

[1] *spreads*

[2] A like reliance upon the word of God is claimed for the provisions of the Book of Discipline. (*Infra*, 280–281)

[3] The numbers of the Chapters are not given in the manuscript. They are here supplied from the first edition of the Confession, printed by Lekprevik in 1561, compared with the Acts of the Parliament of 1567, printed in 1568. (Laing's *Knox*, ii, 97, *note*)

[4] In all cases the words supplied in square brackets are so supplied from the 1561 printed editions and from the version of the Confession printed in the Acts of the Parliament of 1567, printed in 1568. (Laing's *Knox*, ii, 97, *note*)

perfection man and woman did both fall ; the woman being deceived by the Serpent, and man obeying to the voice of the woman, both conspiring against the Sovereign Majesty of God, who in expressed words of before had threatened death, if they presumed to eat of the forbidden tree.

Cap. III.—Of Original Sin

By which transgression, commonly called Original Sin, was the image of God utterly defaced in man ; and he and his posterity of nature became enemies to God, slaves to Sathan, and servants to sin ; in samekill that death everlasting has had, and shall have power and dominion over all that has not been, are not, or shall not be regenerate from above : which regeneration is wrought by the power of the Holy Ghost, working in the hearts of the elect of God an assured faith in the promise of God, revealed to us in his word ; by which faith they apprehend Christ Jesus, with the graces and benefits promised in him.

Cap. IV.—Of the Revelation of the Promise

For this we constantly believe, that God, after the fearful and horrible defection of man from his obedience, did seek Adam again, call upon him, rebuke his sin, convict him of the same, and in the end made unto him a most joyful promise, to wit, " That the seed of the woman should break down the serpent's head " ; that is, he should destroy the works of the Devil. Which promise, as it was repeated and made more clear from time to time, so was it embraced with joy, and most constantly retained of all the faithful, from Adam to Noah, from Noah to Abraham, from Abraham to David, and so forth to the incarnation of Christ Jesus : who all (we mean the faithful Fathers under the law), did see the joyful days of Christ Jesus, and did rejoice.

Cap. V.—The Continuance, Increase, and Preservation of the Kirk

We most constantly believe that God preserved, instructed, multiplied, honoured, decoired,[1] and from death called to life his Kirk in all ages, from Adam, till the coming of Christ Jesus in the flesh : for Abraham he called from his father's country, him he instructed, his seed he multiplied, the same he marvellously preserved, and more marvellously delivered from the bondage [and tyranny] of Pharaoh ; to them he gave his laws, constitutions, and ceremonies ; them he possessed in the land of Canaan ; to them, after Judges and after Saul, he gave David to be king, to whom he made promise, " That of the fruit of his loins should one sit for ever upon his regal seat." To this same people from time to time he sent prophets to reduce[2] them to the right way of their God, from the which often times they declined by idolatry. And albeit for their stubborn contempt of justice, he was compelled to give them in the hands of their

[1] *decorated*, that is, *adorned* [2] *lead back*

enemies, as before was threatened by the mouth of Moses, in samekill that the holy city was destroyed, the temple burnt with fire, and the whole land left desolate the space of seventy years; yet of mercy did he reduce them again to Jerusalem, where the city and temple were re-edified, and they, against all temptations and assaults of Sathan, did abide till the Messiah came, according to the promise.

Cap. vi.—Of the Incarnation of Christ Jesus

When the fullness of time came, God sent his Son, his Eternal Wisdom, the substance of his own glory, in this world, who took the nature of manhood of the substance of a woman, to wit, of a Virgin, and that by the operation of the Holy Ghost. And so was born the just seed of David, the angel of the great council of God; the very Messiah promised, whom we acknowledge and confess Emanuel; very God and very man, two perfect natures united and joined in one person. By which our confession we damn[1] the damnable and pestilent heresies of Arius, Marcion, Eutyches, Nestorius,[2] and such others, as either deny the eternity of his Godhead, or the verity of his human nature, either confound them, or yet divide them.

Cap. vii.—Why it behoved the Mediator to be very God and very Man

We acknowledge and confess that this most wondrous conjunction betwix the Godhead and the Manhead in Christ Jesus did proceed from the eternal and immutable decree of God, whence also our salvation springs and depends.

Cap. viii.—Election

For that same Eternal God and Father, who of mere mercy elected us in Christ Jesus his Son, before the foundation of the world was laid, appointed him to be our Head, our Brother, our Pastor, and great Bishop of our Souls. But because that the enmity betwix the justice of God and our sins was such, that no flesh by itself could or might have attained unto God, it behoved that the Son of God should descend unto us, and take himself a body of our body, flesh of our flesh, and bone of our bones, and so become the perfect Mediator betwix God and man; giving power to so many as believe in Him to be the sons of God, as Himself does witness—"I pass up to my Father and unto your Father, to my God and unto your God." By which most holy fraternity, whatsoever we have lost in Adam is restored to us again. And for this cause are we not effrayed to call God our Father, not so much in that He has created us (which we have common with the reprobate), as for that He has given to us his only Son to be our brother, and given unto us grace to [acknowledge and] embrace Him for our only Mediator, as before is said. It behoved further the Messiah and

[1] *condemn*

[2] Accounts of these heresies will be found in Adolph Harnack, *History of Dogma* (Eng. trans., London, 1894–99), i, 266–286; iv, 7–20, 180–190, 190ff.

Redeemer to [be] very God and very Man, because He was to underlie the punishment due for our transgressions, and to present Himself in the presence of his Father's judgment, as in our person, to suffer for our transgression and inobedience, by death to overcome him that was author of death. But because the only Godhead could not suffer death, neither could the only Manhead overcome the same, He joined both together in one person, that the imbecility of the one should suffer, and be subject to death (which we had deserved), and the infinite and invincible power of the other, to wit, of the Godhead, should triumph and purchase to us life, liberty, and perpetual victory. And so we confess, and most undoubtedly believe.

Cap. ix.—Christ's Death, Passion, Burial, &c.

That our Lord Jesus Christ offered Himself a voluntary sacrifice unto his Father for us ; that He suffered contradiction of sinners ; that He was wounded and plagued for our transgressions ; that He being the clean and innocent Lamb of God, was damned in the presence of an earthly judge, that we might be absolved before the tribunal seat of our God ; that He suffered not only the cruel death of the cross (which was accursed by the sentence of God), but also that He suffered for a season the wrath of his Father, which sinners had deserved. But yet we avow, that He remained the only and well-beloved and blessed Son of his Father, even in the midst of his anguish and torment, which He suffered in body and soul, to make the full satisfaction for the sins of his people. After the which, we confess and avow, that there remains no other sacrifice for sins ; which if any affirm, we nothing doubt to avow that they are blasphemers against Christ's death, and the everlasting purgation and satisfaction purchased to us by the same.

Cap. x.—Resurrection

We undoubtedly believe that insamekill as it was impossible that the dolours of death should retain in bondage the Author of life, that our Lord Jesus Christ crucified, died, and buried, who descended into hell, did rise again for our justification, and destroying [of] him who was [the] author of death, brought life again to us that were subject to death and to the bondage of the same. We know that his resurrection was confirmed by the testimony of his very enemies ; by the resurrection of the dead, whose sepultures did open, and they did arise and appeared to many within the City of Jerusalem. It was also confirmed by the testimony of [his] Angels, and by the senses and judgments of his Apostles, and [of] others, who had conversation, and did eat and drink with Him after his resurrection.

Cap. xi.—Ascension

We nothing doubt but that the self-same body, which was born of the Virgin, was crucified, died, and buried, and which did rise again, did ascend into the heavens for the accomplishment of all things ; where, in our names, and for our comfort He has received all power in heaven and in earth, where He sits at the right hand of the Father inaugurate in his kingdom, advocate and only Mediator for us; which glory, honour, and prerogative He alone amongst the brethren shall possess, till that all his enemies be made his footstool, as that we undoubtedly believe they shall be in the final judgment; to the execution whereof we certainly believe that the same our Lord Jesus shall visibly return, as that He was seen to ascend. And then we firmly believe, that the time of refreshing and restitution of all things shall come, in samekill that they that from the beginning have suffered violence, injury, and wrong for righteousness' sake, shall inherit that blessed immortality promised from the beginning; but contrariwise, the stubborn, inobedient, cruel oppressors, filthy persons, adulterers, and all sorts of unfaithful [men] shall be cast in the dungeon of utter darkness, where their worm shall not die, neither yet their fire [shall] be extinguished. The remembrance of the which day, and of the judgment to be executed in the same, is not only to us a bridle whereby our carnal lusts are refrained; but also such inestimable comfort, that neither may the threatening of worldly princes, neither yet the fear of temporal death and present danger move us to renounce and forsake that blessed society, which we the members have with our Head and only Mediator Christ Jesus, whom we confess and avow to be the Messiah promised, the only Head of his Kirk, our just Lawgiver, our only High Priest, Advocate, and Mediator. In which honours and offices, if man or angel presume to intrude themselves, we utterly detest and abhor them, as blasphemous to our Sovereign and Supreme Governor, Christ Jesus.

Cap. xii.—Faith in the Holy Ghost

This our Faith, and the assurance of the same, proceeds not from flesh and blood, that is to say, from no natural powers within us, but is the inspiration of the Holy Ghost: Whom we confess God, equal with the Father and with the Son; who sanctifieth us, and bringeth us in all verity by his own operation; without whom we should remain for ever enemies to God, and ignorant of his Son, Christ Jesus. For of nature we are so dead, so blind and so perverse, that neither can we feel when we are pricked, see the light when it shines, nor assent to the will of God when it is revealed; only the Spirit of the Lord Jesus quickeneth that which is dead, removeth the darkness from our minds, and boweth our stubborn hearts to the obedience of his blessed will. And so as we confess that God the Father created us when we were not; as his Son, our Lord Jesus redeemed us when we were enemies to Him: so also do we confess that the Holy Ghost does sanctify and regenerate us, without all respect of any merit proceeding from us, be it before or be it after our regeneration. To speak this one thing yet in more plain words, as we willingly spoil ourselves of all honour and glory of our own creation and redemption, so do we also of our regeneration and sanctification: For of ourselves we are not sufficient to think one good thought; but He who has begun the good work in us, is only He that continueth us in the same, to the praise and glory of his undeserved grace.

Cap. xiii.—The Cause of Good Works

So that the cause of Good works we confess to be, not our free will, but the Spirit of the Lord Jesus who, dwelling in our hearts by true faith, brings forth such good works as God hath prepared for us to walk into: for this we most boldly affirm, that blasphemy it is to say that Christ Jesus abides in the hearts of such as in whom there is no spirit of Sanctification. And therefore we fear not to affirm that murderers, oppressors, cruel persecuters, adulterers, whoremongers, filthy persons, idolaters, drunkards, thieves, and all workers of iniquity, have neither true faith, neither any portion of the spirit of Sanctification, which proceedeth from the Lord Jesus, so long as they obstinately continue in their wickedness. For how soon that ever the spirit of the Lord Jesus (which God's elect children receive by true faith), takes possession in the heart of any man, so soon does He regenerate and renew the same man; so that he begins to hate that which before he loved, and begins to love that which before he hated; and from thence comes that continual battle which is betwix the flesh and the spirit in God's children; while the flesh and natural man (according to its own corruption) lusts for things pleasing and delectable unto the self, grudges [1] in adversity, is lifted up in prosperity, and at every moment is prone and ready to offend the Majesty of God. But the Spirit of God, which giveth witnessing to our spirit, that we are the sons of God, makes us to resist the devil, to abhor filthy pleasures, to groan in God's presence for deliverance from this bondage of corruption; and finally, so [to] triumph over sin that it reign not in our mortal bodies. This battle has not the carnal men, being destitute of God's Spirit; but do follow and obey sin with greediness, and without repentance, even as the devil and their corrupt lusts do prick them. But the sons of God (as before is said) do fight against sin, do sob and mourn, when they perceive themselves tempted to iniquity; and if they fall, they rise again with earnest and unfeigned repentance. And these things they do not by their own power, but the power of the Lord Jesus (without whom they were able to do nothing) worketh in them all that is good.

Cap. xiv.—What Works are reputed Good before God

We confess and acknowledge that God has given to man his holy law, in which not only are forbidden all such works which displease and offend his Godly Majesty; but also are commanded all such as please Him, and as He hath promised to reward. And these works be of two sorts; the one are done to the honour of God, the other to the profit of our neighbours; and both have the revealed will of God for their assurance. To have one God, to worship and honour Him; to call upon Him in all our troubles; to reverence his holy name; to hear his word; to believe the same; to communicate with his holy sacraments;—are the works of the First Table. To honour father, mother, princes, rulers, and superior powers; to love them; to support them, yea, to obey their

[1] *murmurs; complains*

charges (not repugning to the commandment of God); to save the lives of innocents; to repress tyranny; to defend the oppressed; to keep our bodies clean and holy; to live in sobriety and temperance; to deal justly with all men, both in word and in deed; and, finally, to repress all appetite of our neighbour's hurt;—are the good works of the Second Table, which are most pleasing and acceptable unto God, as those works that are commanded by Himself. The contrary whereof is sin most odious, which always displeases Him, and provokes Him to anger,—as, not to call upon Him alone when we have need; not to hear his word with reverence; to contemn and despise it; to have or to worship idols; to maintain and defend idolatry; lightly to esteem the reverent name of God; to profane, abuse, or contemn the sacraments of Christ Jesus; to disobey or resist any that God has placed in authority (while they pass not over [1] the bounds of their office); to murder, or to consent thereto, to bear hattrent,[2] or to suffer innocent blood to be shed if we may gainstand it; and, finally, the transgressing of any other commandment in the First or Second Table, we confess and affirm to be sin, by the which God's hot displeasure is kindled against the proud and unthankful world. So that good works we affirm to be these only that are done in faith, [and] at God's commandment, who in his law has expressed what be the things that please Him: And evil works, we affirm, not only those that are expressedly done against God's commandment, but those also that, in matters of religion and worshipping of God, have no [other] assurance but the invention and opinion of man, which God from the beginning has ever rejected; as by the prophet Isaiah, and by our master Christ Jesus, we are taught in these words—" In vain do they worship me, teaching the doctrine being precepts of men."

Cap. xv.—The Perfection of the Law and Imperfection of Man

The Law of God we confess and acknowledge most just, most equal, most holy, and most perfect; commanding those things which, being wrought in perfection, were able to give life, and [able] to bring man to eternal felicity. But our nature is so corrupt, so weak, and imperfect, that we are never able to fulfil the works of the Law in perfection; yea, " If we say we have no sin (even after we are regenerate), we deceive ourselves, and the verity of God is not into us." And therefore it behoved us to apprehend Christ Jesus, with his justice and satisfaction, who is the end and accomplishment of the Law, to all that believe, by whom we are set at this liberty, that the curse and malediction of God fall not upon us, albeit that we fulfil not the same in all points. For God the Father beholding us in the body of his Son Christ Jesus, accepteth our imperfect obedience as it were perfect, and covereth our works, which are defiled with many spots, with the justice of his Son. We do not mean that we are so set at liberty, that we owe no obedience to the Law (for that before we have plainly confessed); but this we affirm, that no man in earth (Christ Jesus only excepted) hath given, giveth, or shall give in work, that obedience

[1] *do not exceed* [2] *hatred*

to the Law which the Law requireth. But when we have done all things, we must fall down and unfeignedly confess, "That we are unprofitable servants." And therefore whosoever boast themselves of the merits of their own works, or put their trust in the works of supererogation, they boast themselves of that which is not, and put their trust in damnable idolatry.

Cap. xvi.—Of the Kirk

As we believe in one God, Father, Son, and Holy Ghost, so do we most earnestly believe that from the beginning there has been, now is, and to the end of the world shall be a Church; that is to say, a company and multitude of men chosen of God, who rightly worship and embrace Him, by true faith in Christ Jesus, who is the only Head of the same Kirk, which also is the body and spouse of Christ Jesus; which Kirk is Catholic, that is, universal, because it contains the Elect of all ages, [of] all realms, nations, and tongues, be they of the Jews, or be they of the Gentiles, who have communion and society with God the Father, and with his Son Christ Jesus, through the sanctification of his Holy Spirit; and therefore it is called [the] communion, not of profane persons but of saints, who, as citizens of the heavenly Jerusalem, have the fruition of the most inestimable benefits, to wit, of one God, one Lord Jesus, one faith, and of one baptism; out of the which Kirk there is neither life, nor eternal felicity. And therefore we utterly abhor the blasphemy of those that affirm that men which live according to equity and justice shall be saved, what religion soever they have professed. For as without Christ Jesus there is neither life nor salvation, so shall there none be participant thereof but such as the Father has given unto his Son Christ Jesus, and those [that] in time come to Him, avow his doctrine, and believe into Him (we comprehend the children with the faithful parents). This Kirk is invisible, known only to God, who alone knoweth whom He has chosen, and comprehends as well (as said is) the Elect that be departed (commonly called the Kirk Triumphant), as those that yet live and fight against sin and Sathan as shall live hereafter.

Cap. xvii.—The Immortality of the Souls

The Elect departed are in peace and rest from their labours; not that they sleep and come to a certain oblivion (as some fantastic heads do affirm), but that they are delivered from all fear, all torment, and all temptation, to which we and all God's elect are subject in this life; and therefore do bear the name of the Kirk Militant. As contrariwise, the reprobate and unfaithful departed, have anguish, torment, and pain, that cannot be expressed; so that neither are the one nor the other in such sleep that they feel not joy or torment, as the Parable of Christ Jesus in the sixteenth of Luke, his words to the thief, and these words of the souls crying under the altar, "O Lord, thou that art righteous and just, how long shalt thou not revenge our blood upon them that dwell upon the earth!" doth plainly testify.

Cap. xviii.—Of the Notes by which the True Kirk is discerned from the false and who shall be judge of the doctrine

Because that Sathan from the beginning has laboured to deck his pestilent Synagogue with the title of the Kirk of God, and has inflamed the hearts of cruel murderers to persecute, trouble, and molest the true Kirk and members thereof, as Cain did Abel ; Ishmael, Isaac ; Esau, Jacob ; and the whole priesthood of the Jews, Jesus Christ Himself, and his apostles after him ; it is a thing most requisite that the true Kirk be discerned from the filthy synagogue, by clear and perfect notes, lest we, being deceived, receive and embrace to our own condemnation the one for the other. The notes, signs, and assured tokens whereby the immaculate spouse of Christ Jesus is known from that horrible harlot the Kirk malignant, we affirm are neither antiquity, title usurped, lineal descent, place appointed, nor multitude of men approving an error ; for Cain in age and title was preferred to Abel and Seth ; Jerusalem had prerogative above all places of the earth, where also were the priests lineally descended from Aaron ; and greater multitude followed the Scribes, Pharisees, and Priests, than unfeignedly believed and approved Christ Jesus and his doctrine ; and yet (as we suppose) no man of sound judgment will grant that any of the forenamed were the Kirk of God. The Notes, therefore, of the true Kirk of God we believe, confess, and avow to be, first, The true preaching of the word of God ; into the which God has revealed himself to us, as the writings of the Prophets and Apostles do declare. Secondly, The right administration of the sacraments of Christ Jesus, which must be annexed to the word and promise of God, to seal and confirm the same in our hearts. Last[ly], Ecclesiastical discipline uprightly ministered, as God's word prescribes, whereby vice is repressed, and virtue nourished.[1] Wheresoever then these former notes are seen, and of any time continue (be the number never so few above two or three) there, but all doubt, is the true Kirk of Christ, who according to his promise is in the midst of them : not that universal (of which we have before spoken) but particular ; such as was in Corinth, Galatia, Ephesus, and other places in which the ministry was planted by Paul, and were of himself named the Kirks of God. And such Kirks we, the inhabitants of the Realm of Scotland, professors of Christ Jesus, confess us to have in our cities, towns, and places reformed ; for the doctrine taught in our kirks is contained in the written word of God, to wit, in the Books of the Old and New Testaments. In those books, we mean, which of the ancient have been reputed canonical, in the which we affirm that all things necessary to be believed for the salvation of mankind, is sufficiently expressed [2] ; the interpretation whereof, we confess, neither appertaineth to private nor public person, neither yet to any kirk for any pre-eminence or prerogative, personal or local, which one has above another ; but appertaineth to the Spirit of God, by the which also the Scripture was written. When controversy then happeneth for the right understanding of any place or sentence of Scripture, or for

[1] These " Notes of the True Kirk " had already been defined in the Confession of the English Congregation at Geneva. (Laing's *Knox*, iv, 172–73)

[2] See the like affirmation in the opening of the Book of Discipline (*infra*, 281)

the reformation of any abuse within the Kirk of God, we ought not so much to look what men before us have said or done, as unto that which the Holy Ghost uniformly speaks within the body of the Scriptures, and unto that which Christ Jesus Himself did, and commanded to be done. For this is a thing universally granted, that the Spirit of God, which is the Spirit of unity, is in nothing contrarious unto Himself. If then the interpretation, determination, or sentence of any doctor, kirk, or council, repugn to the plain word of God written in any other place of [the] Scripture, it is a thing most certain, that theirs is not the true understanding and meaning of the Holy Ghost, supposing that Councils, Realms, and Nations have approved and received the same: For we dare not receive and admit any interpretation which directly repugneth to any principal point of our faith, [or] to any other plain text of Scripture, or yet unto the rule of charity.

Cap. xix.—The Authority of the Scriptures

As we believe and confess the Scriptures of God sufficient to instruct and make the man of God perfect, so do we affirm and avow the authority of the same to be of God, and neither to depend on men nor angels. We affirm therefore that such as allege the Scripture to have no [other] authority, but that which is received from the Kirk, to be blasphemous against God, and injurious to the true Kirk, which always heareth and obeyeth the voice of her own Spouse and Pastor, but taketh not upon her to be mistress over the same.

Cap. xx.—Of General Councils, of their Power, Authority, and Causes of their Convention

As we do not rashly damn that which godly men, assembled together in General Councils, lawfully gathered, have approved unto us; so without just examination dare we not receive whatsoever is obtruded unto men, under the name of General Councils: for plain it is, that as they were men, so have some of them manifestly erred, and that in matters of great weight and importance. So far then as the Council proveth the determination and commandment that it giveth by the plain word of God, so far do we reverence and embrace the same. But if men, under the name of a Council, pretend to forge unto us new articles of our faith, or to make constitutions repugning to the word of God, then utterly we must refuse the same as the doctrine of devils, which draws our souls from the voice of our only God to follow the doctrines and constitutions of men. The cause, then, why [that] General Councils convened, was neither to make any perpetual law (which God before had not made), neither yet to forge new articles of our belief, neither to give the word of God authority, mekle less to make that to be his word, or yet the true interpretation of the same, which was not before by his holy will expressed in his word. But the cause of Councils (we mean of such as merit the name of Councils), was partly for confutation of heresies, and for giving public confession of their faith to the posterity following; which both they did by the authority of God's written word, and not by any opinion or prerogative that they could not err, by reason of their General assembly. And this we judge to have been the chief cause of General Councils. The other was for good policy and order to be constituted and observed in the Kirk, in which (as in the house of God) it becomes all things to be done decently and into order.[1] Not that we think that one policy and one order in ceremonies can be appointed for all ages, times, and places; for as ceremonies (such as men has devised) are but temporal, so may and ought they to be changed, when they rather foster superstition than that they edify the Kirk using the same.

Cap. xxi.—Of the Sacraments

As the Fathers under the Law, besides the verity of the sacrifices, had two chief Sacraments, to wit, Circumcision and the Passover, the despisers and contemners whereof were not reputed for God's people; so [do] we acknowledge and confess that we now, in the time of the Evangel, have two [2] Sacraments only, instituted by the Lord Jesus, and commanded to be used of all those that will be reputed members of his body, to wit, Baptism and the Supper, or Table of the Lord Jesus, called The Communion of his body and blood. And these sacraments (as well of the Old as of the New Testament) were instituted of God, not only to make a visible difference betwix his people, and those that were without his league; but also to exercise the faith of his children; and by participation of the same sacraments, to seal in their hearts the assurance of his promise, and of that most blessed conjunction, union, and society, which the Elect have with their head, Christ Jesus. And thus we utterly damn the vanity of those that affirm Sacraments to be nothing else but naked and bare signs. No, we assuredly believe that by Baptism we are ingrafted in Christ Jesus to be made partakers of his justice, by the which our sins are covered and remitted [3]; and also, that in the Supper, rightly used, Christ Jesus is so joined with us, that he becomes the very nourishment and food of our souls. Not that we imagine any transubstantiation of bread into Christ's natural body, and of wine in his natural blood (as the Papists have perniciously taught and damnably believed); but this union and communion which we have with the body and blood of Christ Jesus in the right use of the sacraments, is wrought by operation of the Holy Ghost, who by true faith carries us above all things that are visible, carnal, and earthly, and makes us to feed upon the body and blood of Christ Jesus, which was once broken and shed for us, which now is in the

[1] *Cf.* The Ninth Head of the Book of Discipline—"Concerning the Policy of the Church" (*infra*, 312).

[2] The ratifications by Parliament in 1560 and 1567 say "two *chief*." (*Acts Parl. Scot.*, ii, 532; iii, 20)

[3] So also the English Congregation at Geneva had declared that Baptism was ordained "to teach us that . . . the virtue of Christ's blood [doth] purge our souls from that corruption and deadly poison wherewith by nature we were infected." (Laing's *Knox*, iv, 188)

heaven, and appeareth in the presence of his Father for us. And yet, notwithstanding the far distance of place, which is betwix his body now glorified in the heaven, and us now mortal in this earth, yet we most assuredly believe, that the bread which we break is the communion of Christ's body, and the cup which we bless is the communion of his blood. So that we confess, and undoubtedly believe, that the faithful, in the right use of the Lord's Table, so do eat the body, and drink the blood of the Lord Jesus, that He remaineth in them and they in Him : yea, that they are so made flesh of his flesh, and bone of his bones, that as the Eternal Godhead hath given to the flesh of Christ Jesus (which of its own condition and nature was mortal and corruptible) life and immortality, so doth Christ Jesus his flesh and blood eaten and drunken by us, give to us the same prerogatives. Which, albeit we confess are neither given unto us at that only time, neither yet by the proper power and virtue of the Sacraments only ; yet we affirm that the faithful in the right use of the Lord's Table have such conjunction with Christ Jesus, as the natural man cannot comprehend : yea, and further we affirm, that albeit the faithful oppressed by negligence, and manly infirmity, do not profit so much as they would at the very instant action of the Supper, yet shall it after bring forth fruit, as lively seed sown in good ground ; for the Holy Spirit, which can never be divided from the right institution of the Lord Jesus, will not frustrate the faithful of the fruit of that mystical action. But all this, we say, comes by true faith, which apprehendeth Christ Jesus, who only makes his Sacraments effectual unto us ; and, therefore, whosoever slandereth us, as that we affirmed or believed Sacraments to be only naked and bare signs, do injury unto us, and speak against a manifest truth. But this liberally and frankly we must confess, that we make a distinction betwix Christ Jesus, in his natural substance, and betwix the elements in the Sacramental signs ; so that we will neither worship the signs in place of that which is signified by them ; neither yet do we despise and interpret them as unprofitable and vain ; but do use them with all reverence, examining ourselves diligently before that so we do, because we are assured by the mouth of the Apostle, " That such as eat of that bread, and drink of that cup, unworthily, are guilty of the body and blood of the Lord Jesus."

Cap. xxii.—Of the Right Administration of the Sacraments

That Sacraments be rightly ministered, we judge two things requisite : the one, That they be ministered by lawful ministers, whom we affirm to be only they that are appointed to the preaching of the word, or into whose mouths God has put some sermon of exhortation, they being men lawfully chosen thereto by some Kirk. The other, That they be ministered in such elements, and in such sort as God hath appointed. Else we affirm, that they cease to be right Sacraments of Christ Jesus. And, therefore, it is, that we flee the society with the Papistical Kirk in participation of their Sacraments ; first, because their ministers are no ministers of Christ Jesus ; yea (which is more horrible) they suffer women, whom the Holy Ghost will not suffer to teach in the congregation, to baptise. And, secondly, Because they have so adulterated, both the one sacrament and the other, with their own inventions, that no part of Christ's action abideth in the original purity; for oil, salt, spittle, and suchlike in baptism, are but men's inventions; adoration, veneration, bearing through streets and towns, and keeping of bread in boxes or buists,[1] are profanation of Christ's Sacraments, and no use of the same: For Christ Jesus said, "Take, eat, &c.; Do ye this in remembrance of me." By which words and charge he sanctified bread and wine to be the sacrament of his body and blood; to the end, that the one should be eaten, and that all should drink of the other; and not that they should be kept to be worshipped and honoured as God, as the blind Papists have done heretofore, who also have committed sacrilege, stealing from the people the one part of the Sacrament, to wit, the blessed cup.[2] Moreover, that the Sacraments be rightly used, it is required that the end and cause why the Sacraments were instituted be understood and observed, as well of the minister as of the receivers; for if the opinion be changed in the receiver, the right use ceaseth; which is most evident by the rejection of the sacrifices (as also if the teacher teach false doctrine) which were odious and abominable unto God (albeit they were his own ordinances), because that wicked men use them to another end than God hath ordained. The same affirm we of the sacraments in the Papistical Kirk, in which we affirm the whole action of the Lord Jesus to be adulterated, as well in the external form, as in the end and opinion. What Christ Jesus did, and commanded to be done, is evident by the three Evangelists and by Saint Paul. What the priest does at his altar we need not to rehearse. The end and cause of Christ's institution, and why the self-same should be used, is expressed in these words,—"Do this in remembrance of me. As oft as ye shall eat of this bread and drink of this cup, ye shall show forth (that is, extol, preach, and magnify), the Lord's death till he come." But to what end, and in what opinion, the priests say their masses, let the words of the same, their own doctors and writings witness, to wit, that they, as mediators betwix Christ and his Kirk, do offer unto God the Father a sacrifice propitiatory for the sins of the quick and the dead. Which doctrine, as blasphemous to Christ Jesus, and making derogation to the sufficiency of his only sacrifice, once offered for purgation of all those that shall be sanctified, we utterly abhor, detest, and renounce.

CAP. XXIII.—TO WHOM SACRAMENTS APPERTAIN

We Confess and acknowledge that Baptism appertaineth as well to the infants of the faithful, as to those that be of age and discretion. And so we damn the error of [the] Anabaptists, who deny baptism to appertain to children, before that they have faith and understanding. But the Supper of the Lord, we confess to appertain only to such as have been of the household of faith, [and] can try and examine themselves, as well in their faith, as in their duty towards their neighbours. Such as eat [and drink] at that holy table without faith, or being at dissension and division

[1] *chests* [2] See *supra*, i, 151 and *note* 2

with their brethren, do eat unworthily: and therefore it is, that in our Kirks our Ministers take public and particular examination of the knowledge and conversation of such as are to be admitted to the table of the Lord Jesus.

Cap. xxiv.—Of the Civil Magistrate [1]

We Confess and acknowledge empires, kingdoms, dominions, and cities to be distincted and ordained by God: the powers and authorities in the same (be it of Emperors in their empires, of Kings in their realms, Dukes and Princes in their dominions, or of other Magistrates in free cities), to be God's holy ordinance, ordained for manifestation of his own glory, and for the singular profit and commodity of mankind. So that whosoever goes about to take away or to confound the whole state of civil policies, now long established, we affirm the same men not only to be enemies to mankind, but also wickedly to fight against God's expressed will. We further Confess and acknowledge, that such persons as are placed in authority are to be loved, honoured, feared, and held in most reverent estimation; because [that] they are the lieutenants of God, in whose session God himself doth sit and judge (yea even the Judges and Princes themselves), to whom by God is given the sword, to the praise and defence of good men, and to revenge and punish all open malefactors. Moreover, to Kings, Princes, Rulers, and Magistrates, we affirm that chiefly and most principally the conservation [2] and purgation of the Religion appertains; so that not only they are appointed for civil policy, but also for maintenance of the true Religion,[3] and for suppressing of idolatry and superstition whatsomever, as in David, Jehoshaphat, Hezekiah, Josiah, and others, highly commended for their zeal in that case, may be espied. And therefore we confess and avow, that such as resist the supreme power (doing that thing which appertains to his charge), do resist God's ordinance, and therefore cannot be guiltless. And further, we affirm, that whosoever deny unto them their aid, counsel, and comfort, while the Princes and Rulers vigilantly travail in the executing of their office, that the same men deny their help, support, and counsel to God, who by the presence of his lieutenant craveth it of them.

Cap. xxv.—The Gifts freely given to the Kirk

Albeit that the word of God truly preached, [and] the Sacraments rightly ministered, and discipline executed according to the word of God, be the certain and infallible signs of the true Kirk [4]; yet do we not so mean, that every particular person joined with such a company, be an

[1] See Randolph's comments in his letter to Cecil of 7 September 1560 (*Calendar of Scottish Papers*, i, No. 902)

[2] In the manuscript (folio 237 *verso*) originally *conversatioun*, which has been scored through and *reformatione* added in the margin. The ratifications by Parliament in 1560 and 1567 say *conservation*.

[3] This was again stressed, in like words, by the General Assembly in 1572. (*Booke of the Universall Kirk*, i, 212)

[4] *Supra*, 266

elect member of Christ Jesus. For we acknowledge and confess, that darnel, cockle, and chaff may be sown, grow, and in great abundance lie in the midst of the wheat ; that is, the reprobate may be joined in the society of the elect, and may externally use with them the benefits of the word and sacraments ; but such being but temporal professors in mouth, but not in heart, do fall back and continue not to the end : and therefore have they no fruit of Christ's death, resurrection, nor ascension. But such as with heart unfeignedly believe, and with mouth boldly confess the Lord Jesus (as before we have said), shall most assuredly receive these gifts—First, In this life, remission of sins, and that by faith only in Christ's blood, insamekle, that albeit sin remain and continually abide in these our mortal bodies, yet it is not imputed unto us, but is remitted and covered with Christ's justice. Secondly, In the general judgment there shall be given to every man and woman resurrection of the flesh ; for the sea shall give her dead, the earth those that therein be inclosed ; yea, the Eternal, our God, shall stretch out his hand upon the dust, and the dead shall arise incorruptible, and that in the substance of the [self]same flesh that every man now bears, to receive according to their works, glory or punishment : for such as now delight in vanity, cruelty, filthiness, superstition, or idolatry, shall be adjudged to the fire inextinguishable, in the which they shall be tormented for ever, as well in their own bodies, as in their souls, which now they give to serve the devil in all abomination. But such as continue in well doing to the end, boldly professing the Lord Jesus [we constantly believe, that they shall receive glory, honour, and immortality, to reign for ever in life everlasting with Christ Jesus], to whose glorified body all his Elect shall be [made] like, when He shall appear again to judgment, and shall render up the kingdom to God his Father, who then shall be, and ever shall remain all in all things, God blessed for ever : To whom, with the Son, and with the Holy Ghost, be all honour and glory, now and ever. AMEN.

Arise, O Lord, and let thy enemies be confounded : Let them flee from thy presence that hate thy godly name : Give thy Servants strength to speak thy word in boldness ; and let all Nations attain to thy true knowledge.

THESE ACTS AND ARTICLES WERE READ IN FACE OF PARLIAMENT, AND RATIFIED BY THE THREE ESTATES OF THIS REALM, AT EDINBURGH, THE SEVENTEEN DAY OF AUGUST, THE YEAR OF GOD 1560.[1]

[1] *Acts Parl. Scot.*, ii, 526, 534. In the manuscript (folio 239 *recto*) the month is given, erroneously, as July.

APPENDIX VII [1]

THE FORM AND ORDER OF THE ELECTION OF SUPERINTENDENTS, ELDERS, AND DEACONS [1]

THE FORM AND ORDER OF THE ELECTION OF THE SUPERINTENDENTS, WHICH MAY SERVE ALSO IN ELECTION OF ALL OTHER MINISTERS. AT EDINBURGH THE 9TH OF MARCH 1560,[2] JOHN KNOX BEING MINISTER.[3]

FIRST was made a Sermon, in the which these Heads were entreated. First, The necessity of Ministers and Superintendents. 2 The crimes and vices that might unable them [of the ministry]. 3 The virtues required in them. And last, whether such as by public consent of the Kirk were called to such Office, might refuse the same.

The Sermon finished, it was declared by the same Minister (maker thereof) that the Lords of Secret Council had given charge and power to the Kirks of Lothian to choose MR. JOHN SPOTTISWOODE Superintendent; and that sufficient warning was made by public edict to the Kirks of Edinburgh, Linlithgow, Stirling, Tranent, Haddington, and Dunbar; as also to Earls, Lords, Barons, Gentlemen, and others, having, or who might claim to have, vote in Election, to be present that day, at that same hour: And, therefore, inquisition was made, Who were present, and who were absent.

After was called the said Mr. John, who answering, the Minister demanded if any man knew any crime or offence to the said Mr. John that might unable him to be called to that office? And this he demanded thrice. Secondly, Question was moved to the whole multitude, If there was any other whom they would put in Election with the said Mr. John. The people were asked, If they would have the said Mr. John Superintendent? If they would honour and obey him as Christ's Minister, and comfort and assist him in everything pertaining to his Charge? They Answered.—We will; and we do promise unto him such obedience as becometh the sheep to give unto their Pastor, so long as he remains faithful in his office.

[1] See the note *supra*, i, 355. See also "Of the Election of Superintendents" in the *Book of Discipline* (*infra*, 293); the election of John Winram to be Superintendent of the Diocese of St. Andrews (*Reg. Kirk Session of St. Andrews*, Scot. Hist. Soc., i, 72–75); and the Manner of Electing Ministers, Elders, and Deacons in the Order of Geneva. (Laing's *Knox*, iv, 175–177)

[2] 9 March 1561

[3] Randolph, writing to Cecil on 5 March 1561, and referring to the election of the Superintendents, says, "Mr. Knox thinks his state honourable enough, if God give him strength to persist in that vocation that he hath placed him in [*i.e.* Minister in Edinburgh], and will receive no other." (*Calendar of Scottish Papers*, i, No. 967)

The Answers of the People, and their consents received, these Questions were proponed unto him that was to be elected :

Question.—Seeing that ye hear the thirst and desire of this people, do ye not think yourself bound in conscience before God to support them that so earnestly call for your comfort, and for the fruit of your labours ?

Answer.—If anything were in me able to satisfy their desire, I acknowledge myself bound to obey God calling by them.

Question.—Do ye seek to be promoted to this Office and charge for any respect of worldly commodity, riches or glory ?

Answer.—God knows the contrary.

Question.—Believe ye not that the doctrine of the Prophets and Apostles, contained in the books of the Old and New Testaments, is the only true and most absolute foundation of the universal Kirk of Christ Jesus, insamekill [1] that in the same Scriptures are contained all things necessary to be believed for the salvation of mankind ?

Answer.—I verily believe the same, and do abhor and utterly refuse all Doctrine alleged necessary to Salvation that is not expressly contained in the same.

Question.—Is not Christ Jesus Man of Man, according to the flesh, to wit, the Son of David, the Seed of Abraham, conceived by the Holy Ghost, born of the Virgin Mary his mother, the only Head and Mediator of his Kirk ?

Answer.—He is, and without Him there is neither salvation to man, nor life to angel.

Question.—Is not the same Lord Jesus [the] only true God, the Eternal Son of the Eternal Father, in whom all that shall be saved were elected before the foundation of the world was laid ?

Answer.—I confess and acknowledge Him in the unity of his Godhead, to be God above all things, blessed for ever.

Question.—Shall not they whom God in his eternal council has elected, be called to the knowledge of his Son, our Lord Jesus ? And shall not they, who of purpose are elected in this life, be justified ? And is not justification and free remission of sins obtained in this life by free grace ? Shall not this glory of the sons of God follow in the general resurrection, when the Son of God shall appear in his glorious majesty ?

Answer.—I acknowledge this to be the doctrine of the Apostles, and the most singular comfort of God's children.

Question.—Will ye not contain yourself in all doctrine within the bounds of this foundation ? Will ye not study to promote the same, as well by your life as by your doctrine ? Will ye not, according to the graces and utterance that God shall grant unto you, profess, instruct, and maintain the purity of the doctrine, contained in the sacred Word of God ? And, to the uttermost of your power, will ye not gainstand and convince the gainsayers and teachers of men's inventions ?

Answer.—That I do promise in the presence of God, and of his congregation here assembled.

Question.—Know ye not that the excellency of this office, to the

[1] *insomuch*

which God has called you, requires that your conversation and behaviour be such as that ye may be irreprehensible ; yea, even in the eyes of the ungodly ?

Answer.—I unfeignedly acknowledge, and humbly desire the Kirk of God to pray with me, that my life be not scandalous to the glorious Evangel of Jesus Christ.

Question.—Because ye are a man compassed with infirmities, will ye not charitably, and with lowliness of spirit, receive admonition of your Brethren ? And if ye shall happen to slide, or offend in any point, will ye not be subject to the Discipline of the Kirk, as the rest of your Brethren ?

The Answer of the Superintendent, or Minister to be elected.—I acknowledge myself to be a man subject to infirmity, and one that has need of correction and admonition ; and therefore I most willingly submit and subject myself to the wholesome discipline of the Kirk ; yea, to the discipline of the same Kirk by the which I am now called to this office and charge ; and here in God's presence and yours do promise obedience to all admonitions, secretly or publicly given ; unto the which, if I be found inobedient, I confess myself most worthy to be ejected not only from this honour, but also from the society of the Faithful, in case of my stubbornness. For the vocation of God to bear charge within his Kirk, maketh not men tyrants, nor lords, but appointeth them Servants, Watchmen, and Pastors of the Flock.

This ended, Question must be asked again of the multitude.

Question.—Require ye any further of this your Superintendent ?

If no man answer, let the Minister proceed. Will ye not acknowledge this your Brother for the Minister of Christ Jesus ? Will ye not reverence the word of God that proceeds from his mouth ? Will ye not receive of him the sermon of exhortation with patience, not refusing the wholesome medicine of your souls, although it be bitter and unpleasing to the flesh ? Will ye not finally maintain and comfort him in his ministry, against all such as wickedly would rebel against God and his holy ordinance ?

The people answereth.—We will, as we will answer to the Lord Jesus, who has commanded his Ministers to be had in reverence, as his ambassadors, and as men that carefully watch for the salvation of our souls.

Let the Nobility also be urged with this.—Ye have heard the duty and profession of this your Brother, by your consents appointed to this charge ; as also the duty and obedience which God requireth of us towards him here in his ministry : But because that neither of both are able to perform anything without the especial grace of our God in Christ Jesus, who has promised to be with us present, even to the consummation of the world ; with unfeigned hearts, let us crave of Him his benediction and assistance in this work begun to his glory, and for the comfort of his Kirk.

The Prayer

O Lord, to whom all power is given in heaven, and in earth, Thou that art the Eternal Son of the Eternal Father, who has not only so loved thy Kirk, that for the redemption and purgation of the same, Thou hast humbled Thyself to the death of the Cross ; and thereupon has shed thy most innocent blood, to prepare to Thyself a Spouse without spot ; but also, to retain this thy most excellent benefit in memory, has appointed in thy Kirk, Teachers, Pastors, and Apostles, to instruct, comfort, and admonish the same : Look upon us mercifully, O Lord, Thou that only art King, Teacher, and High Priest to thy own flock ; and send unto this our Brother, whom in Thy name we have charged with the chief care of thy Kirk, within the bounds of Lothian, such portion of thy Holy Spirit, as thereby he may rightly divide thy word to the instruction of thy flock, and to the confutation of pernicious errors, and damnable superstitions. Give unto him, good Lord, a mouth and wisdom, whereby the enemies of thy truth may be confounded, the wolves expelled, and driven from thy fold, thy sheep may be fed in the wholesome pastures of thy most holy word, the blind and ignorant may be illuminated with thy true knowledge : Finally, That the dregs of superstition and idolatry which yet rest within this Realm, being purged and removed, we may all not only have occasion to glorify Thee our only Lord and Saviour, but also daily to grow in godliness and obedience of thy most holy will, to the destruction of the body of sin, and to the restitution of that image to the which we were once created, and to the which, after our fall and defection, we are renewed by participation of thy Holy Spirit, which by true faith in Thee, we do profess as the blessed of thy Father, of whom the perpetual increase of thy graces we crave, as by Thee our Lord and King, and only Bishop, we are taught to pray, saying, " Our Father that art in heaven, &c."

The prayer ended, the rest of the Ministers, if any be, and Elders of that Kirk present, in sign of their consents, shall take the elected by the hand, and then the chief Minister shall give the benediction, as follows :—

God, the Father of our Lord Jesus Christ, who has commanded his Evangel to be preached, to the comfort of his Elect, and has called thee to the office of a Watchman over his people, multiply his graces with thee, illuminate thee with his Holy Spirit, comfort and strengthen thee in all virtue, govern and guide thy ministry, to the praise of his holy Name, to the propagation of Christ's kingdom, to the comfort of his Kirk, and finally, to the plain discharge and assurance of thy own conscience in the day of the Lord Jesus ; to whom, with the Father, and the Holy Ghost, be all honour, praise, and glory, now and ever. So be it.

The last Exhortation to the Elected

Take heed to thy self, and unto the Flock committed to thy charge ; feed the same carefully, not as it were of compulsion, but of very love, which thou bearest to the Lord Jesus. Walk in simplicity and pureness of life, as it becometh the true servant and ambassador of the Lord Jesus. Usurp not dominion nor tyrannical empire over thy brethren. Be not discouraged in adversity, but lay before thyself the example of Prophets, Apostles, and of the Lord Jesus, who in their ministry sustained contradiction, contempt, persecution and death. Fear not to rebuke the world of sin, justice, and judgment. If anything succeed prosperously in thy vocation, be not puffed up with pride ; neither yet flatter thyself as that the good success proceeded from thy virtue, industry, or care : But let ever that sentence of the Apostle remain in thy heart ; " What has thou, which thou has not received ? If thou hast received, why gloriest thou ? " Comfort the afflicted, support the poor, and exhort others to support them. Be not solist [1] for things of this life, but be fervent in prayer to God for increase of his Holy Spirit. And finally, behave thyself in this holy vocation with such sobriety as God may be glorified in thy ministry : And so shall thou shortly obtain the victory, and shall receive the crown promised, when the Lord Jesus shall appear in his glory, whose Omnipotent Spirit assist thee and us unto the end. AMEN.

Then sing the 23rd Psalm.

THE ORDER OF THE ELECTION OF ELDERS AND DEACONS IN THE PRIVY KIRK OF EDINBURGH, IN THE BEGINNING, WHEN AS YET THERE WAS NO PUBLIC FACE OF A KIRK, NOR OPEN ASSEMBLIES, BUT SECRET AND PRIVY CONVENTIONS IN HOUSES, OR IN THE FIELDS.

BEFORE that there was any public face of a true Religion within this Realm, it pleased God of his great mercy, to illuminate the hearts of many private persons, so that they did perceive and understand the abuses that were in the Papistical Kirk, and thereupon withdrew themselves from participation of their idolatry. And because the Spirit of God will never suffer his own to be idle and void of all religion, men began to exercise themselves in reading of the Scriptures secretly within their own houses ; and variety of persons could not be kept in good obedience and honest fame, without Overseers, Elders, and Deacons : And so began that small flock to put themselves in such order, as if Christ Jesus had plainly triumphed in the midst of them by the power of his Evangel. And they did elect some to occupy the supreme place of exhortation and reading, some to be Elders and helpers unto them, for the oversight of the flock : And some to be Deacons for the collection of alms to be distributed to the poor of their own body. Of this small beginning is that Order, which now God of his great mercy has given unto us publicly within this Realm. Of the principals of them that were known to be men of good conversation and honest fame in the privy Kirk, were chosen Elders and Deacons to rule with the Minister in the public Kirk ; which burden they patiently sustained a year and more : And then, because they could not (without neglecting of their own private houses) longer wait upon the public charge, they desired that they might be relieved, and that others might be burdened in their room : Which was thought a petition reasonable of the whole Kirk. And therefore it was granted unto them that they should nominate and give up in election such personages as they in their consciences thought most apt and able to serve in that charge ; providing that they should nominate double more persons than were sufficient to serve in that charge, to the end that the whole Congregation might have their free vote in their Election.

[1] *solicitous*

And this Order has been ever observed since that time in the Kirk of Edinburgh ; that is, that the old Session before their departure nominate twenty-four in Election for Elders, of whom twelve are to be chosen, and thirty-two for Deacons, of whom sixteen are to be elected ; which persons are publicly proclaimed in the audience of the whole Kirk, upon a Sunday before noon, after sermon ; with admonition to the Kirk, that if any man knew any notorious crime or cause that might unable any of these persons to enter in such vocation, that they should notify the same unto the Session the next Thursday : Or if any knew any persons more able for that charge, they should notify the same unto the Session, to the end that no man either present or absent (being one of the Kirk) should complain that he was spoiled of his liberty in election.

The Sunday following before noon, in the end of the Sermon, the whole Communicants are commanded to be present after noon, to give their votes, as they will answer before God, to such as they esteem most able to bear the charge of the Kirk with the Ministers. The votes of all being received, the scrolls of all are delivered to any of the Ministers, who keeps the same secret from the sight of all men till the next Thursday ; and then in the Session he produces them, that the votes may be counted, where the moniest [1] votes, without respect of persons, have the first place in the Eldership, and so proceeding till the number of twelve be complete ; so that if a poor man exceed the rich man in votes, he precedes him in place ; and it is called the first, second, and third Elder, even as the votes answereth. And this same is observed in the election of Deacons.

The Friday after the judgment is taken what persons are elected for Elders and Deacons to serve for that year, the Minister after his sermon reads the same names publicly, and gives commandment openly, that such persons be present the next Sunday at sermon before noon, in the place to be appointed for them, to accept of that charge that God by plurality of votes had laid upon them. Who being convened, the Minister after sermon reads the names publicly, the absents (if any be) are noted, and those who are present are admonished to consider the dignity of that vocation, whereunto God has called them ; the duty that they owe to the people ; the danger that lies upon them, if they be found negligent in their vocation : And finally, the duty of the people towards the persons elected. Which being done, this Prayer is read :—

The Prayer in the Election of the Elders

O Eternal and everlasting God, Father of our Lord Jesus Christ, who, of thy infinite goodness and mercy, has chosen to thyself a Kirk of the lost seed of Adam, which Thou hast ever ruled by the inspiration of Thy Holy Spirit ; and yet not the less, hast always used the ministry of men, as well in preaching of thy word, and administration of thy sacraments, as in guiding of thy flock, and providing for the poor within the same, as in the Law, Prophets, and in thy glorious Evangel we have witnesses : Which order, O Lord, Thou of thy mercy hast now restored unto us again

[1] *most*

after that the public face of the Kirk has been deformed by the tyranny of that Roman Antichrist. Grant unto us, O heavenly Father, hearts thankful for the benefits which we have received, and give unto these our brethren, elected unto these charges within thy Kirk, such abundance of thy Holy Spirit, that they may be found vigilant and faithful in that vocation whereunto Thou of thy mercy hast called them. And albeit, O Lord, these small beginnings are contemned of the proud world, yet, O Lord, do Thou for thy own mercy's sake, bless the same in such sort that thy godly name may be glorified, superstition and idolatry may be rooted out, and virtue may be planted, not only in this generation, but also in the posterity to come. AMEN. Grant us this, merciful Father, for Christ Jesus thy Son's sake, in whose name we call unto Thee, as He has taught us, saying, *Our Father*, &c.

And so after the rehearsal of the belief, after the which shall be sung this portion of the 103 Psalm, verse 19. *The heavens high are made the seat*,[1] and so forth to the end of that Psalm. After the which shall this short Admonition be given to the elected :—

Magnify God, who has of his mercy called you to rule within his Kirk : Be thankful in your vocation : Show yourselves zealous to promote verity : Fear not the faces of the wicked, but rebuke their wickedness : Be merciful to the poor, and support them to the uttermost of your power ; and so shall ye receive the benediction of God, present and everlasting. God save the King's Majesty,[2] and give unto him the Spirit of sanctification in his young age : Bless his Regent,[2] and such as assist him in upright counsel, and either fruitfully convert, or suddenly confound the enemies of true religion, and of this afflicted Commonwealth. AMEN.

[1] That is, according to the old version of the Psalms, by Sternhold and others, which continued in general use until the authorization of the present version in May 1650. (See the note in Laing's edition of *The Gude and Godlie Ballates* (Edinburgh 1868), Preface, xxvi–xliii)

[2] These words must have been introduced after Mary's surrender of the Crown, 24 July 1567.

APPENDIX VIII [1]

THE BOOK OF DISCIPLINE [2]

THE PREFACE

TO THE GREAT COUNCIL OF SCOTLAND NOW ADMITTED TO [THE] REGIMENT,[3] BY THE PROVIDENCE OF GOD, AND BY THE COMMON CONSENT OF THE ESTATES THEREOF, YOUR HONOURS' HUMBLE SERVITORS AND MINISTERS OF CHRIST JESUS WITHIN THE SAME, WISH GRACE, MERCY, AND PEACE FROM GOD THE FATHER OF OUR LORD JESUS CHRIST, WITH THE PERPETUAL INCREASE OF THE HOLY SPIRIT

From your Honours we received a charge,[4] dated at Edinburgh, 29 April, in the year of God 1560, requiring and commanding us, in the name of the Eternal God, as we will answer in his presence, to commit to writing, and in a Book to deliver unto your Wisdoms our judgments touching the Reformation of Religion, which heretofore in this Realm (as in others), has been utterly corrupted. Upon the receipt whereof, so many of us as were in this town [5] did convene, and in unity of mind do offer unto your Wisdoms these Heads subsequent for common order and uniformity to be observed in this Realm, concerning Doctrine, administration of Sacraments, [election of Ministers, provision for their sustentation],[6] Ecclesiastical Discipline, and Policy of the Kirk. Most humbly requiring your Honours that, as ye look for participation with Christ Jesus, that neither ye admit anything which God's plain word shall not approve, neither yet that ye shall reject such ordinances as

[1] See *supra*, i, 374

[2] No title is given in the manuscript. Knox "registered" The Book of Discipline in his *History* in order that "posterity to come may judge as well what the worldlings refused as what Policy the godly Ministers required" (*supra*, i, 374). Although Vautrollier's edition of the *History* contained part of the Book of Discipline (see *infra*, 288, *note* 3, and Laing's *Knox*, i, xxxii, xxxix–xlii) the whole Book was not published until 1621 when it was apparently printed in Holland and published anonymously by David Calderwood the historian. (Laing's *Knox*, ii, 183, *note*)

[3] Writing to Railton on 23 October 1559, Knox informs him of the deposition of the Queen Regent (*supra*, i, 251–255) and adds "There shall be appointed to occupy the authority a great Council; the president and chief head whereof shall be my Lord Duke [Châtelherault]". (Laing's *Knox*, vi, 86–87) See also, *supra*, i, 256, *note* 1.

[4] *Cf. supra*, i, 343 and *note* 3

[5] That is, Edinburgh. (*Cf. infra*, 323) On 8 May 1560, Knox is said to have returned to Edinburgh "by the space of xv days last bypast." (*Edinburgh Burgh Records*, iii, 64)

[6] These words are omitted in the manuscript, but are contained in Vautrollier's edition and in the edition of 1621.

equity, justice, and God's word do specify. For as we will not bind your Wisdoms to our judgments, further than we be able to prove the same by God's plain Scriptures,[1] so must we most humbly crave of you, even as ye will answer in God's presence (before whom both ye and we must appear to render account of all our facts), that ye repudiate nothing, for pleasure nor affection of men, which ye be not able to improve [2] by God's written and revealed Word.

THE BOOK OF DISCIPLINE

The First Head, of Doctrine.

Seeing that Christ Jesus is He whom God the Father has commanded only to be heard, and followed of his sheep, we urge it necessary that his Evangel be truly and openly preached in every Kirk and Assembly of this Realm ; and that all doctrine repugning to the same be utterly suppressed as damnable to man's salvation.

The Explication of the First Head

Lest upon this our generality ungodly men take occasion to cavil, this we add for explication. By preaching of the Evangel, we understand not only the Scriptures of the New Testament, but also of the Old ; to wit, the Law, Prophets, and Histories, in which Christ Jesus is no less contained in figure, than we have Him now expressed in verity. And, therefore, with the Apostle, we affirm that " All Scripture inspired of God is profitable to instruct, to reprove, and to exhort." In which Books of Old and New Testaments we affirm that all things necessary for the instruction of the Kirk, and to make the man of God perfect, are contained and sufficiently expressed.[3]

By the contrary Doctrine, we understand whatsoever men, by Laws, Councils, or Constitutions have imposed upon the consciences of men, without the expressed commandment of God's word : such as be vows of chastity, foreswearing of marriage, binding of men and women to several and disguised apparels, to the superstitious observation of fasting days, difference of meat for conscience sake, prayer for the dead ; and keeping of holy days of certain Saints commanded by man, such as be all those that the Papists have invented, as the Feasts (as they term them) of Apostles, Martyrs, Virgins, of Christmas, Circumcision, Epiphany, Purification, and other fond feasts of our Lady. Which things, because in God's scriptures they neither have commandment nor assurance, we judge them utterly to be abolished from this Realm ; affirming further, that the obstinate maintainers and teachers of such abominations ought not to escape the punishment of the Civil Magistrate.

[1] A similar reliance upon the Word of God is claimed for the Confession of Faith. (*Supra*, 258) [2] *disprove*

[3] See the like affirmation in the Confession of Faith. (*Supra*, 266)

THE SECOND HEAD, OF SACRAMENTS.

To Christ Jesus his holy Evangel truly preached, of necessity it is that his holy Sacraments be annexed, and truly ministered, as seals and visible confirmations of the spiritual promises contained in the word. And they be two, to wit, Baptism, and the Holy Supper of the Lord Jesus: which are then rightly ministered when, by a lawful Minister, the people, before the administration of the same, are plainly instructed and put in mind of God's free grace and mercy offered unto the penitent in Christ Jesus; when God's promises are rehearsed, the end and use of the Sacraments declared, and that in such a tongue as the people do understand; when further to them is nothing added, from them nothing diminished, and in their practice nothing changed beside [1] the institution of the Lord Jesus, and practice of his holy Apostles.

The number of sacraments

And albeit the Order of Geneva,[2] which now is used in some of our kirks, is sufficient to instruct the diligent reader how that both these Sacraments may be rightly ministered, yet for an uniformity to be kept, we have thought good to add this as superabundant.

In Baptism, we acknowledge nothing to be used except the element of water only (that the word and declaration of the promises ought to precede, we have said before). Wherefore, whosoever presumeth in baptism to use oil, salt, wax, spittle, conjuration, or crossing, accuseth the perfect institution of Christ Jesus of imperfection; for it was void of all such inventions devised by men. And such as would presume to alter Christ's perfect ordinance you ought severely to punish.

The Table of the Lord is then most rightly ministered when it approacheth most nigh to Christ's own action. But plain it is, that at that Supper Christ Jesus sat with his disciples, and therefore do we judge that sitting at a table is most convenient to that holy action [3]: that bread and wine ought to be there; that thanks ought to be given; distribution of the same made; and commandment given that the bread should be taken and eaten; and that all should drink likewise of the cup of wine, with declaration what both the one and the other is, [which] we suppose no godly man will doubt. For as touching the damnable error of the

[1] *beyond*; that is, *away from*

[2] That is, "The Form of Prayers and Ministration of the Sacraments, etc. used in the English Church at Geneva." It was approved and accepted by the Church of Scotland; and the Geneva edition of 1556 was reprinted at Edinburgh in 1562. (See Laing's *Knox*, iv, 141–214; vi, 275–333) Although, in a later passage, it is referred to as "the Book of *our* Common Order, called the Order of Geneva" (*infra*, 296), and "*our* Book of Common Order" (*infra*, 313), its authority was not declared by the General Assembly until 1562. (*Booke of the Universall Kirk*, i, 30) Later in 1564, enlarged and reprinted with the metrical Psalms, it was again prescribed by the General Assembly (*ibid.*, i, 54). As the Book of Common Order, or "Knox's Liturgy" it was a guide to the Minister rather than a liturgy: and Calderwood states "None are tyed to the prayers of that book; but the prayers are set down as samplers." Laud's attempt to introduce a more set liturgical form in the Scottish Church and the method of the attempted introduction formed the background of the well-known events of 1637 and 1638.

[3] In a later passage (*infra*, 321) "tables for the ministration of the Lord's Supper" are included in the necessary furnishings of a church.

Papists, who can defraud the common people of the one part of that holy Sacrament, to wit, of the cup of the Lord's blood, we suppose their error to be so manifest that it needeth no confutation. Neither yet intend we to confute anything in this our simple confession, but to offer public disputation to all that list oppugn anything affirmed by us.

That the Minister break the bread, and distribute the same to those that be next unto him, commanding the rest, every one with reverence and sobriety, to break with other, we think it nighest to Christ's action, and to the perfect practice of the Apostles, as we read it in Saint Paul. During the which action, we think it necessary that some comfortable places of the Scriptures be read, which may bring in mind the death of Christ Jesus, and the benefit of the same. For seeing that in that action we ought chiefly to remember the Lord's death, we judge the Scriptures making mention of the same most apt to stir up our dull minds then, and at all times. Let the discretion of the ministers appoint the places to be read as they think good. What times we think most convenient for the administration of the one and of the other of these Sacraments, shall be declared in the Policy of the Kirk.[1]

The Third Head, touching the Abolishing of idolatry.

As we require Christ Jesus to be truly preached, and his holy Sacraments to be rightly ministered ; so can we not cease to require idolatry, with all monuments and places of the same, as abbeys, monasteries, friaries, nunneries, chapels, chantries, cathedral kirks, canonries, colleges, other than presently [2] are parish Kirks or Schools, to be utterly suppressed in all bounds and places of this Realm (except only the palaces, mansions, and dwelling places adjacent thereto, with orchards and yards of the same) : as also that idolatry may be removed from the presence of all persons, of what estate or condition that ever they be, within this Realm.

For let your Honours be assuredly persuaded, that where idolatry is maintained or permitted where it may be suppressed, that there shall God's wrath reign, not only upon the blind and obstinate idolater, but also upon the negligent sufferers of the same ; especially if God have armed their hands with power to suppress such abomination.

By idolatry we understand, the Mass, invocation of saints, adoration of images, and the keeping and retaining of the same ; and, finally, all honouring of God not contained in his holy Word.[3]

The Fourth Head, concerning Ministers and their Lawful Election.

In a Kirk reformed or tending to reformation, none ought to presume either to preach, either yet to minister the Sacraments, till that orderly they be called to the same. Ordinary vocation consisteth in Election,

[1] See *infra*, 313 [2] *at present*
[3] *Cf.* the definition of "Evil Works" in the Confession of Faith (*supra*, 264).

Examination, and Admission. And because that Election of Ministers in this cursed Papistry has altogether been abused, we think expedient to entreat it more largely.

It appertaineth to the people, and to every several congregation, to elect their Minister. And in case that they be found negligent therein the space of forty days, the best reformed kirk, to wit, the church of the Superintendent with his Council, may present unto them a man whom they judge apt to feed the flock of Christ Jesus, who must be examined as well in life and manners, as in doctrine and knowledge.

And that this may be done with more exact diligence, the persons that are to be examined must be commanded to compear before men of soundest judgment, remaining in some principal town next adjacent unto them: as they that be in Fife, Angus, Mearns, or Strathearn, to present themselves in Saint Andrews; those that be in Lothian, Merse, or Teviotdale, to Edinburgh; and likewise those that be in other countries must resort to the best reformed cities or towns, that is, to the city of the Superintendent. Where first in the schools, or failing thereof in open assembly, and before the congregation, they must give declaration of their gifts, utterance, and knowledge, by interpreting some place of Scripture to be appointed by the ministry. Which, being ended, the person that is presented, or that offered himself to the administration of the kirk, must be examined by the ministers and elders of the kirk, and that openly, and before all that list to hear, in all the chief points that now lie in controversy betwix us and the Papists, Anabaptists, Arians, or other such enemies to the Christian religion. In which, if he be found sound, able to persuade by wholesome doctrine, and to convince the gainsayers, then must he be directed to the Kirk and Congregation where he should serve, that there, in open audience of his flock, in divers public sermons, he may give confession of his faith in the articles of Justification, of the office of Christ Jesus, of the number, effect, and use of the Sacraments; and, finally, of the whole religion which heretofore hath been corrupted by the Papists.

If his doctrine be found wholesome, and able to instruct the simple, and if the Kirk justly can reprehend nothing in his life, doctrine, nor utterance, then we judge the kirk, which before was destitute, unreasonable if they refuse him whom the Kirk did offer; and that they should be compelled, by the censure of the Council and Kirk, to receive the person appointed and approved by the judgment of the godly and learned; unless that the same kirk have presented a man better or as well qualified to the examination, before that this foresaid trial was taken of the person presented by the council of the whole Kirk. As, for example, the Council of the Kirk presents to any kirk a man to be their minister, not knowing that they are otherwise provided: in the meantime, the kirk is provided of another, sufficient in their judgment for that charge, whom they present to the learned Ministers and next reformed kirk to be examined. In this case the presentation of the people, to whom he should be appointed pastor, must be preferred to the presentation of the Council or greater Kirk; unless the person presented by the inferior kirk be judged unable for the regiment by the learned. For altogether this is to be avoided, that any man be violently intruded or thrust in upon any Congregation. But this liberty with all care must be reserved to every several kirk, to have their votes and suffrages in election of their Ministers. But violent intrusion we call [it] not, when the Council of the Kirk, in the fear of God, and for the salvation of the people, offereth unto them a sufficient man to instruct them; whom they shall not be forced to admit before just examination, as before is said.

IV (2). What may unable any person that he may not be admitted to the Ministry of the Kirk

It is to be observed that no person, noted with public infamy, or being unable to edify the Kirk by wholesome doctrine, or being known [to be] of corrupt judgment, be either promoted to the regiment of the Kirk, or yet received in ecclesiastical administration.

Explication

By public infamy we understand not the common sins and offences which any has committed in time of blindness,[1] by fragility (if of the same, by a better and more sober conversation, he hath declared himself verily penitent); but such capital crimes as the civil sword ought and may punish with death by the word of God. For besides that the Apostle requireth the life of Ministers to be so irreprehensible that they have a good testimony from those that be without, we judge it a thing unseemly and dangerous that he shall have public authority to preach to others the life everlasting from whom the civil Magistrate may take the life temporal for a crime publicly committed. And if any object, that the Prince has pardoned his offence, and that he has publicly repented, and so is not only his life in assurance, but also that he may be received to the Ministry of the Kirk, we answer, That repentance does not take away the temporal punishment of the law, neither doth the pardon of the Prince remove his infamy before man.

That the life and conversation of the person presented, or to be elected, may be the more clearly known, public edicts must be directed to all parts of this Realm, or at the least to those parts where the person hath been most conversant—as where he was nourished in letters, or where he continued from the years of infancy, and childhood was passed. Strait commandment would be given, that if any capital crimes were committed by him, that they should be notified; as, if he hath committed wilful murder, adultery, [were] a common fornicator, if he were a thief, a drunkard, a fighter, brawler, or contentious person. These edicts ought to be notified in the chief cities, with the like charge and commandment, with declaration that such as concealed his sins known did deceive and betray (so far as in them lay) the Kirk, which is the spouse of Jesus Christ, and did communicate with the sins of that wicked man.

[1] A similar exception of "sins committed in our former blindness" is given in the section devoted to Marriage. (*Infra*, 319)

IV (3). Admission of Ministers[1]

The admission of Ministers to their offices must consist in consent of the people and Kirk whereto they shall be appointed, and in approbation of the learned Ministers appointed for their examination.

We judge it expedient that the admission of Ministers be in open audience; that some especial Minister make a sermon touching the duty and office of Ministers, touching their manners, conversation, and life; as also touching the obedience which the Kirk oweth to its Ministers. Commandment should be given as well to the Minister as unto the people, both being present, to wit, that he with all careful diligence attend upon the flock of Christ Jesus, over the which he is appointed preacher: that he will walk in the presence of God so sincerely that the graces of the Holy Spirit may be multiplied into him; and in the presence of men so soberly and uprightly that his life may confirm, in the eyes of men, that which by tongue and word he persuadeth unto others. The people would be exhorted to reverence and honour their Ministers chosen, as the servants and ambassadors of the Lord Jesus, obeying the commandments which they pronounce from God's mouth and book, even as they would obey God himself[2]; for whosoever heareth Christ's Ministers heareth himself, and whosoever rejecteth them, and despiseth their ministry and exhortation, rejecteth and despiseth Christ Jesus.

Other ceremony than the public approbation of the people, and declaration of the chief minister, that the person there presented is appointed to serve that Kirk, we cannot approve; for albeit the Apostles used the imposition of hands, yet seeing the miracle is ceased, the using of the ceremony we judge is not necessary.

The Minister, elected or presented, examined, and, as said is, publicly admitted, must neither leave the flock at his pleasure, to the which he has promised his fidelity and labours, neither yet may the flock reject nor change him at their appetite, unless they be able to convict him of such crimes as deserve deposition; whereof we shall after speak. We mean not but that the whole Kirk, or the most part thereof, for just considerations, may transfer a Minister from one kirk to another; neither yet mean we that men who now do serve, as it were of benevolence, may not be appointed and elected to serve in other places; but once being solemnly elected and admitted, we cannot approve that they should change at their own pleasure.

We are not ignorant that the rarity of godly and learned men shall seem to some a just reason why that so strait and sharp examination should not be taken universally; for so it shall appear that the most part of the kirks shall have no Minister at all. But let these men understand that the lack of able men shall not excuse us before God if, by our consent, unable men be placed over the flock of Christ Jesus; as also that, amongst

[1] *Cf.* the Geneva form in Laing's *Knox*, iv, 174–176.

[2] Unfortunately the pronouncements of the ministers, resting upon their individual interpretations of "God's mouth and book," later tended to be political in character, and so led to that struggle which has been aptly described as one between the "Divine Right of Kings" and the "Divine Right of Presbyteries."

the Gentiles, godly, learned men were as rare as they be now amongst us, when the Apostle gave the same rule to try and examine Ministers which we now follow. And last, let them understand that it is alike to have no minister at all, and to have an idol in the place of a true minister, yea and in some cases, it is worse: for those that be utterly destitute of ministers will be diligent to search for them; but those that have a vain shadow do commonly, without further care, content themselves with the same, and so remain they continually deceived, thinking that they have a Minister, when in very deed they have none. For we cannot judge him a dispensator of God's mysteries that in no wise can break the bread of life to the fainting and hungry souls; neither judge we that the Sacraments can be rightly ministered by him, in whose mouth God has put no sermon of exhortation.

The chiefest remedy left to your Honours and to us, in all this rarity of true ministers, is fervent prayer unto God that it will please his mercy to thrust out [1] faithful workmen into this his harvest; and next, that your Honours, with consent of the Kirk, are bound by your authority to compel such men as have gifts and graces able to edify the Kirk of God that they bestow them where greatest necessity shall be known. For no man may be permitted to live idle, or as himself list, but must be appointed to travail where your Wisdoms and the Kirk shall think expedient.

We cannot prescribe unto your Honours certain rule how that ye shall distribute the ministers and learned men whom God has already sent unto you. But hereof we are assured, that it greatly hindereth the progress of Christ's Evangel within this poor Realm that some altogether abstract their labours from the Kirk, and others remain together in one place, the most part of them being idle. And therefore of your Honours we require, in God's name, that by your authority which ye have of God, ye compel all men to whom God has given any talent to persuade, by wholesome doctrine, to bestow the same, if they be called by the Kirk to the advancement of Christ's glory, and to the comfort of his troubled flock; and that ye, with the consent of the Kirk, assign unto your chiefest workmen, not only towns to remain into, but also provinces, that by their faithful labours kirks may be erected, and order established, where none is now. And if on this manner ye will use your power and authority, chiefly seeking God's glory, and the comfort of your brethren, we doubt not but God shall bless you and your enterprises.

IV (4). For Readers

To the kirks where no ministers can be had presently, must be appointed the most apt men that distinctly can read the Common Prayers and the Scriptures, to exercise both themselves and the kirk, till they grow to greater perfection; and in process of time he that is but a Reader may attain to the further degree, and by consent of the kirk and discreet ministers, may be permitted to minister the sacraments; but not before that he be able somewhat to persuade by wholesome doctrine, besides his

[1] *thrust forward*

reading, and be admitted to the ministry, as before is said. Some we know that of long time have professed Christ Jesus, whose honest conversation deserved praise of all godly men, and whose knowledge also might greatly help the simple, and yet they only content themselves with reading. These must be animated, and by gentle admonition encouraged, by some exhortation to comfort their brethren, and so they may be admitted to administration of the sacraments.[1] But such Readers as neither have had exercise, nor continuance in Christ's true religion, must abstain from ministration of the sacraments till they give declaration and witnessing of their honesty and further knowledge.

*Additio

* For the Lords think that none be admitted to preach, but they that are qualified therefor, but rather be retained readers; and such as are preachers already, not found qualified therefor by the Superintendent, be placed to be readers.[2]

THE FIFTH HEAD, CONCERNING THE PROVISION FOR THE MINISTERS, AND FOR THE DISTRIBUTION OF THE RENTS AND POSSESSIONS JUSTLY APPERTAINING TO THE KIRK.

Seeing that of our Master Christ Jesus and his Apostle Paul we have, "That the workman is worthy of his reward," and that, "The mouth of the labouring ox ought not to be muzzled," of necessity it is that honest provision be made for the Ministers, which we require to be such that they have neither occasion of solicitude, neither yet of insolence and wantonness. And this provision must be made not only for their own sustentation during their lives but also for their wives and children after them. For we judge it a thing most contrarious to reason, godliness, and equity, that the widow and children of him who, in [3] his life, did faithfully serve the Kirk of God, and for that cause did not carefully make provision for his family, should, after his death, be left comfortless of all provision.

*Additio

* Provision for the wives of Ministers after their decease, to be remitted to the discretion of the Kirk.

Difficult it is to appoint a several stipend to every Minister, by reason that the charges and necessity of all will not be like; for some will be continuers in one place, [and] some will be compelled to travel, and oft to change dwelling place (if they shall have charge of divers kirks). Amongst these, some will be burdened with wife and children, and one with more than another; and some perchance will be single men. If equal stipends should be appointed to all those that in charge are so unequal, either should the one suffer penury, or else should the other have superfluity and too much.

*Additio

* We judge, therefore, that every Minister have sufficient whereupon to keep an house, and be sustained honestly in all things necessary, as well

[1] This implies the intermediate office of *Exhorter*. (See *infra*, 290)

[2] This is the first of the "notes and additions" referred to in the "Act of Secret Council" of 27 January 1561. (*Infra*, 324)

[3] Vautrollier's suppressed edition ends at this point with the words, "the widow and the children of him who in."

for keeping of his house, as clothes, flesh, fish, books, fuel, and other things necessary, forth of the rents and treasury of the kirk, where he serveth, at the discretion of the congregation, conform to the quality of the person and necessity of the time. Wherein it is thought good that every Minister shall have at least forty bolls [of] meal, and twenty-six bolls [of] malt, to find his house bread and drink [1]; and more, sa mekill as the discretion of the kirk finds necessary; besides money for buying of other provision to his house, and other necessaries, the modification whereof is referred to the judgment of the kirk, to be made every year at the choosing of the elders and deacons of the kirk. Providing always, that there be advanced to every Minister sufficient provision for one quarter of a year beforehand of all things.

To him that travelleth from place to place, whom we call Superintendents, who remain, as it were, a month or less in one place, for the establishing of the kirk, and for the same purpose changing to another place, must further consideration be had. And, therefore, to such we think six chalders [of] bear,[2] nine chalders [of] meal, three chalders [of] oats for his horse, 500 marks [of] money, to be eiked and pared [3] at the discretion of the Prince and Council of the Realm; to be payed to him yearly, in manner foresaid.[4]

The children of the Ministers must have the liberties of the cities next adjacent where their fathers labour, freely granted. They must have the privileges in schools, and bursaries in colleges. That is, that they shall be sustained at learning, if they be found apt thereto. And failing thereof, that they be put to some handicraft, or exercised in some virtuous industry, whereby they may be profitable members in a commonwealth.

* And the same we require for their daughters; to wit, that they be virtuously brought up, and honestly doted [5] when they come to maturity of years, at the discretion of the Kirk. **Additio*

And this in God's presence we witness, we require not so much for ourselves, or for any that to us appertaineth, as that we do for the increase of virtue and learning, and for the profit of the posterity to come. It is not to be supposed that all men will dedicate themselves and children so to God, and to serve his kirk, that they look for no worldly commodity. But this cankered nature, which we bear, is provoked to follow virtue when it seeth honour and profit annexed to the same; as, contrarily, then is virtue of many despised, when virtuous and godly men live without honour. And sorry would we be that poverty should discourage men from study, and from following the way of virtue, by the which they might edify the Kirk and flock of Christ Jesus.

Nothing have we spoken of the stipend of Readers, because, if they

[1] In 1644 it was calculated that fifteen gallons of ale or twenty gallons of beer could be brewed from one boll of malt. (*Acts Parl. Scot.*, vi, pt. i, 243*b*)

[2] *barley* (of an inferior quality)

[3] *to be increased or decreased*; that is, *with more or less*

[4] Dr. G. Donaldson's calculation is that this was equivalent in all to about £700 a year—no mean stipend for the year 1560. Although it was never paid in full, it is no wonder that later there were those who said "many lords have not so much to spend" (*supra*, 31).

[5] *dowered*

can do nothing but read, they neither can be called nor judged true ministers. And yet regard must be had to their labours ; but so that they may be spurred forward to virtue, and not by a stipend appointed for their reading, to be retained still in that estate. To a Reader, therefore, that is lately entered we think forty marks, or more or less as the parishioners and Reader can agree, sufficient : providing that he teach the children of the parish, which he must do, besides the reading of the Common Prayers, and Books of the New and Old Testaments.[1] If from Reading he begin to Exhort,[2] and explain the Scriptures, then ought his stipend to be augmented ; till finally he come to the honour of a Minister. But and if he be found unable after two years, then must he be removed from that office, and discharged of all stipend, that another may be proven as long. For this always is to be avoided, that none who is judged unable to come at any time to some reasonable knowledge, whereby he may edify the Kirk, shall be perpetually nourished upon the charge of the Kirk. Farther, it must be avoided that no child or person within age, that is, within 21 years of age, be admitted to the office of a Reader ; but Readers ought to be endued with gravity, wit,[3] and discretion, lest by their lightness the Prayers or Scriptures read be of less price and estimation. It is to be noted that the Readers be put in by the kirk, and [the] admission of the Superintendent.

Nota

[For] the other sort of Readers, who have long continued in godliness, and have some gift of exhortation, who are in hope to attain to the degree of a minister, and teach the children, we think an hundred marks, or more, at the discretion of the kirk, may be appointed ; so that difference, as said is, be betwix them and the ministers that openly preach the Word, and minister the Sacraments.

Rests yet other two sorts of people to be provided for, [out] of that which is called the patrimony of the Kirk[4] : to wit, the Poor, and Teachers of the youthhead. Every several kirk must provide for the poor within the self ; for fearful and horrible it is, that the poor, whom not only God the Father in his law, but Christ Jesus in his Evangel, and the Holy Spirit speaking by Saint Paul, hath so earnestly commended to our care, are universally so contemned and despised. We are not patrons for stubborn and idle beggars who, running from place to place, make a craft of their begging, whom the Civil Magistrate ought to punish ; but for the widow and fatherless, the aged, impotent, or lamed, who neither can nor may travail for their sustentation, we say that God commandeth his people to be careful. And therefore, for such, as also for persons of honesty fallen in[to] decay and penury, ought such provision be made that [of] our abundance should their indigence be relieved. How this most conveniently and most easily may be done in every city and other parts of this Realm, God shall show you wisdom and the means, so that your

[1] For a description of the work of a Reader, see *Autobiography and Diary of Mr. James Melvill* (Wodrow Soc.), 22

[2] For Exhorters, see the succeeding paragraph

[3] *knowledge*

[4] See the Sixth Head—of the Rents and Patrimony of the Kirk (*infra*, 302–306) ; see also the third head of the Supplication presented to the Reformation Parliament of 1560 (*supra*, i, 337)

minds be godly thereto inclined. All must not be suffered to beg that gladly so would do ; neither yet must beggars remain where they choose ; but the stout and strong beggar must be compelled to work, and every person that may not work, must be compelled to repair to the place where he or she was born (unless of long continuance they have remained in one place), and there reasonable provision must be made for their sustentation, as the church shall appoint. The order nor sums, in our judgments, cannot be particularly appointed, unto such time as the poor of every city, town, or parish be compelled to repair to the places where they were born, or of their residences, where their names and number must be taken and put in [a] roll ; and then may the wisdom of the Kirk appoint stipends accordingly.

V (1). Of the Superintendents

Because we have appointed a larger stipend to those that shall be Superintendents than to the rest of the Ministers, we have thought good to signify unto your Honours such reasons as moved us to make difference betwix preachers at this time [1] ; as also how many Superintendents we think necessary, with their bounds, office, [the manner of their] election, and [the] causes that may deserve deposition from that charge.

We consider that if the Ministers whom God hath endued with his [singular] graces amongst us should be appointed to several and certain places, there to make their continual residence, that then the greatest part of this Realm should be destitute of all doctrine ; which should not only be occasion of great murmur, but also should be dangerous to the salvation of many. And therefore we have thought it a thing most expedient for this time that, from the whole number of godly and learned [men], now presently in this Realm, be selected twelve or ten (for in so many Provinces have we divided the whole), to whom charge and commandment shall be given to plant and erect churches, to set order and appoint ministers (as the former Order prescribeth) to the countries that shall be appointed to their care where none are now. And by these means [your] love and common care over all the inhabitants of this Realm (to whom ye are equal debtors) shall evidently appear ; as also the simple and ignorant (who perchance have never heard Christ Jesus truly preached) shall come to some knowledge by the which many that now be dead in superstition and ignorance shall attain to some feeling of godliness, by the which they may be provoked to search and seek further knowledge of God, and his true religion and worshipping. Where, by the contrary, if they shall be neglected, they shall not only grudge,[2] but also they shall seek the means whereby they may continue in their blindness, or return to their accustomed idolatry. And therefore nothing desire we more earnestly, than that Christ Jesus be universally once preached throughout this Realm ; which shall not suddenly be unless that, by you, men be appointed and compelled faithfully to travail in such Provinces as to them shall be assigned.

[1] That is, when there were still too few preachers for the work of the Church.

[2] *complain*

V (2). The Names of the Places of Residence, and several Dioceses of the Superintendents

Imprimis, the Superintendent of Orkney; whose Diocese shall be to the Isles of Orkney, Shetland, Caithness, and Strathnaver.[1] His residence to be in the town of Kirkwall.

2 The Superintendent of Ross; whose Diocese shall comprehend Ross, Sutherland, Moray, with the North Isles of the Skye, and the Lewis, with their adjacents. His residence to be in [the] Canonry of Ross.[2]

3 The Superintendent of Argyll; whose Diocese shall comprehend Argyll, [Kintyre,] Lorne, the South Isles, Arran [and] Bute, with their adjacents, with Lochaber. His residence to be in [Argyll].

4 The Superintendent of Aberdeen; whose Diocese is betwix Dee and Spey, containing the sheriffdom of Aberdeen and Banff. His residence to be in Old Aberdeen.

5 The Superintendent of Brechin; whose Diocese shall be the whole sheriffdoms of Mearns and Angus, and the Brae of Mar to Dee. His residence to be in Brechin.

6 The Superintendent of Saint Andrews; whose Diocese shall comprehend the whole sheriffdom of Fife and Fotheringham,[3] to Stirling; and the whole sheriffdom of Perth.[4] His residence to be in Saint Andrews.

7 The Superintendent of Edinburgh; whose Diocese shall comprehend the whole sheriffdoms of Lothian, and Stirling on the south side of the Water of Forth; and thereto is added, by consent of the whole Church, Merse, Lauderdale, and Wedale. His residence to be in [Edinburgh].

8 The Superintendent of Jedburgh; whose Diocese shall comprehend Teviotdale, Tweeddale, Liddesdale, with the Forest of Ettrick. His residence to be [in Jedburgh].

9 The Superintendent of Glasgow; whose Diocese shall comprehend Clydesdale, Renfrew, Menteith, Lennox, Kyle, and Cunningham. His residence to be in Glasgow.

10 The Superintendent of Dumfries; whose Diocese shall comprehend Galloway, Carrick, Nithsdale, Annandale, with the rest of the Dales in the West. His residence to be in Dumfries.

These men must not be suffered to live as your idle Bishops have done heretofore; neither must they remain where gladly they would. But they must be preachers themselves, and such as may make no long residence in any one place, till their churches be planted and provided of Ministers, or at the least of Readers.

Charge must be given to them that they remain in no one place above twenty or thirty days in their visitation, till they have passed through their whole bounds. They must thrice every week, at the least, preach; and when they return to their principal town and residence, they must be

[1] Thus including part of Sutherland [2] Fortrose

[3] The old archdeaconry of St. Andrews (in the diocese of St. Andrews) had contained the deaneries of Fife, Fothric, Gowrie, Angus, and Mearns. Fothric, here called Fotheringham, embraced the parishes running along the northern shore of the Forth.

[4] And also the sheriffdom of Kinross

likewise exercised in preaching and in edification of the church there. And yet they must not be suffered to continue there so long, as they may seem to neglect their other churches : but after that they have remained in their chief town three or four months at most, they shall be compelled (unless by sickness only they be retained), to re-enter in visitation, in which they shall not only preach, but also examine the life, diligence, and behaviour of the Ministers ; as also the order of their churches, [and] the manners of the people. They must further consider how the poor be provided ; how the youth be instructed. They must admonish where admonition needeth ; dress such things as by good counsel they be able to appease ; and, finally, they must note such crimes as be heinous that, by the censure of the Church, the same may be corrected.

If the Superintendent be found negligent in any of these chief points of his office, and especially if he be noted negligent in preaching of the word, and in visitation of his churches, or if he be convicted of any of those crimes which in the common Ministers are damned, he must be deposed, without respect of his person or office.[1]

V (3). Of the Election of Superintendents [2]

In this present necessity, the nomination, examination, and admission of Superintendents cannot be so strait as we require, and as afterwards it must be.[3]

For this present, therefore, we think [it] sufficient that either your Honours, by yourselves, nominate so many as may serve the fore-written provinces, or that ye give commission to such men as in whom ye suppose the fear of God [to be] to do the same ; and that the same men, being called in your presence, shall be by you, and by such as your Honours please [to] call unto you for consultation in that case, appointed to their provinces. We think it expedient and necessary, that as well the gentlemen, as burgesses of every diocese, be made privy at the same time to the election of the Superintendent, as well to bring the Church in some practice of her liberty, as to make the pastor better favoured of the flock whom themselves have chosen. If your Honours cannot find for this present so many able men as the necessity requireth, then, in our judgments, more profitable it is that those provinces vaik [4] till God provide better, than that men unable to edify and govern the Church be suddenly placed in that charge. For experience hath taught us what pestilence hath been engendered in the Church by men unable to discharge their offices.

When, therefore, after three years any Superintendent shall depart, or chance to be deposed, the chief town within that province, to wit, the Ministers, Elders, and Deacons, with the Magistrate and Council of the same town, shall nominate and by public edicts proclaim, as well to

[1] See also *infra*, 294

[2] See the Form and Order of the Election of the Superintendents, etc. (*supra*, Appendix VII)

[3] "After that the Church be established, and three years be passed," two years' faithful labour in the ministry was to be a prerequisite (*infra*, 295).

[4] *remain vacant*

the Superintendent, as to two or three provinces next adjacent, two or three of the most learned and most godly Ministers within the whole realm, that from amongst them, one, with public consent, may be elected and appointed to the office then vaiking. And this the chief town shall be bound to do within the term of twenty days. Which being expired and no man presented, then shall three of the next adjacent provinces with consent of their Superintendents, Ministers, and Elders, enter in into the right and privileges of the chief town, and shall present every one of them one, or two if they list, to the chief town, to be examined as the Order requireth. As also, it shall be lawful for all the churches of the Diocese to nominate within the same time such persons as they think worthy to stand in election ; which must be put in edict.

After the nominations be made, public edicts must be sent, first warning all men that have any objection against the persons nominated, or against any one of them, to be present in the chief town at day and place affixed, to object what they can against the election of any one of them. Thirty days we think sufficient to be assigned thereto ; thirty days, we mean, after that the nomination be made.

Which day of election being come, the whole Ministers of that Province, with three or more of the Superintendents next adjacent, or that shall thereto be named, shall examine not only the learning, but also the manners, prudence, and ability to govern the Church, of all those that are nominated ; that he who shall be found most worthy may be burdened with the charge. If the Ministers of the whole Province should bring with them the votes of those that were committed to their care, the election should be the more free ; but always, the votes of all those that convene must be required. The examinations must be publicly made ; those that stand in election must publicly preach ; and men must be charged in the name of God, to vote according to conscience, and not after affection. If anything be objected against any that stand in election, the Superintendents and Ministers must consider whether the objection be made of conscience or of malice, and they must answer accordingly. Other ceremonies than sharp examination, approbation of the Ministers and Superintendents, with the public consent of the Elders and people then present, we cannot allow.

The Superintendent being elected, and appointed to his charge, must be subjected to the censure and correction of the Ministers and Elders, not only of his chief town, but also of the whole Province over the which he is appointed overseer.

If his offences be known, and the Ministers and Elders of his Province be negligent in correcting him, then the next one or two Superintendents, with their Ministers and Elders, may convene him, and the Ministers and Elders of his chief town (provided that it be within his own Province or chief town), and may accuse and correct as well the Superintendent in those things that are worthy of correction, as the Ministers and Elders for their negligence and ungodly tolerance of his offences.

Whatsoever crime deserve correction or deposition of any other Minister, deserveth the same in the Superintendent, without exception of person.

After that the Church be established, and three years be passed, we require that no man be called to the office of a Superintendent who hath not two years, at the least, given declaration of his faithful labours in the ministry of some church.

No Superintendent may be transferred at the pleasure or request of any one Province ; no, not without the consent of the whole council of the Church,[1] and that for grave causes and considerations.

Of one thing, in the end, we must admonish your Honours, to wit, that, in appointing Superintendents for this present, ye disappoint not your chief towns, and where learning is exercised, of such Ministers as more may profit by residence in one place, than by continual travel from place to place. For if ye so do, the youth in those places shall lack the profound interpretation of the Scriptures ; and so shall it be long before that your gardens send forth many plants ; where, by the contrary, if one or two towns be continually exercised as they may, the Commonwealth shall shortly taste of their fruit, to the comfort of the godly.

V (4). For the Schools

Seeing that the office and duty of the godly Magistrate is not only to purge the Church of God from all superstition, and to set it at liberty from bondage of tyrants, but also to provide, to the uttermost of his power, how it may abide in the same purity to the posterities following, we cannot but freely communicate our judgments with your Honours in this behalf.

V (5). The Necessity of Schools [2]

Seeing that God hath determined that his Church here in earth shall be taught not by angels but by men ; and seeing that men are born ignorant of all godliness, and seeing also [that] God now ceaseth to illuminate men miraculously, suddenly changing them, as that he did his Apostles and others in the Primitive Church : of necessity it is that your Honours be most careful for the virtuous education and godly upbringing of the youth of this Realm, if either ye now thirst unfeignedly [for] the advancement of Christ's glory, or yet desire the continuance of his benefits to the generation following. For as the youth must succeed to us, so ought we to be careful that they have the knowledge and erudition to profit and comfort that which ought to be most dear to us, to wit, the Church and Spouse of the Lord Jesus.

Of necessity therefore we judge it, that every several church have a

[1] The " whole council " of the Church is also referred to in relation to Church funds (*infra*, 305), and, later still, it is called the " Assembly of the Universal Kirk gathered within the Realm " (*infra*, 320). It was, in effect, the General Assembly.

[2] Earlier, in his *Brief Exhortation to England*, Knox had written that " for the preservation of religion, it is most expedient, That Scholes be universally erected in all cities and chief townes, the oversight whereof to be committed to the magistrates and godly learned men of the said cities and townes ; that of the youth godly instructed amongst them, a seade may be reserved and continued, for the profet of Christes Church in all ages." (Laing's *Knox*, v, 520)

Schoolmaster appointed, such a one as is able, at least, to teach Grammar and the Latin tongue, if the town be of any reputation. If it be upland,[1] where the people convene to doctrine but once in the week, then must either the Reader or the Minister there appointed, take care over the children and youth of the parish, to instruct them in their first rudiments, and especially in the Catechism,[2] as we have it now translated in the Book of our Common Order, called the Order of Geneva.[3] And further, we think it expedient that in every notable town, and especially in the town of the Superintendent, [there] be erected a College, in which the Arts, at least Logic and Rhetoric, together with the Tongues, be read by sufficient Masters, for whom honest stipends must be appointed : as also provision for those that be poor, and be not able by themselves, nor by their friends, to be sustained at letters, especially such as come from landward.[4]

The fruit and commodity hereof shall suddenly appear. For, first, the youth-head and tender children shall be nourished and brought up in virtue, in presence of their friends ; by whose good attendance many inconvenients may be avoided, in the which the youth commonly falls, either by too much liberty, which they have in strange and unknown places, while they cannot rule themselves, or else for lack of good attendance, and of such necessities as their tender age requireth. Secondly, the exercise of the children in every church shall be great instruction to the aged.

Last, the great Schools, called Universities, shall be replenished with those that be apt to learning ; for this must be carefully provided, that no father, of what estate or condition that ever he be, use his children at his own fantasy, especially in their youth-head ; but all must be compelled to bring up their children in learning and virtue.

The rich and potent may not be permitted to suffer their children to spend their youth in vain idleness, as heretofore they have done. But they must be exhorted, and by the censure of the Church compelled to dedicate their sons, by good exercise, to the profit of the Church and to the Commonwealth ; and that they must do of their own expenses, because they are able. The children of the poor must be supported and sustained on the charge of the Church, till trial be taken whether the spirit of docility[5] be found in them or not. If they be found apt to letters and learning, then may they not (we mean, neither the sons of the rich, nor yet the sons of the poor), be permitted to reject learning ; but must be charged to continue their study, so that the Commonwealth may have some comfort by them. And for this purpose must discreet, learned, and grave men be appointed to visit all Schools for the trial of their exercise, profit, and continuance ; to wit, the Ministers and Elders, with the best learned in every town, shall every quarter take examination how the youth hath profited.

[1] in the *countryside*, or *to landward*, as distinguished from the town

[2] That is, the translation of Calvin's Catechism. (See Laing's *Knox*, iv, 143–144, 167–168 ; vi, 277–286, 341–345 ; and the note, *supra*, 282, *note* 2)

[3] See *supra*, 282, *note* 2

[4] That is, from country districts

[5] *aptitude for learning*

A certain time must be appointed to Reading, and to learning of the Catechism ; a certain time to the Grammar, and to the Latin tongue ; a certain time to the Arts, Philosophy, and to the Tongues ; and a certain [time] to that study in which they intend chiefly to travail for the profit of the Commonwealth. Which time being expired, we mean in every course, the children must either proceed to further knowledge, or else they must be sent to some handicraft, or to some other profitable exercise ; provided always, that first they have the form of knowledge of Christian religion, to wit, the knowledge of God's law and commandments, the use and office of the same, the chief articles of our belief, the right form to pray unto God, the number, use, and effect of the sacraments, the true knowledge of Christ Jesus, of his office and natures, and such other [points] as without the knowledge whereof, neither deserveth [any] man to be named a Christian, neither ought any to be admitted to the participation of the Lord's Table. And therefore, these principals ought and must be learned in the youth-head.

V (6). The Times appointed to every Course

Two years we think more than sufficient to learn to read perfectly, to answer to the Catechism, and to have some entry in the first rudiments of Grammar [1] ; to the full accomplishment whereof (we mean of the Grammar), we think other three or four years, at most, sufficient. To the Arts, to wit, Logic and Rhetoric, and to the Greek tongue, four years ; and the rest, till the age of twenty-four years, to be spent in that study wherein the learner would profit the Church or Commonwealth, be it in the Laws, or Physic or Divinity. Which time to twenty-four years being spent in the schools, the learner must be removed to serve the Church or Commonwealth, unless he be found a necessary Reader in the same College or University. If God shall move your hearts to establish and execute this Order, and put these things in practice, your whole Realm (we doubt not), within [a] few years, shall serve the self of true preachers, and of other officers necessary for your Commonwealth.

V (7). The Erection of Universities

The Grammar Schools and of the Tongues being erected as we have said, next we think it necessary there be three Universities in this whole Realm, established in the towns accustomed. The first in Saint Andrews, the second in Glasgow, and the third in Aberdeen.

And in the first University and principal, which is Saint Andrews, there be three Colleges. And in the first College, which is the entry of the University, there be four classes or seiges [2] : the first, to the new Supposts,[3] shall be only Dialectics ; the next, only Mathematics ; the third, of

[1] "Grammar" generally means Latin.

[2] *seats*, or, in modern parlance, *Chairs*

[3] The term "supposts" meant non-graduate scholars, but might be extended to include all members of the University (even its servants) and university "clients" (such as booksellers).

Physics only ; the fourth of Medicine. And in the second College, two classes or seiges : the first, in Moral Philosophy ; the second in the Laws. And in the third College, two classes or seiges : the first, in the Tongues, to wit, Greek and Hebrew [1] ; the second, in Divinity.

V (8). Of Readers, and of the Grees,[2] of Time, and Study

Item, In the first College, and in the first class, shall be a Reader of Dialectics, who shall accomplish his course thereof in one year. In the Mathematics, which is the second class, shall be a Reader who shall complete his course of Arithmetic, Geometry, Cosmography, and Astrology, in one year. In the third class, shall be a Reader of Natural Philosophy, who shall complete his course in a year. And who, after these three years, by trial and examination, shall be found sufficiently instructed in these aforesaid sciences, shall be Laureate and Graduate in Philosophy. In the fourth class, shall be a Reader of Medicine, who shall complete his course in five years : after the study of the which time, being by examination found sufficient, they shall be graduate in Medicine.

The first gree

Second degree

Item, In the second College, in the first class, one Reader only in the Ethics, Economics, and Politics, who shall complete his course in the space of one year. In the second class, shall be two Readers in the Municipal and Roman Laws, who shall complete their courses in four years ; after the which time, being by examination found sufficient, they shall be graduate in the Laws.

Third degree

Item, In the third College, in the first class, a Reader of the Hebrew, and another of the Greek tongue, who shall complete the grammars thereof in half a year, and the remanent of the year the Reader of the Hebrew shall interpret a book of Moses, [or of] the Prophets, or the Psalms ; so that his course and class shall continue one year. The Reader of the Greek shall interpret some book of Plato, together with some place of the New Testament. And in the second class, shall be two Readers in Divinity, that one in the New Testament, that other in the Old, who shall complete their course in five years. After which time, who shall be found by examination sufficient, shall be graduate in Divinity.

Fourth degree

Item, We think expedient that none be admitted unto the first College, and to be Supposts of the University unless he have from the Master of the School, and the Minister of the town where he was instructed in the tongues, a testimonial of his learning, docility, age, and parentage ; and likeways trial to be taken by certain Examinators, depute by the Rector and Principals of the same, and, if he be found sufficiently instructed in Dialectics, he shall incontinent, that same year, be promoted to the class of Mathematics.

Item, That none be admitted to the class of the Medicine but he that shall have his testimonial of his time well spent in Dialectics, Mathematics, and Physics, and of his docility in the last.

[1] Scholars coming up to the University were expected to be already well " founded " in Latin, learned in school.

[2] *degrees*

Item, That none be admitted unto the class of the Laws, but he that shall have sufficient testimonials of his time well spent in Dialectics, Mathematics, Physics, Ethics, Economics, and Politics, and of his docility[1] in the last.

Item, That none be admitted unto the class and seige of Divines but he that shall have sufficient testimonials of his time well spent in Dialectics, Mathematics, Physics, Ethics, Economics, Moral Philosophy, and the Hebrew tongue, and of his docility in the Moral Philosophy and the Hebrew tongue. But neither shall such as will apply them to hear the Laws, be compelled to hear Medicine ; neither such as apply them to hear Divinity be compelled to hear either Medicine or yet the Laws.

Second University

Item, In the Second University, which is GLASGOW, shall be two Colleges alanerlie.[2] In the first shall be a class of Dialectics, another in Mathematics, the third in Physics, ordered in all sorts as [in] Saint Andrews.

Item, In the Second College, four classes ; the first in Moral Philosophy, Ethics, Economics, and Politics ; the second of the Municipal and Roman Laws ; the third of the Hebrew tongue ; the fourth in Divinity. Which shall be ordered in all sorts, conform to it we have written in the order of the University of Saint Andrews.

Third University

The Third University of ABERDEEN shall be conform to this University of Glasgow, in all sorts.

Item, We think needful, that there be chosen of the body of the University to every College a man of learning, discretion, and diligence, who shall receive the whole rents of the College, and distribute the same according to the erection of the College ; and shall daily hearken the diet accounts, adjoining to him weekly one of the Readers or Regents. Above whom[3] he shall [take] attendance upon their diligence, as well in their reading as exercition of the youth in the matter taught ; upon the policy and upholding of the place ; and for punishment of crimes, [he] shall hold a weekly convention with the whole members of the College. He shall be comptable[4] yearly to the Superintendent, Rector, and rest of the Principals convened, about the first of November. His election shall be in this sort : There shall be three of the most sufficient men of the University (not Principals already), nominated by the members of the College, whose Principal is departed, sworn to follow their conscience, and publicly proponed through the whole University. After the which time eight days,[5] the Superintendent, by himself or his special Procurator, with the Rector and rest of the Principals, as a chapter convened, shall confirm one of the three they think most sufficient, being aforesworn to do the same with single eye, but respect to feud or favour.

Item, In every College, we think needful at the least one Steward, a Cook, a Gardener,[and] a Porter, who shall be subject to [the] discipline of the Principal, as the rest.

[1] *aptitude to learning* [2] *only*
[3] That is, " the body of the University "
[4] *accountable* [5] That is, *eight days later*

Item, That every University have a Beadle subject to serve at all times throughout the whole University, as the Rector and Principals shall command.

Item, That every University have a Rector chosen from year to year as shall follow. The Principals, being convened with the whole Regents chapterly, shall be sworn that every man in his roume [1] shall nominate such one as his conscience shall testify to be most sufficient to bear such charge and dignity ; and three of them that shall be oftest nominated shall be put in edict publicly, fifteen days afore Michaelmas. And then shall on Michaelmas Even convene the whole Principals, Regents, and Supposts that are graduate, or at the least studied their time in Ethics, Economics, and Politics, and no others younger ; and every nation,[2] first protesting in God's presence to follow the sincere ditement [3] of their consciences, shall nominate one of the said three, and he that has monyest [4] votes shall be confirmed by the Superintendent and Principal, and his duty with an exhortation proponed unto him. And this to be the 28 day of September ; and thereafter oaths to be taken, *hinc inde*, of his just and godly government, and of the remanent lawful submission and obedience. He shall be propined [5] to the University, at his entry with a new garment, bearing *Insignia Magistratus* ; and be held monthly to visit every College, and with his presence decore [6] and examine the lections and exercition thereof. His assessors shall be a lawyer and a theologue, with whose advice he shall decide all questions civil, betwix the members of the University. If any without [7] the University pursue a member thereof, or be pursued by a member of the same, he shall assist the Provost and Bailies in those cases, or other judges competent, to see justice be ministered. In likewise, if any of the University be criminally pursued, he shall assist the Judges competent, and see that justice be ministered.

Summa of bursars in the three Universities

Item, We think it expedient that in every College in every University there be twenty-four bursars, divided equally in all the classes and seiges, as is above expressed : that is, in Saint Andrews, seventy-two bursars ; in Glasgow, forty-eight bursars ; in Aberdeen, forty-eight ; to be sustained only in meat upon the charges of the College ; and [to] be admitted at the examination of the Ministry and chapter of Principals in the University, as well in docility [8] of the persons offered, as of the ability of their parents to sustain them their selves, and not to burden the Commonwealth with them.

V (9). Of Stipends and Expenses necessary

Item, We think expedient that the Universities be doted [9] with temporal lands, with rents and revenues of the Bishoprics' temporality, and of the Kirks Collegiate, so far as their ordinary charges shall require ; and

[1] *place* ; that is, in his *turn* or *order*

[2] For a brief note on "nations" in the Scottish universities, see Rashdall, *Universities of Europe in the Middle Ages* (new edn., 1936), ii, 307.

[3] *dictate* [4] *most*

[5] *presented with* in the sense of a formal gift upon acceptance of office

[6] *adorn*, in the sense of *honour* [7] *outwith* ; *outside*

[8] *aptitude to learning* [9] *endowed*

therefore, that it would please your Honours, by advice of your Honours' Council and vote of Parliament, to do the same. And to the effect the same may be shortly expediate,[1] we have recollected [2] the sums we think necessary for the same.

Imprimis, For the ordinary Stipend of the Dialectician Reader, the Mathematician, Physician, and Moral Philosophy, we think sufficient one hundred pounds for every one of them.

Item, For the Stipend of every Reader in Medicine and Laws, one hundred and thirty-three pounds, 6s. 8d.

Item, To every Reader in Hebrew, Greek, and Divinity two hundred pounds.

Item, To every Principal of a College, two hundred pounds.[3]

Item, To every Steward, sixteen pounds of fee.

Item, To every Gardener, to every Cook, and Porter, ilkane,[4] ten marks.

Item, To the Board of every Bursar, without the Classes of Theology and Medicine, twenty pounds.

Item, [To every Bursar] in the Class of Theology, which will be only twelve persons in Saint Andrews, twenty-four pounds.

Summa of yearly and ordinary expenses in the University of Saint Andrews, extends to	3796 lib.
Summa of yearly and ordinary expenses of Glasgow .	2922 lib.
Aberdeen, asmekill	2922 lib.
Summa of the Ordinary Charges of the whole . .	9640 lib.

Item, the Beadle's Stipend shall be of every entrant and suppost of the University, two shillings; of every one graduate in Philosophy, three shillings; of every one graduate in Medicine or Laws, four shillings; in Theology, five shillings; all Bursars being excepted.

Item, We have thought good for building and upholding of the places, [that] a general collection be made; and that every Earl's son, at his entry to the University, shall give forty shillings, and siclike at every graduation, forty shillings. *Item*, Every Lord's son sicklike at ilk[4] time, thirty shillings; ilk freeholding Baron's son, twenty shillings: every Feuar and substantious Gentleman's son, one mark. *Item*, Every substantious Husband[5] and Burgess son, at ilk time, ten shillings: *Item*, Every one of the rest (excepting the Bursars), five shillings at ilk time.

And that this be gathered in a common box, put in keeping to the Principal of the Theologians, every Principal having a key thereof, to be counted ilk year once, with the relicts[6] of the Principals to be laid into the same, about the fifteenth day of November, in presence of the Super-

[1] *expedited* [2] *brought together*

[3] In the manuscript (*folio* 281 *verso*), "to everie Principall of a Colledge, ij c. lb"; Laing's text reads, erroneously, "ij lb" [4] *each*

[5] That is, the holder of a *husbandland* which was nominally, but not necessarily, twenty-six acres.

[6] *residue* or *balances*

intendent, Rector, and the whole Principals; and, at their whole consent, or at the least the most part thereof, reserved and employed only upon the building and upholding of the places, and repairing of the same, as ever necessity shall require. And therefor the Rector, with his assistants, shall be held to visit the places ilk year once, incontinent after he be promoted, upon the last of October, or thereby.

V (10). Of the Privilege of the University

Seeing we desire that Innocence shall defend us rather than Privilege, we think that ilk person of the University should answer before the Provost and Bailies of ilk town where the Universities are, of all crimes whereof they are accused, only that the Rector be Assessor to them in the said actions. In civil matters if the question be betwix members of the University on ilk side, making their residence and exercition therein for the time, in that case the party called shall not be held to answer but only before the Rector and his Assessors heretofore expressed. In all other cases of civil pursuit, the general rule of the Law to be observed, *Actor sequatur forum rei, &c.*[1]

Item, That the Rector and all inferior members of the University be exempted from all taxations, imposts, charges of war, or any other charge that may onerate or abstract him or them from the care of their office: such as Tutory, Curatory, Deaconry, or any siclike, that are established, or hereafter shall be established in our Commonwealth. To the effect, that but [2] trouble, that the one may wait upon the upbringing of the youth in learning, that the other bestow his time only in that most necessary exercition.

All other things touching the books to be read in each class, and all such particular affairs, we refer to the discretion of the Masters, Principals, and Regents, with their well-advised Councils: not doubting but if God shall grant quietness, and if your Wisdoms grace to set forward letters in the sort prescribed, ye shall leave wisdom and learning to your posterity, a treasure more to be esteemed nor any earthly treasure ye are able to provide for them; which, without wisdom, are more able to be their ruin and confusion, than help or comfort. And as this is most true, so we leave it with the rest of the commodities to be weighed by your Honours' wisdom, and set forward by your authority to the most high advancement of this Commonwealth, committed to your charge.

The Sixth Head, of the Rents and Patrimony of the Kirk.

These two sorts of men, that is to say, the Ministers and the Poor, together with the Schools, when order shall be taken thereanent, must be sustained upon the charges of the Church.[3] And therefore provision must

[1] That is, "A pursuer shall follow the court of the defender"; in other words, the pursuer must pursue in a court to the jurisdiction of which the defender is subject. (See Trayner's *Latin Maxims*) [2] *without*

[3] *Cf.* the third head of the Supplication presented to the Reformation Parliament of 1560 (*supra*, i, 337).

be made, how and of whom such sums must be lifted. But before we enter in this head, we must crave of your Honours, in the name of the Eternal God and of his Son Christ Jesus, that ye have respect to your poor brethren, the labourers and manurers of the ground; who by these cruel beasts, the Papists, have been so oppressed that their life to them has been dolorous and bitter. If ye will have God author and approver of your reformation, ye must not follow their footsteps; but ye must have compassion upon your brethren, appointing them to pay so reasonable teinds, that they may feel some benefit of Christ Jesus now preached unto them.

With the grief of our hearts we hear that some Gentlemen are now as cruel over their tenants as ever were the Papists, requiring of them whatsoever before they paid to the Church; so that the Papistical tyranny shall only be changed in the tyranny of the lord or of the laird.[1] We dare not flatter your Honours, neither yet is it profitable for you that so we do. If you permit such cruelty to be used, neither shall ye, who by your authority ought to gainstand such oppression, neither [shall] they that use the same, escape God's heavy and fearful judgments. The Gentlemen, Barons, Earls, Lords, and others, must be content to live upon their just rents, and suffer the Church to be restored to her liberty, that, in her restitution, the poor, who heretofore by the cruel Papists have been spoiled and oppressed, may now receive some comfort and relaxation.

* Concluded by the Lords: That these teinds and other exactions, to be clean discharged, and never to be taken in time coming; as, the uppermost Cloth, the Corpse-present, the Clerk-mail, the Pasche offerings, Teind Ale, and all handlings Upland,[2] can neither be required nor received of godly conscience.[3]

**Additio*

Neither do we judge it to proceed from justice that one man shall possess the teinds of another; but we think it a thing most reasonable, that every man have the use of his own teinds, provided that he answer to the Deacons and Treasurers of the Church of that which justly shall be appointed unto him. We require Deacons and Treasurers rather to receive the rents, nor the Ministers themselves; because that of the teinds must not only the Ministers be sustained, but also the Poor and Schools. And therefore we think it most expedient that common Treasurers, to wit, the Deacons, be appointed from year to year, to receive the whole rents appertaining to the Church; and that commandment be given, that no man be permitted either to receive either yet to intromet with anything appertaining to the sustentation of the persons foresaid, but such as by common consent of the Church are thereto appointed.

Additio

The lords agree with this head of the receiving of the deacons

If any think this prejudicial to the tacks and assedations [4] of those that now possess the teinds, let them understand that an unjust possession is no possession before God; for those of whom they received their title and presupposed right, were and are thieves and murderers, and had no power so to alienate the patrimony and common-good of the Church.

[1] That this continued is clear from the Supplication of 1562 (*supra*, 49–50).

[2] all *takings* from the *countryside*

[3] For these exactions, see *Statutes of the Scottish Church* (Scot. Hist. Soc.), 178, *note* 2; Robertson, *Concilia Scotiæ*, ii, 305–306.

[4] *holdings and leases*

And yet we are not so extreme, but that we wish just recompense to be made to such as have disbursed sums of money to those unjust possessors (so that it has not been of late days in prejudice of the Church) : but such as are found and known to be done of plain collusion in no wise ought to be maintained of you. And for that purpose, we think it most expedient that whosoever have assedation of teinds or churches be openly warned to produce their assedation and assurance, that cognition being taken, the just tacksman [1] may have a just and reasonable recompense for the years that are to run, the profit of the years passed being considered and deducted ; and the unjust and surmised [2] may be served accordingly. So that the Church, in the end, may recover her liberty and freedom, and that only for relief of the Poor.

Your Honours may easily understand that we speak not now for ourselves, but in favour of the Poor and the labourers defrauded and oppressed by the priests, and by their confederate pensioners. For while that the priest's pensioner's idle belly is delicately fed, the Poor, to whom a portion of that appertains, were pined with hunger ; and moreover the true labourers were compelled to pay that which [they] ought not : for the labourer is neither debtor to the dumb dog called the Bishop, neither yet unto his hired pensioner ; but is debtor only unto the Church. And the Church is only bound to sustain and nourish her charges, the persons before mentioned, to wit, the Ministers of the word, the Poor, and the Teachers of the youth.

But now to return to the former Head. The sums able to sustain these forenamed persons, and to furnish all things appertaining to the preservation of good order and policy within the Church, must be lifted off the teinds, to wit, the teind sheaf, teind hay, teind hemp, teind lint, teind fish, teind calf, teind foal, teind lamb, teind wool, teind cheese, &c. And because that we know that the tithes reasonably taken, as is before expressed, will not suffice to discharge the former necessity, we think that all things doted [3] to hospitality,[4] all annual rents, both in burgh and [to] land, pertaining to Priests, Chantries, Colleges, Chaplainries, and to Friars of all Orders, to the Sisters of the Seans,[5] and to all others of that Order, and such others within this Realm, be received still to the use of the Church or Churches within the towns or parishes where they were doted. Furthermore to the upholding of the Universities and sustentation of the Superintendents,[6] the whole revenue of the temporality of the Bishops', Deans', and Archdeans' lands, and all rents of lands pertaining to the Cathedral Churches whatsoever. And further, merchants and rich craftsmen in free Burghs, who have nothing to do with the manuring of the ground, must make some provision in their cities, towns, or dwelling places, for to support the need of the Church.

Agreed also by the Lords

[1] *leaseholder* [2] That is, without legal right

[3] *gifted in endowment ; mortified*

[4] to *hospitals*, that is, *almshouses*. But only the old endowed hospitals of the Roman Church. (See *infra*, 305, *note* 3)

[5] That is, the Sisters of the Convent of St. Katherine of Sienna. The district in Edinburgh where the convent was located is still known as The Sciennes.

[6] As given, *supra*, 289, 300–301

To the Ministers, and failing thereof the Readers, must be restored their manses and their glebes ; for else they cannot serve their flock at all times as their duty is. If any glebe exceed six acres of land, the rest to remain in the possessor's hands, while order be taken therein.

The Lords condescend that the Manses and Yards be restored to the Ministers : and all the Lords consent that the Ministers have six acres of lands, except Marischal, Morton, Glencairn, and Cassillis, where Manses are of great quantity.[1] [*Additio*]

The receivers and collectors of these rents and duties must be the Deacons or Treasurers appointed from year to year in every church,[2] and that by common consent and free election of the church. The Deacons may distribute no part of that which is collected, but by commandment of the Ministers and Elders ; and they may command nothing to be delivered, but as the Church before hath determined. To wit, the Deacons shall, of the first, pay the sums, either quarterly, or from half year to half year, to the Ministers which the Kirk hath appointed. The same they shall do to the Schoolmasters, Readers, and Hospitals [3] (if any be), always receiving acquittances for their discharge.

If any extraordinary sums lie to be delivered, then must the Ministers, Elders, and Deacons consult whether the deliverance of those sums doth stand with the common utility of the Church or not ; and if they do universally agree and condescend either upon the affirmative or the negative, then because they are in credit and office for the year, they may do as best seemeth unto them. But if there be controversy amongst themselves, the whole Church must be made privy ; and after that the matter be exponed, and the reasons heard, the judgment of the Church with the Minister's consent shall prevail.

The Deacons shall be bound and compelled to make accounts to the Ministers and Elders of that which they have received, as oft as the Policy shall appoint. And the Elders when they are changed (which must be every year), must clear their accounts before such auditors as the Church shall appoint. And both the Deacons and Elders being changed, shall deliver to them that shall be now elected, all sums of money, corns, and other profits resting in their hands ; the tickets [4] whereof must be delivered to the Superintendents in their visitation, and by them to the great Council of the Church, that as well the abundance as the indigence of every church may be evidently known, that a reasonable equality may be had throughout the whole Realm. If this order be precisely kept, corruption cannot suddenly enter. For the free and yearly election of Deacons and Elders [5] shall suffer none to usurp a perpetual dominion over the Church ; the knowledge of the rental shall suffice them to receive no more than whereof they shall be bound to make accounts ; the deliverance of the money to

[1] In the manuscript (folio 285 *recto*) this paragraph is a marginal addition. It is indicative of the discussions that took place in relation to the " policy " advocated by the " godly ministers." See also the Bibliographical Note, *supra*, i, cii–ciii.

[2] *Supra*, 303

[3] That is, to the *new* almshouses to be newly established or newly maintained by the Reformed Church.

[4] *vouchers*

[5] See *infra*, 309–310

the new officers shall not suffer private men [to] use in their private business that which appertaineth to the public affairs of the Church.

The Seventh Head, of Ecclesiastical Discipline.

As that no Commonwealth can flourish or long endure without good laws, and sharp execution of the same, so neither can the Church of God be brought to purity, neither yet be retained in the same, without the order of Ecclesiastical Discipline, which stands in reproving and correcting of those faults which the civil sword doth either neglect, either may not punish. Blasphemy, adultery, murder, perjury, and other crimes capital, worthy of death, ought not properly to fall under censure of the Church; because all such open transgressors of God's laws ought to be taken away by the civil sword. But drunkenness, excess (be it in apparel, or be it in eating and drinking), fornication, oppression of the poor by exactions, deceiving of them in buying or selling by wrong mete or measure, wanton words and licencious living tending to slander, do properly appertain to the Church of God, to punish the same as God's word commandeth.

Consented on by the Council

But because this accursed Papistry hath brought in such confusion in the world, that neither was virtue rightly praised, neither vice severely punished, the Church of God is compelled to draw the sword, which of God she hath received, against such open and manifest offenders, cursing and excommunicating all such, as well those whom the civil sword ought to punish as the others, from all participation with her in prayers and sacraments, till open repentance manifestly appear in them. As the order of Excommunication and proceeding to the same ought to be grave and slow, so, being once pronounced against any person, of what estate and condition that ever they be, it must be kept with all severity. For laws made and not kept engendereth contempt of virtue and brings in confusion and liberty to sin. And therefore this order we think expedient to be observed before and after excommunication.

First, if the offence be secret and known to few, and rather stands in suspicion than in manifest probation, the offender ought to be privately admonished to abstain from all appearance of evil; which, if he promises to do, and to declare himself sober, honest, and one that feareth God, and feareth to offend his brethren, then may the secret admonition suffice for his correction. But if he either contemn the admonition, or, after promise made, do show himself no more circumspect than he was before, then must the Minister admonish him; to whom if he be found inobedient, they must proceed according to the rule of Christ, as after shall be declared.

If the crime be public, and such as is heinous, as fornication, drunkenness, fighting, common swearing, or execration, then ought the offender to be called in the presence of the Minister, Elders, and Deacons, where his sin and offence ought to be declared and agredged,[1] so that his conscience may feel how far he hath offended God, and what slander he hath raised in the Church. If signs of unfeigned repentance appear into him, and if he require to be admitted to public repentance, the Ministry may

[1] *shown to be grave*

appoint unto him a day when the whole Church conveneth together, that in presence of all he may testify the repentance which before them he professed. Which, if he accept, and with reverence do, confessing his sin, and damning the same, and earnestly desiring the Congregation to pray to God with him for mercy, and to accept him in their society, notwithstanding his former offence, then the Church may, and ought [to] receive him as a penitent. For the Church ought to be no more severe than God declareth himself to be, who witnesseth, that "In whatsoever hour a sinner unfeignedly repenteth, and turns from his wicked way, that he will not remember one of his iniquities." And therefore the Church ought diligently to advert that it excommunicate not those whom God absolveth.

If the offender called before the Ministry be found stubborn, hard-hearted, or one in whom no sign of repentance appeareth, then must he be dismissed with an exhortation to consider the dangerous estate in which he stands ; assuring him, if they find into him no other token of amendment of life, that they will be compelled to seek a further remedy. If he within a certain space show his repentance to the Ministry, they must present him to the Church as before is said.

But if he continue in his impenitence, then must the Church be admonished that such crimes are committed amongst them, which by the Ministry hath been reprehended, and the persons provoked to repent ; whereof, because no signs appeareth unto them, they could not but signify unto the Church the crimes, but not the person, requiring them earnestly to call to God to move and touch the hearts of the offenders, so that suddenly and earnestly they may repent.

If the person malign,[1] then, the next day of public assembly, the crime and the person must be both notified unto the Church, and their judgment must be required, if that such crimes ought to be suffered unpunished amongst them. Request also would be made to the most discreet and to the nearest friends of the offender to travail with him to bring him to knowledge of himself, and of his dangerous estate ; with a commandment given to all men to call to God for the conversion of the impenitent. If a solemn and a special prayer were made and drawn for that purpose, the thing should be the more gravely done.

The third Sunday, the Minister ought to require if the impenitent have declared any signs of repentance to any of the Ministry ; and if he hath, then may the Minister appoint him to be examined by the whole Ministry, either then instantly, or at another day affixed to the consistory : and if repentance appear, as well of the crime, as of his long contempt, then may he be presented to the Church, and make his confession, and to be accepted as before is said. But if no man signify his repentance, then ought he to be excommunicate ; and by the mouth of the Minister, consent of the Ministry, and commandment of the Church, must such a contemner be pronounced excommunicate from God, and from the society of his Church.

After which sentence may no person (his wife and family only excepted) have any kind of conversation with him, be it in eating and drinking,

[1] That is, remains contumacious

buying or selling, yea, in saluting or talking with him, except that it be at the commandment or licence of the Ministry for his conversion ; that he by such means confounded, seeing himself abhorred of the faithful and godly, may have occasion to repent and be so saved. The sentence of his Excommunication must be published universally throughout the Realm, lest that any man should pretend ignorance.

His children begotten or born after that sentence and before his repentance, may not be admitted to baptism, till either they be of age to require the same, or else that the mother, or some of his especial friends, members of the Church, offer and present the child, abhorring and damning the iniquity and obstinate contempt of the impenitent. If any think it severe that the child should be punished for the iniquity of the father, let them understand that the sacraments appertain only to the faithful and to their seed : But such as stubbornly contemn all godly admonition, and obstinately remain in their iniquity, cannot be accounted amongst the faithful.

VII (2). The Order for Public Offenders

We have spoken nothing of those that commit horrible crimes, as murderers, man-slayers, and adulterers ; for such (as we have said) the Civil sword ought to punish to death. But in case they be permitted to live, then must the Church, as before is said, draw the sword which of God she hath received, holding them as accursed even in their very fact ; the offender being first called, and order of the Church used against him, in the same manner as the persons that for obstinate impenitence are publicly excommunicated. So that the obstinate impenitent, after the sentence of excommunication, and the murderer or adulterer, stand in one case as concerning the judgment of [the Church] ; that is, neither of both may be received in the fellowship of the Church to prayers or sacraments (but to hearing of the word they may), till first they offer themselves to the Ministry, humbly requiring the Ministers and Elders to pray to God for them, and also to be intercessors to the Church, that they may be admitted to public repentance, and so to the fruition of the benefits of Christ Jesus, distributed to the members of his body.

Consented to by the Lords

If this request be humbly made, then may not the Ministers refuse to signify the same unto the Church, the next day of public preaching, the Minister giving exhortation to the Church to pray to God to perform the work which he appeared to have begun, working in the heart of the offender unfeigned repentance of his grievous crime, and the sense and feeling of his great mercy, by the operation of his Holy Spirit. Thereafter a day ought publicly to be assigned unto him to give open confession of his offence and contempt, and so to make a public satisfaction to the Church of God. Which day, the offender must appear in presence of the whole Church, and with his own mouth damn his own impiety, publicly confessing the same ; desiring God of his grace and mercy, and his congregation, that it will please them to accept him in their society, as before is said. The Minister must examine him diligently whether he find a haitrent and displeasure of his sin, as well of his crime as of his contempt : which if he confess, he must travail with him, to see what hope he hath of God's mercy.

And if he find him reasonably instructed in the knowledge of Christ Jesus [and] in the virtue of his death, then may the Minister comfort him by God's infallible promises, and demand of the Church if they be content to receive that creature of God (whom Sathan before had drawn in his nets), in the society of their body, seeing that he declares himself penitent. Which, if the Church grant, as they may not justly deny the same, then ought the Minister in public prayer to commend him to God, confess the sin of that offender, and of the whole Church desire mercy and grace for Christ Jesus' sake. Which prayer being ended, the Minister ought to exhort the Church to receive that penitent brother in their favour, as they require God to receive themselves when they have offended; and in sign of their consent, the Elders and chief men of the Church shall take the penitent by the hand, and one or two in name of the whole shall kiss and embrace him with all reverence and gravity, as a member of Christ Jesus.

Which being done, the Minister shall exhort the reconciled to take diligent heed in times coming that Sathan trap him not in such crimes, admonishing him that he will not cease to tempt and try [by] all means possible to bring him from that obedience which he hath given to God, and to the ordinance of his Son Christ Jesus. The exhortation being ended, the Minister ought to give public thanks unto God for the conversion of that their brother, and for the benefits which we receive by Jesus Christ, praying for the increase and continuance of the same.

If the penitent, after that he have offered himself to the Ministry, or to the Church, be found ignorant in the principal points of our religion, and chiefly in the article of Justification, and of the office of Christ Jesus, then ought he to be exactly instructed before he be received. For a mocking of God it is to receive them in repentance who knoweth not wherein stands their remedy, when they repent their sin.

VII (3). Persons subject to Discipline

Consented to likewise

To Discipline must all Estates within this Realm be subject if they offend, as well the rulers as they that are ruled; yea and the Preachers themselves, as well as the poorest within the Church. And because the eye and mouth of the Church ought to be most single and irreprehensible, the life and conversation of the Ministers ought most diligently to be tried. Whereof we shall speak, after that we have spoken of the election of Elders and Deacons, who must assist the Ministers in all public affairs of the Church, &c.

The Eighth Head, touching the Election of Elders and Deacons, &c.[1]

Men of best knowledge in God's word, of cleanest life, men faithful, and of most honest conversation that can be found in the Church, must

[1] See also *supra*, Appendix VII

be nominated to be in election; and the names of the same must be publicly read to the whole Kirk by the Minister, giving them advertisement that from amongst these must be chosen Elders and Deacons. If any of the nominated be noted with public infamy, he ought to be repelled; for it is not seemly that the servant of corruption shall have authority to judge in the Church of God. If any man knows others of better qualities within the Church than those that be nominated, let them be put in election, that the Church may have the choice.

What churches may be joined let the policy judge

If churches be of smaller number than that Seniors and Deacons can be chosen from amongst them, then may they well be joined to the next adjacent church. For the plurality of churches, without ministers and order, shall rather hurt than edify.

The election of Elders and Deacons ought to be used every year once (which we judge to be most convenient the first day of August); lest that by long continuance of such officers, men presume upon the liberty of the Church.[1] It hurts not that one man be retained in office more years than one, so that he be appointed yearly, by common and free election; provided always, that the Deacons, treasurers, be not compelled to receive the office again for the space of three years.

How the votes and suffrages may be best received, so that every man may give his vote freely, every several Church may take such order as best seemeth to them.

The Elders being elected, must be admonished of their office, which is to assist the Minister in all public affairs of the Church; to wit, in judging and decerning causes; in giving of admonition to the licentious liver; [and] in having respect to the manners and conversation of all men within their charge. For by the gravity of the Seniors ought the light and unbridled life of the licentious [to] be corrected and bridled.

Yea, the Seniors ought to take heed to the life, manners, diligence, and study of their Ministers. If he be worthy of admonition, they must admonish him; of correction, they must correct him. And if he be worthy of deposition, they with consent of the Church and Superintendent, may depose him, so that his crime so deserve. If a Minister be light in conversation, by his Elders and Seniors he ought to be admonished. If he be negligent in study, or one that vaketh [2] not upon his charge and flock, or one that proponeth not fruitful doctrine, he deserveth sharper admonition and correction. To the which if he be found stubborn and inobedient, then may the Seniors of one Church complain to the Ministry of the two next adjacent Churches, where men of greater gravity are; to whose admonition if he be found inobedient, he ought to be discharged from his ministry till his repentance appear, and a place be vacant for him.

If any Minister be deprehended [3] in any notable crime, as whoredom, adultery, murder, manslaughter, perjury, teaching of heresy, or any such as deserve death, or [that] may be a note of perpetual infamy, he ought to be deposed for ever. By heresy, we mean pernicious doctrine plainly taught, and obstinately defended, against the foundation and principles

[1] *Cf. supra*, 305–306 [2] *attendeth* [3] *apprehended*

of our faith. And such a crime we judge to deserve perpetual deposition from the ministry; for most dangerous we know it to be, to commit the flock to a man infected with the pestilence of heresy.

Some crimes deserve deposition for a time, and while [1] the person give declaration of greater gravity and honesty. As if a minister be deprehended drunk, in brawling or fighting, an open slanderer, an infamer of his neighbour, [or] factious and [a] sower of discord, he may be commanded to cease from his ministry, till he declare the signs of repentance; upon the which, the Church shall abide him the space of twenty days or further, as the Church shall think expedient, before that they proceed to a new election.

Every inferior Church shall by one of their Seniors and one of their Deacons, once in the year, notify unto the ministry of the Superintendent's Church, the life, manners, study, and diligence of their Ministers, to the end that the discretion of some may correct the lenity of others.

Not only may the life and manners of the Ministers come under censure and judgment of the Church, but also of their wives, children, and family. Judgment must be taken, that he neither live riotously, neither yet avariciously; yea, respect must be had how they spend the stipend appointed to their living. If a reasonable stipend be appointed, and they live avariciously, they must be admonished to live so as they receive; for as excess and superfluity is not tolerable in a minister, so is avarice and the careful solicitude of money and gear utterly to be damned in Christ's servants, and especially in those that are fed upon the charge of the Church. We judge it unseemly and not tolerable that ministers shall be boarded in common ale-houses or taverns.

Neither yet must a Minister be permitted to frequent and commonly haunt the Court, unless it be for a time, when he is either sent by the Church, either yet called for by the Authority for his counsel and judgment. Neither yet must he be one of the council in Civil affairs, be he never judged so apt for that purpose; but either must he cease from the ministry (which at his own pleasure he may not do), or else from bearing charge in Civil affairs, unless it be to assist the Parliament if he be called.

The office of the Deacons, as is before declared, is to receive the rents and gather the alms of the Church, to keep and distribute the same, as by the ministry of the Kirk shall be appointed. They may also assist in judgment with the Ministers and Elders, and may be admitted to read in the assembly if they be required, and be found able thereto.

The Elders and Deacons, with their wives and households must be under the same censure that is prescribed for the Ministers: for they must be careful over their office; and seeing that they are judges to the manners of others, their own conversation ought to be irreprehensible. They must be sober, humble, lovers and entertainers of concord and peace; and, finally, they ought to be the example of godliness to others. And if the contrary thereof appear, they must be admonished by the Minister, or by some of their brethren of the ministry, if the fault be secret; and if it be open and known, it must be rebuked before the

[1] *until*

ministry, and the same order kept against the Senior or Deacon, that before is described against the Minister.

We think it not necessary that any public stipend shall be appointed either to the Elders or yet to the Deacons, because their travail continues but for one year; and also because that they are not so occupied with the affairs of the Church, but that reasonably they may attend upon their domestical business.

The Ninth Head, concerning the Policy of the Church.

Policy we call an exercise of the Church in such things as may bring the rude and ignorant to knowledge, or else inflame the learned to greater fervency, or to retain the Church in good order. And thereof there be two sorts. The one [is] utterly necessary; as that the word be truly preached, the sacraments rightly ministered, [and] common prayers publicly made; that the children and rude persons be instructed in the chief points of religion, and that offences be corrected and punished. These things, we say, be so necessary, that without the same there is no face of a visible Kirk. The other is profitable, but not of mere necessity; as, that Psalms should be sung; that certain places of the Scriptures should be read when there is no sermon; [and] that this day or that day, few or many in the week, the Church should assemble. Of these and such others we cannot see how a certain order can be established. For in some churches the Psalms may be conveniently sung; in others, perchance, they cannot.[1] Some churches may convene every day; some thrice or twice in the week; some perchance but once. In these, and such like, must every particular Church, by their own consent, appoint their own policy.

In great towns we think expedient that every day there be either Sermon, or else Common Prayers, with some exercise of reading the Scriptures. What day the public Sermon is, we can neither require or greatly approve that the Common Prayers be publicly used, lest that we shall either foster the people in superstition, who come to the Prayers as they come to the Mass; or else give them occasion to think that those be no prayers which are made before and after Sermon.

In every notable town, we require that one day, besides the Sunday, be appointed to the Sermon and Prayers; which, during the time of Sermon, must be kept free from all exercise of labour, as well of the master as of the servants. In smaller towns, as we have said, the common consent of the Church must put order. But the Sunday must straitly be kept, both before and after noon, in all towns. Before noon, must the word be preached and sacraments ministered, as also marriage solemnised, if occasion offer. After noon, must the young children be publicly examined in their Catechism in audience of the people,[2] in doing whereof the

[1] Though men and women were to be exhorted to exercise themselves in the Psalms that they might the more ably praise God with heart and voice (*infra*, 314).

[2] See *Selections from the Records of the Kirk Session, Presbytery and Synod of Aberdeen* (Spalding Club), 23 (*anno* 1578).

Minister must take great diligence, as well to cause the people to understand the questions proponed, as the answers, and the doctrine that may be collected thereof. The order and how much is appointed for every Sunday, is already distincted in our Book of Common Order [1]; which Catechism is the most perfect that ever yet was used in the Church. At afternoon also may Baptism be ministered, when occasion is offered of great travail before noon. It is also to be observed, that prayers be used at afternoon upon the Sunday, where there is neither preaching nor catechism.

It appertaineth to the Policy of the Church to appoint the times when the Sacraments shall be ministered. Baptism may be ministered whensoever the word is preached; but we think it more expedient, that it be ministered upon the Sunday,[2] or upon the day of prayers, only after the sermon; partly to remove this gross error by the which many deceived think that children be damned if they die without Baptism; and partly to make the people assist the administration of that sacrament with greater reverence than they do. For we do see the people begin already to wax weary by reason of the frequent repetition of those promises.

Four times in the year we think sufficient to the administration of the Lord's Table,[3] which we desire to be distincted, that the superstition of times may be avoided so far as may be. Your Honours are not ignorant how superstitiously the people run to that action at Pasche, even as [if] the time gave virtue to the Sacrament; and how the rest of the whole year they are careless and negligent, as [if] that it appertaineth not unto them but at that time only. We think therefore most expedient, that the first Sunday of March be appointed for one [time]; the first Sunday of June for another; the first Sunday of September for the third; and the first Sunday of December for the fourth. We do not deny but that any several church, for reasonable causes, may change the time, and may minister ofter; but we study to suppress superstition. All Ministers must be admonished to be more careful to instruct the ignorant than ready to satisfy their appetites; and more sharp in examination than indulgent in admitting to that great Mystery such as be ignorant of the use and virtue of the same. And therefore we think that the administration of the Table ought never to be without that examination pass before, especially of those whose knowledge is suspect. We think that none are apt to be admitted to that Mystery who cannot formally say the Lord's Prayer, the Articles of the Belief, and declare the sum of the Law.

Further, we think it a thing most expedient and necessary, that every Church have a Bible in English, and that the people be commanded to

[1] See the note, *supra*, 282, *note* 2

[2] Baptism on Sundays was apparently being observed in September 1562. (See de Gouda's report in Pollen, *Papal Negotiations with Mary Queen of Scots*, Scot. Hist. Soc., 123, 135)

[3] In the Geneva Order the rubric lays down "The day when the Lord's Supper is ministered, which commonly is used once a month, or so oft as the Congregation shall think expedient. . . ." (Laing's *Knox*, iv, 191); but, in December 1562, the General Assembly ordained that the Communion should be ministered "four times in the year within burghs, and twice in the year to landward." (*Booke of the Universall Kirk*, i, 30)

convene to hear the plain reading or interpretation of the Scripture, as the Church shall appoint; that by frequent reading this gross ignorance, which in the cursed Papistry hath overflowed all, may partly be removed. We think it most expedient that the Scriptures be read in order, that is, that some one Book of the Old and the New Testament be begun and orderly read to the end. And the same we judge of preaching, where the Minister for [the] most part remaineth in one place. For this skipping and divagation from place to place of the Scripture, be it in reading, or be it in preaching, we judge not so profitable to edify the Church, as the continual following of one text.

Every Master of household must be commanded either to instruct, or else cause [to] be instructed, his children, servants, and family, in the principles of the Christian religion; without the knowledge whereof ought none to be admitted to the Table of the Lord Jesus. For such as be so dull and so ignorant, that they can neither try themselves, neither yet know the dignity and mystery of that action, cannot eat and drink of that Table worthily. And therefore of necessity we judge it, that every year at least, public examination be had by the Ministers and Elders of the knowledge of every person within the Church; to wit, that every master and mistress of household come themselves and their family so many as be come to maturity, before the Ministers and Elders, to give confession of their faith, and to answer to such chief points of Religion as the Ministers shall demand. Such as be ignorant in the Articles of their Faith, understand not, nor cannot rehearse the Commandments of God, [and] know not how to pray, neither whereinto their righteousness consists, ought not to be admitted to the Lord's Table. And if they stubbornly continue, and suffer their children and servants to continue in wilful ignorance, the discipline of the Church must proceed against them unto excommunication; and then must the matter be referred to the Civil Magistrate. For seeing that the just liveth by his own faith, and that Christ Jesus justifieth by knowledge of Himself, insufferable we judge it that men shall be permitted to live and continue in ignorance as members of the Church of God.

Moreover, men, women, and children would be exhorted to exercise themselves in the Psalms, that when the Church conveneth, and does sing, they may be the more able together with common heart and voice to praise God.[1]

In private houses we think it expedient, that the most grave and discreet person use the Common Prayers at morn and at night, for the comfort and instruction of others.[2] For seeing that we behold and see the hand of God now presently striking us with divers plagues, we think it a contempt of his judgments, or a provocation of his anger more to be kindled against us, if we be not moved to repentance of our former unthankfulness, and to earnest invocation of his name, whose only power

[1] See the young James Melville's appreciation of the Psalms and the tunes thereof, which ever thereafter he found "a great blessing and comfort." (*Autobiography and Diary of Mr. James Melvill*, Wodrow Soc., 22)

[2] Knox had earlier stressed this in his brief *Letter of Wholesome Counsel* addressed to the Protestants of Scotland on his departure from them in 1556. (Laing's *Knox*, iv, 137)

may (and great mercy will), if we unfeignedly convert unto Him, remove from us these terrible plagues which now for our iniquities hang over our heads. "Convert us, O Lord, and we shall be converted."

IX (2). For Preaching, and Interpreting of Scriptures, &c.[1]

To the end that the Church of God may have a trial of men's knowledge, judgments, graces, and utterances; and also, that such as somewhat have profited in God's word may from time to time grow to more full perfection to serve the Church, as necessity shall require: it is most expedient that in every town, where schools and repair of learned men are, that there be one certain day every week appointed [to] that exercise, which Saint Paul calleth prophesying. The order whereof is expressed by him in these words: "Let two or three prophets speak; and let the rest judge: But if anything be revealed to him that sitteth by, let the former keep silence: [For] ye may, one by one, all prophesy, that all may learn, and all may receive consolation. And the spirits (that is, the judgments) of the prophets, are subject to the prophets." Of which words of the Apostle, it is evident that in Corinth, when the Church did assemble for that purpose, some place of Scripture was read; upon the which, first one gave his judgment to the instruction and consolation of the auditors, after whom did one other either confirm what the former had said, or did add what he had omitted, or did gently correct or explain more properly where the whole verity was not revealed to the former. And in case some things were hid from the one and from the other, liberty was given to the third to speak his judgment for edification of the Church. Above the which number of three (as appeareth), they passed not, for avoiding of confusion.

Cor. 14, 29

These exercises, we say, are things most necessary for the Church of God this day in Scotland. For thereby (as said is) shall the Church have judgment and knowledge of the graces, gifts, and utterances of every man within their own body; the simple, and such as have somewhat profited, shall be encouraged daily to study and proceed in knowledge; the Church shall be edified (for this exercise must be patent to such as list to hear and learn); and every man shall have liberty to utter and declare his mind and knowledge to the comfort and edification of the Church.

But lest that of a profitable exercise might arise debate and strife, curious, peregrine and unprofitable questions are to be avoided. All interpretation disagreeing from the principles of our faith, repugning to charity, or that stands in plain contradiction to any other manifest place of Scripture, is to be rejected. The interpreter in that exercise may not take to himself the liberty of a public preacher, yea, although he be a Minister appointed; but he must bind himself to his text, that he enter not by disgression in explaining common-places. He may use no invective in that exercise unless it be with sobriety in confuting heresies. In exhortations or admonitions he must be short, that the time may be spent in opening of the mind of the Holy Ghost in that place, in following the

[1] See the Geneva Order, in Laing's *Knox*, iv, 178–179

file [1] and dependence of the text, and in observing such notes as may instruct and edify the auditure.[2] For avoiding of contention, neither may the interpreter, neither yet any of the assembly, move any question in open audience, whereto himself is not content to give resolution without reasoning with any other ; but every man ought to speak his own judgment to the edification of the Church.

If any be noted with curiosity, or bringing in any strange doctrine, he must be admonished by the moderators, the Ministers and Elders, immediately after that the interpretation is ended. The whole members and number of them that are of the Assembly ought to convene together, where examination should be had, how the persons that did interpret did handle and convey the matter ; they themselves being removed till every man have given his censure ; after the which, the persons being called, the faults (if any notable be found) are noted, and the person gently admonished. In that last Assembly all questions and doubts (if any arise) should be resolved without contention.

The Ministers of the parish churches to landward, adjacent to every chief town, and the Readers, if they have any gift of interpretation, within six miles must assist and concur to those that prophesy within the towns ; to the end that they themselves may either learn, or else others may learn by them. And moreover, men in whom are supposed any gifts to be which might edify the Church if they were well applied, must be charged by the Ministers and Elders to join themselves with that session and company of interpreters, to the end that the Church may judge whether they be able to serve to God's glory, and to the profit of the Church in the vocation of Ministers, or not. And if any be found disobedient, and not willing to communicate the gifts and spiritual graces of God with their brethren, after sufficient admonition, discipline must proceed against them ; provided that the Civil Magistrate concur with the judgment and election of the Church. For no man may be permitted to live as best pleaseth him within the Church of God ; but every man must be constrained, by fraternal admonition and correction, to bestow his labours, when of the Church they are required, to the edification of others.

What day in the week is most convenient for that exercise, and what books of the Scriptures shall be most profitable to be read, we refer to the judgment of every particular Church, we mean, to the wisdom of the Ministers and Elders.

IX (3). Of Marriage

Because that Marriage, the blessed ordinance of God, in this cursed Papistry hath partly been contemned, and partly hath been so infirmed, that the persons conjoined could never be assured of continuance, if the Bishops and Prelates list to dissolve the same, we have thought good to show our judgments how such confusion in times coming may be best avoided.

And first, public inhibition must be made that no persons under the

[1] *thread* [2] *audience*

power and obedience of others, such as sons and daughters, [and] those that be under curators, neither men nor women, contract marriage privily and without knowledge [of their parents, tutors, or curators, under whose power they are for the time] : which if they do, the censure and discipline of the Church [ought] to proceed against them. If the son or daughter, or other, have their heart touched with desire of marriage, they are bound to give that honour to the parents that they open unto them their affection, asking of them counsel and assistance, how that motion, which they judge to be of God, may be performed. If the father, friend, or master, gainstand their request, and have no other cause than the common sort of men have (to wit, lack of goods, or because they are not so high-born as they require), yet must not the parties whose hearts are touched make any covenant till further declaration be made unto the Church of God. And, therefore, after they have opened their minds to their parents, or such others as have charge over them, they must declare it also to the Ministry, or to the Civil Magistrate, requiring them to travail with their parents for their consent, which to do they are bound. And if they, to wit, the Magistrate or Ministers, find no just cause why the marriage required may not be fulfilled, then, after sufficient admonition to the father, friend, master, or superior, that none of them resist the work of God, the Ministry or Magistrate may enter in the place of the parent, and by consenting to their just requests may admit them to marriage. For the work of God ought not to be hindered by the corrupt affections of worldly men. The work of God we call, when two hearts (without filthiness before committed) are so joined that both require and are content to live together in that holy bond of matrimony.

If any man commit fornication with the woman whom he required in marriage, then do both lose this foresaid benefit, as well of the Church as of the Magistrate ; for neither of both ought to be intercessors or advocates for filthy fornicators. But the father, or nearest friend, whose daughter being a virgin is deflowered, hath power by the law of God to compel the man that did that injury to marry his daughter. Or if the father will not accept him by reason of his offence, then may he require the dot [1] of his daughter ; which if the offender be not able to pay, then ought the Civil Magistrate to punish his body by some other punishment.

And because that fornication, whoredom, and adultery, are sins most common in this Realm, we require of your Honours, in the name of the Eternal God, that severe punishment, according as God hath commanded, be executed against such wicked offenders. For we doubt not but such enorme crimes openly committed, provoke the wrath of God, as the Apostle speaketh, not only upon the offenders, but also upon such places as where, without punishment, they are committed.

Agrees to the head of marriage

But to return to our former purpose : Marriage ought not to be contracted amongst persons that have no election for lack of understanding; and therefore we affirm, that bairns and infants cannot lawfully be married in their minor age, to wit, the man within fourteen years of age,

[1] *dowry*

and the woman within twelve years, at the least.[1] Which if it chance any to have been, and have kept their bodies always separate, we cannot judge them bound to adhere as man and wife, by reason of that promise, which in God's presence was no promise at all. But if in the years of judgment they have embraced the one the other, then by reason of their last consent, they have ratified that which others did promise for them in their youth-head.

In a Reformed Church, marriage ought not to be secretly used, but in open face and public audience of the Church. And for avoiding of dangers, expedient it is that the banns be publicly proclaimed three Sundays (unless the persons be [so] known, that no suspicion of danger may arise, and then may the banns be shortened at the discretion of the Ministry). But in no wise can we admit marriage to be used secretly, how honourable that ever the persons be. The Sunday before sermon we think most convenient for marriage, and it to be used no day else without the consent of the whole Ministry.

Marriage once lawfully contracted, may not be dissolved at man's pleasure, as our master Christ Jesus doth witness, unless adultery be committed; which, being sufficiently proven in presence of the Civil Magistrate, the innocent (if they so require) ought to be pronounced free, and the offender ought to suffer the death as God hath commanded. If the Civil sword foolishly spare the life of the offender, yet may not the Church be negligent in their office, which is to excommunicate the wicked, and to repute them as dead members, and to pronounce the innocent party to be at freedom, be they never so honourable before the world. If the life be spared (as it ought not to be) to the offenders, and if the fruits of repentance of long time appear in them, and if they earnestly desire to be reconciled with the Church, we judge that they may be received to participation of the Sacraments, and of the other benefits of the Church, (for we would not that the Church should hold those excommunicate whom God absolved, that is, the penitent).

If any demand, whether that the offender after reconciliation with the Church, may not marry again, we answer, That if they cannot live continent, and if the necessity be such as that they fear further offence of God, we cannot forbid them to use the remedy ordained of God.[2] If the party offended may be reconciled to the offender, then we judge that in nowise

[1] In 1568 we find the Superintendent of Fife forbidding the solemnization of a marriage until the man had completed fourteen years of age. (*St. Andrews Kirk Session Register*, Scot. Hist. Soc., i, 299–300). In 1600 the General Assembly lamented that there was "untimeous marriage of young and tender persons" and "no law nor statute of the Kirk, [made] as yet defining the age of persons to be married"; and thereafter it ordained the ages for marriage to be those that are given above, and desired the Commissioners of the Assembly to have its decision ratified by the Convention of Estates. (*Booke of the Universall Kirk*, iii, 953)

[2] In 1600, however, the General Assembly had to note that the marriage of persons convicted of adultery was a great temptation to married persons to commit that crime, thinking thereby to be separated by divorce and thereafter to enjoy those with whom they had committed adultery. Accordingly the Assembly thought it expedient to crave an Act at the next Convention of Estates "discharging all marriages of such persons as are convicted of adultery." (*Booke of the Universall Kirk*, iii, 953)

it shall be lawful to the offender to marry any other, except the party that before hath been offended; and the solemnization of the latter marriage must be in the open face of the Church like as the former, but without proclamation of banns.

This we do offer as the best counsel that God giveth unto us in so doubtsome a case. But the most perfect Reformation were, if your Honours would give to God his honour and glory, that ye would prefer his express commandment to your own corrupt judgments, especially in punishing of those crimes which he commandeth to be punished with death. For so should ye declare yourselves God's true and obedient officers, and your Commonwealth should be redd [1] of innumerable troubles.

We mean not, that sins committed in our former blindness [2] (which be almost buried in oblivion) shall be called again to examination and judgment. But we require that the law may now and hereafter be so established and executed, that this ungodly impunity of sin have no place within this Realm. For in the fear of God we signify unto your Honours, that whosoever persuadeth unto you that ye may pardon where God commandeth death, deceiveth your souls, and provokes you to offend God's Majesty. *Nota*

IX (4). Of Burial

Burial in all ages hath been held in estimation, to signify that the same body that was committed to the earth should not utterly perish, but should rise again. And the same we would have kept within this Realm, provided that superstition, idolatry, and whatsoever hath proceeded of a false opinion, and for advantage sake, may be avoided; as singing of Mass, Placebo, and Dirige, and all other prayers over or for the dead, are not only superfluous and vain, but also are idolatry, and do repugn to the plain Scriptures of God. For plain it is, that everyone that dieth departeth either in the faith of Christ Jesus, or else departeth in incredulity. Plain it is, that they that depart in the true faith of Christ Jesus, rest from their labours, and from death [do] go to life everlasting, as by our Master and by his Apostle we are taught. But whosoever departs in unbelief or in incredulity, shall never see life, but the wrath of God abideth upon him. And so, we say that prayers for the dead are not only superfluous and vain, but do expressly repugn to the manifest Scriptures and verity thereof.

For avoiding all inconvenients, we judge it best, that neither singing nor reading be at the burial. For albeit things sung and read may admonish some of the living to prepare themselves for death, yet shall some superstitious and ignorant persons ever think that the works, singing, or reading of the living do and may profit the dead. And therefore, we think most expedient that the dead be conveyed to the place of burial with some honest company of the Church, without either singing or reading; yea, without all kind of ceremony heretofore used, other than that the dead be committed to the grave, with such gravity and sobriety, as those that *Refers this article to the judgment of the Church*

[1] *cleared* [2] So also *supra*, 285

be present may seem to fear the judgments of God, and to hate sin, which is the cause of death.

*[*Additio*] * And yet, notwithstanding, we are not so precise, but that we are content that particular Kirks use them in that behalf, with the consent of the Ministry of the same, as they will answer to God, and [the] Assembly of the Universal Kirk gathered within the Realm.[1]

We are not ignorant that some require a sermon at the burial, or else some places of Scriptures to be read, to put the living in mind that they are mortal, and that likewise they must die. But let those men understand that the sermons which be daily made, serve for that use ; which if men despise, the preaching of the funeral sermons shall rather nourish superstition and a false opinion (as before is said), than that they shall bring such persons to any godly consideration of their own estate. Attour, either shall the Ministers for the most part be occupied in preaching funeral sermons, or else they shall have respect to persons, preaching at the burial of the rich and honourable, but keeping silence when the poor or despised departeth ; and this with safe conscience cannot the Ministers do. For, seeing that before God there is no respect of persons, and that their ministry appertaineth to all alike, whatsoever they do to the rich, in respect of their ministry, the same they are bound to do to the poorest under their charge.

In respect of divers inconvenients, we think it neither seemly that the Church appointed to preaching and ministration of the Sacraments shall be made a place of burial ; but that some other secret and convenient place, lying in the most free air, be appointed for that use ; the which place ought to be well walled and fenced about, and kept for that use only.[2]

IX (5). For Reparation of Churches

Lest that the word of God, and ministration of the Sacraments, by unseemliness of the place come in contempt, of necessity it is that the churches and places where the people ought publicly to convene be with expedition repaired in doors, windows, thatch, and with such preparations within, as appertaineth as well to the majesty of the word of God as unto

Agreed on the ease and commodity of the people. And because we know the slothfulness of men in this behalf, and in all other which may not redound to their private commodity, strait charge and commandment must be given that within a certain day the reparations must be begun, and within another day, to be affixed by your Honours, that they be finished. Penalties and sums of money must be enjoined, and without pardon taken from the contemners.

[1] That particular Kirks availed themselves of this dispensation seems to be clear from "The Forme and Maner of Buriall usit in the Kirk of Montrois" (*Wodrow Soc. Miscellany*, i, 293–300). This service, which may be dated between 1560 and 1581, includes an address by the Minister or Reader, a Prayer, and a Funeral Hymn—this last being one of the Gude and Godly Ballatis particularly appropriate to the occasion.

[2] In addition to this recommendation, far advanced for the time, we should note that in 1563 the General Assembly ordained that the dead were to be buried "six feet under the earth." (*Booke of the Universall Kirk*, i, 43)

The reparation would be according to the possibility and number of the Church. Every Church must have doors, close windows of glass, thatch or slate able to withhold rain, a bell to convocate the people together, a pulpit, a basin for baptism, and tables for the ministration of the Lord's Supper.[1] In greater churches, and where the congregation is great in number, must reparation be made within the Church for the quiet and commodious receiving of the people. The expenses to be lifted partly of the people, and partly of the teinds, at the consideration of the Ministry.

IX (6). For Punishment of those that profane the Sacraments and do contemn the Word of God, and dare presume to minister them, not being thereto lawfully called

As Sathan hath never ceased from the beginning to draw mankind in one of two extremities, to wit, that men should either be so ravished with gazing upon the visible creatures that, forgetting the cause why they were ordained, they attributed unto them a virtue and power which God hath not granted unto them ; or else that men should so contemn and despise God's blessed ordinance and holy institutions, as [if] that neither in the right use of them were there any profit, neither yet in their profanation were there any danger. As this wise, we say, Sathan hath blinded the most part of mankind from the beginning ; so doubt we not, but that he will strive to continue in his malice even to the end. Our eyes have seen, and presently do see the experience of the one and of the other. What was the opinion of most part of men of the Sacrament of Christ's body and blood, during the darkness of superstition, is not unknown ; how it was gazed upon, kneeled unto, borne in procession, and finally worshipped and honoured as Christ Jesus Himself. And so long as Sathan might then retain man in that damnable idolatry, he was quiet, as one that possessed his kingdom of darkness peaceably. But since that it hath pleased the mercies of God to reveal unto the unthankful world the light of his word, the right use and administration of his sacraments, he assays [2] man upon the contrary part. For where (not long ago), men stood in such admiration of that idol in the Mass that none durst presume to have said the Mass but the foresworn shaven sort, the Beast's marked men, some dare now be so bold as, without all convocation,[3] to minister (as they suppose), the true sacraments in open assemblies. And some idiots[4] (yet more wickedly and more impudently), dare counterfeit in their houses that which the true Ministers do in the open congregation ; they presume, (we say), to do it in houses without reverence, without word preached, and without Minister, other than of companion to companion.[5] This contempt proceedeth, no doubt, from the malice and craft of that

[1] For the Lord's Supper was to be taken "sitting at a table" (*supra*, 282), though no seats are specified in the furnishings.

[2] *tests*

[3] That is, without a proper *calling*

[4] Here used in the sense of *private persons, laymen*, rather than in the sense of *uneducated, ignorant* persons.

[5] But see Winzet's pertinent questions on this point in *Certane Tractatis* (Maitland Club), [18], 89.

Serpent who first deceived man, of purpose to deface the glory of Christ's Evangel, and to bring his blessed sacraments in a perpetual contempt. And further, your Honours may clearly see how proudly and stubbornly the most part despise the Evangel of Christ Jesus offered unto you ; whom unless that sharply and stoutly ye resist, we mean as well the manifest despiser as the profaner of the sacraments, ye shall find them pernicious enemies ere it be long. And therefore, in the name of the Eternal God, and of his Son Christ Jesus, we require of your Honours that, without delay, strait Laws be made against the one and the other.

Optima collatio

We dare not prescribe unto you what penalties shall be required of such : But this we fear not to affirm, that the one and the other deserve death ; for if he who doth falsify the seal, subscription, or coin of a king is adjudged worthy of death ; what shall we think of him who plainly doth falsify the seals of Christ Jesus, Prince of the kings of the earth ? If Darius pronounced that a balk should be taken from the house of that man, and he himself hanged upon it, that durst attempt to hinder the re-edification of the material Temple,[1] what shall we say of those that contemptuously blaspheme God, and manifestly hinder the [spiritual] Temple of God (which is the souls and bodies of the elect) to be purged, by the true preaching of Christ Jesus, from the superstition and damnable idolatry in which they have been of long plunged and held captive ? If ye (as God forbid), declare yourselves careless over the true Religion, God will not suffer your negligence unpunished. And therefore, more earnestly require we, that strait laws may be made against the stubborn contemners of Christ Jesus, and against such as dare presume to minister his Sacraments, not orderly called to that office, lest that while there be none found to gainstand impiety, the wrath of God be kindled against the whole.

The Papistical priests have neither power nor authority to minister the Sacraments of Christ Jesus ; because that in their mouth is not the sermon of exhortation.[2] And therefore, to them must strait inhibition be made, notwithstanding any usurpation which they have had in that behalf in the time of blindness. It is neither the clipping of their crowns, the crossing of their fingers, nor the blowing of the dumb dogs called the Bishops, neither yet the laying on of their hands, that maketh them true Ministers of Christ Jesus. But the Spirit of God inwardly first moving the hearts to seek Christ's glory and the profit of his Church, and thereafter the nomination of the people, the examination of the learned, and public admission (as before is said), makes men lawful Ministers of the word and sacraments. We speak of an ordinary vocation, where churches are reformed, or at least tend to reformation, and not of that which is extraordinary, when God by Himself, and by his only power, raiseth up to the Ministry such as best pleaseth his wisdom.

The Conclusion

Thus have we, in these few Heads, offered unto your Honours our judgments, according as we were commanded, touching the Reformation

[1] Ezra, vi, 11 [2] *Cf. supra*, 287

of things which heretofore have altogether been abused in this cursed Papistry. We doubt not but some of our petitions shall appear strange unto you at the first sight. But if your Wisdoms deeply consider that we must answer not only unto men, but also before the throne of the Eternal God, and of his Son Christ Jesus, for the counsel which we give in this so grave a matter, your Honours shall easily consider that more assured it is to us to fall in the displeasure of all men in earth, than to offend the Majesty of God, whose justice cannot suffer flatterers and deceitful counsellors unpunished.

That we require the Church to be set at such liberty that she neither be compelled to feed idle bellies, neither yet to sustain the tyranny which heretofore by violence hath been maintained, we know will offend many. But if we should keep silence hereof, we are most assured to offend the just and righteous God, who by the mouth of his Apostle hath pronounced this sentence: "He that laboureth not, let him not eat." If we in this behalf, or in any other, require or ask any [other] thing than by God's expressed commandment, by equity, and good conscience ye are bound to grant, let it be noted, and after repudiated [1]; but if we require nothing which God requireth not also, let your Honours take heed how ye gainstand the charge of Him whose hand and punishment ye cannot escape.

If blind affection rather lead you to have respect to the sustentation of those your carnal friends, who tyrannously have empired above the poor flock of Christ Jesus, than that the zeal of God's glory provoke and move you to set his oppressed Church at freedom and liberty, we fear your sharp and sudden punishments, and that the glory and honour of this enterprise be reserved unto others.

And yet shall this our judgment abide to the generations following for a monument and witness, how lovingly God called you and this Realm to repentance, what counsellors God sent unto you, and how ye [have] used the same. If obediently ye hear God now calling, we doubt not but He shall hear you in your greatest necessity. But if, following your own corrupt judgments, ye contemn his voice and vocation, we are assured that your former iniquity, and present ingratitude, shall together crave just punishment from God, who cannot long delay to execute his most just judgments, when, after many offences and long blindness, grace and mercy offered is contemptuously refused.

God the Father of our Lord Jesus Christ, by the power of his Holy Spirit, so illuminate your hearts that ye may clearly see what is pleasing and acceptable in his presence; so bow the same to his obedience that ye may prefer his revealed will to your own affections; and so strengthen you by the spirit of fortitude that boldly ye may punish vice and maintain virtue within this Realm, to the praise and glory of his Holy name, to the comfort and assurance of your own consciences, and to the consolation and good example of the posterities following. Amen. So be it.

By your Honours'

Most humble Servitors, etc.

From Edinburgh, The 20 of May 1560

[1] *Cf. supra*, 280–281

Act of Secret Council, 27 January 1560 [1]

We, who have subscribed these Presents, having advised with the Articles herein specified, as is above mentioned from the beginning of this Book, think the same good, and conform to God's Word in all points; conform to the Notes and Additions thereto eikit [2]; and promise to set the same forward at the uttermost of our powers: Providing that the Bishops, Abbots, Priors, and other prelates and beneficed men, which else [3] have adjoined them to us, bruik [4] the revenues of their benefices during their lifetimes, they sustaining and upholding the Ministry and Ministers, as is herein specified, for preaching of the Word, and ministering of the Sacraments of God.

(*Sic Subscribitur*) [5]

James [6]
James Hamilton [7]
Ard. Argyll [8]
James Stewart [9]
Rothes [10]
James Haliburton [11]
R. Boyd [12]
Alexr. Campbell, Dean of Moray [13]
William of Culross [14]
Master Alexr. Gordon [15]
Bargany Younger [16]
George Corrie of Kelwood [17]
John Shaw of Haily [18]
Andrew Hamilton of Letham [19]
Glencairn [20]
Ochiltree [21]
Sanquhar [22]
Saint John [23]
William Lord Hay [24]
Drumlanrig [25]
Cunninghamhead [26]
John Maxwell [27]
Andro Ker of Fawdonside [28]
T. Scott of Haining [29]
John Lockhart of Barr [30]
George Fentoun of that Ilk [31]
Lochinvar [32]

[1] That is, 27 January 1561; the new year, at this time, did not begin until 25 March. See also *supra*, i, 345.

[2] *added*. The "notes and additions" are marked on pages 288, 289, 290, 303, 305, 320; but attention should also be paid to such marginal comments as "Consented on by the Council" (*supra*, 306), or "Agreed on" (*supra*, 320)

[3] *otherwise*, in the sense of *already*

[4] *possess*

[5] In the manuscript (folio 300 *recto*) a rough attempt has been made to write the first few signatures in facsimile.

[6] James, Duke of Châtelherault

[7] James, Lord Hamilton, eldest son of the Duke of Châtelherault

[8] Archibald, fifth Earl of Argyll

[9] Lord James Stewart, Commendator of St. Andrews and Pittenweem; afterwards Earl of Moray, and Regent of Scotland.

[10] Andrew, fifth Earl of Rothes

[11] James Haliburton, sometimes styled Tutor of Pitcur. He was Provost of Dundee. (See Laing's *Knox*, vi, 678–679)

[12] Robert, fifth Lord Boyd

[13] Alexander Campbell, Dean of Moray, third son of Colin, third Earl of Argyll

[14] William Colville, Commendator of Cuiross

[15] Alexander Gordon, titular Archbishop of Athens, second son of John, Lord Gordon (eldest son of Alexander, third Earl of Huntly). He had been Archbishop of Glasgow (1550–51); Bishop of the Isles, and Abbot of Inchaffray and Icolmkill; and became Elect of Galloway, after the death of Andrew Durie, in 1558.

[16] Thomas Kennedy, of Bargany, Ayrshire
[17] George Corrie of Kelwood (Ayrshire)
[18] John Shaw of Haily (Ayrshire)
[19] Andrew Hamilton of Letham (Lanarkshire)
[20] Alexander, fourth Earl of Glencairn
[21] Andrew Stewart, second Lord Ochiltree
[22] Robert, sixth Lord Crichton of Sanquhar
[23] James Sandilands, second son of Sir James Sandilands of Calder; Lord St. John, and afterwards Lord Torphichen.
[24] William, fifth Lord Hay of Yester
[25] Sir James Douglas of Drumlanrig
[26] William Cunningham of Cunninghamhead (Ayrshire)
[27] Sir John Maxwell of Terregles (became Lord Herries in 1566)
[28] Andrew Ker of Fawdonside (Selkirkshire). He married for his second wife, Margaret Stewart, daughter of Lord Ochiltree, and widow of John Knox.
[29] Thomas Scott of Haining (Selkirkshire)
[30] John Lockhart of Barr (Ayrshire)
[31] George Fentoun of Fentoun. In the manuscript this name appears as "George Setoun of that ilk." There was no Seton of that Ilk; and George, fifth Lord Seton, never joined the Reformers. Fentoun of that Ilk is the most likely alternative reading.
[32] Sir John Gordon of Lochinvar (Kirkcudbrightshire)

Knox informs us (*supra*, i, 345), that the Book of Discipline was also subscribed by, among others,

William, Earl Marischal *
John, Earl of Menteith
James, Earl of Morton *
John, Lord Lindsay of the Byres
Patrick, Master of Lindsay
Sir Alexander Stewart of Garlies

* These Lords are referred to in the discussion anent glebes (*supra*, 305).

APPENDIX IX [1]

ACTS OF THE PRIVY COUNCIL RELATING TO THE THIRDS OF THE BENEFICES

APUD EDINBURGH, XXII DECEMBRIS, ANNO 1561

[SEDERUNT

Jacobus Dux de Châtelherault
Georgius Comes de Huntlie
Archibaldus Ergadie Comes
Willelmus Marescalli Comes
Johannes Atholie Comes
Willelmus Comes de Montross
Jacobus Comes de Morton
Alexander Comes de Glencairn
Jacobus Commendatarius St. Andree et Pittenweem
Johannes Dominus Erskine
Magister Robertus Richardson Thesaurarius
Magister Jacobus Makgill de Nether Rankeillour Clericus Registri
Johannes Bellenden de Auchnoull miles Clericus Justiciarie
Willelmus Maitland de Lethington junior Secretarius

Presentibus etiam Dominis subscriptis ratione Conventionis, viz. Johanne Comite de Sutherland, Georgio Comite de Cathenes, Andrea Comite de Rothes, Johanne Domino de Menteith, Johanne Domino Glamis, Hugone Domino Somerville, Roberto Domino Boyd, Johanne Domino Fleming, Georgio Domino Seton, Johanne Domino Innermeath, Alexandro Domino Hume, Davide Domino Drummond, Andrea Domino Stewart de Ochiltree, Jacobo Domino Sancti Johannis, Johanne Magistro de Maxwell, et Jacobo Douglas de Drumlanrig, militibus] [2]

The same day, forsamekle as the Queen's Majesty, by the advice of the Lords of her Secret Council, foreseeing the imminent trouble which apparently was to arise amongst the lieges of her realm for matters of Religion: to stay the same, and to evade all inconvenients that may follow thereupon, intercommuned with a part of the Clergy and Estate Ecclesiastical, with whom then reasoning being had, it was thought good and expedient by her Highness, that a General Convention should be appointed the xv day of December instant, whereto the rest of the Estates might have repaired and, by the advice of the whole, a reasonable overture made and order taken for staying of the apparent trouble, and quieting of the whole country. Which Convention being by her Majesty appointed, and sundry days of Council kept, and the said Ecclesiastical Estate ofttimes required that the said order might be taken and overture made for staying of trouble

[1] See *supra*, 28, *note* 3

[2] The *sederunt* has been supplied from *Reg. Privy Council of Scotland*, i, 192, where also the Act will be found. In the manuscript this first Act is incorrectly dated 20 December 1561. Knox's entries have been collated with the *Register*, but only one or two minor details have been corrected.

and quieting of the country; first[1] of all, in presence of the Queen's Majesty, and Lords of Council foresaid, and others of the Nobility of this Realm, compeared[2] John, Archbishop of Saint Andrews, Robert, Bishop of Dunkeld, Patrick, Bishop of Moray, and Henry, Bishop of Ross, and for themselves *respective* offered to the Queen's Grace to be content of three parts[3] of the rents of their benefices, and the fourth[4] part thereof to be employed as her Grace thought expedient. And because the certainty thereof was not known, nor yet what sums of money would sufficiently sustain the Ministry and Ministers of God's word within this Realm, nor yet how mekle was necessary to support the Queen's Majesty above her own rents for the common affairs of the country: Therefore, it is concluded, decerned, and determined by the Queen's Grace and Lords of Council foresaid, and others of the Nobility present, that if the fourth part[5] of the fruits of the whole benefices ecclesiastical within this Realm may be sufficient to sustain the Ministry through the whole Realm, and support the Queen's Majesty to entertain and set forward the common affairs of the country, failing thereof, the third part of he said fruits, or more, while[6] it be found sufficient to the effect foresaid, to be taken up yearly in time coming, while[6] a general order be taken therein; samekle thereof to be employed to the Queen's Majesty for entertaining and setting forward of the common affairs of the country, and samekle thereof unto the Ministers and sustentation of the Ministry, as may reasonably sustain the same, at the sight and discretion of the Queen's Majesty and Council foresaid: and the excrescence and superplus to be assigned unto the old possessors. And to that effect that the rents and yearly avail of the whole benefices within this Realm may be clearly known to the Queen's Majesty and Council foresaid, It is statute and ordained, that the whole rentals of all benefices within this Realm be produced before her Grace and Lords foresaid, at the times underwritten; That is to say, of the benefices on this side of the Mounth,[7] the xxiv day of January next to come, and beyond the Mounth, the tenth of February next thereafter. And ordains letters to be directed to officers of the Queen's sheriffs in that part, to pass, charge, and require all and sundry Archbishops, Bishops, Abbots, Commendators and Priors of this Realm on this side of the Mounth personally, if they can be apprehended, and failing thereof, at the said Archbishops', Bishops', Abbots', Commendators' and Priors' dwelling-places, cathedral kirks, or abbeys; and all Deans, Sub-

[1] The manuscript (folio 313 *recto*) has *last of all.*

[2] To *compear* is a legal term meaning to present oneself in court either in response to a summons or in fulfilment of an obligation to attend under the burden of rendering suit or presence.

[3] In the manuscript, " to be content of the two parte," thus anticipating the arrangement eventually reached.

[4] In the manuscript, corrected from *fourth* to *third*, and then back again by a marginal correction to *fourth.*

[5] In the manuscript, again corrected from *fourth* to *third,* and then back again, by a marginal correction to *fourth.*

[6] *until*

[7] *The Mounth* is the old name for the range of mountains extending across Scotland from Aberdeenshire on the east to northern Argyll on the West.

deans, Archdeans, Chantors, Sub-chantors, Provosts, Parsons, Vicars, and other beneficed men [whatsomever],[1] their Chamberlains and Factors, personally or at their dwelling-places, or at their parish kirks, where they should remain, to exhibit and produce before the Queen's Majesty and Lords foresaid, the said xxiv day of January next to come, the just and true rental of the avail and rents of their benefices to the effect foresaid; and to charge the prelates and other beneficed men on the yond [2] side of the Mounth in manner *respective* foresaid, to [exhibit and] [1] produce the just and true rental of their benefices before the Queen's Majesty and Lords foresaid the said tenth day of February next to come, to the effect above rehearsed, With certification to them that fails, the Queen's Grace and Council will proceed against [them] as accords: And siclike to charge the whole Superintendents, Ministers, Elders, and Deacons of the principal towns and shires of this Realm, to give in before the Queen's Grace and Lords of Council foresaid, the said xxiv day of January next to come, a formal and sufficient roll and memorial, what may be sufficient and reasonable to sustain the Ministry and whole Ministers of this Realm, that her Majesty and Lords of Council foresaid may take order therein as accords: And further, that the Queen's Majesty and Lords of Council foresaid [may] [1] ryplie [3] and digestly weigh and consider what necessary support is required to be taken yearly of the fruits of the said benefices by [4] her Grace's own yearly rent, to entertain and set forward the common affairs of this Realm, against the said xxiv day of January next to come, that then it may be proceeded in the said matter, all parties be satisfied, and the whole country and lieges thereof set in quietness.

[The same day, forsamekle as the weighty and debatable causes standing amongst the lieges of this Realm, which might give occasion of break and inquieting of the whole estate of the same—for eschewing thereof the Queen's Majesty appointed a Convention of the Nobility and Clergy of her Grace's Realm foresaid, to compear the xv day of December instant: which being held, and divers times continued, compeared, John, Archbishop of Saint Andrews, Robert, Bishop of Dunkeld, Patrick, Bishop of Moray, and Henry, Bishop of Ross, and offered as after follows; That is to say, that they being restored to their benefices and privileges and answered thereof, offers to the Queen's Majesty for the space of one year, the fourth part of the rents of their benefices, to be employed as her Grace thinks expedient: And this they offered, and no further.] [5]

APUD LINLITHGOW, 24 JANUARII, ANNO &C. 1561 [6]

Forsamekle as the Queen's Majesty, by the advice of the Lords of her Secret Council, directed her Letters commanding all and sundry

[1] The words within square brackets do not appear in the entry in the *Register of the Privy Council*. [2] *beyond*, that is *further*

[3] *maturely*, through being *fully informed* [4] *besides, apart from*

[5] This entry does not appear in the manuscript. It is taken from the *Register of the Privy Council* (i, 194) and serves to connect the preceding Act with those that follow.

[6] That is, 24 January 1562. No *sederunt* appears in the *Register of the Privy Council* (i, 196).

Archbishops, Bishops, Abbots, [Commendators],[1] Priors, Deans, Archdeans, [Subdeans, Chantors, Subchantors],[1] Parsons, Vicars, and all other beneficed men, their factors, fermorars,[2] and tacksmen,[3] to compear before her Highness and Lords foresaid, at Edinburgh, or where it shall happen them to be for the time, so many as dwells upon this side of the Mounth, the xxiv day of January instant ; and them that dwells beyond the Mounth, the tenth day of February next to come ; that the just avail of their benefices may be known, so that thereafter her Grace might take order for the sustaining of the Ministry of the Kirk,[4] and public business of the Realm : And because the Queen's Majesty is presently occupied in other affairs, and may not attend herself upon the receipt of the said rentals, Therefore her Highness has given and granted, and by these presents gives and grants, full power and commission to Master James McGill of Rankeillor Nether, Clerk of Register, Sir John Bellenden of Auchinoull, knight, Justice Clerk, Treasurer, Secretary, Advocate, and Laird of Pittarrow,[5] To call before them, within the burgh of Edinburgh, all and sundry prelates and beneficed men who are charged by virtue of the said letters, and now being in Edinburgh, or that hereafter shall happen to repair thereto, their factors and fermorars, and there inquire of them the rentals of their benefices, and receive the same from them, to the effect foresaid : And siclike that the said Commissioners cause warn all Superintendents, [Ministers] [1] Elders, and Deacons, to give unto them the names of the whole Ministers of this Realm, that the just calculation being considered and made by the said Commissioners of the avail of the said benefices, they may report the same to the Queen's Majesty, that her Highness may take order therein ; according to the [just] [1] tenor of the first Ordinance made thereupon.

APUD EDINBURGH, XII FEBRUARII, ANNO &C. 1561 [6]

[SEDERUNT

Georgius Comes de Huntlie	Alexander Comes de Glencairn
Archibaldus Comes Ergadie	Jacobus Comes de Morton
Jacobus Comes de Mar	Johannes Dominus Erskine
Willelmus Marescalli Comes	Johannes Bellenden de Auchnoull
Johannes Atholie Comes	miles Clericus Justiciarie.] [7]

THE which day, forsamekle as by Statute and Ordinance made by the Queen's Majesty and Lords of Secret Council, and her Highness's letters

[1] The words within square brackets do not appear in the entry in the *Register of the Privy Council.* [2] Tenants holding by a money-rent or *ferme*

[3] Tenants holding on a *tack* or lease

[4] In the *Register of the Privy Council* (i, 196) the wording runs "ministers of the poor and public business of the realm."

[5] These officials were Mr. Robert Richardson, Treasurer ; William Maitland of Lethington, Secretary ; and Mr. John Spens of Condie, Advocate. Sir John Wishart of Pittarrow was appointed as Comptroller less than a month later, namely on 16 February 1562. (MS. Reg. Secreti Sigilli, xxxi, 3) [6] That is, 12 February 1562

[7] The *sederunt* is supplied from the *Register of the Privy Council of Scotland*, i, 199.

directed thereupon, All and sundry Archbishops, [Bishops] [1] Abbots, Commendators, Priors, Archdeans, Deans, Subdeans, Chantors, Subchantors, Provosts, Parsons, Vicars, and other beneficed men of this Realm, were charged to exhibit and produce the rentals of their benefices before her Majesty and Lords foresaid, in manner following : That is to say, the said beneficed men, [dwelling] [1] on this side of the Mounth, the xxiv day of January last bypast, and on the other side of the Mounth, the tenth of February instant, to that effect that order might be taken therein conform to the said Ordinance ; with certification to them, and they failed, the Queen's Majesty and Council [foresaid] [1] would take order therein, as the same Ordinance bears : Notwithstanding the which, and that the Queen's Majesty and Council, and others appointed by her for receiving of the said rentals, has continually, since the said xxiv day of January, awaited upon the receiving thereof ; yet a very small number of them has produced the said rentals, contemning therethrough not only her Grace's Ordinance and Proclamation foresaid, but also herself and her authority, like as they were princes and not subjects, express against reason, equity, and justice : For remedy whereof, the Queen's Majesty ordains by advice of the Lords of her Secret Council that Factors and Chamberlains be appointed to intromet, gather, uplift and receive to our Sovereign Lady's use all and sundry mailles,[2] fermes,[3] teinds,[4] rents, provents,[5] emoluments, cains,[6] profits and duties of whatsomever benefices, whereof the rentals are not produced, conform to the said Ordinance : And if any rental else [7] produced bears not the just avail, but is fraudfully made, to intromet and uptake samekle of the fruits and profits of the said benefices as are omitted forth of the said rental ; and the ingivers of the rentals, and possessors of the benefices thereof, shall never have action to crave, clame, or receive from the tenants and possessors, further nor is contained in the said rentals else [7] produced by them : and the said tenants and possessors shall nowise be held to pay any more for their rowmes [8] to the possessors of the said benefices and ingivers of the said rentals, nor is contained in the same rentals else produced, as said is : And that the said Factors and Chamberlains to be appointed by the Queen's Majesty shall have sufficient power to intromet and uptake the fruits and profits foresaid, siclike as if special letters of Factory and Chamberlainry were granted to them thereupon. And ordains the Lords of Session to direct forth letters at the said Factors' and Chamberlains' instance, either horning or poinding,[9] as shall be thought expedient, for causing of them to be answered of the fruits of the said benefices, to be forthcoming to the Queen's Majesty's behalf, while further order be taken therein.

[1] The words in square brackets do not appear in the entry in the *Register of the Privy Council.*

[2] *farm-rents* [3] *rents* [4] *tithes* [5] *profits*, or *issues*

[6] *duties paid in kind* [7] *already* [8] *holdings*

[9] That is, either letters declaring a person a rebel and *at the horn*, or letters ordering his moveable goods to be distrained or *poinded.*

APUD EDINBURGH, XV FEBRUARII, ANNO &C. 1561 [1]

[SEDERUNT

Georgius Comes de Huntlie	Johannes Atholie Comes
Archibaldus Ergadie Comes	Jacobus Comes de Morton
Jacobus Comes de Mar	Willelmus Marescalli Comes] [2]

THE which day, forsamekle as the Queen's Majesty, by the advice of the Lords of her Secret Council and others divers of the Nobility, had of before, upon the xxii day of December last bypast, ordained that if the fourth part of the fruits and rents of all the benefices within this Realm were not sufficient for the support of her Majesty and other particular charges underwritten necessary to be borne for the tranquillity of the country; then the third part of the said fruits, more or less, should be taken up to the effects foresaid. And attour [3] ordained letters to be directed charging all and sundry beneficed men, on this side of the Mounth, to produce their rentals upon the xxiv day of January last bypast; and the tenth day of February instant was prefixed by the said letters for in-bringing of all rentals of the benefices beyond the Mounth; with certification that who produced not the said rentals at the days foresaid *respective*, the Queen's Majesty and her Council would provide remedy. According to the which certification, her Highness, with advice of her Council foresaid, has ordained that those who have not produced their rentals, whole and full intromission shall be had of their fruits, by them whom her Majesty shall direct thereto; and who have not given in their just rentals, whatsomever part omitted in their said rentals shall be intrometted with in like manner. And further, having consulted ryply,[4] and diligently advised upon the common affairs and necessities concerning the Queen's Majesty, and charges to be borne, for the common weal of the Realm, and sustentation of the Preachers and Readers, conform to the said Ordinance made thereupon of before, has found and declared the whole third parts of all benefices within this Realm, of which the rentals are produced, to be taken up by the person or persons to be nominated by her Majesty, and to begin upon this last crop of the year of God 1561, the same to be employed to the effect foresaid: together with the whole fruits of the benefices whereof the rentals are not produced; and also of samekle as is omitted in the rentals produced: And that order be directed by the Queen's Majesty to the Lords of Session that the old possessors may be answered of the remaining fruits of the said benefices; providing that the third part foresaid be fully and wholly taken up by the persons to be deputed to the uptaking thereof: And this order to continue and stand ay and whill [5] further order be taken by the Queen's Majesty with advice of her Estates. Moreover her Highness by the advice of her Council foresaid, has statute and ordained that all

[1] That is, 15 February 1562

[2] The *sederunt* has been supplied from the *Register of the Privy Council of Scotland*, i, 201.

[3] *moreover* [4] *maturely*, through being *fully informed*

[5] *until*

annuals,[1] mailles,[2] and duties within free burghs, or other towns of this Realm, as well pertaining to Chaplainries, Prebendaries, as to Friars, together with the rents of the Friars' lands, wherever they be, [and the] setting and disponing [3] thereupon, be intrometted with, and taken up by such as her Grace shall depute thereto ; for employing of the same by her Highness, to Hospitals, Schools, and other godly uses, as shall seem best to her Highness, by the advice of her Council : And knowing that nothing is more commodious for the said Hospitals, nor the places of Friars as [are] yet standing undemolished, as also to the entertaining of Schools, Colleges, and other uses foresaid : Ordains the Provost and Bailies of Aberdeen, Elgin in Moray, Inverness, Glasgow, and other burghs of this Realm, where the same are not demolished, to entertain and uphold the said Friars' places standing in the said towns, upon the common good [4] thereof, and to use the same to the common-weal and service of the said towns, ay and quhill [5] the Queen's Majesty be further advised and take final order in such things, notwithstanding any other gift, title, or interest given to whatsomever persons of the said places, with their yards, orchards, and pertinents, by our Sovereign Lady of before.[6]

[1] *annual rents* [2] here meaning *burgage-rents* [3] *leasing* or *conveying*

[4] The *common good* of a burgh was the property and income belonging *in common* to the whole community of the burgh.

[5] *until*

[6] For a final Act of the Privy Council in relation to the ingathering of the Thirds of the Benefices, passed to prevent a fraudulent prior-ingathering of fruits and rents, see *Register of the Privy Council of Scotland*, i, 204–206.

APPENDIX X

ANE EPISTLE DIRECT FRA THE HOLYE ARMITE OF ALLARIT,[1] TO HIS BRETHEREN THE GRAY FREIRES[2]

I, THOMAS, Armite in Larite,[3]
Sainct Frances brether do hartlie greit,
Beseiking yow with ferme intent,
To be walkryfe[4] and diligent;
For thir Lutherians, rissen of new,
Our Ordour daylie dois persew:
Thay smaikis[5] do sett their haill intent,
To reid this English New Testament;
And sayes, We have thame clene disceavit.
Therefore, in haist, they man be stoppit.
Our stait[6] hypocrisie they prysse,[7]
And us blaspheamis on this wyse,
Sayand, That we are heretikes,
And fals, loud, liand, mastif tykes;
Cumerars[8] and quellars[9] of Christes kirk,
Sueir swongeouris[10] that will not wirk,
But ydlelie our living wynnes,
Devouring woulves into sheip skynnes,
Hurkland with huides[11] into our neck,
Wyth Judas mynd to jouck and beck,[12]
Seikand Christes peple to devoir,
The down thringars[13] of God his glore,
Professouris of hipocrisie,
And doctouris in idolatrie,
Stout fyschares with the Feindis nett,
The upclosars of Heavins yett,[14]
Cankcarit corruptars of the Creid,
Homlok sawares[15] amangest good seid,
To trow[16] in traytouris, that do men tyiste,[17]
The hie way kennand thame fra Chryst,

[1] *Holy Hermit of Alareit*, that is, of Loretto, near Musselburgh
[2] See *supra*, i, 30, *note* 5
[3] Thomas Douchtie, founder of the Chapel of Our Lady of Loretto (1533). (See *Diurnal of Occurrents*, 17)
[4] *watchful* [5] *Those poltroons* [6] *estate* [7] *account*
[8] *troublers* [9] *slayers* [10] *lazy sluggards*
[11] *hulking beneath our hoods* [12] *bow and cringe* [13] *overthrowers*
[14] *gate* [15] *hemlock sowers* [16] *believe* [17] *entice*

Monstouris with the Beast his mark,
Dogges that never stintes to bark,
Kirk men that are with Christ unkend,
A sect that Sathane self hes send,
Lurkand in holes, lyke traytour toddes,[1]
Mantenaris of idoles and false goddes,
Fantastik fooles and feynzeit fleachearis,[2]
To turne fra the treuth the verie teachearis.
For to declair thair haill sentence,
Wald mekle cummer [3] your conscience.
They say your fayth it is sa stark,
Your cord and lowsie coit [4] and sark,
Ye lippin [5] it may bring yow to salvatioun,
And quyte excludes Christ his passioun.
I dreid this doctryne, yf it last,
Sall other gar us either wirk or fast ;
Therfor, with speid we mon provyde,
And not our proffit to oureslyde.
I schaip my selfe, within schort quhyle,
To turse [6] our Ladie in Argyle ;
And their, uncraftie wyse to wirk,
Till that we bigged [7] have ane kirk ;
Syne [8] miracles mak be your avyse.
Thay kettereles,[9] though they had but lyse,
The twa part to us they will bring :
But ordourlie to dress this thing,
A gaist [10] I pu[r]pose to gar gang,
Be counsall of Freir Walter Lang,[11]
Quhilk sall mak certane demonstrations,
To help us in our procurations,
Your haly Ordour to decoir :
That practik he proved anes before,
Betuix Kirkcaldie and Kingorne [12] ;
But lymmars [13] made therat sic skorne,
And to his fame maide sic degressioun,
Sensyne he hard not the Kinges confessioun.
Thoicht at that tyme he came na speid,
I pray yow tak guid will as deid ;

[1] *foxes* [2] *dissembling flatterers* [3] *much trouble* [4] *coat*
[5] *trust* [6] *to carry off hastily* [7] *built* [8] *afterwards*
[9] *those low fellows* [10] *ghost*

[11] Friar Walter [William] Laing was a chaplain attached to James V's court. According to Foxe he betrayed Henry Forrest's confession to Cardinal Beaton. Friar Laing's "conjuring of a ghost" is referred to by Calderwood (*History*, i, 142), and by Buchanan (see *infra*, *note* 13)

[12] Buchanan says at Dysart.

[13] *rogues.* And among the "rogues" who made scorn of Friar Laing's "ghaist" was undoubtedly George Buchanan. (See the analysis of his *Franciscanus*, lines 823–911, in *Glasgow Quatercentenary Studies of George Buchanan*, 312–321)

And him amongest your selves receave,
As ane worth mony of the leave.[1]
Quhat I obteyne may, through his arte,
Ressoun wald ye had your parte.
Your Ordour handles na monye,
But for uther casualitie,
As beif, meill, butter, and cheiss,
Or quhat that we have, that ye plese,
Send your Bretheren *et habete.*
As now nocht elles, but *valete.*

Be THOMAS your brother at command,
A cullurune kythed[2] throw many a land.

[1] *the rest, the others*

[2] *a rascal known*

GLOSSARY

A reference within brackets indicates that an explanatory note has been supplied on that page

abuse deceive (by word or by writing)
advise consider; take under consideration
aefald honest, sincere; (literally, one-fold
after according to
aggreage, aggredge aggravate; make graver; lay stress upon
allanerly only
allutterly utterly, entirely
allya alliance
almous alms
aneuch enough
annual annual-rent
aposthume aposteme (abscess)
arguessin lieutenant of a galley (i, 108)
armite eremite, hermit
attour moreover
aucht owed
auditour, auditure auditory, audience
ayre early

backs, to give backs to turn one's back, to retreat
barratry the purchase or sale of an ecclesiastical benefice or pension (i, 341)
bawbie a small coin of base metal, worth at one time six pence (Scots), and hence worth about a halfpenny (English); vulgarly equated with a halfpenny
bear barley (of an inferior quality)
beck cringe; bow down
beddrelles bedridden
beetle a heavy wooden mallet
begould began
bewray distort
besides apart from
big, bigg build
bigane bygone; in the past
birse bristle; used metaphorically for the beard
boast, boist threaten
bordel, bordell brothel
boss disreputable fellow; drunkard (i, 44)
bourd jest
Bowes [papal] Bulls
box gift
brag boast
brod board; a 'painted brod' is thus a picture
brook, bruik, bruke possess, hold; enjoy
bruit report, rumour
bud increase
budd bribe
buist, bust chest, coffer (i, 130)
bukkill buckle, hence engage, grapple
bundin bound
burne deceive; play false
but without
butting plunder; or, perhaps, household gear (i, 32)
by without regard to; despite; apart from; without
bye-lyers 'sitters on the fence'

cagot hypocrite (ii, 190)
caiche catch-ball
cain duty paid in kind
calsay causeway; street
cammoise coarse linen (ii, 62)
cannabie canopy
carters card-players
censement judgment; opinion
charge maintain (a use derived from the meaning 'to cause to bear')
cheek-mate boon companion
claw-backs 'back-scratchers'; flatterers; toadies
cockle corn-cockle (the weed, *Lychnis Githago* or *Agrostemma Githago*)
coft bought
coloured pretended; disguised; sham
compear to present oneself in response to a formal summons (ii, 327)
compte account
conceit conception
conferring comparing

conjured sworn
contentation satisfaction ; contentment
course, by course in turn
cowhuby cow-boy, cow-herd ; hence, a stupid fellow
cowp up tip up
craig rock ; neck
cuide chrisom
cullurune poltroon
cummer trouble
cummerer troubler
cunning wise
cunzie coinage
cunzie-house mint
cure a narrow passage
cursing excommunication

dadding dashing
dagg pistol
dagged shot thickly ; let fly
danton daunt, intimidate, subdue
deambulatour place for a stroll
debtful due
decern determine, judge
decoir, decore adorn, in the sense of honour
deface defame
delation formal accusation
deprave defame
deprehend apprehend, take
dictament phraseology
dicton saying
ding drive, smash, overcome, defeat
discovering uncovering, disclosing, exposing
dispone convey
divagation wandering
docility aptitude for learning
document admonition ; intimation ; evidence
dontybours, dountybours hangers-on ; courtesans (ii, 9)
dortour dormitory
doted endowed ; dowered
doung driven, struck, overcome
dounthring overthrow
dule weed mourning weeds
dung driven, struck, overcome

effeiring pertaining to, proportionate to
effeirs concerns ; *as effeirs* as accords
effray fright
eik increase ; add
eird earth
eirdit buried
else otherwise ; already
eme kinsman
emplesour pleasure
ene eyes
engine genius ; mother-wit
enseignzie, ensenzie ensign, standard ; used also for the men under an ensign, that is, a company
entracted detracted
entres entry ; interest
espials spies
ethnick gentile, that is, heathen
everilk each and every
expone explain ; represent
extrye axle-tree

fact act, deed ; matter
falcon a cannon, of about three inches calibre
falsett falseness, deceit
fard fervour, vehemence
fashery trouble, vexation
fate act, deed ; matter
feals faithful followers ; dependants ; vassals
fear slowly ; solemnly
fenzeit, feynzeit feigned ; dissembled
ferilie wonderfully ; marvellously
ferme rent
fermorar a tenant holding on a money-rent
fertour reliquary (i, 127)
fessned fixed, fastened
file thread
fleachearis flatterers
fleiche flatter
fleyed afraid
flingers dancers
flirt scoff
flyre ridicule
foiranent, foranent directly opposite
forfaltour forfeiture
forsamekle forasmuch
forsars galley-slaves (i, 108)
foryett forgot
fow full
frack resolute ; active ; *to make frack* to make ready
fray frighten
freammed, fremmed distant ; foreign ; strange
furiors billeting officers (i, 183)

gait road
gaper aspirant
garnish fortify ; garrison
gart caused

gawfe guffaw
gawmound gambol
gernal, girnal, girnel granary
gett brat ; child
girn snarl (ii, 237)
glaise a short sharp burst of heat
glondours ill-favour (i, 71)
glowming scowling
good-daughter step-daughter (ii, 33)
goodsire grandfather
gossips god-parents ; sponsors
graith harness ; ware ; fittings, furnishings
grandsire great-grandfather
gree degree ; step
greet, greit weep
gretumly greatly
grew shudder
gyrth sanctuary

hackbut of crock arquebus-à-croc (i, 320)
haitrent hatred
hamesucken violent breaking into a house and the assault of a man (or woman) within his (or her) house
hant haunt ; frequent
happ skip
harberous providing shelter or protection ; hospitable
hard-head a small coin of base metal (i, 222)
hards coarse linen (i, 88)
harle drag ; draw
haterent, hatterent hatred
hecht promise ; engagement
helsum wholesome
herschip ravaging
hetterent hatred
horn, to put to the horn to denounce as a rebel (ii, 59)
host cough
how deep
hulie cautiously, carefully
hurkland crouching

idiot a private person ; hence, a layman
ilk each
ilkane each one
incredulity unbelief
indifferent impartial
indurate hardened ; impenitent
inlaik lack, want
intend direct towards
intromet intermeddle ; interfere

jack a quilted coat for war
jackmen armed followers ; liveried retainers
jefwells knaves, rascals (i, 34)
joise enjoy
jouk bow ; stoop down ; duck
jow move from side to side ; *to jow the bell* to ring the bell
justified executed ; put to death

ken know
kepp intercept
kettereles low-down fellows
kist chest
kithed practised
knapped cracked, struck
knapscall head-piece
kythed known, shown

lapped wrapped up
lardon sarcasm ; *double-entendre* (i, 366)
lared bogged
lavachre purification ; baptism (i, 151)
lawtie loyalty
layit alloyed ; *layit money* money of base alloy
leasings, lesings lies, falsehoods
leave, lave rest, remainder
leif live
lesum lawful
limmer rogue
lippen trust, expect ; *lippen to* rely upon, confidently expect

maill rent
manck lack ; be deficient
manrent, bond of a bond or engagement to support a superior in all his quarrels and affairs
marmouset a small grotesque image (i, 127)
marrow one of a pair ; one's equal, or opponent (in a contest)
mean, meane, mene complain
mean design ; intent
mekle much
mell meddle
menzie company ; retinue ; following
mint threat
mister need
modify assess
monzeons minions
monzeors ? monsieurs, that is, messieurs
morrion steel-cap ; helm
mot may
mowes jest
mummers mutterers

neff fist
neffeling fisticuffs
non-sunt a small coin of base metal (i, 222)
notour notorious ; well-known

oblisse bind ; that is, be under obligation
oblist bound ; obliged ; under obligation
offerand offering ; receipts from offerings
once at one time ; at once ; at one and the same time ; once and for all
or ere
orison oration
orphelingis orphans
oulk week
over-thorte athwart ; across
oxter arm-pit

padgean pageant ; mummery
pair, *pare* impair ; decrease
palzean, *palzeon* pavilion ; tent
panel the accused in court
pasche Easter
pasementit laced
pasquil lampoon
patrociny patronage
paucks cunning ; slyness
pined punished
placebo 'yes-man' (i, 15)
plack a small coin of base metal (i, 16)
plain complain
platt plan ; scheme
pleuch plough
pley debate
pock bag
poise, *pose* hoard ; hoard of money ; treasure
pottingar apothecary
presently now ; at present
pretence intent
pretend intend
prevent come before ; forestall ; forgo
prick point
prickers light horsemen
propine to offer a gift
proport purport
provents issues ; revenues
purpose, *to hold purpose with* to enter into conversation with
pynours pioneers ; labourers

raik track (i, 320)
rang reigned
reacuntar rencontre
reason question
reclame call upon ; reclaim
recollect bring together
red rid, free
reduce bring back
regiment rule ; government
reif theft
remanent remainder, rest
remit put back ; re-instate ; send back
reparelling plenishing ; furnishing
repone place back ; restore
repugn impugn
respect respite ; postpone
retrahibition countermand
ring reign
ripely, *reply*, *ryply* maturely
roung, *rung* reigned
rouped, *rowped* croaked
rowme place ; turn ; holding (of land)—hence, inheritance
rownged filed ; worn away
ruse boast
ryped searched

scabrously rudely
scaill disperse
scantly scarcely
schone shoes
scoupars skippers
scripped mocked
scruiff a thin covering ; thus used for thin or worn money, or money of a very base alloy (i, 221)
seige seat
seinze synod, session
sen since ; thereafter
sensyne since ; later
shackle-bones wrists
shavelings a contemptuous term for the Roman clergy with their shaven tonsures
shopped struck
siclyke suchlike ; likewise
silly weak
sithence since
skaill disperse
skair part
skeife section ; division (i, 94)
skrimpled scorched
skybalds worthless fellows ; ragamuffins
sloghorne slogan ; war-cry
smaiks poltroons
smote strain
snappers mishaps
sned lop
solist solicitous
souter shoe-maker

sparse spread
speir inquire
splint leg-armour
spuilzie, spulzie spoil
spurtill a large wooden stick used for stirring
stammered staggered
stancheour stanchion
steik shut
stog stab ; *stog-sword* a thrusting-sword
stop interfere with
stopped holed
stoup prop
stowen stolen
stowth theft
stracked clasped (of hands)
sture at to be discontented with
sua so
sueir loth ; lazy
suppost supporter (i, 232)
swash drum
swing sway
swongeours 'lead-swingers'; sluggards
syne after ; afterwards ; moreover—that is, after all that

tack lease
tacksman leaseholder
tane taken
targatting tasselling
teinds tithes
tender have regard to ; safeguard
tentation trial
thai, thay those
thir these
thocht though
thoill, thole suffer, endure ; allow ; undergo
thrist thirst
tinsall, tynsall loss
toddes foxes
to-look prospect
toome, tume empty
tor arm (of a chair)
tred path ; direction
trowan trusted
tyiste entice
tynsall, tinsall loss
tynt lost
turse carry

umquhile late, deceased
unable disqualify
unhap misfortune, mischance
unprovided unprepared ; unforeseen
upfall relapse

vaik become, or remain, vacant
vake attend to
vissorne vizor ; mask

wa unhappy
wadset, wodset mortgage
wait know
walking awake
walkryfe watchful
want do without ; lack
wanton extravagant
war worse
waring expense
warsling, warstling wrestling
wat know
while until
whinger short sword, or dagger ; (literally, a *hanger*)
wit know ; knowledge
wite blame
witty wise
wodness, woodness rage ; anger
wolter overturning ; revolution
wote know
wrech niggardly ; avaricious (i, 344)

yead, yeid went
yett gate
yond beyond ; further

A NOTE ON AUTHORITIES

The intention of this Note is to give the general reader some guidance with regard to the literature on Knox and the history of his time. The Note does not pretend to be exhaustive, and no attempt has been made to include all the works cited in the Introduction and in the footnotes to the Text. The works have been grouped as follows :

(1) The Works of John Knox
(2) Biographies of John Knox
(3) Contemporary Documents and Records
(4) Contemporary or near-contemporary Narrative Sources, Literary Works, and Polemical Writings
(5) Modern Works

(1) THE WORKS OF JOHN KNOX

The Works of John Knox; Collected and edited by David Laing. 6 vols. Edinburgh, 1846–1864.

Vols. I and II, which contain the 'History of the Reformation of Religion within the Realm of Scotland,' were published by the Bannatyne Club (and issued also to members of the Wodrow Society) ; vols. III, IV, V, and VI were not published by the Bannatyne Club, but were printed on Club paper and provided for the members. A reprint of the six volumes, with new title-pages, was issued by James Thin in 1895.

The general arrangement of the six volumes is :

Vol. I	*The History of the Reformation,* Books I and II. This volume contains a valuable note on the 'Manuscript Copies of the History.'
Vol. II	*The History of the Reformation,* Books III, IV, and V.
Vol. III	Early Writings, from 1548 to 1554, including Letters to Mrs. Elizabeth Bowes and her daughter Marjory, 1553–1554.
Vol. IV	Writings from 1555 to 1558, including the *First Blast of the Trumpet against the Monstrous Regiment of Women,* the two versions of the *Letter* to the Queen Regent, and Familiar Epistles, 1555–1558.
Vol. V	Further Writings, 1558–1560.
Vol. VI	Letters written 1559–1572 ; the *Reasoning* with Quintin Kennedy ; the Sermon preached in St. Giles, 19 August 1565 ; the *Book of Common Order* ; and other documents and writings. This volume contains an Editorial Preface giving a brief outline of Knox's life and work.

This monumental collection is unlikely ever to be superseded. Throughout, the notes and the editorial comments reflect the learning and scholarship of David Laing, then " easily the Prince of all living authorities in all matters of Scottish history and biography."

The text of the *History of the Reformation* is based upon the so-called 'MS.

of 1566'—the earliest of the manuscripts—and has been used for the present edition. (See *supra*, i, xcv-cix)

[Cited throughout as 'Laing's *Knox*']

(2) BIOGRAPHIES OF JOHN KNOX

The principal biographies are:

P. Hume Brown. *John Knox, A Biography.* 2 vols. London, 1895

A careful and well-documented biography including, for the period of Knox's exile abroad, the results of original research into Continental sources. Because of its scope, the work is also a study of the Reformation period in Scottish history.

A. Taylor Innes. *John Knox.* Edinburgh, 1896. (Famous Scots Series)

An admirable survey, within a limited compass, of the main aspects of Knox's life and work. Based largely on Knox's own writings, the book captures something of the essential spirit of the man.

Andrew Lang. *John Knox and the Reformation.* London, 1905

Like all Andrew Lang's work, this 'biography' is lively and provocative. In the Preface Lang states that he has tried "to get behind Tradition," while Knox's *History of the Reformation* is to be regarded "as the work of an old-fashioned advocate rather than as the summing up of a judge." The book is a useful corrective: it compels the reader to re-assess Knox's work and to determine for himself how much of the 'new criticism' is accurate and fair.

Thomas M'Crie. *Life of John Knox.* 2 vols. Edinburgh, 5th ed., 1831

This was the first important biography of Knox, and it has enjoyed a deservedly high reputation. Even to-day it is still useful. Admittedly it represents the 'Tradition' to which Andrew Lang took exception; but it is a work of scholarship and, while the bias can be easily detected, there is no attempt to distort the evidence or to suppress important facts.

Lord Eustace Percy. *John Knox.* London, 1937

This is the most recent biography and in many ways it is the best; certainly it is the best for the general reader. It is honest and impartial; it understands the 'spirit of the time'; and it provides the necessary European background. Although the Preface opens with the words, "This is not a work of original research," full advantage has been taken of the research of others, and an attempt has been made to evaluate the results. Finally, and not unimportant, the book is written in an attractive and easy style. The absence of any *apparatus criticus* is to be regretted.

(3) CONTEMPORARY DOCUMENTS AND RECORDS

Accounts of the Lord High Treasurer of Scotland. Vol. VII 1538–41; vol. VIII 1541–46; vol. IX 1546–51; vol. X 1551–59; vol. XI 1559–66. (H.M. Stationery Office)

Acts and Proceedings of the General Assemblies of the Kirk of Scotland, from the year 1560. Edited by Thomas Thomson. 3 vols. (Bannatyne Club and Maitland Club, 1839–1845)

[Cited as *Booke of the Universall Kirk*]

Acts of the Parliaments of Scotland. Vol. II 1424–1567; vol. III 1567–92. (Record Commission)

Ancient Criminal Trials in Scotland; compiled from the original Records and MSS. Edited by Robert Pitcairn. 3 vols. (Bannatyne Club and Maitland Club, 1833)
[Cited as Pitcairn, *Criminal Trials*]

Booke of the Universall Kirk. See *Acts and Proceedings of the General Assemblies of the Kirk of Scotland*

Calendar of State Papers, Foreign Series, of the Reign of Elizabeth. (H.M. Stationery Office)
[Cited as *Foreign Calendar, Elizabeth.* The relevant volumes are: Vol. I 1558–59; vol. II 1559–60; vol. III 1560–61; vol. IV 1561–62; vol. V 1562; vol. VI 1563; vol. VII 1564–65.]

Calendar of State Papers relating to Scotland and Mary, Queen of Scots. Vol. I 1547–63; vol. II 1563–69. (H.M. Stationery Office)
[Cited as *Calendar of Scottish Papers*]

Concilia Scotiæ. See *Statuta Ecclesiæ Scoticanæ*

Criminal Trials. See *Ancient Criminal Trials*

Edinburgh Records: The Burgh Accounts. Edited by Robert Adam. 2 vols. (Printed for the Lord Provost, Magistrates, and Council; Edinburgh, 1899)

Extracts from the Council Register of the Burgh of Aberdeen. Edited by John Stuart. 2 vols. (Spalding Club, 1844, 1848)

Extracts from the Records of the Burgh of Edinburgh. Edited by Sir James D. Marwick. 4 vols. (Scottish Burgh Records Society, 1869–1882). Vol. I 1403–1528 (see *Scottish Historical Review*, xxvi, 190); vol. II 1528–57; vol. III 1557–71; vol. IV 1573–89. A general index to the four volumes was published separately in 1892.
[Cited as *Edinburgh Burgh Records*]

Hamilton Papers. Vol. I 1532–43; vol. II 1543–90. (H.M. Stationery Office)

Inventaire Chronologique des Documents relatifs à l'Histoire d'Écosse conservés aux Archives du Royaume à Paris. Edited by Alexandre Teulet. (Abbotsford Club, 1839)

Inventaires de la Royne Descosse. Edited by Joseph Robertson. (Bannatyne Club, 1863)
This work has a long, fully documented and exceedingly valuable Preface, which is, unfortunately, unindexed.

Mission de Beccarie de Pavie, Baron de Fourquevaux, en Écosse, 1549: Documents originaux du fonds Fourquevaux. Edited by G. Dickinson. Oxford, 1948

Papal Negotiations with Mary Queen of Scots during her Reign in Scotland, 1561–1567. Edited by John Hungerford Pollen. (Scottish History Society, 1901)

Papiers d'État, Pièces et Documents inédits ou peu connus relatifs à l'Histoire de l'Écosse au XVIe Siècle. Edited by Alexandre Teulet. Vol. I 1513–60; vol. II 1561–87; vol. III 1563–1603. (Bannatyne Club, 1852–1860)
[Cited as *Papiers d'État*]

Register of the Minister, Elders and Deacons of the Christian Congregation of St Andrews, 1559–1600. Edited by David Hay Fleming. 2 vols. (Scottish History Society, 1889, 1890)
[Cited as *St Andrews Kirk Session Register*]

Register of the Privy Council of Scotland. Vol. I 1545–69; vol. II 1569–78. (H.M. Stationery Office)

Relations Politiques de la France et de l'Espagne avec l'Écosse au XVIe Siècle. Edited by Alexandre Teulet. 5 vols. Paris, 1862
[Cited as *Relations Politiques*]

Rentale Dunkeldense, 1505–1517. Edited by Robert Kerr Hannay. (Scottish History Society, 1915)

Rentale Sancti Andree, 1538–1546. Edited by Robert Kerr Hannay. (Scottish History Society, 1913)

Sadler's State Papers. See *State Papers and Letters of Sir Ralph Sadler*

St. Andrews Kirk Session Register. See *Register of the Minister, Elders and Deacons of the Christian Congregation of St. Andrews*

State Papers and Letters of Sir Ralph Sadler. Edited by A. Clifford. 2 vols. Edinburgh, 1809

Scottish Correspondence of Mary of Lorraine, 1543–1560. Edited by Annie I. Cameron. (Scottish History Society, 1927)

Statuta Ecclesiæ Scoticanæ (Concilia Scotiæ). Edited by Joseph Robertson. 2 vols. (Bannatyne Club, 1866)

Vol. I consists entirely of an exceedingly valuable and fully documented Preface.

Statutes of the Scottish Church, 1225–1559. Translated and edited by David Patrick. (Scottish History Society, 1907)

This is a translation of Joseph Robertson's collection, *Statuta Ecclesiæ Scoticanæ*, but the translator has provided his own Introduction, Notes and Appendices.

(4) CONTEMPORARY OR NEAR-CONTEMPORARY NARRATIVE SOURCES, LITERARY WORKS, AND POLEMICAL WRITINGS

The Autobiography and Diary of Mr. James Melvill. Edited by Robert Pitcairn. (Wodrow Society, 1842)

James Melville (1556–1614), nephew of the more celebrated Andrew Melville, was a student at St. Andrews at the time of Knox's sojourn there.

The Catechism set forth by Archbishop Hamilton [1552]; together with the Two-Penny Faith [1559].

A facsimile edition with a Preface by Alexander F. Mitchell. Edinburgh, 1882.

A Compendious Book of Psalms and Spiritual Songs [? 1570]—commonly known as "The Gude and Godlie Ballates." Edited by David Laing. Edinburgh, 1868

See *supra*, i, xxi–xxii

A Diurnal of Remarkable Occurrents that have passed within the Country of Scotland since the Death of King James the Fourth till the year 1575. Edited by Thomas Thomson. (Bannatyne Club and Maitland Club, 1833)

An anonymous, independent and exceedingly valuable contemporary record of events, of which by far the greater part covers the important period 1559–73. Unfortunately the Bannatyne and Maitland Club editions are unindexed, though a separate, but not wholly satisfactory, index was prepared by A. G. Scott and others, and published in 1938. A critical edition of the *Diurnal* has been long overdue.

[Cited as *Diurnal of Occurrents*]

Fragments of Scotish History. [Edited by Sir John Graham Dalyell.] Edinburgh, 1798

The last three 'Fragments' are the contemporary 'Diary of Robert Birrel, Burgess of Edinburgh, 1532–1605,' 'The Late Expedition in Scotland under the Earl of Hertford, 1544,' and Patten's 'Account of the Expedition into Scotland under the Duke of Somerset, 1547.'

The Gude and Godlie Ballates. See *A Compendious Book of Psalms and Spiritual Songs*

Historie and Chronicles of Scotland, written and collected by Robert Lindesay of Pitscottie. Edited by Æneas J. G. Mackay. 3 vols. (Scottish Text Society, 1899, 1911)

Lindsay of Pitscottie (? 1500–? 1565) was sympathetic to the Reformers and to the English party. His narrative is lively and often amusing, and he is the source of many of the romantic stories of Scottish history. A work to be used with the greatest caution, but to be read with the greatest pleasure.

[Cited as Pitscottie, *Chronicles*]

A History of Greater Britain, by John Major. Translated and edited by Archibald Constable. (Scottish History Society, 1892)

The *Historia Majoris Britanniae* of John Major (1469–1550) was first published at Paris in 1521, and is in many ways a remarkable book for its time. It is particularly valuable for its observations on the corruption within the Church and on the urgent need for reform.

The Historie of Scotland, wrytten first in Latin by the most reverend and worthy Jhone Leslie, Bishop of Rosse, and translated in Scottish by Father James Dalrymple. Edited by E. G. Cody and William Murison. 2 vols. (Scottish Text Society, 1888, 1895), and

The History of Scotland, from the Death of King James I to the year 1561, by John Lesley, Bishop of Ross. Edited by Thomas Thomson. (Bannatyne Club, 1830)

The *De Origine, moribus, et rebus gestis Scotorum* of John Leslie, or Lesley (1527–96), was published at Rome in 1578, and contains ten Books, of which the concluding three Books bear the separate title *De rebus gestis Scotorum posteriores libri tres, recentiorum regum historiam, quæ hucusque desiderabatur, ab ANNO DOMINI MCCCCXXXVI. usque ad annum MDLXII. fusius continentes.* These last three Books were originally written (1570) in the vernacular (Bannatyne Club edition, above); they were then rewritten by Lesley in Latin with the addition of the earlier Books, and from the Latin of the whole ten Books a very poor translation into the vernacular was made by Father James Dalrymple in 1596 (Scottish Text Society edition, above).

Lesley was a loyal servant to Mary and to the Roman Church. His account of the history of his own time is useful and, upon occasion, well reasoned; but he is never able to forget his allegiances.

The History of Scotland, by George Buchanan. Translated from the Latin, with Notes, by James Aikman. 4 vols. Glasgow, 1827

A critical edition of that part of Buchanan's *Rerum Scoticarum Historia* (1582), which covers the history of his own time would be welcome. Although a 'party history' (and, with Buchanan's Lennox connections, doubly hostile to Mary because of the murder of Darnley), Buchanan's account of the period

1559 to 1567 is still useful if only as the account of a contemporary revealing the passions and prejudices of that difficult time.

[Cited as Aikman's *Buchanan*]

History of the Church of Scotland, by John Spottiswoode. Edited by M. Russell (vol. I) and Mark Napier (vols. II–III). 3 vols. (Spottiswoode Society, 1851)

John Spottiswoode (1565–1637) was Archbishop of Glasgow, and later Archbishop of St. Andrews, in the 'First Episcopacy.' His *History*, written at the command of James VI, is that of a moderate Episcopalian, and his comments are naturally influenced in the same direction. But he is more charitable than Calderwood (*q.v.*), and it is difficult to find, in his own words, anything written "out of humour." He undoubtedly had access to a copy of Knox's *History*, but he did not borrow heavily in the manner of Calderwood.

[Cited as Spottiswoode, *History*]

A Historie of the Estate of Scotland, from the year 1559 to the year 1566. See *Miscellany of the Wodrow Society*

The History of the Kirk of Scotland, by Mr. David Calderwood. Edited by the Rev. Thomas Thomson (vols. I–VII) and David Laing (vol. VIII). 8 vols. (Wodrow Society, 1842–1849)

David Calderwood (1575–1650) wrote as a perfervid Presbyterian and an opponent of Episcopacy (see his *Altare Damascenum*, 1621), and his *History* received the encouragement and support of the General Assembly. This bias being borne in mind, his *History* is particularly valuable in that he gives *in extenso* many documents of which the originals have since been lost. A shorter version, entitled *The True History of the Church of Scotland*, preceded publication of the full work; the full work certainly gave him a right to be regarded, in the words of the contemporary Robert Baillie, as the "living magazine of our ecclesiastical history." For the period to 1564 he borrows heavily from Knox.

[Cited as Calderwood, *History*]

Memoirs of his own Life, by Sir James Melville of Halhill. Edited by Thomas Thomson. (Bannatyne Club and Maitland Club, 1827, 1833)

Sir James Melville (1535–1617) was frequently entrusted with diplomatic missions in the reign of Mary, and in the earlier part of the reign of James VI. His *Memoirs* cover the period 1549–93. Undoubtedly he had much 'inside knowledge'; he writes with zest; and we are indebted to him for many interesting details. But he compiled his *Memoirs* late in life, and, upon occasion, his memory may have played him false.

Miscellany of the Wodrow Society. Vol. I (all published). Edited by David Laing. (1844)

Among other material this volume contains:

A Historie of the Estate of Scotland, from the year 1559 to the year 1566

This is a late seventeenth-century transcript of part of an earlier manuscript by an unknown author. The part that has thus survived covers the period July 1558 to April 1560. It is of considerable value as relating "a number of minute circumstances at the period of the Reformation not elsewhere to be met with," and serving "to corroborate the statements of other writers." Laing was of opinion that the original manuscript was not written by "a person living at the time and describing events as an eye-witness," but by a later writer deriving his information "from some contemporary authority."

Ane Compendius Tractive, &c., set furth be Maister Quintine Kennedy, 1558

Quintin Kennedy (1520–64) was one of the few meritorious churchmen in the pre-Reformation Church, and it is significant that his *Compendius Tractive* stands alone as the one work written during the period 1558–60 in support of the cause of Rome. In it Kennedy strives to encourage each " Christian man " to a continuance of faith and belief in the old Church, basing his arguments on the Scriptures (to answer the Reformers' appeal to the Word of God) and on the decisions of the Councils of the Church.

The Poetical Works of Sir David Lyndsay. Edited by David Laing. 3 vols. Edinburgh, 1879

Sir David Lindsay, or Lyndsay (? 1490–1555) saw service at the court of James V, was Lyon King of Arms, and was regarded with affection by his contemporaries as a man of upright life " invariably opposed to falsehood." His poetical works are a valuable source for the social history of his time; they illustrate the baronial disorders within Scotland, the party factions and the family feuds, the weakness of the central authority, and, above all, the licentious lives of the clergy and the corruption within the Church. Essentially Lindsay was the people's poet; he wrote for the people and to the people; and his sympathies are always with the people against Nobility and Church alike.

Two Missions of Jacques de la Brosse. Edited by Gladys Dickinson. (Scottish History Society, 1942)

This volume contains (1) *Discours des affaires du Royaume descosse*: a report by La Brosse and Ménage of the state of Scotland, social, military, and political, in the autumn of 1543; and (2) *Journal*: a day-to-day account of the siege of Leith from 22 January to 15 June 1560.

Both these documents are important. The first is a reasoned summary which throws new light on the part played by Matthew, fourth Earl of Lennox, in the political intrigue following the death of James V. The second is a graphic and detailed description of the closing episode in the 'uproar for religion.'

(5) MODERN WORKS

Peter Hume Brown. *History of Scotland to the Present Time.* 3 vols. Cambridge, 1911

George Brunton and David Haig. *An Historical Account of the Senators of the College of Justice.* Edinburgh, 1836

John Hill Burton. *The History of Scotland.* 8 vols. and Index. New (Second) edition, Edinburgh, 1873

George Gordon Coulton. *Scottish Abbeys and Social Life.* Cambridge, 1933

John Dowden. *The Bishops of Scotland.* Glasgow, 1912

An invaluable work of reference.

David Hay Fleming. *Mary Queen of Scots: from her Birth to her Flight into England.* Second edition, London, 1898

An exceedingly careful and fully documented work. The text occupies pages 1–176; the " Notes and References " and the " Documents hitherto unpublished " occupy pages 177–514; and an Itinerary occupies pages 515–543. It is much to be regretted that this wealth of evidence, analysed with critical scholarship, has no index.

David Hay Fleming. *The Reformation in Scotland.* London, 1910

A standard work by a scholar who had an unrivalled knowledge of the history of the Scottish Church in the sixteenth and seventeenth centuries. Hay Fleming, like Knox, could find little that was good in the Church of Rome, while on the other hand, " inspired by the vital principles of a pure Scottish Calvinism," he strove in all his writings " to vindicate the character of the Reformers and the Covenanters."

Robert Kerr Hannay. *The Scottish Crown and the Papacy, 1424–1560.* Edinburgh, 1931. (Historical Association of Scotland, Pamphlets, New Series, No. 6)

An admirable summary of the relations of Church and State.

Thomas F. Henderson. *Mary Queen of Scots.* 2 vols. London, 1905

John Herkless and Robert Kerr Hannay. *The Archbishops of St. Andrews.* 5 vols. Edinburgh, 1907–1915

Robert Keith. *History of Affairs of Church and State in Scotland.* Edited by John Parker Lawson (vols. I and II) and C. J. Lyon (vol. III). 3 vols. (Spottiswoode Society, 1844–1850)

Robert Keith (1681–1757) was Bishop of Fife, 1733–43. In 1743 he was chosen as Primus of the Scottish Episcopal Church. His work betrays a strong episcopal bias—" avoiding Rome on the one hand, and Geneva on the other " —but he had a keen and critical mind, and he supported his *History* with a full apparatus of letters and documents. Although beginning at 1527, by far the greater part of the work is devoted to the period 1560–68.

[Cited as Keith's *History*]

Andrew Lang. *History of Scotland.* 4 vols. Edinburgh, 1903–1907

Andrew Lang. *The Mystery of Mary Stewart.* London, 1901

Peter Lorimer. *Knox and the Church of England, etc.* London, 1875

Peter Lorimer. *Patrick Hamilton.* Edinburgh, 1857

Alexander R. MacEwen. *A History of the Church in Scotland.* 2 vols. London, 1913, 1918

A valuable and scholarly ecclesiastical history of Scotland covering the period from the earliest times to the success of the Reformation movement in 1560.

Janet Girdwood Macgregor. *The Scottish Presbyterian Polity.* Edinburgh, 1926

William Law Mathieson. *Politics and Religion.* 2 vols. Glasgow, 1902

A history of Scotland from the eve of the Reformation to the Revolution Settlement.

Alexander Ferrier Mitchell. *The Scottish Reformation.* Edinburgh, 1900

James Balfour Paul (*ed.*). *The Scots Peerage.* 9 vols. Edinburgh, 1904–1914

An indispensable work of reference, though not all the contributions are of equal merit. The *Addenda et Corrigenda* in vol. IX should be consulted in conjunction with the main articles.

Hew Scott. *Fasti Ecclesiæ Scoticanæ.* 7 vols. New and revised edition, Edinburgh, 1915–1928

An indispensable work of reference for the " succession of ministers in the Church of Scotland from the Reformation." Unfortunately the contributions are of unequal merit; the arrangement leaves much to be desired; and a volume of *Addenda et Corrigenda* is sadly needed.

Patrick Fraser Tytler. *History of Scotland.* 9 vols. Second edition, Edinburgh, 1841–1843

HAMILTONS, LENNOX-STEWARTS, AND THE SCOTTISH SUCCESSION

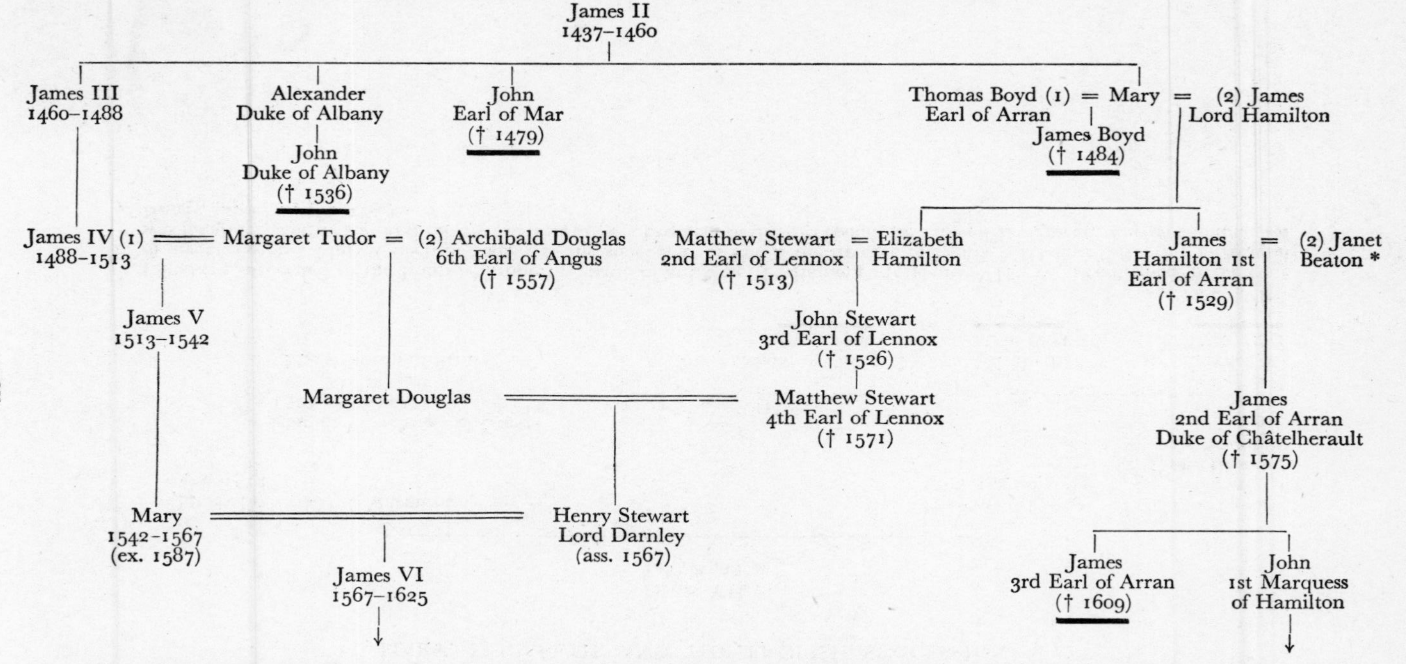

* James, 1st Earl of Arran, was married, firstly, to Elizabeth Home (from whom he was divorced), and, secondly, to Janet Beaton. James, 2nd Earl of Arran, was the son of this second marriage. It will be seen from the Table that, during the whole of Mary's reign until the birth of James [VI] in 1566, James, 2nd Earl of Arran (Duke of Châtelherault) was next in succession to the Crown. The Hamiltons were thus naturally " interested " in any " uproar " that might affect Mary's tenure of the throne.

On the other hand, the divorce of James, 1st Earl of Arran, from Elizabeth Home was not above suspicion, and if, indeed, it had been irregular and was invalid, then James, 2nd Earl of Arran and Duke of Châtelherault, was illegitimate, and Matthew Stewart, 4th Earl of Lennox, was next in succession to the Crown. This explains the antipathy between the Hamiltons and the Lennox-Stewarts ; it explains the action taken by both houses ; and finally it explains the significance of the marriage of Mary and Darnley.

MARY, ELIZABETH, AND THE ENGLISH SUCCESSION

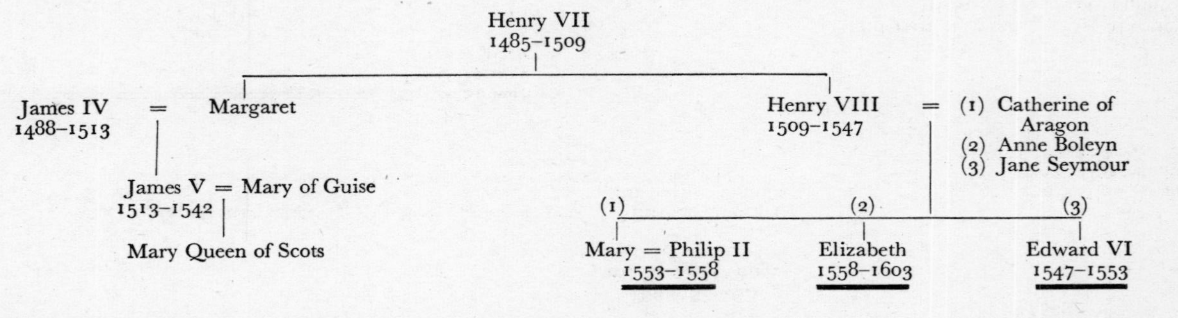

Elizabeth succeeded to the English throne by virtue of an Act of Parliament (35 Henry VIII, c.1), confirmed at the time of her accession. Mary Queen of Scots was the strict heir of line if the divorce of Henry VIII and Catherine of Aragon was invalid. (For a clear and succinct account of the problem of the succession, *see* Taswell-Langmead, *English Constitutional History*, 9th edn., 186–189.)

INDEX

The form of the names chosen for the headings follows the usually accepted rules. References are given from alternative forms.

Brief biographical details (in square brackets immediately after the heading) are given in certain cases, either because the persons played important parts in the history of Scotland or because such details are required for purposes of identification. They make no pretence to biographical research and are derived from easily accessible books, to which the reader is referred for further information.

The items within each entry are arranged chronologically and, especially in the longer entries, dates have been inserted at frequent intervals to facilitate quick reference.

PRINTED IN GREAT BRITAIN AT
THE PRESS OF THE PUBLISHERS